THE QUESTION PRESENTED:
MODEL
APPELLATE
BRIEFS

THE QUESTION PRESENTED:
MODEL
APPELLATE
BRIEFS

Maria L. Ciampi

William H. Manz

ISBN: 9781422415535

Editorial Offices
121 Chanlon Rd., New Providence, NJ 07974 (908) 464-6800
201 Mission St., San Francisco, CA 94105-1831 (415) 908-3200
www.lexisnexis.com

(Pub.3566)

Table of Contents

Preface

The appellate attorney has one goal in writing an appellate brief: to persuade the court to adopt the client's position. Telling law students and lawyers this fundamental fact is easy; showing them how to put it into practice is difficult. Our book, *The Question Presented: Model Appellate Briefs,* was written to "show" rather than to "tell."

In determining which briefs to "show" in this volume, we researched briefs that appellate judges themselves said were excellently written. The briefs are from both state and federal courts and address a variety of issues: theft of Native-American artifacts, freedom of speech, securities fraud, and conflict of interest. After the brief(s), we have included the court's opinion so that its relation to the brief(s) can be examined and discussed.

We did not include briefs to the United States Supreme Court in this volume. Briefs to the Supreme Court do not represent issues typically addressed by the overwhelming majority of lawyers. We have, however, included excerpts from some famous Supreme Court briefs in the introductory chapter.

The Question Presented is dedicated to those who teach appellate advocacy. It can be used as a supplement to any of the excellent primers that now exist on appellate advocacy, such as *Winning on Appeal: Better Briefs and Oral Argument* by the Honorable Ruggero Aldisert or *Brief Writing and Oral Argument* by the Honorable Edward Re and Joseph Re. It can also stand alone, especially in an introductory course, because of its introductory chapter.

We hope the materials are helpful and interesting. Good luck!

Introduction:
The Art and Science of
Appellate Advocacy

*"If oral advocacy is an art, brief writing can be
called a combination of art and science."*
The Honorable Chief Justice William H. Rehnquist[1]

Writing an excellent, that is, *persuasive* appellate brief requires more than merely knowing the rules of appellate procedure, the rules of the court the brief is to be filed with, and the various sections of the brief. It requires learning how to craft every sentence of the brief to logically and concisely persuade the court to accept the client's position, even in the face of apparent adverse authority.

Few lawyers master the art and science of appellate brief writing in law school. There is the story of the first-year associate at a major Manhattan law firm who worked until all hours of the morning to write her first appellate brief. Bleary-eyed from hours at her word processor, the associate placed the finished product on the assigning partner's chair and returned to her office to catch a few winks before the new day began. When she awoke—several hours later—she stepped out of her office only to overhear the assigning partner ranting to another partner about her work. "This brief has no punch!" was all she heard him say over and over again.

Yet it is precisely this "punch" that appellate judges clamor for. Apart from wanting to read briefs that are grammatically correct and typographical-error free, judges want to read well-organized briefs that sting them between the eyes with the client's strongest position.

And so the briefs included in this volume are the ones that appellate judges from federal and state appellate courts told us "punched" them between the eyes. The briefs cover a range of topics: theft of Native-American artifacts, freedom of speech, securities fraud, and conflict of interest. All of the briefs have one thing in common: they captured the attention of the appellate judges deciding the case and played a role in the courts' final decisions.

Part One of this book is an introductory chapter discussing what appellate judges say are the ingredients for a well-written brief. Part Two consists of four chapters; each chapter is devoted to one of the four cases included in the volume. Each "case" chapter includes at least one brief and the appellate court's judicial opinion. We believe that a careful study of these briefs and the corresponding appellate court decisions will help the law student see

---

[1] William H. Rehnquist, *From Webster to Word Processing: The Ascendance of the Appellate Brief*, 1 J. APPELLATE PRACTICE & PROCESS 1, 1 (1999).

how a well-written brief can help a judge write the final decision and possibly even decide in the client's favor.

General Principles of Persuasive Advocacy

Appellate judges agree on certain basic principles for writing an effective appellate brief.

First General Principle: Length

A shorter brief is generally more effective. Look at Thurgood Marshall's winning United States Supreme Court brief in *Brown v. Board of Education*. The text of the brief is a mere thirteen pages long, its supporting appendix only an additional twenty-four pages.

Shorter briefs can be more effective for several reasons. First, a shorter brief will keep the attention of a tired and often overworked judge. Second, it ensures that the attorney has focused the court's attention on the strongest arguments and eliminated weaker points. It therefore heeds Justice Oliver Wendell Holmes' advice—"Strike for the jugular, let go of the rest." Finally, a shorter brief is probably more concisely written so that the strongest points shine forth.

Second General Principle: Organization

Law students and lawyers, both often pressed for time, overlook the importance of this critical element of the well-written brief. Appellate judges do not, as the Honorable William Rehnquist recently underscored:

> When a case first lands on an appellate lawyer's desk, it more often than not is a confusing and complicated jumble of facts, lower court rulings, procedural questions and rules of law. The brief writer must immerse himself in this chaos of detail and bring order to it by organizing—and I cannot stress that term enough—by organizing, organizing, and organizing, so that the brief is a coherent presentation of the arguments in favor of the writer's client.[2]

Third General Principle: Persuasiveness

The sole purpose of the appellate brief is to persuade the court. It is not an academic exercise. To write a persuasive appellate brief, the attorney must do several things.

First, lawyers and law students must write the brief from the *client's point of view*. Law students, possibly because they do not see and talk to the actual client, have a particularly difficult time writing from the client's point of view. Their questions presented, statements of the case, statements of the facts, point headings, and summaries of the relevant legal rules and policies are often written neutrally so that the reader does not know what side they represent. To write from the client's point of view, law students must take Atticus Finch's advice in *To Kill a Mockingbird*: step inside their clients' shoes and walk around in them.

---

[2]   *Id.* at 4.

Second, to write persuasively, lawyers and law students must write offensively rather than defensively. Too often briefs focus on presenting and defending against the other side's arguments. While the adversary's arguments must be addressed, the brief writer should first make the client's best case. Furthermore, some commentators suggest that adverse arguments should be addressed indirectly and not attacked head on; interestingly, the briefs in this volume use both approaches.

Third, the law student and lawyer must write with "punch." "Punch" can be accomplished by strategically placing short, succinct, direct reminders of the client's position throughout the brief, particularly in the opening sentence of paragraphs. It can also be accomplished by interjecting the "well-turned phrase":

> The well-turned phrase in a brief can capture a judge's attention, which tends to wane after 60 or so words of legalese; the surprising allusion can set her thinking along different lines. . . . Pepper your brief . . . with relevant metaphors or quotations, and I guarantee the best ones will reappear in the judges' opinions.[3]

Benjamin Cardozo's opinions are famous for their style and memorable quotes. His briefs, written during his career as an appellate attorney, also contain phraseology that seizes the reader's attention. In *Zimmermann v. Timmermann*, a case involving the non-delivery of bonds, Cardozo summarized his client's position in the following terms:

> We are concerned at this time with the interests of justice. The defendants have had their day before a tribunal, where the accused were without the benefit of counsel, where there was no compulsory process to secure the attendance of witnesses, where the rules of evidence were unheeded, and where the power and wealth and influence were arrayed on the side of the complainants. The plaintiffs are now to have *their* day in the calm atmosphere of the courts. They submit the case with the consciousness that they have done no wrong,—unless it be a wrong to have brought the wealth and power of the Stock Exchange before the ordinary tribunals of justice, to be judged, not by the favor of friends and associates, but by the law of the land.[4]

Finally, judges agree that persuasiveness is not making general statements attacking the opponent's brief or person. Direct your disagreement with particular statements of fact, legal rules, policies, and/or applications and present the reason your position is correct instead. Cardozo does this at the start of his argument in *Zimmerman*, stating:

> The defendant's have taken their stand upon the single proposition that not til the full $20,000,000 of bonds had been distributed by Brown Brothers & Company did their contracts mature. Such a construction of the obligations of the parties is without warrant of law. A contract to deliver the bonds when issued is a con-

---

[3]   Patricia M. Wald, *19 Tips From 19 Years on the Appellate Bench*, 1 J. APPELLATE PRACTICE & PROCESS 7, 21 (1999).

[4]   Appellant's Brief at 50, *Zimmerman v. Timmermann*, 86 N.E. 540 (N.Y. 1908).

tract to deliver them when issued in such reasonable quantities as to render it possible for the promisor with the exercise of due diligence to procure them. To attribute any other meaning to it is to involve the parties in obvious absurdities.[5]

Fourth General Principle: Theme

The appellate court is concerned with applying the law not only in a technically correct manner, but also in a just one. Using a theme in an appellate brief aids the court in deciding whether it is doing justice to the parties in the controversy. This valuable device, however, is often overlooked by both law students and attorneys.

Each of the briefs in this volume articulates a theme. The theme is sometimes stated directly and sometimes indirectly, but it is ever-present. It is interwoven in virtually every part of the brief, even in the question presented and the point headings. It is like the central message in a well-made movie, a message stated in every "scene" and tying the whole brief together.

To identify the theme, law students and lawyers must step back and think about what picture of the client and case they want to present to the court. They must then ask whether the chosen theme will be able to tie all of the different parts of the brief together, including the different arguments that will be made. Finally, they must strategize about how to incorporate this "picture" into each part of the brief.

Harvard Law Professor Laurence Tribe is the master at using themes in his appellate briefs to the United States Supreme Court. Professor Tribe's themes are often articulated right up front. For example, in *Bowers v. Hardwick*, Professor Tribe opens the brief and the Statement of the Case with this sentence:

> At issue in this case is whether the State of Georgia may send its police into private bedrooms to arrest adults for engaging in consensual, noncommercial sexual acts, with no justification beyond the assertion that those acts are immoral.[6]

Similarly, the Statement of the Case in *Richmond Newspaper, Inc. v. Virginia* opens:

> When on September 11, 1978, as the murder trial of John Paul Stevenson began, the Hanover County Circuit Court granted defense counsel's request for an order clearing the courtroom of all members of the public and press, and directing that the entire trial be conducted in secret, centuries of faithful adherence under Anglo-American law to the principle of open criminal trials came to an abrupt end.[7]

In a single sentence Professor Tribe articulates the theme for the brief, a theme that is interwoven into each of the ensuing sections.

---

[5]   *Id*. at 11.

[6]   Respondent's Brief at 1, *Bowers v. Hardwick,* 478 U.S. 186 (1986).

[7]   Appellant's Brief at 4, *Richmond Newspapers,* 448 U.S. 555 (1979).

Fifth General Principle: Opportunity

Law students, novice, and even experienced lawyers are sometimes surprised to hear that each part of an appellate brief should be viewed as an *opportunity* to *limit length, provide organization, add persuasiveness* and *incorporate a theme*. But the attorneys who authored the briefs in this volume would not be surprised, and that is the reason that their briefs stand out.

So, law students and lawyers alike should keep the following post-it on their computers or typewriters:

> Every Part of the Brief is an Opportunity
> To Limit Length
> To Provide Organization
> To Add Persuasiveness
> To Incorporate a Theme
> (Point Headings Included!)

These are the *general* principles for effective brief writing. Now, let's look specifically at how to write each section effectively.

Specific Principles of Appellate Advocacy

Know the Required Sections of the Brief

To know what sections of the brief the appellate court requires, look at both the general appellate rules for the jurisdiction and the specific rules for your particular court. In general, most appellate courts require the following sections in the brief:

Question Presented
Table of Contents
Table of Authorities
Jurisdictional Statement
Opinions Below
Standard of Review
Statement of the Case
Statement of Facts
Summary of Argument
Argument
Conclusion

Let's take a look at each section individually.

Question Presented

The rules for the United States Supreme Court require that the Question Presented be placed first. The Court wants to know immediately what issue lies at the heart of the appeal. While not all courts require the Question Presented to be placed first, they do require that it be close to the beginning of the brief to give the court a glimpse of the nature of the controversy.

When drafting the Question Presented, remember that it is an opportunity to persuade. As a result, make sure your Question Presented includes, where relevant, the governing law, facts, and policies as your client sees them. Where the issue involves statutory law, let the court know it by including the relevant statutory language that is in issue and a reference to the statute itself. For particularly well-drafted examples, analyze the Questions Presented in the *United States v. Gerber* and *United States v. Mulheren* briefs in this volume.

Table of Contents

The Table of Contents plays two important roles in the brief. First, it tells the reader where each part of the brief can be found. Second, by including all the Point Headings from the brief, the Table provides the court with a summary of the entire argument. Because the Table is at the beginning of the brief, it usually gives the court the first view of the client's position and, therefore, is an excellent opportunity to persuade.

Table of Authorities

The Table of Authorities provides the court with an index of the primary, secondary, and other authority cited in the brief. The use of headings to divide up the different types of authority is very helpful here. Be careful to check your citations; a judge's clerk uses the Table to gather and then read the relevant authority, so typographical errors or incomplete citations make a clerk's job harder—and may make the clerk less favorably disposed toward your client.

Jurisdictional Statement

Appellate courts have the power to dismiss a case *sua sponte* for lack of jurisdiction. As a result, appellate courts want to see the basis for their jurisdiction right up front.

Opinions Below

Many appellate judges read the opinion(s) below before they even read the briefs. Here, again, make sure the citations to the opinions are accurate even though the opinions themselves will be included in the Record or Joint Appendix.

Statutes

Some jurisdictions require that the text of any relevant statute be placed in a separate section at the beginning of the brief or in an appendix. If a jurisdiction does not have such a requirement, but the brief involves one or more statutory issues, include the relevant statutory language in the text of the brief, or at least in a footnote. Quoting the relevant statutory language not only makes the court's job easier, but also adds to your credibility, because the court will not think that the text was excluded because the client had something to hide.

Standard of Review

The Standard of Review is one of the most important parts of the brief. It determines whether the appellate court has full, limited or very limited power to review the issue before it. As a general rule, the court's review power is full, or plenary, if the question is one of law; limited if it is a question of fact; and very limited if it is a question of discretion.[8] Where an issue involves a mixed question of law and fact, the court will apply plenary review to the question of law and limited review to the question of fact.

Because the standard of review the appellate court adopts plays a critical role in the court's ultimate decision, it must be drafted carefully. Despite this section's importance, however, many law school writing courses do not emphasize this part of the brief, and some first-year programs do not require that it be included at all. Because this section is so important, the Standard of Review should be taught and practiced in law school.

For a case in this volume in which the Standard of Review creates one of the issues on appeal, see *In re Holtzman*.

Statement of the Case

In some jurisdictions, the Statement of the Case and the Statement of Facts are combined. Whether combined or in separate sections, the juridical history of the case (Statement of the Case) and the story the court is going to review (Statement of Facts) must be set forth early on in the appellate brief.

The Statement of the Case gives the side that won below an opportunity to emphasize that fact to the appellate court. At the same time, however, the side that lost below should try to find whatever it can that was favorable in the lower court decision(s) and emphasize these points to the appellate court.

An excellent example of the losing side making the most of an unfavorable decision below can be found in Professor Laurence Tribe's brief in *Bowers v. Hardwick*.[9] Here Professor Tribe notes the weakness of the authority cited by the district court where his client lost and emphasizes the favorable reasoning contained in the Eleventh Circuit's reversal:

> The district court ruled that Hardwick had standing, but disposed of his constitutional claims in two sentences, by the citation, without more, of this Court's summary affirmance in *Doe v. Commonwealth's Attorney*, 403 F. Supp. 1199 (E.D. Va. 1975), *aff'd*, 425 U.S. 901 (1976). App. 2-3.
>
> The Court of Appeals for the Eleventh Circuit reversed the district court's dismissal, holding that the statute implicates fundamental constitutional rights by regulating citizens' conduct in their own bedrooms, and involves none of the "public ramifications" that attend "sexual activity with children or with persons who are coerced either through physical force or commercial inducement." App. 26. Indeed, the court held, "[t]he activity [Hardwick] hopes to engage in is quintessentially private and lies at the heart of an intimate association beyond the proper reach of state regulation." *Id.*[10]

---

[8]   For an excellent discussion of the different standards of review, see Ruggero J. Aldisert, WINNING ON APPEAL: BETTER BRIEFS AND ORAL ARGUMENT (rev. 1st ed. 1996) or Edward Re & Joseph Re, BRIEF WRITING AND ORAL ARGUMENT (7th ed. 1999).

[9]   478 U.S. 186 (1986).

[10]   Respondent's Brief at 2-3, *Bowers*.

Professor Tribe does what excellent appellate brief writers do: he finds whatever he can in the opinion below to help his client and crafts it into the Statement of the Case.

Statement of Facts

The attorney's job is to present, not a lack-luster recitation of facts, but a *living, breathing story*. The attorney is the master storyteller, not a mere compiler of information. If the attorney can make the client's facts come to life and capture the court's imagination in this early section of the brief, the court may be willing to follow along throughout the remainder of the document.

The story the attorney/master storyteller recounts is from the client's point of view. Thus, the story told in the appellant's brief and that in the appellee's brief, *for the most part*, should be different.

For an example of how the appellant and appellee can present two very different "stories" of the facts, look at the "stories" in *Palsgraf v. Long Island Railroad*.[11] Every law student is familiar with the case as it is presented by Benjamin Cardozo in his landmark opinion. However, when related in the opposing briefs, more detailed and totally divergent versions of the *Palsgraf* tale emerge.

The brief for Mrs. Palsgraf related the following version of the famous accident:

> It clearly appears that the defendant's two agents, to wit: the platform man and the guard were jointly attempting to forcibly push and pull the passenger on board a moving train. There was no good reason for their acts. The train was equipped with a door and a guard purposely kept the door open to permit the platform man to push the passenger through the opening.
>
> > "He held the door open and the other man on the platform pushed him in" (fol. 117).
>
> In addition, the guard attempted to assist the platform man by pulling the intending passenger on to the platform of the moving train.
>
> > "The platform man tried to push him on and the guard of the train tried to pull him in while the train was in motion." (fol. 85).
>
> While these two agents of the defendant were thus acting in concert the bundle was pushed from the [passenger's] arm. The [passenger] did not drop the bundle of his own volition or from haste, intention or fright, but it was knocked from under his arm by defendant's agent, to wit: the platform man.
>
> > "The man on the station took his arm to assist him in, in grabbing the arm he knocked the bundle out" (fol. 117).
>
> The train was in motion and the guard inside was trying to help his fellow on, and the platform man was trying to help him on from the outside and as he has

---

[11]   162 N.E. 99 (N.Y. 1928).

the bundle in his right hand the platform man pushed his arm and the bundle fell between the platform and the train" (fols. 75-76).

Again

> "Q. The man standing on the platform with the uniform on, you say, pushed this man in?
>
> "A: Yes. When the man in the station took his arm to assist him in, grabbing the arm he knocked the bundle out.
>
> "Q. Well, did you see the platform man's hand strike the bundle?
>
> "A. Yes" (fol. 118).[12]

Not surprisingly, a completely different story emerged in the brief for the Long Island Railroad:

> The undisputed evidence shows that the man carrying the package and his companion entered upon the station platform in great haste and attempted to board the train as it started to leave the station. That the first of the two men boarded the train without difficulty or assistance. As the man with the package jumped aboard the train he had difficulty retaining his balance and defendant's employees took hold of him to help him and prevent his falling from the train. In his efforts to get safely aboard the train he dropped the package which exploded (fols. 85, 116, 140).
>
> It is clearly established from the testimony of the plaintiff's witnesses that the two men rushed upon the platform determined to board the train. Their actions were voluntary and were not induced by defendant's employees, who it does not appear had any opportunity to prevent the men from boarding the train or to warn them against such action. Moreover, it affirmatively appears that defendant's employees took no part in the passenger's attempt until it appeared that the man was in danger of falling (fol. 85). They then took hold of him and prevented his falling from the train. They had no knowledge or notice of the contents of the package and that they acted prudently under the circumstances is demonstrated by the fact that the man retained his position on the train in safety (fol. 116). Nor does it appear that their action caused injury to any of the persons upon the platform. Faced with such an emergency they cannot be charged with negligence because they elected to assist the man in danger other than stand idly by and leave him to his fate.[13]

Whichever picture the court adopts will affect the final outcome. Accordingly, the version of the facts related by Cardozo's opinion holding the Long Island Railroad not liable is essentially a simplified rendition of the story as presented in its brief.

---

[12]   Plaintiff-Respondent's Brief at 6-8, *Palsgraf v. Long Island Railroad,* 162 N.E.2d 99 (1928).

[13]   Appellant's Brief at 5, *Palsgraf.*

Plaintiff was standing on a platform of defendant's railroad after buying a ticket to go to Rockaway Beach. A train stopped at the station, bound for another place. Two men ran forward to catch it. One of the men reached the platform of the car without mishap, though the train was already moving. The other man, carrying a package, jumped aboard the car, but seemed unsteady as if about to fall. A guard on the car, who had held the door open, reached forward to help him in, and another guard on the platform pushed him from behind. In this act, the package was dislodged, and fell upon the rails.[14]

In contrast, Judge Andrews' dissent adopts the view presented in Mrs. Palsgraf's brief that the negligence of the railroad employee caused the explosion, stating, "Assisting a passenger to board a train, the defendant's servant negligently knocked a package from his arms. It fell between the platform and the cars."[15]

Some final rules for drafting the Statement of the Facts. One frequently overlooked rule is to write a smashing first sentence to open the Statement and to orient the court to your client's story. See, for example, the opening sentences in the Statements of Fact in the briefs for *United States v. Gerber* in this volume.

Second, the first sentence of every paragraph is an opportunity to create a sound and persuasive structure for this section of the brief. For each Statement of Facts in this volume, pluck out the first sentences of the paragraphs and analyze how they are crafted to structure and persuade. Third, while a chronological recitation of the facts is often logical, do not be wed to that structure if another fits your Statement better. Fourth, use headings in a particularly long Statement to give the reader a psychological rest and to highlight your persuasive structure. As an example, see the *Holtzman* brief. Finally, remember that in drafting the Statement, you are bound by the record and by the findings of fact below. To rely on facts not in the record or not found below—unless the facts are legislative or judicially noticed—will immediately destroy your credibility with the court and probably result in an adverse decision.

Summary of Argument

All law students and lawyers should learn to do the Summary of Argument well. Some appellate judges consider the Summary the most important part of the brief. The Summary "summarizes" the major and supporting arguments in the brief. A particularly strong Summary begins with a smash-bang sentence sometimes referred to as the *exordium.*

Again, the Summaries of Argument in Professor Laurence Tribe's appellate briefs contain powerful openings. Thus, for example, the Summary in *Bowers v. Hardwick* begins:

---

[14]   *Palsgraf*, 162 N.E. at 99.

[15]   *Id.* at 101 (Andrews, J., dissenting).

> The State of Georgia would extend its criminal law into the very bedrooms of it citizens, to break up even wholly consensual, noncommercial sexual relations between willing adults.[16]

The Summary of Argument in *Richmond Newspapers* has a similarly powerful opening:

> For centuries, it has been an axiom of every just society that the people may enter freely into its halls of justice.[17]

Each first sentence not only is powerful, but also embodies the *theme* that is interwoven throughout the rest of the brief.

Argument

This portion of the brief is probably the most difficult to write. Here the brief writer must combine law, facts and policies in just the right proportion; create a tightly knit organization; craft every sentence for maximum persuasiveness; and demonstrate the client's story to be a winner under the relevant law and applicable policies. In writing this section of the brief, use: (i) point headings; (ii) thesis sections; (iii) first sentences; (iv) supporting legal rules; (v) adverse authority; (vi) relevant policies; (vii) a theme; and (viii) the facts.

(i) Point Headings

Point headings state the major arguments and supporting subarguments for each section of the brief. They are specific statements combining the relevant legal rules and facts from your client's perspective. They should not be overbroad, vague or so general that they could appear in any one of a thousand briefs. They provide both organization and persuasiveness to the brief.

An example of a point heading that clearly summarizes the brief writer's legal position is the first heading from Thurgood Marshall's brief in *Brown v. Board of Education*:

> The State of Kansas in affording opportunities for elementary education to its citizens has no power under the Constitution of the United States to impose racial restrictions and distinctions.[18]

The most important clause in the Point Heading is the frequently AWOL "because" clause. Appellate judges bemoan the failure of brief writers to give the reason for the arguments they make both in the text of the Argument and in the point headings. If a major point heading does not have minor subheadings, the "because" clause must be included in the major heading. Where the major heading has minor subheadings, the "because" clause is included in the subheadings.

Analyze the point headings for the appellate briefs contained in this volume. All of them state both the client's position and the *reason* for that position.

---

[16]   Respondent's Brief at 4, *Bowers.*

[17]   Appellant's Brief at 9, *Richmond Newspapers.*

[18]   Appellants' Brief at 6, *Brown v. Board of Education,* 347 U.S. 483 (1954).

(ii) Thesis Section

Where the Argument contains both major and minor headings, consider using a thesis section between the two to give the reader a roadmap of the reasons supporting the major contention. The thesis can summarize the issue to be addressed in this portion of the brief, your conclusion on the issue, and the reasons for your conclusion. Each reason will be a summary of one of the minor headings to follow.

(iii) First Paragraphs

The first paragraph following a major or minor heading can be used as an opportunity to persuade. Brief writers often construct their first paragraphs to set forth relevant legal principles and/or policies. When possible, however, consider using your first paragraph to capture the court's attention rather than to merely set forth dry legal rules/policies.

(iv) First Sentences

The first sentence of each paragraph in the Argument is critical to the organization, unity and persuasiveness of the appellate brief. When writing a first sentence, ask yourself the following questions:

- Does the sentence state the topic I intend to focus on in this particular paragraph?
- Does the paragraph that follows flesh out what is stated in the first sentence?
- Is the first sentence directly related to the major or minor point heading in this portion of the Argument?
- Does the first sentence support that major or minor point heading?
- Does the first sentence connect to, or logically flow from, the paragraph preceding it?
- Is the first sentence stated in the most persuasive way?

Both trial and appellate judges criticize briefs as being poorly written, poorly organized and unpersuasive. Rewriting first sentences to meet the above criteria is a sound step toward writing both an organized and persuasive brief.

(v) Supporting Legal Rules

All too often appellate briefs are written defensively rather than offensively. Instead of defending against your client's position first, set forth your client's strongest position first and then directly or indirectly address the adversary's position. This offensive strategy requires that you set forth the supporting legal rules first.

Finding the supporting legal rules may require creativity, such as using a trend in the law to support your position or interpreting controlling authority broadly or narrowly. In *Muller v. Oregon*, Justice Brandeis developed his argument based on a trend in the law, stating, "The statute under which the information herein was drawn is only one of the innumerable instances wherein the legislative arm of the state has in its wisdom invoked and applied the police power of the state, when the best interests of the state at large demanded it."[19]

---

[19]   Defendant in Error's Brief at 7, *Muller v. Oregon,* 208 U.S. 412 (1908).

The important points here are to present the relevant legal rules offensively rather than defensively and to rely on creativity within the bounds of credibility in interpreting legal rules when not much authority exists in favor of your client's position.

(vi) Adverse Authority

For ethical and credibility purposes, the brief writer must inform the court of adverse legal authority from the controlling jurisdiction. Where no controlling adverse authority exists, it is probably also advisable to inform the court of persuasive adverse authority.

The damage from adverse authority can be diminished in several ways. First, address adverse authority only after you have presented favorable law and facts. For example, in *Brown v. Board of Education*, Thurgood Marshall dealt with *Plessy v. Ferguson* only after presenting his client's arguments.

Second, distinguish the adverse authority based on the facts, the issue and/or the holding, which can be interpreted broadly or narrowly. In *Brown*, Thurgood Marshall handled the adverse case *Gong Lum v. Rice* by stating:

> *Gong Lum v. Rice* is irrelevant to the issues in this case. There a child of Chinese parentage was denied admission to a school maintained exclusively for white children and was ordered to attend a school for Negro children. The power of the state to make racial distinctions was not in issue.[20]

Third, distinguish by a trend that developed after the adverse authority was decided. Thurgood Marshall used this technique as well, stating, "*Plessy v. Ferguson* is not applicable. Whatever doubts may once have existed in this respect were removed by this Court in *Sweatt v. Pointer...*."[21]

Fourth, distinguish adverse authority by emphasizing social changes that have taken place and here made the legal rule out of step with the times. For example, in *Dawson v. White & Case*, the New York Court of Appeals stated that a blanket prohibition against recovery of good will as a partnership asset was no longer the law in the state because of social and economic changes in the times.

Whether you use the above or other methods to diminish damage from adverse authority, be sure to craft the first sentences of the applicable paragraphs to ward off the damage. Analyze the briefs in this volume to see how the various authors did just that. Finally, where possible, interpret the adverse authority in such a way that you can argue that it is actually consistent with your client's position, and inconsistent with your adversary's.

(vii) Relevant Policies

An appellate court wants to make a "just" decision based on relevant legal and/or social policies. Many arguments, however, fail to use supporting policies in drafting the Argument.

---

[20] Appellant's Brief at 11, *Brown*.

[21] *Id.*

The Brandeis Brief from *Muller v. Oregon* provides a famous example of the policy argument:

> More than twenty states of the Union, including nearly all those in which women are largely employed in factory or similar work, have found it necessary to take action for the protection of their health and safety and the public welfare, and have enacted laws limiting the hours of labor for adult women.
>
> This legislation has not been the result of sudden impulse of passing humor,—it has followed deliberate consideration, and been adopted in the face of much opposition. More than a generation has elapsed between the earliest and the latest of these new acts.
>
> In no instance has any such law been repealed. Nearly every amendment in any law has been in the line of strengthening the law or further reducing the working time.[22]

Try to interweave the policy with your discussion of the law and facts. Even though the "Brandeis Brief" and some briefs included in this volume separate out policy arguments, generally all legal rules are based on policy and so your legal arguments should be intertwined with your policy arguments.

(viii) Theme

Policy arguments also help to create, or at least support, the underlying theme for the appellate brief. Remember the theme is like a thread that holds the fabric of the entire brief together. It crystallizes for the court the reason that your client should win.

For example, suppose the issue in an appellate brief is whether a statute criminalizing threats to the life of the President requires that the criminal defendant not only make the threat, but also intend to carry it out. The government's theme would be the national security interest in protecting the President; the criminal defendant's would be the freedom of speech concerns in finding criminal culpability. Each side would weave its theme into every section of the appellate brief.

(ix) The Facts

Many briefs do not make effective use of the client's favorable facts. Unless the issue is a purely legal one, such as whether state and federal concurrent jurisdiction exists, the Argument must use the facts to show the court why the client should win. The brief writer should be careful here to explain all the steps in the writer's analysis so the court is not left to connect the dots itself.

---

[22]   Defendant in Error's Brief at 16, *Muller*.

Conclusion

The Conclusion contains the prayer for relief, that is, the relief you are requesting from the court. Some attorneys also use the Conclusion to reiterate in summary form the major arguments in the brief.

A word of caution for law students who decide to include such a summary. Very often law students muff here, failing to accurately summarize the points they made in the Argument or reiterating their position at too great length. In the beginning, the law student should probably opt for the prayer for relief alone.

Some Final Thoughts

Just two.

Write the brief for the naive reader, that is, assume the court knows nothing about the law and facts involved in the case. You must make connections clear, fill in the dots so to speak.

Second, be careful to eliminate typographical errors. Judges read enormous amounts of material on a daily basis. To their trained eye, every typographical error—including citation errors—stands out and, therefore, distracts. The appellate brief writer does not want to *distract*, but to *attract* the judge's attention. Believe it or not, even proofreading is part of the persuasive process.

Bibliography

Books:

Arthur L. Alarcon, *Points on Appeal in* APPELLATE PRACTICE MANUAL (1992).

Ruggero J. Aldisert, WINNING ON APPEAL: BETTER BRIEFS AND ORAL ARGUMENT (rev. 1st ed. 1996).

Ruggero J. Aldisert, LOGIC FOR LAWYERS: A GUIDE TO CLEAR LEGAL THINKING (3d ed. 1997).

Kenneth E. Andersen, PERSUASION THEORY AND PRACTICE (1971).

Ursula Bentele & Eve Cary, APPELLATE ADVOCACY: PRINCIPLES AND PRACTICE (3d ed. 1998).

Carole C. Berry, EFFECTIVE APPELLATE ADVOCACY: BRIEF WRITING AND ORAL ARGUMENT (1998).

E. Bettinghaus, PERSUASIVE COMMUNICATION (3d ed. 1980).

Board of Student Advisers, Harvard Law School, INTRODUCTION TO ADVOCACY: RESEARCH, WRITING, AND ARGUMENT (6th ed. 1996).

Charles D. Breitel, *A Summing Up*, *in* COUNSEL ON APPEAL (Arthur A. Charpentier ed. 1968).

Charles R. Calleros, LEGAL METHOD AND LEGAL WRITING (3d ed. 1998).

Jim R. Carrigan, *Some Nuts and Bolts of Appellate Advocacy in* APPELLATE PRACTICE MANUAL (1992).

P. Carrington, D. Meador & M. Rosenberg, JUSTICE ON APPEAL (1976).

Jordan B. Cherrick, *Issues, Facts, and Appellate Strategy in* APPELLATE PRACTICE MANUAL (1992).

Frank Morey Coffin, THE WAYS OF A JUDGE: REFLECTIONS FROM THE FEDERAL APPELLATE BENCH (1980).

Linda Holdeman Edwards, LEGAL WRITING: PROCESS, ANALYSIS, AND ORGANIZATION (1996).

Toni M. Fine, AMERICAN LEGAL SYSTEMS: A RESOURCE AND REFERENCE GUIDE (1997).

Daniel M. Friedman, *Winning on Appeal in* APPELLATE PRACTICE MANUAL (1992).

Bryan A. Garner, *The Language of Appellate Advocacy in* APPELLATE PRACTICE MANUAL (1992).

Bryan A. Garner, THE WINNING BRIEF (1999).

John C. Godbold, *Twenty Pages and Twenty Minutes in* APPELLATE PRACTICE MANUAL (1992).

Margaret Z. Johns, PROFESSIONAL WRITING FOR LAWYERS (1998).

Miriam Kass, *The Ba Theory of Persuasive Writing in* APPELLATE PRACTICE MANUAL (1992).

Whitman Knapp, *The Civil and the Criminal Appeal Compared in* COUNSEL ON APPEAL (Arthur A. Charpentier ed. 1968).

L.H. La Rue, A STUDENT'S GUIDE TO THE STUDY OF LAW: AN INTRODUCTION (1987).

Donald P. Lay, LAW: A HUMAN PROCESS (1996).

Christopher T. Lutz, *Why Can't Lawyers Write? in* APPELLATE PRACTICE MANUAL (1992).

Thurgood Marshall, *The Federal Appeal in* COUNSEL ON APPEAL (Arthur A. Charpentier ed. 1968).

Robert J. Martineau, MODERN APPELLATE PRACTICE: FEDERAL AND STATE CIVIL APPEALS (1983).

John E. Nelson, III, *Building the Brief in* APPELLATE PRACTICE MANUAL (1992).

Richard K. Neumann, Jr., LEGAL REASONING AND LEGAL WRITING: STRUCTURE, STRATEGY, AND STYLE (3d ed. 1998).

New York State Bar Association, PRACTITIONER'S HANDBOOK FOR APPEALS TO THE COURT OF APPEALS OF THE STATE OF NEW YORK (2d ed. 1991).

Laurel Currie Oates, Anne Enquist & Kelly Kunsch, THE LEGAL WRITING HANDBOOK: ANALYSIS, RESEARCH, AND WRITING (2d ed. 1998).

Dennis J.C. Owens, *Second and Third Chances on Appeal in* APPELLATE PRACTICE MANUAL (1992).

Girvan Peck, *Strategy of the Brief in* APPELLATE PRACTICE MANUAL (1992).

Girvan Peck, WRITING PERSUASIVE BRIEFS (1984).

Mario Pittoni, BRIEF WRITING AND ARGUMENTATION (3d ed. 1967).

Milton Pollack, *The Civil Appeal in* COUNSEL ON APPEAL (Arthur A. Charpentier ed. 1968).

Edward Re & Joseph Re, *Brief Writing and Oral Argument* (7th ed. 1999).

Simon H. Rifkind, *Appellate Courts Compared, in* COUNSEL ON APPEAL (Arthur A. Charpentier ed. 1968).

James L. Robertson, *Reality on Appeal in* APPELLATE PRACTICE MANUAL (1992).

David S. Romantz & Kathleen Elliott Vinson, LEGAL ANALYSIS: THE FUNDAMENTAL SKILL (1998).

Marjorie Dick Rombauer, LEGAL PROBLEM SOLVING: ANALYSIS, RESEARCH AND WRITING (5th ed. 1991).

Gary L. Sasso, *Anatomy of the Written Argument in* APPELLATE PRACTICE MANUAL (1992).

Priscilla Anne Schwab, ed., APPELLATE PRACTICE MANUAL (1992).

Nancy L. Schultz & Louis J. Sirico, Jr., LEGAL WRITING AND OTHER LAWYERING SKILLS (3d ed. 1998).

Helene S. Shapo, Marilyn R. Walter & Elizabeth Fajans, WRITING AND ANALYSIS IN THE LAW (3d ed. 1995).

Louis J. Sirico, Jr. & Nancy L. Schultz, PERSUASIVE WRITING FOR LAWYERS AND THE LEGAL PROFESSION (1995).

L. Stebbing, A MODERN INTRODUCTION TO LOGIC (7th ed. 1961).

Harris B. Steinberg, *The Criminal Appeal, in* COUNSEL ON APPEAL (Arthur A. Charpentier ed. 1968).

Robert L. Stern, APPELLATE PRACTICE IN THE UNITED STATES (1981).

Robert L. Stern & Eugene Gressman, SUPREME COURT PRACTICE (5th ed. 1978).

Robert L. Stern, *Tips for Appellate Advocates in* APPELLATE PRACTICE MANUAL (1992).

Albert Tate, Jr., *The Art of Brief Writing: What a Judge Wants to Read in* APPELLATE PRACTICE MANUAL (1992).

Michael E. Tigar, FEDERAL APPEALS: JURISDICTION AND PRACTICE (1987).

UCLA Moot Court Honors Program, HANDBOOK OF APPELLATE ADVOCACY (3d ed. 1993).

Irving Younger, PERSUASIVE WRITING (1990).

Frederick Bernays Wiener, BRIEFING AND ARGUING FEDERAL APPEALS (1961).

Robin S. Wellford, LEGAL ANALYSIS AND WRITING (1997).

Articles:

Ruggero Aldisert, *The Appellate Bar: Professional Responsibility and Professional Competence—A View from the Jaundiced Eye of One Appellate Judge*, 11 CAP. U. L. REV. 444 (1982).

Ruggero Aldisert, *Precedent: What It Is and What It Isn't; When Do We Kiss It and When Do We Kill It?*, 17 PEPP. L. REV. 605 (1990).

William A. Bablitch, *Writing to Win,* THE COMPLEAT LAWYER (Winter 1988).

Alice M. Batchelder, *Some Brief Reflections of a Circuit Judge*, 54 OHIO ST. L.J. 1453 (1993).

Myron H. Bright, *Appellate Brief Writing: Some "Golden" Rules*, 17 CREIGHTON L. REV. 1069 (1983-1984).

Harold G. Christensen, *How to Write for the Judge*, 9 LITIGATION 25 (Spring 1983).

Frank E. Cooper, *Stating the Issue in Appellate Briefs*, 49 A.B.A. J. 180 (1963).

R. Kirkland Cozine, *The Emergence of Written Appellate Briefs in the Nineteenth-Century United States*, 38 AM. J. LEGAL HIST. 482 (1994).

John Davis, *The Argument of an Appeal*, 26 A.B.A. J. 895 (1940).

William O. Douglas, *Stare Decisis*, 49 COLUM. L. REV. 735 (1949).

Christine M. Durham, *Writing a Winning Appellate Brief*, 10 UTAH B.J., October 1997, at 34.

Judith D. Fischer, *Bareheaded and Barefaced Counsel: Courts React to Unprofessionalism in Lawyers' Papers*, 31 SUFFOLK U. L. REV. 1 (1997).

Murray L. Gurfein, *Appellate Advocacy, Modern Style*, 4 LITIGATION 8 (Winter 1978).

Christopher H. Hoving, *The Art of the Appellate Brief*, 72 A.B.A. J. 52 (1986).

Robert H. Jackson, *Advocacy Before the Supreme Court: Suggestions for Effective Case Presentation*, 37 A.B.A. J. 801 (1951).

Irving R. Kaufman, *Appellate Advocacy in the Federal Courts*, 79 F.R.D. 165 (1978).

Alex Kozinski, *In Praise of Moot Court—Not!*, 97 COLUM. L. REV. 178 (1997).

Lay, *The Crisis in Appellate Advocacy*, 16 INT'L SOC. OF BARRISTERS Q. 321 (1981).

James W. McElhaney, *A Matter of Style: What It Takes To Make Legal Writing Look Persuasive*, A.B.A. J. 84 (Apr. 1996).

James W. McElhaney, *Powers of Persuasion: How You Argue Will Affect Whether the Judge Sees Things Your Way*, A.B.A. J. 92 (Oct. 1995).

Morris, *Oral Arguments and Written Briefs—DCA Judges Comment*, 62 FLA. B.J. 23 (1988).

S. Eric Ottesen, *Effective Brief-Writing for California Appellate Courts*, 21 SAN DIEGO L. REV. 371 (1984).

Raymond E. Peters, *The Preparation and Writing of Briefs on Appeal*, 22 CAL. ST. B.J. 175 (1947).

Diana Pratt, *Representing Non-Mainstream Clients to Mainstream Judges: A Challenge of Persuasion*, 4 J. LEGAL WRITING INST. 79 (1998).

Harry Pregerson, *The Seven Sins of Appellate Brief Writing and Other Transgressions,* 34 UCLA L. REV. 431 (1986).

E. Barrett Prettyman, *Some Observations Concerning Appellate Advocacy*, 39 VA. L. REV. 285 (1953).

Report and Recommendations of the Committee on Appellate Skills Training Appellate Judges' Conference Judicial Administration Division American Bar Association, 54 U. CIN. L. REV. 129 (1985).

Alvin B. Rubin, *What Appeals to the Court* (Book Review), 67 TEX. L. REV. 225 (1988).

Mark Rust, *Mistakes to Avoid on Appeal*, 74 A.B.A. J. 78 (Sept. 1988).

Wiley B. Rutledge, *The Appellate Brief*, 28 A.B.A. J. 251 (1942).

Pamela Samuelson, *Good Legal Writing: Of Orwell and Window Panes*, 46 U. PITT. L. REV. 149 (1984).

Walter V. Schaefer, *Appellate Advocacy*, 23 TENN. L. REV. 471 (1954).

Walter V. Schaefer, *Precedent and Policy*, 34 U. CHI. L. REV. 3 (1966).

Walter V. Schaefer, *The Appellate Court*, 3 U. CHI. L.S. REC. 1 (1954).

Morey L. Sear, *Briefing in the United States District Court for the Eastern District of Louisiana*, 70 TUL. L. REV. 207 (1995).

James van R. Springer, *Some Suggestions on Preparing Briefs on the Merits in the Supreme Court of the United States*, 33 CATH. U. L. REV. 593 (1984).

Arthur Vanderbilt, *Forensic Persuasion*, 7 WASH. & LEE L. REV. 1 (1950).

Charles Alan Wright, *The Doubtful Ominiscience of Appellate Courts*, 41 MINN. L. REV. 751 (1957).

UNITED STATES v. GERBER

No. 92-2741

IN THE UNITED STATES COURT OF APPEALS
FOR THE SEVENTH CIRCUIT

United States of America,

    Plaintiff-Appellee,

        v.

Arthur Joseph Gerber,

    Defendant-Appellant.

Appeal from the United States
District Court for the
Southern District of Indiana,
Evansville Division

No. EV 91-19-CR

Honorable Gene E. Brooks
Judge Presiding

BRIEF OF APPELLANT

Harvey M. Silets
Kenneth M. Kliebard
KATTEN MUCHIN & ZAVIS
525 West Monroe Street
Suite 1600
Chicago, Illinois 60661
(312) 902-5200

Jeffrey L. Lantz
525 Sycamore
P.O. Box 1087
Evansville, Indiana 47706
(812) 464-0044

*Attorneys for
Defendant-Appellant
Arthur Joseph Gerber*

CERTIFICATE OF INTEREST

Cause No. 92-2741

Short Title: <u>United States of America v. Arthur Joseph Gerber</u>
To enable the judges to determine whether recusal is necessary or appropriate, an attorney for nongovernmental party or amicus curiae, or a private attorney representing a government party, mush furnish a certificate of interest stating the following information:

(1) The full name of every party or amicus the attorney represents in the case:

<u>Arthur Joseph Gerber</u>

(2) If any such party or amicus is a corporation:

    i)   Its parent corporation, if any:

       <u>N/A</u>

    ii) A list of its stockholders which are publicly held companies owning 10% or more of the stock in the party or amicus:

       <u>N/A</u>

(3) The names of all law firms whose partners or associates have appeared for the party in the district court or are expected to appear for the party in this court:

<u>Jeffery L. Lantz</u>

<u>Katten Muchin & Zavis</u>

<u>Ober, Symmes, Cardwell, Voyles & Zahn</u>

This certificate shall be filed with the appearance form or upon the filing of a motion in this court, whichever occurs first. The text of the certificate (i.e., caption omitted) shall also be included in the front of the table of contents of the party's main brief.*

*If an attorney changes law firm affiliation after the filing of the main brief, an original and three copies of an amended certificate of interest must be filed.

Attorney's Signature: <u>/s/ Kenneth M. Kliebard</u>
              Date: <u>August 6, 1992</u>

CERTIFICATE OF INTEREST

Cause No. 92-2741

Short Title: <u>United States of America v. Arthur Joseph Gerber</u>

To enable the judges to determine whether recusal is necessary or appropriate, an attorney for nongovernmental party or amicus curiae, or a private attorney representing a government party, mush furnish a certificate of interest stating the following information:

(1) The full name of every party or amicus the attorney represents in the case:

<u>Arthur Joseph Gerber</u>

(2) If any such party or amicus is a corporation:

    i)   Its parent corporation, if any:

    <u>N/A</u>

    ii) A list of its stockholders which are publicly held companies owning 10% or more of the stock in the party or amicus:

    <u>N/A</u>

(3) The names of all law firms whose partners or associates have appeared for the party in the district court or are expected to appear for the party in this court:

<u>Jeffery L. Lantz, sole practitioner</u>

<u>J. J. Paul, III, OBER, SYMMES, CARDWELL, VOYLES & ZAHN</u>

<u>Harvey M. Silets, KATTEN MUCHIN & ZAVIS</u>

<u>Kenneth M. Kliebard, KATTEN MUCHIN & ZAVIS</u>

This certificate shall be filed with the appearance form or upon the filing of a motion in this court, whichever comes first. The text of the certificate (i.e., caption omitted) shall also be included in the front of the table of contents of the party's main brief.*

*If an attorney changes law firm affiliation after the filing of the main brief, an original and three copies of an amended certificate of interest must be filed.

Attorney's Signature: <u>/s/ Jeffery L. Lantz</u>
              Date: <u>July 30, 1992</u>

TABLE OF CONTENTS

TABLE OF AUTHORITIES
Cases

Statutes And Legislative Material

I. STATEMENT OF THE CASE

In 1979, Congress passed the Archaeological Resources Protection Act of 1979, 16 U.S.C. §§ 470aa-470ll ("ARPA"), in order "to secure, for the present and future benefit of the American people, the protection of archaeological resources and sites which are on *public lands and Indian lands*." 16 U.S.C. § 470aa(b) (emphasis added.) On July 11, 1991, Defendant-Appellant, Arthur Joseph Gerber ("Gerber"), was indicted under Section 470ee(c) of ARPA for purchasing, removing, and selling Indian artifacts that were removed from *private land* in alleged violation of State or local law.[1] These artifacts were recovered by Gerber after a road construction crew, which had been digging for fill soil on property owned by the General Electric Company, excavated an Indian mound, thereby unearthing the artifacts. The Government alleged that Gerber's acts constituted conversion and trespassing under Indiana law and thereby could serve as predicate state or local law violations for purposes of Section 470ee(c). In the thirteen years between the enactment of ARPA and the indictment of Gerber and several others involved in the same incident, there had been no reported prosecution under Section 470ee of ARPA except where the Government proved that the archaeological resources at issue were taken from public or Indian lands. Nor are there any reported decisions where the Government sought to extend ARPA to violations of ordinary state laws, as opposed to violations of state archaeological resources protection laws.

Note how a key argument for Gerber—that ARPA does not apply to private lands—appears in the very first sentence.

Because there is clear support that ARPA is inapplicable to artifacts removed from non-public, non-Indian lands, Gerber filed a Motion to Dismiss the Indictment with the District Court on December 2, 1991, in which he presented that argument. Gerber also sought dismissal of the Indictment based on the fact that the alleged violation of a state or local law, which is required under Section 470ee(c), was not a violation of an archaeological resource protection law. Without that requirement, Section 470ee(c) cannot be saved from absurd and unconstitutional constructions. Also relevant here, Gerber argued below that Section 470ee(c) was unconstitutionally vague.

The Honorable Gene E. Brooks, in an Order and Memorandum dated January 28, 1992, summarily rejected all grounds raised in Gerber's Motion to Dismiss. With respect to the argument that ARPA is inapplicable to non-public, non-Indian lands, the Court reaffirmed its holding in the companion case of *United States v. Way*, No. EV 90-32-CR,

---

[1]   Section 470ee(c) provided at all relevant times as follows:

No person may sell, purchase, exchange, transport, receive, or offer to sell, purchase, or exchange, in interstate or foreign commerce, any archaeological resource excavated, removed, sold, purchased, exchanged, transported, or received in violation of any provision, rule, regulation, ordinance, or permit in effect under State or local law.

16 U.S.C. § 470ee(c).

that Section 470ee(c) applies to private lands. (R. 7: Court's Order of Jan. 28, 1992, at 6.; *United States v. Way*, No. EV 90-32-CR, slip. op. at 4 (S.D. Ind. Oct. 25, 1990).) The District Court in *Way* noted that subsection (a) addresses violations of ARPA's regulatory section and that subsection (b) prohibits trafficking in archaeological resources obtained from public or Indian lands in violation of subsection (a). (*Way*, No. EV 90-32-CR, slip. op. at 4.) The court determined that to limit subsection (c) to public and Indian lands would make that subsection superfluous. (*Id*. at 5.) As to the argument that Section 470ee(c) requires a violation of a state or local archaeological resource protection law, the Court held that the plain meaning of that section contained no such requirement since it refers to the violation of "any" law. (R. 7: Court's Order of Jan. 28, 1992, at 4-5.) Finally, the Court rejected the vagueness argument, simply holding that ARPA makes clear what conduct is prohibited and would not lead police, prosecutors, or juries to pursue their personal predilections. (*Id*. at 5.) In reaching its holdings, the District Court refused to examine the legislative history of ARPA under the belief that ARPA was unambiguous, even though its interpretation of ARPA created inconsistencies within ARPA and would lead to absurdities. (*Id*. at 3.)

Because the District Court rejected the legal arguments raised in the Motion to Dismiss, and because the factual matters in this case are largely undisputed, Gerber entered into a conditional plea agreement, pursuant to Rule 11(a)(2) and Rule 11(e)(1)A) of the Federal Rules of Criminal Procedure. Under the terms of that plea agreement, Gerber reserved his right to appeal the judgment of the District Court and that Court's denial of the Defendant's Motion to Dismiss the Indictment and all issues raised therein. (R. 9: Guilty Plea Agreement ¶ 10.) As part of that plea agreement, Gerber entered pleas of guilty to five counts of the Indictment, all of which alleged violations of Section 470ee(c). (*Id*. ¶ 2.)

Following a sentencing hearing, Judge Brooks sentenced Gerber to 12 months on each of the five counts, to run concurrently, imposed a fine of $5,000.00, and imposed a period of supervised release during which Gerber will not be allowed to attend or promote archaeological shows. (R. 15: Judgment at 3-4.) The Court stayed the judgment pending the outcome of this appeal.

II. <u>STATEMENT OF ISSUES PRESENTED</u>

(1)   Whether the anti-trafficking provision contained in Section 470ee(c) of the Archaeological Resources Protection Act of 1979, 16 U.S.C. §§ 470ee, applies to archaeological resources that were not removed from federal or Indian lands?

(2)   Whether the anti-trafficking provision contained in Section 470ee(c) of the Archaeological Resources Protection Act of 1979, 16 U.S.C. §§ 470aa-470ee, is unconstitutionally vague?

(3)   Whether the anti-trafficking provision contained in Section 470ee(c) of the Archaeological Resources Protection Act of 1897, 16 U.S.C. §§ 470-aa-470ee, requires the violation of a state or local archaeological resource protection law?

III. RELEVANT STATUTE

At the time of the acts complained of in the Indictment, Section 470ee provided:

(a)   Unauthorized excavation, removal, damage, alteration, or defacement archaeological resources

No person may excavate, remove, damage, or otherwise alter or deface any archaeological resource on public lands or Indian lands unless such activity is pursuant to a permit issued under section 470cc of this title, a permit referred to in section 470cc(h)(2) of this title, or the exemption contained in section 470cc(g)(1) of this title.

(b)   Trafficking in archaeological resources the excavation or removal of which was wrongful under Federal law

No person may sell, purchase, exchange, transport, receive, or offer to sell, purchase, or exchange any archaeological resource if such resource was excavated or removed from public or Indian lands in violation of—

(1)   the prohibition contained in subsection (a) of this section, or

(2)   any provision, rule, regulation, ordinance, or permit in effect under any other provision of Federal law.

(c)   Trafficking in interstate or foreign commerce in archaeological resources the excavation, removal, sale, purchase, exchange, transportation or receipt of which was wrongful under State or local law

No person may sell, purchase, exchange, transport, receive, or offer to sell, purchase, or exchange in interstate or foreign commerce, any archaeological resource excavated, removed, sold, purchased, exchanged, transported, or received in violation of any provision, rule regulation, ordinance, or permit in effect under State or local law.

(d)   Penalties

Any person who knowingly violates or counsels, procures, solicits, or employs any other person to violate, any prohibition contained in subsection (a), (b) , or (c) of this section shall, upon conviction, be fined not more than $10,000 or imprisoned no more than one year, or both: Provided, however, That if the commercial or archaeological value of the archaeological resources involved exceeds the sum of $5,000 such person shall be fined not more than $20,000 or imprisoned not more than two years, or both.

In the case of a second or subsequent such violation upon conviction such person shall be fined not more than $100,000, or imprisoned not more than five years, or both.

(e)   Effective date

The prohibitions contained in this section shall take effect on October 31, 1979.

(f)   Prospective application

Nothing in subsection (b)(1) of this section shall be deemed applicable to any person with respect to an archaeological resource which was in the lawful possession of such person prior to October 31, 1979.

(g)   Removal of arrowheads located on ground surface

Nothing in subsection (d) of this section shall be deemed applicable to any person with respect to the removal of arrowheads located on the surface of the ground.

IV. STATEMENT OF JURISDICTION

This appeal is from the conviction of Gerber in the United States District Court for the Southern District of Indiana, Evansville Division. The District Court had jurisdiction over this case pursuant to 18 U.S.C. § 3231 because the Indictment charged Gerber with offenses against the laws of the United States. This Court has jurisdiction over the present appeal pursuant to 28 U.S.C. § because the appeal is from a final decision of the United States District Court. The sentencing is considered to be a final judgment. *See Berman v. United States*, 302 U.S. 211, 212 (1937). The Judgment was entered by the District Court on July 14, 1992, and the Notice of Appeal was filed on July 23, 1992.

V. STATEMENT OF FACTS

Sometime prior to the summer of 1987, the Indiana Department of Highways authorized plans for the construction of a new road in Posey County, Indiana known as County Road 850S. (R. 2: Indictment ¶ 13.) County Road 850S was intended to connect Old State Road 69 with New State 69 so as to improve traffic conditions near the GE Plastics Manufacturing Division, Mount Vernon Plant Site ("GE"), which is located near Old State Road 69. (*Id*. ¶¶ 13, 10.) GE is owned by the General Electric Company and manufactures plastic materials and resins at the Mount Vernon Plant. (*Id*. ¶ 10.)

The general contract for construction of Count Road 850S was awarded to J.H. Rudolph & Company, Inc., which in turn subcontracted some of the earthmoving work to Boyd Brothers, Incorporated ("Boyd Brothers"). (*Id*. ¶ 16.) As part of the road construction process, Boyd Brothers obtained an archaeological survey to determine whether there were any archaeological

Unlike the brief for the United States, this statement of facts does not dwell on the number or value of the artifacts involved. Instead, it emphasizes that the land was not posted. It also attempts to put Gerber's actions in a better light by noting that the site had already been despoiled and that many other persons were also taking artifacts.

sties in the are affected by the new road. (*Id.* ¶ 17.) The survey disclosed no archaeo-logical sites. (*Id.*) The survey required, however, that the State of Indiana be notified immediately in the event that archaeological sites were discovered during excavation of the new road. (*Id.*)

During the course of the construction of County Road 805S the need arose for fill soil, which was removed by Boyd Brothers' employees from a large mound located on the GE site. (*See* Sentencing Hearing Tr. at 79, 80-82). Testimony of one of the Boyd Brothers employees who assisted in bulldozing the mound indicates that some of the soil removed from the mound may have been used for the road bed, but some of the soil was also used for other purposes at the GE Mount Vernon Site. (*See* Sentencing Hearing Tr. at 80-82.) The mound razed for this fill soil was in fact a significant Hopewell Indian ceremonial site from the Middle Woodland period. (*See* R. 2: Indictment ¶ 14.)

One of Boyd Brothers' bulldozer operators involved in the road project was John William Way ("Way"). (R. 2: Indictment ¶ 17.) On approximately June 3, 1998, Way was bulldozing the mound on the GE site to obtain soil, and in the process unearthed thousands of Indian artifacts. (*Id.* ¶ 19.) Without notifying the authorities of his discov-ery, Way removed a large number of the artifacts and brought them to this home in Illi-nois. (*Id.* ¶¶ 20, 21.) No other agent or employee of Boyd Brothers notified the proper authorities of the discovery of the artifacts. (*Id.* ¶ 20.)

Later, Way spoke with Gerber over the telephone and asked Gerber if he would be interested in viewing the artifacts removed from the GE mound. (R 11: Stipulated Facts at 2.) Gerber told Way that he would be interested in viewing the artifacts. (*Id.*) Gerber's interest in the artifacts was understandable. At that time Gerber, a photographer by pro-fession, had collected prehistoric Indian artifacts for more than thirty-five years and dur-ing that time he had become knowledgeable about the prehistoric civilizations that inhabited North America. (*Id.* at 1.) Accordingly, Gerber made arrangements to view the artifacts in Way's possession. (*Id.* at 2.)

Gerber subsequently drove to Way's residence in Grayville, Illinois to examine the artifacts in Way's possession. (*Id.*) Upon examining the artifacts, Gerber determined that Way's collection consisted of Hopewell artifacts from the Middle Woodland period. (*Id.*) This excited Gerber because he held a special interest in Hopewell artifacts and materials. (*Id.* at 1.) Gerber expressed an interest in purchasing the artifacts from Way, who ultimately agreed to sell the artifacts to Gerber for $6,000.00. (*Id.*) Way also told Gerber that he would show Gerber the site from which the artifacts had been removed. (*Id.* at 2-3)

On approximately July 21, 1988, a few days after Gerber's initial visit with Way, Gerber returned to Way's residence to consummate the purchase of Way's artifacts. (*Id.* at 3.) That evening, after the purchase of the artifacts was concluded, Way drove Ger-ber to the GE site in Indiana from which Way had obtained the artifacts. (*Id.*) It was undisputed that at the time of Gerber's visit, GE's property was unfenced and was not posted with "No Trespassing" signs. (*Id.*)

The two men then walked on GE's property to the Mound, where they encountered other people digging for artifacts on the mound. (*Id.*) There had been so much digging and activity at the site that Gerber described it as looking "like a bombed out battle zone," and thought that it might be too late to recover any artifacts from the site. (Sentencing Hearing Tr. at 201-202.) In fact, Gerber's expert witness later testified at the sentencing hearing that the construction equipment—not the collectors—caused the bulk of the damage to the mound and that as much as 70% of the mound's cap had been removed by that equipment. (*See* Sentencing Hearing Tr. at 159-50.) After examining what remained of the mound, Gerber returned to his home in Tell City, Indiana. (R. 11: Stipulated Facts at 3.)

Several days after his initial visit to the GE site, Gerber contacted two of his long-time acquaintances, John David Towery and Danny Gene Glover, to obtain their assistance in recovering additional artifacts from the mound. (*Id.*) On four occasions, Gerber went to the mound accompanied each time by Towery, and on all but one occasion he was accompanied by Glover. (*Id.* at 4-5.) The three men recovered artifacts from the mound on each of their visits to the mound. (*Id.* at 4-6.) Gerber, Towery, and Glover divided their shares of the recovered artifacts equally, although Glover on each occasion sold his one-third share to Towery and Gerber. (*Id.* at 5, 6.) Some of those artifacts were subsequently sold for of total of $450-$900 at an Indiana Relic show sponsored by the Owensboro-Kentucky Indian Art Show, Inc. in Owensboro, Kentucky. (*Id.* at 7-8, 2.) Also, because Gerber was particularly interested in Hopewell artifacts, Gerber purchased Towery's share of the artifacts for $2,000. (*Id.* at 8.)

Gerber was subsequently indicted on July 11, 1991, for his participation in the recovery of artifacts at the GE site, and he entered into a conditional guilty plea to five counts of the Indictment alleging violations of Section 470ee(c) or ARPA. (*See generally* R. 2: Indictment; R. 9: Guilty Plea Agreement ¶ 10.) Following a sentencing hearing, Judge Brooks sentenced Gerber to twelve months on each of the five Counts of Section 470ee(c) violations, to run concurrently, imposed a fine of $5,000.00, and imposed a period of supervised release during which Gerber will be banned from attending or promoting archaeological shows. (R. 15; Judgment at 3.) This appeal timely followed.

VI. STANDARD OF REVIEW

This Court's determination of whether Gerber violated Section 470ee(c) or ARPA involves statutory interpretation of ARPA, which is a question of law. *E.g.*, *United States v. Montoya*, 827 F.2d 143, 146 (7th Cir. 1987). The legal determinations made by the District Court are reviewed *de novo*. *Id.*

VII. SUMMARY OF ARGUMENT

There are three primary reasons why the Indictment against Gerber should have been dismissed: (1) ARPA does not apply to artifacts removed from non-public, non-Indian lands; (2) Section 470ee(c) is void for vagueness; and (3) the predicate act required under Section 470ee(c) must necessarily be a violation of an archaeological resource protection law. Each of these arguments was presented to the District Court in the Motion to Dismiss. Gerber is mindful of the fact that the District Court rejected his constructions as contrary to what that court perceived as the plain meaning of Section 470ee(c) or as resulting in a superfluous construction of that subsection. In so holding, the District Court ignored the contrary intent indicated in ARPA itself, the valuable and insightful legislative history of ARPA, and the absurdities that would result from a literal reading of Section 470ee(c). When these factors are taken into consideration, it is clear that the Indictment against Gerber should have been dismissed.

First and foremost, the Indictment should have been dismissed because application of Section 470ee(c) to artifacts removed from non-public, non-Indian lands is beyond the scope of ARPA. Section470ee(c) admittedly does not state whether it is limited to archaeological resources removed from public or Indian lands. That section cannot be viewed in isolation, however. The language of ARPA, the framework or ARPA, ARPA's legislative history, and subsequent congressional hearings addressing what is rightly perceived by Congress and experts in the area, including the United States Department of the Interior, as ARPA's inapplicability to non-public, non-Indian lands, all evidence that Section 470ee(c) does not extend to archaeological resources removed from private lands. The Indictment should have been dismissed for that reason.

At a minimum, Section 470ee(c) of ARPA is unconstitutionally vague in that it does not provide citizens with adequate notice of the proscribed acts. As such, ARPA's vagueness allows law enforcement, prosecutors, and juries to pursue their personal predilections. In fact, this confusion over the application of ARPA to private property and the arbitrary and inequitable enforcement that will result is perhaps best evidenced by the statements in the Technical Brief prepared by the Department of the Interior concerning ARPA and the statements of current and former United States Attorney and others in recent articles and Congressional hearings to the effect that ARPA is inapplicable to non-federal lands. This is strong evidence that without clarification from Congress or a limiting interpretation by the courts, Section 470ee(c) will be arbitrarily applied. For this reason, ARPA is unconstitutionally vague and the Indictment should have been dismissed.

Finally, even ignoring the fact that ARPA is in applicable to archaeological resources removed from non-federal lands, the predicate state or local law violation required under 16 U.S.C. § 470ee(c) must be the violation of an archaeological or cultural resource protection law. This requirement, although not apparent from a purely literal reading of Section 470ee(c), is necessary as a matter of construction and on constitutional grounds. In fact, if such a requirement is not read into Section 470ee(c), a whole host of absurd violations and prosecutions under ARPA could result in a manner completely unintended by Congress. This limiting interpretation is equally supported by the framework of ARPA and the legislative history of that section.

VIII. <u>ARGUMENT</u>

A. Section 470ee(c) Does Not Apply to Archaeological Resources Removed From Non-Public, Non-Indian Lands

1. <u>Introduction</u>

Section 470ee(c) is narrow in scope, and there are several reasons why that section's reach must be limited to artifacts removed from public and Indian lands. First, by examining ARPA, its structure, and its legislative history, it is clear that Congress had no intention of addressing excavations on non-federal lands or archaeological resources obtained from those excavations. It is also easily demonstrated that there is no basis for concluding that a construction limited to federal lands would render subsection (c) superfluous, as the District Court held. Second, the uniform consensus of the commentators and even the United States Department of the Interior is that ARPA does not extend to non-federal lands. Third, a construction of ARPA limiting Section 470ee(c) to public and Indian lands is dictated by established principles of federalism, which call for a narrow construction of federal laws that interfere with state sovereign powers absent unmistakably clear language in a statute. There is no such unmistakably clear language here. Finally, the conclusion that Section 470ee(c) does not extend to artifacts removed from non-public, non-Indian lands is also mandated by the rule of lenity.

Here, each point heading and sub-heading asserts that the statute does not apply to Gerber's actions. Note also how the final paragraph of Section 2(a) points to "inconsistencies and absurdities" which would result from ruling against the client's position.

2. ARPA And Its Legislative History Reveal That Section 470ee(c) Is Inapplicable To Archaeological Resources Removed From Non-Public, Non-Indian Lands

As a general rule, the starting point for analyzing a statute is the language of the statute itself. *Ernst & Ernst v. Hochfelder*, 425 U.S. 185, 197 (1976). It is frequently said that where statutory language is plain, the inquiry ends and there is no need to further examine legislative intent. *E.g., Indiana Port Commission v. Bethlehem Steel Corp.*, 835 F.2d 1207, 1210 (7th Cir. 1987). "Yet plain meaning, like beauty, is sometimes in the eye of the beholder." *Florida Power & Light Co. v. Lorion*, 470 U.S. 729, 737 (1985). For that reason, "the statute is to be read as a whole [citation omitted], since the meaning of statutory language, plain or not, depends on context." *King v. St. Vincent's Hospital*, 112 S. Ct. 570, 574 (1991); *accord Crandon v. United States*, 494 U.S. 152, 158 (1990) (courts must look "to the design of the statute as a whole and to its object and policy.").

In some instances, examination of the statute as a whole as well as its legislative history will require an interpretation that is at odds with a literal reading of the section at issue. *See, e.g., Nupulse, Inc. v. Schlueter Co.*, 853 F.2d 545, 549 (7th Cir. 1988) (Court rejected literal interpretation of section of the Lanham Act in light of statute's overriding purpose and its legislative history). Courts must also reject a literal construction "if it would lead to absurd results or would thwart the obvious purpose of the statute." *Smith v. Brown*, 815 F.2d 1152, 1154 (7th Cir. 1987) (citing *In re Trans Alaska Pipeline Rate Cases*, 436 U.S. 631, 643 (1978)).

In addition, where the statute is ambiguous or where the statute has not been judicially interpreted, the court must also be guided by Congressional intent, as evidenced by the statute's legislative history. *See, e.g., Blum v. Stenson*, 465 U.S. 886, 896 (1984); *Janowski v. International Brotherhood of Teamsters Local No. 710 Pension Fund*, 673 F.2d 931, 936 (7th Cir. 1982) (*vacated on other grounds*, 463 U.S. 1222 (1983)).

a.   The Design And Object Of ARPA Indicate That Section 470ee(c) Is Limited To Public And Indian Lands

In the context of ARPA as a whole, it is clear that Section 470ee(c) is inapplicable to trafficking in artifacts that were removed from non-public, non-Indian lands. Admittedly, subsection (c) is silent as to whether it applies to artifacts removed from non-public, non-Indian lands. Unlike subsections (a) and (b), which mention resources removed from "public lands or Indian lands" as a basis for federal jurisdiction, subsection (c) simply refers to the prohibited acts in terms of occurring "in interstate or foreign commerce." 16 U.S.C. § 470ee(c). That omission does not end the inquiry, however. Resolution of the issue facing this Court requires an analysis of the structure, object, and purpose of ARPA. Several sections of ARPA are valuable in providing a more complete understanding of ARPA, help place section 470ee(c) in its proper context, and demonstrate that ARPA does not extend to non-public, non-Indian lands.

Of perhaps the greatest significance, ARPA begins with a section entitled "Congressional findings and declaration of purpose." That section provides as follows:

(a)   The Congress finds that—

(1)   archaeological resources on *public lands and Indian lands* are an accessible and irreplaceable part of the Nation's heritage;

(2)   these resources are increasingly endangered because of their commercial attractiveness;

(3)   existing Federal laws do not provide adequate protection to prevent the loss and destruction of these archaeological resources and sites resulting from uncontrolled excavation and pillage;

* * *

(b)   The purpose of this chapter is to secure, for the present and future benefit of the American people, the protection of archaeological resources which are on *public lands and Indian lands*, and to foster increased cooperation and exchange of information between governmental authorities, the professional archaeological community, and private individuals having collections of archaeological resources and data which were obtained before October 31, 1979.

16 U.S.C. § 470aa (emphasis added).

The significance of Section 470aa cannot be overstated, for the purpose of ARPA and the proper context of Section 470ee(c) are set forth in plain and unambiguous terms: "the protection of archaeological resources which are on *public lands and Indian lands. . . .*" *Id*. Significantly, there is absolutely no mention of protection resources on non-public, non-Indian lands, or or simply protecting archaeological resources generally. ARPA's stated purpose and protections are plainly limited to archaeological resources on "public lands and Indian lands." In fact, so persuasive is this statement of Congress purpose that the District Court held in the companion case of *United States v. Way* that Section 470aa was "compelling" support for limiting Section 470ee(c) to public and Indian lands.[5] *United States v. Way*, No. EV 90-32-CR, slip. op. at 4 (S.D. Ind. Oct. 25, 1990). The language reversal of the District Court.

The definitional section of ARPA also provides insight into the design and object of ARPA. Section 470bb defines, *inter alia*, "archaeological resource," "Federal land manager," "public lands," and "Indian lands." 16 U.S.C. § 470bb. It is noteworthy that the definition of "public lands" excludes state-owned land. 16 U.S.C. § 470bb(2). It is also noteworthy that where there is no individual or agency "having primary management authority" over public or Indian lands, the Federal land manager is deemed to be the Secretary of the Interior, yet there is no mention of a comparable person or agency for non-public, non-Indian lands. 16 U.S.C. § 470bb(2). One would think that a comparable state agency or the state could fill such a role. The significance of this omission becomes apparent since other sections of ARPA depend on the role of the Federal land manager, and this results in certain inconsistencies if ARPA is held applicable to non-public, non-Indian lands.[6]

Also relevant to proper understanding of the framework of ARPA is section 470cc. Section 470cc sets up a permitting system, whereby a person can apply to a Federal land manager for a permit to excavate archaeological resources located on public or Indian lands. 16 U.S.C.§ 470cc(a). That section also provides guidelines for issuing permits,

---

[4]   All citations to the Transcript on Appeal and the appropriate document numbers are indicated by "R. _:" followed by the title for the document and page or paragraph reference.

[5]   As already noted, the District Court refused to construe Section 470ee(c) as limited to federally owned lands because it was concerned that subsection (c) would be superfluous under that construction. As demonstrated below, subsection (c) is not superfluous when limited to federally owned lands. *See infra* at 27 to 32.

[6]   For example, as further discussed [ ] *infra* only a Federal land manager can certify rewards to informants under Section 470gg, and only a Federal land manager can impose civil fines under Section 470ff.

along with terms and conditions and various notification requirements. 16 U.S.C. § 470cc(b-e, g-j). Section 470cc(f) requires that a Federal land manager suspend a permit if it is determined that the permittee violated the criminal prohibitions contained in subsections (a), (b), or (c) of Section 470ee. 16 U.S.C. § 470cc(f). As discussed more fully below, this section clearly contemplates that violations of Section 470ee(c) may occur on public lands, since there are not Federal land managers or permits in connection with non-public, non-Indian lands.[7] This fact undercuts the District Court's belief that subsection (c) would be superfluous if limited to public or Indian lands.

Section 470dd is interesting because it evidences one of several statutory "holes" that exist if ARPA is held to extend to resources on non-public, non-Indian lands. That section provides the Secretary of the Interior with the power to promulgate regulations concerning the custody and ultimate disposition of archaeological resources removed from public or Indian lands. 16 U.S.C. § 470dd. ARPA is silent on the custody or ultimate disposition of artifacts removed from non-public, non-Indian lands. If ARPA extends to artifacts removed from private or state lands, as the Government contends, then any recovered artifacts should presumably be returned to the state if taken from state property, or to the landowner did not unlawfully remove the archaeological resources from the landowner's property). But there are no provisions in ARPA stating who is entitled to ultimate possession of the archaeological resources in such cases. It is illogical that a thief would be able to maintain possession of archaeological resources unlawfully removed from private or state lands but not those removed from public or Indian lands. ARPA is silent on this issue presumably because Congress did not contemplate or intend ARPA's application to archaeological resources removed from non-public, non-Indian lands.

Another significant section in terms of providing the proper context and understanding of the workings of ARPA is Section 470ff. That section sets forth civil penalties that may be assessed by a Federal land manager. 16 U.S.C. § 470ff. These civil penalties apply to "[a]ny person who violates any prohibition contained in an applicable regulation or permit. . . ." 16 U.S.C. § 470ff(1). Although this section does not state that it is limited to violations relating to public or Indian lands, as a practical matter it is so limited because there is no Federal land manager or substitute for a Federal land manager for non-public, non-Indian lands. *See* 16 U.S.C. § 470bb(2). Thus, if ARPA is in fact applicable to non-public, non-Indian lands, one can only conclude that Congress made a conscious determination that offenders on public and Indian land could receive a penalty as light as a fine, whereas the minimum penalty for an infraction on non-public, non-Indian lands is a criminal sanction.[8] A would-be thief who engaged in a cost-benefit

---

[7]   See [ ] *infra* for a discussion of possible violations of a state resource protection law on public or Indian land that do not violate the prohibitions contained in Section 470ee(a) or (b).

[8]   As a practical matter, the Government must be careful as to whether to choose civil or criminal penalties because of double jeopardy concerns. *See, e.g., United States v. Halper,* 490 U.S. 435, 447-48 (1989).

analysis would chose to steal from public or Indian lands, with the possibility of only a civil penalty. From the perspective of deterrence, this would hardly promote the stated purpose of ARPA: protecting archaeological resources on public and Indian lands. 16 U.S.C. § 470aa. Thus, Section 470ff underscores another absurdity if ARPA is held applicable to non-public, non-Indian lands.

Further evidence that Congress never envisioned ARPA applying to archaeological resources removed from non-public, non-Indian lands is contained in Section 470gg. That section, which is entitled "Enforcement," provides for payment of rewards to informants following "the certification of the Federal land manager concerned . . . ." 16 U.S.C. 470gg(a). Subsection (b) provides for forfeitures of archaeological resources obtained in violation of ARPA as well as forfeiture of vehicles and equipment used in obtaining those archaeological resources. 16 U.S.C. 470gg(b). If ARPA extends to resources removed from non-public, non-Indian lands, then ARPA provides *no* rewards to informants in non-federal land cases (because only a Federal land manager can certify such rewards and there are no Federal land managers or statutory equivalents for non-public, non-Indian lands). It makes no sense that Congress would act in such an arbitrary and capricious manner.

Also, on parallel with section 470cc(f), Section 470gg clearly contemplates that violations of Section 470ee(c) may occur on Indian lands.[9] Specifically, that section provides that if archaeological resources are removed from Indian lands in "violation of the prohibition contained in subsection (a), (b), *or (c)* or section 470ee of this title," all penalties collected pursuant to section 470ff and all items forfeited under Section 470gg(b) are to be transferred to the affected Indian or Indian tribe. *Id*. (emphasis added). This again undercuts the District Court's belief that subsection (c) would be superfluous if limited to public or Indian lands, for Congress clearly contemplated such subsection (c)'s application to Indian lands.

Finally, section 470kk, entitled "Savings provisions," provides in relevant part that "[n]othing in this chapter shall be construed to affect any land other than public land or Indian land or to affect the lawful recovery, collection, or sale of archaeological resources from land other than public land or Indian land." 16 U.S.C. § 470kk(c). This provides further support that ARPA is limited to public and Indian lands.

The combined effect of the sections discussed about is apparent: Congress simply did not intend for ARPA to extend to non-public, non-Indian lands, or artifacts removed from such lands. If Congress had intended that ARPA extend beyond such lands, Congress would not have limited its statements of purpose and findings to "public and Indian lands," but instead would have referred to protection of archaeological resources generally. At a minimum there would have been some discussion of private or state

---

[9]   It is certainly possible to violate a state archaeological resource protection law with respect to archaeological resources removed from public or Indian land without violating the prohibitions contained in Section 470ee(a) or (b). *See [ ] infra.*

lands, yet there is none. Congress presumably would have also addressed the custody and ultimate disposition of artifacts removed from non-public non-Indian lnads if ARPA extended to such lands. It is also incongruous that ARPA would allow for payments of rewards to informants and civil penalties for violations of ARPA on public and Indian lands, but not on state or private lands.

These inconsistencies and absurdities that would result if section 470ee(c) is extended beyond public and Indian lands place Section 470ee(c) in the proper perspective. One simply cannot reconcile a construction of that section extending beyond public and Indian lands with the rest of the statute. Thus, when Section 470ee(c) is placed in the context of the entire statute there is, at a minimum, uncertainty as to whether Section 470ee(c) applies to artifacts removed from non-public, non-Indian lands. And in light of Congress' strong statement of purpose in Section 470aa, it is incontrovertible that Congress did not intend to extend ARPA beyond public and Indian lands.

b.   ARPA's Legislative History Demonstrates That Section 470ee(c) Is Limited To Public And Indian Lands

The conclusion that ARPA does not apply to non-public, non-Indian lands is strongly supported by ARPA's legislative history. In the present case, the legislative history of ARPA must be examined since the prohibition contained in Section 470ee(c) is at a minimum unclear and, in addition, Section 470ee(c) has not yet been subject to judicial interpretation. *See, e.g.*, *Blum*, 465 U.S. at 896; *Janowksi*, 673 F.2d at 936.

Both the House of Senate reports analyzing ARPA are replete with signs Congress did not intend for ARPA to extend to archaeological resources removed from lands other than public and Indian lands. The House Report states the purpose of H.R. 1825 as "provid[ing] protection for archaeological resources found on public lands and Indian lands of the United States." H.R. Rep. No. 96-311, 92th Cong., 1st Sess. 7 (1979); *accord* S. Rep. No. 96-179, 1st Sess. 6 (1979) (purpose is to "provide greater protection than now exists for archaeological resources on public lands and Indian lands of the United States."). Moreover, addressing the problem sought to be resolved by ARPA, the Report speaks only in terms of public and Indian lands. For example, the House Report notes that unfavorable court decisions concerning the Antiquities Act of 1906 (16 U.S.C. §§ 431-433) "promoted members of the House of Senate to introduce legislation intended to provide adequate protection to archaeological resources located on public lands and Indian lands." House Report at 7; *accord* Senate Report at 7. This is yet another unambiguous expression of Congress' intention that ARPA does not extend to resources located on non-public, non-Indian lands.

In addition, the House Report recognizes "that it is often difficult to delineate public land from private or state land on the ground. . . ." House Report at 8. For that reason, the Report clarifies that the definition of "public lands" excludes privately owned lands within the boundaries of federally held lands. *Id.* The same exclusion was made for the definition of "Indian lands," which was changed to exclude private and state owned lands within the exterior boundaries of Indian lands. *Id*. at 17. The reason for this exclusion was that the term "Indian lands" would otherwise "be broader than intended" by Congress. *Id*. Obviously, if removal of archaeological resources from state owned or privately owned lands was unlawful under ARPA, then there would be no reason to exclude certain private or state lands from the operation of the statute. Also, there would be no need to recognize the fact that it is physically difficult to delineate public lands from non-public lands. Accordingly, it is plain that Congress did not intend to address *any* private or state lands or archaeological resources removed therefrom.

Finally in terms of costs associated with the legislation, the House Report states that "[t]he lands involved are entirely Federally owned or Indian lands. . . ." *Id*. at 13. This comment in the Report further shows that Congress did not intend to include non-federal lands within ARPA.

Statements in the floor debate also evidence Congress' intention that ARPA not extend beyond public and Indian lands. For example, Representative Udall, a chief sponsor of ARPA, stated that ARPA "prohibits the wanton destruction of archaeological sites and resources located on the *public domain or Indian lands*," and that ARPA "provides that recovered archaeological resources will remain the property of the United States." 125 Cong. Rec. 17, 393-94 (1979) (emphasis added). Significantly, Representative Udall added the following remarks:

I want to emphasize in the boldest terms what the bill does not do:

* * *

It does not affect any lands other than the public lands of the United States and lands held in trust by the United States for Indian tribes or individual Indian allottees.

Id.; *accord* 125 Cong. Rec. S10,832 (1979) (statement of Sen. Bumper) ("The purpose of S. 490 is to provide greater protection than currently exists for archaeological resources located on public and Indian lands."); 125 Cong. Rec. S14,721 (1979) (statement of Sen. Bumper) ("this measure will protect archaeological resources located on public and Indian lands.").

Thus, the legislative history of ARPA further confirms what is already apparent from a reading of ARPA, namely, that ARPA is only applicable to public and Indian lands and archaeological resources removed from such lands. As with the stated purpose in ARPA itself, the legislative history provides no support for the notion that ARPA protects archaeological resources generally, or that it protects archaeological resources on private or state lands. In fact, one can scour the legislative history and find no mention of ARPA applying to private or state lands or to archaeological resources removed from private or state lands. The legislative history of ARPA therefore provides further compelling support that Congress had no intention of extending ARPA beyond the public and Indian lands.[10]

3.   Subsection (c) Is Not Superfluous When Limited To Public And Indian Lands

The District Court expressed concern that subsection (c) would be superfluous if it did not extend beyond public and Indian lands. *Way*, slip. op. at 5. But for this concern, the District Court was persuaded that Section 470ee(c) is inapplicable to non-public, non-Indian lands, but felt compelled to reject that construction under the mistaken belief that subsection (c) would be superfluous if it did not extend beyond public and Indian lands. *Id.* That subsection would be superfluous, according to the District Court, because subsections (a) and (b) address public and Indian lands. ARPA itself, as well as a few illustrations, show that the District Court was mistaken.

As we have seen, ARPA itself clearly contemplates that subsection (c) includes violations occurring on public or Indian lands. Section 470cc(f), for example, allows a Federal land manager to suspend a permit "upon his determination that the permittee has violated any provision of subsection (a), (b), *or (c)* of section 470ee of this title." 16 U.S.C. § 470cc(f) (emphasis added). Since there is no Federal land manager for non-federal lands, Section 470ee clearly envisions violations of subsection (c) occurring on federal lands. Similarly, Section 470gg(b) clearly contemplates that subsection (c) will apply to violations on Indian land. That section provides that "[i]n cases in which a violation of the prohibition contained in subsection (a), (b), *or (c)* of section 470ee of this title *involve archaeological resources excavated or removed from Indian lands*, the Federal land manager or the court, as the case may be, shall provide for the payment to the Indian or Indian tribe involved of all penalties collected pursuant to section 470ff of this title for the transfer to such Indian or Indian tribe of all items forfeited under this section." 16 U.S.C. § 470gg(b) (emphasis added). These sections could no be clearer in evidencing Congress' assumption that subsection (c) applies to public and Indian lands. For that reason, subsection (c) would not be superfluous if limited to public and Indian lands.

Furthermore, some examples easily demonstrate that subsection (c) can apply to resources removed from public or Indian lands without overlapping with subsections (a) and (b). For instance, subsection (c) could be used where a state statute provides broader

---

[10]   Although technically not "legislative history," it is interesting that post-enactment Congressional reports concerning proposed amendments of ARPA emphasize that Congress limited ARPA to public and Indian lands. For example, a recent Senate Report states that ARPA "toughened the laws protecting archaeological resources on *federal and Indian lands* by imposing criminal penalties for unauthorized excavation, damage, destruction or removal of archaeological resources. However, looting and damaging of cultural resources on federal lands have continued." S. Rep. No. 100-569, 100th Cong. 2d Sess. 1 (1988) (emphasis added).

protection for archaeological resources removed from lands within its borders, includ-ing federal and Indian lands, than ARPA's regulations. A state resource protection statute could be broader than ARPA by making removal of archaeological resources a per se violation of the law, whereas ARPA has a general intent requirement of performing the acts knowingly.[11] 16 U.S.C. § 470ee(d). Thus, an individual who removed artifacts from federal lands but denied knowing that he or she was on federal lands at the time of the removal could be prosecuted under subsection (c) but not under subsections (a) or (b) of Section 470ee. A state statute could also be broader than ARPA by making mere pos-session of archaeological resources an offense, whereas ARPA does not prohibit mere possession.[12] *See* 16 U.S.C. § 470ee.

In cases where a state statute is broader than ARPA, subsection (c) would allow the federal government to prosecute violations of state resource protection laws that would otherwise escape prosecution. For example, if an individual obtained archaeological resources in violation of a state statute but not in violation of Section 470ee(a), either by committing a per se violation or by violating a possession statute, and then sold those artifacts to a buyer in another state who knew that the resources at issues had been removed in violation of the state or local resource protection law, the buyer could perhaps only be prosecuted under ARPA, having never set foot in the state from which the arti-facts were removed.

Section 470ee(c) could also be used where a violator of a state archaeological resource protection law flees to another state to avoid prosecution. In fact, this applica-tion of Section 470ee(c) is mentioned in the legislative history. Specifically, Senator Pete Domenici, the Senate sponsor of ARPA, stated that ARPA "would dovetail with existing state laws, such as New Mexico's, so that offenders could not skip to another state to avoid prosecution." 125 Cong. Rec. S10,834 (1979) (statement of Sen. Domenici).

Subsection (c) could also be used to prosecute an individual who obtained artifacts from federal lands in violation of a state or local resource protection law prior to the

---

[11] For example, New Mexico's Cultural Properties Act appears to lack an intent element by provid-ing that "[i]t is a misdemeanor for any person or his agent to: (1) appropriate, excavate, injure or destroy . . . any historic or prehistoric ruin or monument. . . ." N.M. Stat. Ann. § 18-6-9 (1992). *See also* Alaska Stat. §§ 41.35.200, 41.35.210 (1991) (no intent or knowledge required); S.D. Codified Laws Ann. § 1-20-35 (1985) (same); Wis. Stat. Ann. § 44.47(7) (West Supp. 1991) (same).

[12] For example, California broadly prohibits the mere possession of Native American artifacts removed from a grave or cairn. Cal. Pub. Res. Code § 5097.99 (West Supp. 1992). In addition, Alaska pro-hibits possession of artifacts removed in violation or the Alaska Historic Preservation Act or ARPA regard-less of whether the person in possession of that artifact knew that it was taken unlawfully. Alaska Stat. §§ 41.35.200(b), 41.35.210 (1991).

effective date of ARPA (but not in violation of any federal law) and then trafficked in the resources after ARPA's effective date.[13] *See* 16 U.S.C. § 470(f) (ARPA's prospective application section only exempts resources that were lawfully obtained prior to the effective date of ARPA); *see also* H.R. Rep. No. 96-311 at 11 ("The Committee notes, however, that archaeological resources which are in a person's possession illegally, are not covered by" Section 470ee(f)'s exception).

The above examples provide only a few of the uses that Congress could have intended for subsection (c). In all of these illustrations, subsection (c) would not be superfluous if limited to public and Indian lands. These illustrations, combined with Congress' clear indication in Sections 470cc(f) and 470gg(b) that violations of subsection (c) could occur on public or Indian lands, eliminate the District Court's only hesitation in refusing to limit ARPA to Congress' stated purpose of protecting archaeological resources located on public and Indian lands. Having removed the only obstacle to what the District Court viewed as the "compelling" proof in Sections 470aa and 470ee(c), the Motion to Dismiss should have been granted. *Way*, No. EV 90-32-CR, slip. op. at 4.

4.   The Commentators Agree That ARPA Is Limited To Public And Indian Lands

Although the issue of whether ARPA extends beyond public and Indian lands has not been judicially determined, it is the uniform consensus of the commentators that ARPA is inapplicable to non-federal lands. In fact, even the United States Department of the Interior issued a technical brief stating that criminal violations of ARPA require that the archaeological resource was removed from public or Indian lands. These conclusions in the commentaries are particularly persuasive because they often come from advocates of increased protection for archaeological resources, and provide further support that ARPA does not extend to non-public, non-Indian lands.

A selective use of secondary authority in an attempt to bolster the client's position.

Most telling are the statements contained in the technical brief issued by the United States Department of the Interior—the department with the closest connection to ARPA. According to that brief:

---

[13]   This scenario is quite possible given the holes in the then existing federal laws that led to t he enactment of ARPA. ARPA's predecessor, the Antiquities Act of 1906, 16 U.S.C. §§ 431-433, was held to be unconstitutional by the United States Court of Appeals for the Ninth Circuit in 1974. *United States v. Diaz*, 499 F.2d 113 (9th Cir. 1974). Thus, prior to ARPA's enactment, an individual could have removed archaeological resources from federal property in the states within the Ninth Circuit wihtout violating the Antiquities Act. The removal of those artifacts may have been in violation of a state archaeological resource protection law, however. Although ARPA cannot be used in an *ex post facto* manner to prosecute the *removal* of those artifacts, Section 470ee(c) could be used to prosecute *trafficking* in those artifacts after ARPA's effective date if the removal was in violation of a state archaeological resource protection law.

ARPA *felony* criminal violations now require four elements of proof:

(1)   that defendant did knowingly excavate, remove, damage, alter, or deface an archaeological resource;

(2)   *that said resource was located on public and Indian lands*;

(3)   that the defendant acted without a permit; and

(4)   that the archaeological value or commercial value and cost of restoration and repair exceeded $500.

C.   Carnett, United States Department of the Interior, *Legal Background of Archaeolgcial Resources Protection* 10 (1991) (emphasis in original and added).[14] Thus, the very department with responsibility over ARPA believes that ARPA only applies to resources located on public and Indian lands.

The view that ARPA is limited to archaeological resources on public and Indian lands is shared by the academic commentators. For example, an article appearing in the Harvard Environmental Law Review, in addressing the lands affected by ARPA, states that "ARPA protects archaeological resources on public lands and Indian lands," and that "[a]s a result, federal jurisdiction under ARPA is no greater than under the Antiquities Act."[15] L. Northey, *The Archaeological Resources Protection Act of 1979: Protecting Prehistory for the Future*, 6 HARVARD ENVIRONMENTAL LAW REVIEW 61, 74-45 (1982). In fact, the article notes that by excluding private lands within Indian lands from the definition of Indian lands, ARPA's definition of Indian lands is more limited than other federal laws, "which include[] private and state lands within reservation boundaries. . . ." *Id*. The author of the article express concern over that exclusion because of the difficulty in determining whether a possible violation occurred on Indian, state, or private lands. *Id*. Of course, this limitation in the definition of Indian lands would more or less be inconsequential if ARPA extended to private and state lands, since a "theft" could be prosecuted no matter where it occurred. Since ARPA does not extend to private and state lands, the author is rightly concerned with enforcement difficulties relating to the situs of the possible violation.

Similarly, former Assistant United States Attorney Kristine Olson Rogers, in referring to the difficulties associated with the criminal provisions of Section 470ee, states that "[t]he hitch comes in proving that an artifact was taken from public or Indian lands." K. Olson, *Visigoths Revisited: The Prosecution of Archaeological Resource Thieves, Traffickers, and Vandals*, 2 JOURNAL OF ENVIRONMENTAL LAW AND LITIGATION

---

[14]   The significance of this statement in the Technical Brief is further discussed *infra* [ ].

[15]   The Antiquities Act was also limited to federal lands, specifically, lands "owned or controlled by the United States." 16 U.S.C. § 432.

47, 72 (1987).[16] Significantly, the article continues with the following advise: "If the artifact's source can be proven, however, then the seller or purchaser must ascertain whether any federal, or in the case of interstate commerce, state or local law was violated." *Id.* This last comment shows that the author is addressing subsections (b) and (c), since only subsection (c) addresses violations of state and local laws, and Ms. Rogers concludes that proof of a federal land source of the artifacts is necessary under both subsections (b) and (c). Thus, it is apparent that he author shares the view that Section 470ee(c) does not extend to archaeological resources obtained from non-public, non-Indian lands.

Other commentators who have examined ARPA have expressly or impliedly come to the same conclusion, namely that ARPA does not extend to archaeological resources obtained from non-public, non Indian lands. *See, e.g.*, L. Jones, *Preserving Utah's Cultural Resources: A Proposal for New Legislation*, 10 JOURNAL OF ENERGY LAW AND POLICY 93, 105 (1989) (noting, in a hypothetical situation that could only arise if ARPA was not applicable to private property, "the ARPA does not address whether a person may be successfully charged under this section if he excavated on public property under the mistaken belief that the property was privately owned."); P. Fish, *Federal Policy and Legislation for Archaeological Conservation*, 22 ARIZONA LAW REV. 681- 695- 96 (1980) (noting that federal protection of resources privately owned is "strictly limited to periphÔeral actions, such as the withholding of federal funds or licenses to projects that might contribute to destruction."); W. Echo-Hawk, *Museum Rights vs. Indian Rights: Guidelines for Assessing Competing Legal Interests in Native Cultural Resources*, 14 NEW YORK UNIVERSITY REVIEW OF LAW & SOCIAL CHANGE 437, 445 (1986) (federal legislation regulates excavation of cultural resources on "federal and Indian lands.").

5.   To Minimize Federal Interference With State Sovereign Powers, And Given The Absence Of Unmistakably Clear Language To The Contrary, ARPA Should Be Narrowly Construed

An example of attempting to persuade the court by noting the broader implications of not adopting the client's position. It contrasts sharply with the United States' position that a broad interpretation of ARPA would "dovetail" with existing state statutes.

Another rule of statutory construction dictates that Section 470ee(c) be limited to federal lands. Absent unmistakably clear language in a statute, principles of federalism requires that the statute be construed narrowly so as to avoid interfering with state sovereign powers. *See, e.g.*, *Gregory v. Ashcroft*, 111 S. Ct. 2395, 2401 (1991); *Evans v. United States*, 112 S. Ct. 1881, 1901 (1992) (Thomas, J. dissenting).

[16]   Ms. Rogers is well known in the area of archaeological law. Ms. Rogers prosecuted several archaeological resource protection cases, is a consultant to federal, state, and tribal agencies on archaeological resource law issues, taught courses at the University or Oregon School of Law and Northwestern School of Law at Lewis & Clarke College, and has taught at the Federal Law Enforcement Training Center in Glynco, Georgia and Marana, Arizona. *Id.* at 47 n.*.

This concern with infringing on state sovereign powers is especially significant here because states traditionally exercise police powers over non-federal lands within their borders, and most states have enacted archaeological resource protection laws.[17] In fact, at the time of the events alleged in the Indictment, Indiana had legislation concerning protection of archaeological resources. *See generally* Ind. Code. § 14-3-3.41 *et seq.* That act, entitled Historic Preservation and Archaeology, contains one criminal provision. That criminal provision, Section 7 of that act, at the time of the events alleged in the Indictment, provided as follows:

> A person who knowingly, without a permit, conducts a field investigation or alters historic property within the boundaries of property owned or leased by the state commits a Class B misdemeanor.

Ind. Code § 14-3-3.4-7. Although not a necessary element of this argument, it is noteworthy that the criminal provisions of the Indiana act did not apply to sites or structures located on private property prior to the act's amendment in 1989. The point here is that a traditional sovereign power of the State of Indiana, as with any other state, is its exercise of police powers over non-federal lands within their borders, whereas the federal government's police powers with respect to land are traditionally limited to federal lands. *See, e.g.*, 16A Am. Jur. 2d *Constitutional Law* § 381 (1979) (Nothing that "Congress has no general power to enact police regulations operative within the territorial limits of a state," but that the federal government can exercise police power over federal lands); L. Northey, *The Archaeological Resources Protection Act of 1979: Protecting Prehistory for the Future*, 6 HARVARD ENVIRONMENTAL LAW REVIEW 61 n.3 (1982) (all 50 states have laws protecting archaeological resources). Indiana made a conscious decision prior to 1989 to protect certain archaeological resources within its borders. Before Congress can override Indiana's legislation in this area, it must do so with "unmistakable clear" language in the statute. *See, e.g.*, *Gregory*, 111 S. Ct. at 2401; *Evans*, 112 S. Ct. at 1901. There is no such "unmistakably clear" language in Section 470ee(c) showing that Congress intended to regulate activities on state and private property. Accordingly, principles of federalism require that ARPA be limited in scope to federal lands.

6.   The Rule of Lenity Dictates A Narrow Construction of Section 470ee(c)

If there is any final doubt as to whether Section 470ee(c) extends to artifacts removed from non-public, non-Indian lands, this Court is required to construe that section in favor of lenity. As the United States Supreme Court has stated on many occasions

---

[17]   All 50 states have at least some law protecting archaeological resources. *See* L. Northey, The *Archaeological Resources Protection Act of 1979: Protecting Prehistory for the Future*, 6 HARVARD ENVIRONMENTAL LAW REVIEW 61 n.3 (1982).

in the context of resolving the substantive scope of criminal statutes, if the language or history of a section of a penal statute is "uncertain" and the court must choose between two readings of a statute, the rule of lenity requires that all doubts be resolved in favor of lenity. *Crandon v. United States*, 494 U.S. 152, 158 (1990). *See also United States v. R.L.C.*, 112 S. Ct. 1329, 1338 (1992) ("the venerable rule of lenity, [citation omitted] is rooted in 'the instinctive distaste against men languishing in prison unless the lawmaker has clearly said they should.'"); *United States v. Campos-Serrano*, 404 U.S. 293, 297 (1971). Because of the ambiguity created when Section 470ee(c) is placed in context, and the fact that the Court must choose between two readings of that Section, the rule of lenity dictates that the Court choose the least harsh interpretation—that Section 470ee(c) does not extend to private lands.

B.   Section 470ee(c) Is Void For Vagueness

At a minimum, the lack of clarity in ARPA, its legislative history, and the uniform consensus of commentators that ARPA is inapplicable to non-public, non-Indian lands, indicate that there are serious constitutional problems stemming from ARPA itself and particularly in its application in this case.

The Supreme Court has made clear that undue vagueness in a statute is constitutionally impermissible where that uncertainty pertains either to the persons within the scope of the statute,[18] the conduct forbidden by the statute,[19] or the punishment that may be imposed by the statute.[20] The void-for-vagueness doctrine is premised upon the due process clauses of the Fifth and Fourteenth Amendments. *See Connally v. General Constr. Co.*, 269 U.S. 385, 391 (1926). As the *Connally* Court stated, "a statute which either forbids or requires the doing of an act in terms so vague that men of common intelligence must necessarily guess at its meaning and differ as to its application violates the first essential of due process of law." *Id.* This early and basic test has remained essentially unchanged; the test focuses both on actual notice to citizens and the potential for arbitrary enforcement. *See, e.g., Kolender v. Lawson*, 461 U.S. 352, 357 (1983). Under this standard, Section 470ee(c) cannot pass constitutional muster.

If the Court determines that ARPA extends to non-public, non-Indian lands, there can be no doubt that ARPA is vague on that issue. As the above discussion indicates, ARPA's statement of purpose is directly at odds with such a construction, and there are sections within ARPA that are inconsistent with ARPA's application to non-public, non-

---

[18]   *See, e.g., Lanzetta v. State of New Jersey*, 306 U.S. 451 (1939) (Court held that a statute that made it a penal offense to be a gangster was unconstiutionally vague).

[19]   *See, e.g., Colautti v. Franklin*, 439 U.S. 379 (1979) (Pennsylvania statute requiring abortionists to exercise the same degree of care to preserve a viable fetus' life and health as in the case of a fetus intended to be born alive was unconstitutional).

[20]   *See, e.g., United States v. Evan*, 333 U.S. 483 (1948) (where statute was vague and inconsistent as to penalty to be applied for its violation, Court refused to enforce the statute).

Indian lands. When people of common intelligence read ARPA in its entirety, including ARPA's statement of purpose as "the protection of archaeological resources and sites which are on public lands and Indian lands," such people "must necessarily guess at [ARPA's] meaning and differ as to its application. . . ." 16 U.S.C. § 470aa; *Connally*, 269 U.S. at 391. As proof of this point, one need only refer to the opinions of the commentators, who expressly state or impliedly assume that ARPA does not extend beyond public and Indian lands.[21]

Moreover, of particular concern in a vagueness analysis is the potential for arbitrary enforcement. *See, e.g.*, *Kolender*, 462 U.S. at 357. In this case, we have the statements from the United States Department of the Interior as well as current and former United States Attorneys to the effect that ARPA is only applicable to resources removed from public or Indian lands.

First and foremost, we have seen that the technical brief prepared by the United States Department of the Interior plainly states that ARPA does not apply to archaeological resources removed from non-public, non-Indian lands. According to that brief, "ARPA *felony* criminal violations now require four elements of proof: . . . (2) that said resource was located on public and Indian lands. . . ." C. Carnett, United States Department of the Interior, *Legal Background or Archaeological Resources Protection* 10 (1991) (emphasis in original). Significantly, the purpose of the Technical Brief "is to provide a convenient summary of archaeological protection and preservation as an issue in law and jurisprudence that will be of use to jurists who may need assistance in their casework." *Id.* at 1. Thus, even the United States Department of the Interior is publicly spreading its conclusion that criminal violations of ARPA can *only* occur where the resource was removed from public or Indian lands.

We have also seen that former Assistant United States Attorney Kristine Olson Rogers' views are inconsistent with an extension of ARPA to non-public, non-Indian lands.[22] Ms. Rogers amplified her views in congressional testimony, where she testified as follows:

> The United States is one of the few nations in the world which does not lay claim to *all* its cultural heritage, wherever found. If this committee really wants to tackle the tough issues, it would address archaeological resources located on private land. . . . I think that protection should be extended to all archaeological sites because of the serious problems of tying objects back to federal sites beyond a reasonable doubt.

Theft of Archaeological Resources From Archaeological Sites: Oversight Hearing Before The Subcommittee On General Oversight And Investigations Of The Commit-

---

[21]   *See supra* at [ ].

[22]   *See supra* at [ ].

tee On Interior And Insular Affairs, House of Representatives, 100th Cong., 1st Sess. 152 (emphasis in original) (testimony of Kristine Olson Rogers).

Similarly, Brent D. Ward, the United States Attorney for the District of Utah, offered several suggestions to improve ARPA, including the suggestion that "Congress. . . make it a criminal offense to purchase or sell an archaeological resource, as defined by ARPA, without written proof that the artifact was removed from nonpublic land." *Id.* at 121 (Statement of Brent D. Ward, United States Attorney for the District of Utah). Proof of provenance, showing that the artifact was removed from non-public lands, obviously assumes that ARPA is inapplicable to archaeological resources removed from non-pub-lic lands. Presumable then, Mr. Ward would not have sought an indictment against a per-son who performed the same acts as Mr. Gerber.

The Department of the Interior Technical Brief and the statements of Rogers and Ward drive home the point that if ARPA extends to non-public and non-Indian lands, it is unconstitutionally vague because it will lead to arbitrary enforcement. The department closest to ARPA is telling jurists that ARPA criminal violations can only occur on pub-lic and Indian lands. Furthermore, Ms. Rogers, who teaches at the Federal Law Enforce-ment Training Center, believes that ARPA does not extend to sites on private lands. Ms. Rogers presumably teaches her law enforcement students that ARPA is inapplicable to resources removed from non-federal sites. Lastly, United States Attorney Brent Ward assumes that ARPA is only applicable where the archaeological resource was removed from public or Indian lands. Thus, this is not a case where anyone has to speculate that ARPA's vagueness will *potentially* lead to arbitrary enforcements, which is the concern in a vagueness analysis. *Kolender*, 461 U.S. at 357. This is a case where there is over-whelming evidence that law enforcement *will* apply ARPA in an arbitrary manner. For this reason, Section 470ee(c) is unconstitutionally vague if extended to non-public, non-Indian lands. In order to avoid an unconstitutional interpretation of Section 470ee(c), this Court should limit that section's scope to archaeological resources removed from pub-lic or Indian lands or declare that Section 470ee(c) is unconstitutionally vague.

C.   Section 470ee(c) Requires As A Predicate Act A Violation Of A Resource Protection Law

Section 470ee(c), in addition to requiring trafficking in archaeological resources removed from public or Indian lands, requires that such trafficking be "in violation of any provision, rule, regulation, ordinance, or permit in effect under State or local law." 16 U.S.C. § 470ee(c). Despite the apparent literal meaning of "any . . . law," the predicate violation of a state or local law needed for a violation of Section 470ee(c) must be the violation of a archaeological resource protection law. Such a requirement must be read into Section 470ee(c) as a matter of construction and in order to avoid the absurdities that would result from a literal reading of that section. Because the Indictment in this case does not allege violations of a state archaeological resource protection law, the indictment should have been dismissed.

A significant clue into the required violation of a state or local law is found in the only portion of the legislative history addressing Section 470ee(c). As noted in the earlier discussion, Senator Pete Domenici, the Senate sponsor of ARPA, stated:

> This proposed federal act contains several features which make it good law which both federal and state officials can use to protect archaeological sites.

> If enacted, the law would dovetail with existing state laws, such as New Mexico's, so that offenders could not skip in another state to avoid prosecution.

125 Cong. Rec. S10,834 (1979).

Significantly, New Mexico had it own archaeological resource protection statute at the time ARPA was enacted. *See generally* N.M. Stat. Ann. §§ 18-6-1 to 18-6-17. Thus, when Senator Domenici was referring to ARPA as dovetailing with "New Mexico's," it is apparent that he was referring to New Mexico's Cultural Properties Act. Senator Domenici's statement plainly shows that Congress did not intend to create a new class of crimes arising out of states' general criminal *and* civil laws, rules, and regulations. Rather, one of the purposes of Section 470ee(c) was to create an enforcement mechanism to assist states is enforcing their archaeological resource protection laws when the resources are removed from the state. As such, a proper interpretation of Section 470ee(c) would require a violation of a state or local resource protection law.[23]

The above construction is also required under the rule that a court must reject a literal construction of a statute if it would lead to absurd results. *E.g.*, *Smith v. Brown*, 815 F.2d 1152, 1154 (7th Cir. 1987) (citing *In re Trans Alaska Pipeline Rate Cases*, 436 U.S. 631, 643 (1978)). A few examples illustrate that the Government's insistence on a literal reading of Section 470ee(c) would lead to grossly absurd results.

Suppose that a person drives from Chicago to Milwaukee with an Indian arrowhead in the car, and suppose that person is driving without insurance or without a valid drivers license in violation of state law. That person will have violated ARPA, because he or she "transport[ed] . . .

The portion of the brief proved ineffective. In its opinion, the court rejected the following scenarios as poor examples.

---

[23] This interpretation is supported by the commentators. For example, Kristine Olson Rogers states that if the resource is taken in violation of "any" state or local law and then transported in interstate commerce, it a violation of ARPA. K. Rogers, *Visigoths Revisited: The Prosecution of Archaeological Resource Thieves, Traffickers, and Vandals,* 2 JOURNAL OF ENVIORNMENTAL LAW AND LITIGATION 47, 71-72 (1987). Significantly, Ms. Rogers follows that comment with a footnote stating that "[a]pproximately 26 states have some form of cultural resource legislation." *Id.* at 72 n.157. The obvious assumption on her part is that only a violation of one of those 26 state cultural resource laws can serve as the basis for a Section 470ee(c) violation.

any archaeological resource . . . transported . . . in violation of any provision, rule, regulation, ordinance or permit in effect under State or local law." 16 U.S.C. § 470ee(c). A purely literal reading of Section 470ee(c) leads to an absurd result in this illustration.

Another illustration shows how a violation of a civil law can constitute a violation of federal criminal law under the Government's purely literal reading of Section 470ee(c). Suppose that a seller in Illinois sells artifacts to a buyer in another state, an in negotiating the sale misstates the nature of the artifacts, thereby violating the Illinois consumer protection law or committing actionable misrepresentation. By selling the artifacts in violation of a civil law, the seller has committed a violation of federal criminal law. Again, Congress could not have intended such absurd applications of ARPA.

Finally, suppose that the Art Institute loaned archaeological resources to an out-of-state museum and used a trucking company that was not properly registered in Illinois. Having transported the archaeological resources in violation of "any" law or rule, one or both museums will have violated the criminal provisions of ARPA if this Court accepts the Government's literal reading of Section 470ee(c).

As these examples demonstrate, a literal reading of Section 470ee(c) as encompassing violations of "any" state or local law, ordinance, or rule is absurd. Particularly in light of the fact that ARPA is a general intent crime, it makes no sense that Congress would use ARPA to criminalize civil or criminal violations of ordinary state and local laws and ordinances. A limiting interpretation is required to prevent such absurd results. *See, e.g., Smith v. Brown*, 815 F.2d at 1154. Moreover, a limiting interpretation of Section 470ee(c) is well grounded in the legislative history of Section 470ee(c). For these reasons, the Court should limit application of Section 470ee(c) to violations of state or local resource protection laws. Since Gerber is not alleged to have violated a state or local resource protection law, the Indictment should have been dismissed.

IX. CONCLUSION

For all of the foregoing reasons, Defendant-Appellant, Arthur Joseph Gerber, respectfully requests that the judgment of the District Court be reversed.

_____

Respectfully submitted,
Harvey M. Silets
Kenneth M. Kliebard
KATTEN MUCHIN & ZAVIS
525 West Monroe Street
Suite 1600
Chicago, Illinois 60661-3693
(312) 902-5200

Jeffrey L. Lantz
525 Sycamore
P.O. Box 1087
Evansville, Indiana 47706-1087
(812) 464-0044

Attorneys for Defendant-Appellant,
Arthur Joseph Gerber

Dated: October 8, 1992

IN THE

UNITED STATES COURT OF APPEALS

FOR THE SEVENTH CIRCUIT

No. 92-2741

UNITED STATES OF AMERICA,	)	Appeal from the
	)	United States District Court
Plaintiff-Appellee,	)	Southern District of Indiana
	)	Evansville Division
v.	)	No. EV 91-19-CR
	)	
ARTHUR JOSEPH GERBER,	)	
	)	Honorable Gene E. Brooks
	)	Chief U.S. District Judge
Defendant-Appellant.	)	

BRIEF OF PLAINTIFF-APPELLEE

DEBORAH J. DANIELS
United States Attorney

SCOTT C. NEWMAN
Assistant United States Attorney

LARRY A. MACKEY
Chief, Criminal Division

Attorneys for Plaintiff-Appellee

Office of the United States Attorney
5th Floor, United States Courthouse
46 East Ohio Street
Indianapolis, Indiana 46204
Telephone: 317-226-6333

TABLE OF CONTENTS

TABLE OF AUTHORITIES

IN THE

UNITED STATES COURT OF APPEALS

FOR THE SEVENTH CIRCUIT

No. 92-2741

UNITED STATES OF AMERICA,	)	Appeal from the
	)	United States District Court
Plaintiff-Appellee,	)	Southern District of Indiana
	)	Evansville Division
v.	)	No. EV 91-19-CR
	)	
ARTHUR JOSEPH GERBER,	)	
	)	Honorable Gene E. Brooks
Defendant-Appellant.)		Chief U.S. District Judge
	)	

BRIEF OF PLAINTIFF-APPELLEE

I. JURISDICTIONAL STATMENT

The appellant's jurisdictional statement, as separately filed and as incorporated into his brief on appeal, is complete and correct.

STATMENT OF THE CASE

The defendant, Arthur Joseph Gerber, appeals his convictions of violating a criminal provision of the Archaeological Resources Protection Act ("ARPA"), specifically Title 16, United States Code, Section 470ee(c), which proscribes trafficking in interstate commerce in archaeological resources excavated or removed in violation of state or local laws, regulations or permits.

On July 11, 1991, a Grand Jury charged defendant Arthur Joseph Gerber with one count of conspiracy to violate ARPA, one substantive ARPA felony count (for trafficking in archaeological resources having a commercial value of over $5,000), and five substantive ARPA misdemeanor counts (for trafficking in archaeological resources having a commercial value of less than $5,000). (O.R. 2).[1]

---

[1]   All references to the original, or "common law," record on appeal will begin with the letters "O.R." followed by the document number as designated by the Clerk of the District Court, *e.g.,* (O.R. 20). Page and/or paragraph numbers will also be supplied where appropriate.

Before trial, on December 2, 1991, Defendant Gerber moved to dismiss the indictment on the grounds that the indictment failed to state an offense, in that as a matter of statutory interpretation, ARPA did not apply to the kinds of conduct Gerber was alleged to have committed, and further that ARPA itself was void for vagueness. (O.R. 4). The matter was fully briefed by both sides, and on January 28, 1992, the district court, Hon. Gene R. Brooks, Chief U.S. District Judge, presiding, issued a written opinion denying defendant Gerber's motion to dismiss. (O.R. 7).

On April 17, 1992, pursuant to a written plea agreement and Rule 11(a)(2), Federal Rules of Criminal Procedure, defendant Gerber entered conditional pleas of guilty to the five misdemeanor counts of the indictment, reserving for appellate review the issues raised in his motion to dismiss and rejected by the district court. (O.R. 9, 10, 11, 12).

At his plea hearing, defendant Gerber admitted that he had entered upon land owned by the General Electric Company without permission and, in a manner that constituted criminal conversion and criminal trespass under Indiana law, knowingly excavated and removed numerous prehistoric artifacts of the Hopewell culture. (O.R. 11; G.P. Tr. 28-30).[2] He further admitted that he knowingly trafficked in a number of these artifacts in interstate commerce for commercial gain (O.R. 11; G.P. Tr. 28-30).

In return for his plea of guilty, the United States agreed to dismiss the two felony counts charged in the indictment, and joined in recommending that the execution of Gerber's sentence be stayed pending the present appeal of the district court's denial of Gerber's motion to dismiss. (O.R. 9).

On July 8, 1992, defendant Gerber was sentenced, pursuant to the Sentencing Reform Act of 1984, to twelve (12) months imprisonment on each count, to run concurrently; a fine of $5,000; special assessments totaling $125.00; and three years of supervised release. (O.R. 14-15; Sent. Tr.). The district court stayed the execution of the sentence pending the present appeal of defendant Gerber's convictions. (O.R. 14). Gerber does not challenge his sentence on appeal.

Judgment was entered by the district court on July 14, 1992 (O.R. 15), and the defendant filed a timely notice of appeal on July 23, 1992 (O.R. 21), from which this appeal results.

III. STATEMENT OF THE ISSUES PERSENTED FOR REVIEW

1.   WHETHER THE ARCHAEOLOGICAL RESOURCES PROTECTION ACT [16 U.S.C. §§ 4700aa *et seq.*] ON ITS FACE PLAINLY PROSCRIBES THE INTERSTATE TRAFFICKING OF ARCHAEOLOGICAL RESOURCES EXCA-

---

[2]   Citations to the transcript of Gerber's guilty plea hearing will be designated by the notation "G.P. Tr." and the pertinent page numbers. Citation to the transcript of Gerber's sentencing hearing will be designated by the notation "Sent. Tr." and the pertinent page numbers.

VATED IN VIOLATION OF STATE OR LOCAL LAW, REGARDLESS OF WHETHER THE LAND FROM WHICH THE RESOURCES WERE EXCAVATED WAS PUBLICLY OR PRIVATELY OWNED.

2.   WHETHER THE LEGISLATIVE HISTORY OF THE ARCHAEOLOGI-CAL RESOURCES PROTECTION ACT [16 U.S.C. §§ 470aa *et seq.*] SUPPORTS THE CONCLUSION THAT THE STATUTE'S ANTI-TRAFFICKING PROVISION APPLIES REGARDLESS OF WHETHER THE LAND FROM WHICH THE RESOURCES WERE UNLAWFULLY EXCAVATED WAS PUBLICLY OR PRI-VATELY OWNED.

3.   WHETHER THE ARCHAEOLOGICAL RESOURCES PROTECTION ACT [16 U.S.C. §§ 470aa *et seq.*] ON ITS FACE PLAINLY PROSCRIBES INTER-STATE TRAFFICKING IN RESOURCES REMOVED IN VIOLATION OF "ANY PROVISION, RULE, REGULATION, ORDINANCE OR PERMIT IN EFFECT UNDER STATE OR LOCAL LAW, REGARDLESS OF WHETHER SUCH PROVI-SION IS OF GENERAL APPLICATION OR SPECIFICALLY DESIGNED TO PRO-MOTE "ARCHAEOLOGICAL RESOURCE PROTECTION."

4.   WHETHER THE ARCHAEOLOGICAL RESOURCES PROTECTION ACT [16 U.S.C. §§ 470aa *et seq.*] IS UNCONSTITUTIONALLY VAGUE OR OVER-BROAD,

IV. STATEMENT OF FACTS

Between the years 100 and 300 A.D., people inhabiting what is now southwestern Indiana, near the confluence of the Ohio and Wabash Rivers, built one of the five largest burial and ceremonial mounds ever seen in eastern North America. M.F. Seeman, REPORT ON THE AGE, AFFILIATION, AND SIG-NIFICANCE OF THE GE MOUND (1992) (Govt. Exh. 3, G.P. Tr. 31) (hereinafter "Seeman Report"), at 19; Sent. Tr. 10. To construct this enormous loaf-shaped mound, these prehistoric inhabitants hauled an estimated 289,000 bushel basket-loads of earth from the river bottoms to nearby ridge, and placed them over a prepared mound floor containing at least two human burials,[3] together with literally thousands of precious ceremonial artifacts and grave goods made of silver, copper, wood, cloth, leather, obsid-ian, flint, mica, quartz, pearl, shell, cannel coal, bone, and drilled, carved or inlaid human and bear canines. (O.R. 24, ¶7).

Here, the statement of facts emphasizes the wrongfulness of Gerber's acts by reiterating the large numbers of artifacts involved and their great historical value. It also stresses Gerber's status as a trespasser on the land and charac-terizes his actions as "looting."

Almost two thousand years later, in 1985, the General Electric Company, Plastics Manufacturing Division, located just outside the town of Mount Vernon in Posey County,

---

[3]   Analysis of the remains indicated that the two bodies were of a large adult male, 20-35 years of age, and a child aged 12-18 years. Copper stains on the bones were consistent with their having worn orna-ments at the chin, hip, ankle, mid-back and knee at the time of burial. (O.R. 24, ¶5).

Indiana, purchased from some farmers a piece of untillable real estate containing a prominent "knob" on top of a "ridge." (O.R. 24, ¶9). Unbeknownst to General Electric, the "knob" was in fact the ancient burial mound, its contents and those who built it long since forgotten. As of early April, 1988, the ancient burial mound and its remarkable contents remained intact, and even its perishable materials (such as wood and leather) unusually well-preserved. (O.R. 24, ¶¶ 12-19).

In archaeological terms, the site implicated in this case (hereinafter, the "GE Mound") is affiliated with something known as the "Hopewell phenomenon," a widespread cultural affiliation dating to the early centuries A.D., and sharing many common characteristics with sites located throughout the central United States, particularly in present-day Ohio, Indiana, and Illinois. (O.R. 24, ¶6). Hopewell represents a period in human prehistory that exhibited the beginnings of settled agriculture, and elaborate pattern of ceremonialism and display, and far-flung trading networks for obtaining the rare materials used to fashion exquisite artifacts and grave goods. (O.R. 24, ¶6; Sent. Tr. 13). The silver used to fashion earspools and musical panpipes found inside the GE Mound, for example, probably was brought from present-day Ontario, Canada, while the obsidian likely came from northwestern Wyoming and adjacent southern Idaho. (O.R. 24, ¶7; Seeman Report 7, 11 Sent. Tr. 20). Taken as a whole, the GE Mound in its pristine condition contained one of the largest and finest assemblages of Hopewell artifacts ever encountered. (Seeman Report 27; Sent Tr. 11).

During the highway construction season ending in November, 1987, work was progressing near the GE Mound along a corridor that was to become new County Road 850 Spur. (O.R. 24, ¶12; G.P. Tr. 25). This project was jointly funded by the federal government and by General Electric, and was administered by the Indiana Department of Highways. (O.R. 24, ¶12). The purpose of the new county road was to connect two existing state roads, thereby routing traffic around and outside the premises of the General Electric Plastics plant. (O.R. 24, ¶12; G.P. Tr. 27). The right-of-way being excavated in 1987 ran alongside, but not through, the GE Mound site, which remained undiscovered. (O.R. 24, ¶12).

As excavation of the County Road 850 Spur right-of-way progressed during the 1987 construction season, problems began to develop at a "saddle cut" where the road was to go through the ridge just to the side of the GE Mound. (O.R. 24, ¶13). The base and slopes in this area could not be stabilized, as the ground continually buckled and slid. (O.R. 24, ¶13).

On April 6 and 7, 1988, before the start of the 1988 construction season, state highway representative met with the general contractor and several subcontractors on the project to adopt a strategy for dealing with the instability of the roadbed beside the ridge. (O.R. 24, ¶14). As a result of these meetings, the parties agreed that subject to an archaeological survey and clearance, as required by federal and state highway regulations, an earth-moving subcontractor known as Boyd Brothers, Inc. ("Boyd Brothers") would "borrow" fill dirt from the nearby mound area for use in stabilizing the slopes and roadbed, as well as for grading low areas within General Electric's property. (O.R. 24, ¶15; G.P. Tr. 26).

On April 12, 1988, Boyd Brothers contacted and retained Dr. C. Russell Stafford, a professional archaeologist from Indiana State University, to conduct an archaeological survey of the proposed borrow area. (O.R. 24, ¶16). On the following day, Dr. Stafford sent his assistant, Mark Cantin, to the site to perform the field work for the survey. (O.R. 24, ¶16). Cantin examined the area, laid out grids, and performed shallow shovel-probes at regular intervals across the mound. (O.R. 24, ¶17). In the archaeological survey produced on April 25, 1988, and forwarded directly to Boyd Brothers, Dr. Stafford concluded that "no archaeological sites were identified by this reconnaissance." He further advised:

> However, if any concentration of archaeological materials or evidence of subsurface features should be encountered during borrow operations, an archaeologist from the Division of Historic Preservation and Archaeology should be immediately notified for an on-site assessment. (O.R. 24, ¶17).

An Indiana statute in effect in 1988 [Indiana Code, Section 8-23-9-52] further required that a state-administered highway contract specifying borrow operations must require the conctractor to conform to Indiana's manual of Standard Specifications. That manual provided as follows:

Rights in and Use of Materials Found on the Property

If archaeological artifacts are encountered during excavation operations, the Contractor shall cease operations in the immediate vicinity and notify the Engineer. An Archaeologist will be provided by the State and a determination will be made as to the significance and the disposition of such findings. In no event will any employee of the Contractor or the State of Indiana share in such ownership, or profit from any salvaged archaeological findings.

Indiana Department of Highways, STANDARD SPECIFICATIONS § 104.06 (1985). (O.R. 2, ¶5).

Shortly after the completion of the survey by Dr. Stafford, Boyd Brothers was given the notice to proceed with borrow operations on the mound. (O.R. 24, ¶18). Boyd Brothers employed pieces of heavy equipment known as "scrapers" to gouge a large trench into the mound, from which earth was removed. (O.R. 24, ¶18). During these scraping operations, two Boyd Brothers employees noticed a concentrated area of "quartz rock" objects packed together in the midst of the borrow area. (O.R. 24, ¶19).

Although the two scraper operators did not know what the concentrated area of "quartz rock" represented, before leaving the project in mid-May, 1988, one of them showed some of the rocks to fellow heavy equipment operator John William ("Bill") Way. (O.R. 24, ¶20). Coincidentally, Way had long been a collector of Indian artifacts, and recognized that these "turtleback"-shaped rocks might be such artifacts. (O.R. 24, ¶20).

On June 3, 1988, Way went to the area of the mound, and proceeded to operate his bulldozer to fill in the pit that had been left by the scraper operators after completion of the borrow operations. (O.R. 24, ¶21). While running the bulldozer, Way observed some unusually shaped objects being pushed out from the sides of the bulldozer blade. (O.R. 24, ¶21). Way stopped the bulldozer and began looking along the ground; the objects he had encountered were prehistoric solid copper axeheads, or "celts." (O.R. 24, ¶21).

As Way continued to examine the pit area, he began to discover and collect hundreds of prehistoric artifacts made of diverse materials. At the end of approximately one hour, he had amassed some 700-900 flint spearpoints, 40 drilled and inlaid bear canines, 14 solid copper axeheads, numerous shell heads and freshwater pearls, and carved pieces of cannel coal (fashioned into effigy spearpoints), obsidian, and tooled leather. (O.R. 24, ¶22). With the acquiesence of his Boyd Brothers foremen, who was the only other person present in the area, Way loaded these items into his pickup truck and transported them to his home in Illinois. (O.R. 24, ¶23). Neither Way, the foreman, nor any other agent of Boyd Brothers notified the project engineer or any other proper authority that a concentration of archaeological material had been encountered. (O.R. 24, ¶25).

Way returned to the site on June 4, 1988, and with the aid of heavy equipment collected approximately 200 more pieces similar to those he had taken the day before. (O.R. 24, ¶24). He then covered the site back up with dirt, and transported these additional artifacts to Illinois. (O.R. 24, ¶24).

In mid-July, 1988, Way told fellow construction worker Harold Sallee that he wanted to sell his collection of artifacts from the GE Mound. (O.R. 24, ¶26). Sallee then contacted the defendant, Arthur Joseph Gerber, of Tell City, Indiana, a well-known collector of Indian artifacts, and promoter of one of the nation's largest annual Indian "relic shows," held each year at a hotel in Owensboro, Kentucky, (O.R, 11, at 1-2 O.R. 24, ¶26). Gerber had in the past been an outspoken advocate of the rights of artifact hunters, and had publicly expressed his disapproval of regulations governing archaeological resources discovered during highway construction projects. In a televised interview, Gerber had stated: "If you have a super highway and they run through [artifacts], then they take the objects and maybe put them in the basement of some university. . . . We'll never see them again." (O.R. 24, ¶21). Gerber's own collection of artifacts was housed in a free-standing, heavily-alarmed vault building located in Cannelton, Indiana. (O.R. 24, ¶41).

On July 18, 1988, following the initial contact from Sallee, defendant Gerber telephoned Bill Way and arranged to view the artifacts uncovered by Way during borrow operations. (O.R. 24, ¶27). Upon arriving at Way's residence and examining his collection, Gerber, a longtime admirer and acquirer of Hopewell artifacts, recognized Way's collection to be Hopewell ceremonial material. (O.R.11, at 2). Way explained to Gerber that he had removed the artifacts while working as a bulldozer operator on a highway project. (O.R. 24, ¶27). Gerber took numerous photographs of the collection, and offered

Way the sum of $6,000.00 to be paid entirely in currency, for all of the materials. (O.R. 24, ¶27; G.P. Tr. 25).

On July 21, 1988, Gerber returned to Way's residence in Illinois, and completed the purchase. (O.R. 11, at 2-3). As part of the transaction, Bill Way agreed to reveal to Gerber the location of the GE Mound site. (O.R. 24, ¶28; O.R. 11, at 2). During the nighttime hours of July 21, Way took Gerber to the site and the two of them walked on the mound. (O.R. 24, ¶28). During this visit, they encountered other people who were digging for artifacts; one of these diggers immediately instructed Way and Gerber to turn off the flashlight they were using to examine the site. (O.R. 24, ¶28; O.R. 11, at 3). Following the artifact purchase and site visit, Gerber transported his newly acquired collection of Hopwell artifacts to the state of Indiana. (O.R. 24, ¶27; G.P. Tr. 29).

For several years before the discovery of the GE Mound, Gerber had associated with two men from western Kentucky, John Towery and Danny Glover. (O.R. 24, ¶29; O.R. 11, at 3). Both men shared Gerber's interest in Hopewell artifacts, and they regularly sold their finds to Gerber in the past. (O.R. 24, ¶29). Within two days of being shown the location of the GE Mound by Bill Way, Arthur Gerber recruited Towery Glover to return to the site in order to dig up more Hopewell artifacts. (O.R. 24, ¶30; O.R. 11, at 3).

On four occasions within the next eight days, Gerber returned to the site with one or both of these men. (G.P. Tr. 29). On each occasion, Towery and Glover performed the heavy digging work, while Gerber stood by, taking numerous photographs, performing lighter digging, directing Towery and Glover as to what items to watch for, and evaluating and maintaining the objects being found. (O.R. 24, ¶37). Gerber told one person persent on the mound that Towery and Glover were "working for" him. (O.R. 24, ¶37).

During their first three visits to the mound, Gerber, Towery, and Glover excavated and removed several hundred flint points or "bifaces," copper axe-heads (one wrapped in the remnants of cloth and encrusted with pearls and beads), copper pins, copper and silver spherical objects made of silver, numerous drilled and inlaid bear canines, pieces of worked leather, cannel coal and obsidian, and sets of rare silver "panpipe" musical instrument, with some of the original reeds still preserved. (O.R, 11, at 3-7; O.R. 24, ¶47).

From the outset of their joint visits to the mound, Gerber, Towery and Glover agreed that they would share equally in all artifacts which any of them located while digging together. (O.R. 24, ¶31; O.R. 11, at 4; Sent. Tr. 235). In each instance, Towery transported to his home in Kentucky all of the large flint artifacts, which the men regarded as the less valuable pieces. (O.R. 24, ¶32). These pieces, they agreed, would be sold later, and the proceeds shared among them. (O.R. 24, ¶32). As to the more valuable "collection pieces," Gerber, Towery and Glover on each occasion negotiated a physical division of the artifacts. (O.R. 11, at 4-6; Sent. Tr. 204-05). Gerber and Towery each time "bought out" Glover's one-third share of the finer pieces for a total of approximately

$1,550 paid in cash, and divided Glover's share of the finer pieces between themselves. (G.P. Tr. 32).

On August 1, 1988, shortly after arriving for their last visit to the GE Mound, defendant Gerber (in the company of Danny Glover) was detected as a General Electric security guard, and was ejected from the property. (O.R. 24, ¶36; O.R. 11, at 6).

Five days after Gerber was ejected from General Electric's property, he held his annual "Indian Relic Show of Shows" at the Executive Inn in Owensboro, Kentucky. (O.R. 11, at 7). As had been agreed, during this show (on August 6 and 7, 1988), Towery and Glover sold all of the flint artifacts that they and Gerber had jointly excavated from General Electric's property during July. (O.R. 24, ¶42) All of the sale proceeds, totalling about $900.00, were received in cash and divided equally among Towery, Glover, and Gerber. (O.R. 24, ¶42). Gerber later sold other GE artifacts at other artifact "shows" for cash, and kept all of the profits. (Sent. Tr. 206-07, 235).

Following the relic show and sale, Gerber repeatedly offered to purchase Towery's remaining finer pieces from the GE Mound. (O.R. 24, ¶43). To that end, Gerber made several trips to Towery's home in Kentucky and, in the spring of 1989, finally convinced Towery to sell his GE artifacts to Gerber for $2,000.00, in currency, together with certain other unrelated artifacts from Gerber's personal collection. (O.R. 24, ¶43; Sent. Tr. 206).

At no time had Gerber, Glover, or Towery sought or obtained permission from General Electric to go onto, or to remove valuable property from, its land. (O.R. 11, at 7). Defendant Gerber has admitted that his conduct constituted criminal conversion under Indiana law, in that he knowingly exerted unauthorized control over property of another. (O.R. 11, at 7). Indiana Code, Section 35-43-4-3. He has further admitted that his entry onto and taking of property violated Indiana's criminal trespass law, in that he knowingly interfered with the possession or use of the property of another person without that person's consent. (O.R. 11, at 7). Indiana Code, Section 35-43-2-2.[4] Gerber was also aware, at all times during the summer of 1988, that when archaeological sites are discovered during the course of road construction projects, work must cease and authorities must be contacted. (O.R. 11, at 7).

Beginning in the fall of 1988, Gerber became aware of published reports in area newspapers which described the looting of the GE Mound and the initiation of a criminal investigation by law enforcement officials. (O.R. 24, ¶44; O.R. 11, at 8). During 1989, Gerber used a prearranged "code name" in telephone conversations with Bill Way to signal that he wished to meet personally at a pre-arranged location in Evansville. (O.R. 24, ¶44; O.R. 11, at 8). During two such meetings, Gerber instructed Way to "stand firm"

---

[4]   4 Gerber has twice previously been convicted of criminal trespass resultiing from his removal of archaeological material from private property without permission. (Sent. Tr. 233-34).

and not to divulge to law enforcement officials Gerber's role in the removal and interstate trafficking of artifacts from General Electric. (O.R. 24, ¶44; O.R. 11, at 8) During a conversation at Gerber's business, Gerber similarly instructed Danny Glover not to divulge Gerber's involvement in the removal of artifacts from the site. (O.R. 24, ¶44).[5]

Gerber was issued a federal Grand Jury subpoena in December, 1989, to produce, among other things, all photographs or visual depictions of artifacts acquired by him during 1988. Despite having taken numerous photographs of Bill Way's artifacts before purchasing them, and numerous photographs at the scene of his own digging activities, Gerber knowingly withheld them from his subpoena response and falsely represented that no such photographs existed. (O.R. 24, ¶46, O.R. 11, at 8-9; Sent. Tr. 226-31).[6]

Pursuant to his plea agreement, defendant Gerber has surrendered all of the General Electric artifacts in his possession (minus the several hundred flint artifacts, which have been sold to numerous unknown individuals) to the government for safekeeping pending the outcome of this appeal. (O.R. 24, ¶47).

V. ARGUMENT

1.   THE ARCHAEOLOGICAL RESOURCES PROTECTION ACT [16 U.S.C. §§ 470aa *et seq.*] ON ITS FACE PLAINLY PROSCRIBES THE INTERSTATE TRAFFICKING OF ARCHAEOLOGICAL RESOURCES EXCAVATED IN VIOLATION OF STATE OR LOCAL LAW, REGARDLESS OF WHETHER THE LAND FROM WHICH THE RESOURCES WERE EXCAVATED WAS PUBLICLY OR *PRIVATELY OWNED.*

Since Gerber is questioning the meaning of the statute, note how the point heading stresses that there can be no doubt about what it means. This tactic is repeated in numerous other point headings.

STANDARD OF REVIEW:

The issue of whether the charged conduct states a violation of the Archaeological Resources Protection Act [16 U.S.C. §§ 470aa *et seq.*] is a legal one, which required the district court, upon defendant's motion to dismiss, to interpret a federal statute in light of facts which were alleged in detail on the face of the indictment. Because the district

---

[5]   John William Way, John David Towery, and Danny G. Glover each entered pleas of guilty to ARPA violations arising out of their conduct on the GE Mound, and transactions with Gerber, in cause numbers EV 91-13-CR, EV 91-21-CR, and EV 91-20-CR, respectively. The execution of their sentences has also been stayed pending the outcome of this appeal.

[6]   As a further act of concealment, the Indictment alleged that Gerber dealt exclusively in currency when trafficking in artifacts removed from General Electric property. (O.R. 2, ¶46). In previous circumstances, wherein Danny Glover had first obtained the owner's permission to remove artifacts from private property, Gerber had paid for Glover's finds by check. (O.R. 24, ¶29).

court's determination was strictly a question of law, its determination will be reviewed by this Court *de novo. See United States v. Montoya,* 827 F.2d 143, 146 (7th Cir. 1987).

A. Background

The Archaeological Resources Protection Act of 1979 (hereinafter, "ARPA") created three new categories of prohibited acts carrying criminal penalties, as follows:

> (a)   No person may excavate, remove, damage, or otherwise alter or deface any archaeological resource located on *public lands or Indian lands* unless such activity is pursuant to a permit . . .
>
> (b)   No person may sell, purchase, exchange, transport, receive, or offer to sell, purchase, or exchange any archaeological resource if such resource was excavated or removed from *public lands or Indian lands* in violation of—
>
> (1)   the prohibition contained in subsection (a). . ., or;
>
> (2)   any provision, rule, regulation, ordinance, or permit in effect under any other provision of Federal law.
>
> (c)   No person may sell, purchase, exchange, transport, receive, or offer to sell, purchase, or exchange, *in interstate or foreign commerce,* any archaeological resource excavated, removed sold, purchased, exchanged, transported, or received in violation of any provision, rule, regulation, ordinance, or permit in effect under State or local law.

16 U.S.C. §§ 470ee(a), (b), (c) (emphasis added).[7] "Knowing" violations of any of the foregoing prohibitions may constitute either ARPA misdemeanor or felony offenses, depending upon the "commercial or archaeological value" of the archaeological resources involved in the violation. Title 16, United States Code, Section 470ee(d).[8]

---

[7]   The Act defines" archaeological resource" as ". . . any material remains of past human life or activities which are of archaeological interest, as determined under uniform regulations promulgated pursuant to this Chapter. Such regulations . . . shall include, but not be limited to: pottery, basketry, bottles, weapons, weapon projectiles, tools, structures or portions of structures, pit houses, rock paintings, rock carvings, intaglios, graves, human skeletal materials, or any portion or piece of any of the foregoing items . . . . No item shall be treated as an archaeological resource under regulations under this paragraph unless such item is at least 100 years of age." 16 U.S.C. § 470bb(1).

Regulations in effect at the time of this offense further refined the definition of "archaeological resource" to include, *inter alia,* "surface or subsurface structures," "ceremonial structures," "artificial mounds," "surface or surface artifact concentrations or scatters," and "[w]hole fragmentary tools, implements, containers, weapons and weapon projectiles, clothing, and ornaments." 18 C.F.R. ¶ 1312; *see also* 49 Federal Register, no. 4, 1016, 1028 (Jan. 6, 1984).

[8]   At the time of the offnse alleged in this case, violations involving archaeological resources valued at over $5,000 were punishable by up to two (2) years imprisonment and a fine, while violations involving archaeological resources of lesser value were misdemeanors punishable by up to one (1) year of imprisonment and a lesser fine. 16 U.S.C. § 470ee(d). Gerber was charged in seven (7) counts, two of which alleged felonies, and five (5) of which alleged misdemeanor violations. (O.R. 2). Pursuant to a plea agreement, Gerber entered his conditional pleas of guilty to the five (5) misdemeanor counts of the indictment. (O.R. 9).

Defendant-appellant Gerber was charged only with violating subsection (c) of the ARPA criminal provisions set forth above, Specifically, the indictment alleged that Gerber knowingly excavated, removed, purchased and transported, in interstate commerce, archaeological resources removed from the GE Mound site in violation of a state highway permit (in the case of the artifacts that Gerber purchased from the highway construction worker, Bill Way), and in violation of Indiana's criminal trespass and criminal conversion statutes. (O.R. 2).

In his conditional plea of guilty, Gerber admitted all of the principal factual occurrences alleged, but essentially demurred to the indictment. He argues on appeal that as a matter of statutory interpretation, ARPA simply does not apply to this kind of conduct. The parties are in agreement that the issue raised is one of first impression.

Here, facts of the case are incorporated to bolster the legal argument and to serve as a lead-in to Section B.

Gerber's involvement with the GE Mound began when he learned of John William ("Bill") Way, a highway construction worker who had bulldozed hundreds of priceless Hopewell artifacts on property of the General Electric Company in southern Indiana. (O.R. 24, ¶¶ 20-26). Instead of ceasing work and notifying appropriate authorities of his find (as well as required by state statute and the permission to proceed granted by the state to his employer), Way furtively gathered up two truckloads of the artifacts and took them to his home in Illinois. (O.R. 24, ¶¶23-25).

Gerber, a well-known artifact collector and promoter of "Indian relic shows," travelled to Illinois, met with Bill Way, and learned the circumstances of Way's removal of the artifacts while operating heavy equipment on a highway project. (.O.R. 24, ¶¶27-28). Despite Gerber's awareness of the notification requirements for archaeological finds made during highway construction[9] he negotiated for the purchase of Way's collection for the sum of $6,000.00 to be paid all in currency. (G.P. Tr. 25). He then transported the unlawfully excavated artifacts from Illinois to Indiana. (G.P. Tr. 29).

After paying Way to learn the location of the GE Mound, Gerber and two "diggers" went there on at least three occasions to excavate and remove[10] hundreds more Hopewell artifacts before being ejected from the property on their fourth visit. (O.R. 24,

---

[9]   Gerber himself, during a televised interview, had perviously criticized such requirements, arguing that they only resulted in consigning archaeological materials to the obscurity of "the basement of some university." (O.R. 24, ¶41).

[10]   In words no doubt intended to be reminiscent of professional archaeological salvage excavations, counsel for the appellant often describes Gerber and his associates as having only "recovered" artifacts from the mound after a construction crew "unearthed" them. *See, e.g.,* Brief of Appellant, at 1, 10, 11. It is undisputed, however, that Gerber's associates under his supervison, themselves "unearthed" numerous artifacts by putting in heavy work with their backs and shovels. (O.R. 11, at 4-6; O.R. 24, ¶37). While counsel for the government have generally avoided the more argumentative term, "looting," that description could fairly be applied to the knowing destruction of an archaeological site, accompanied by the removal of materials in violation of state law for commercial gain.

¶¶36, 47). Gerber's entry upon General Electric's property, and his taking of valuable property, were without permission or authorization, and were in violation of Indiana's criminal conversion and criminal trespass statutes. (O.R. 11, at 7).

Following these unlawful takings, Gerber caused hundreds of the artifacts to be transported to Kentucky, where they were sold for cash at Gerber's own "Indian Relic Show of Shows." (O.R. 24, ¶42). He later purchased over $2,000.00 worth of the valuable GE Mound "collection pieces" from John Towery, one of the diggers whom he had brought to the site, and transported them from Towery's home in Kentucky to Inidana, where Gerber maintained a large, freestanding vault for Indian artifacts. (O.R. 24, ¶¶41, 43).

B. The Plain Language of § 470ee Applies to the Conduct Admitted by Gerber.

The foregoing brief overview of the facts underlying the present indictment demonstrates this defendant's persistent and concerted efforts knowingly to traffic, in interstate commerce, in archaeological resources excavated and removed in violation of state laws and permits. As a factual matter, the defendant concedes that this is precisely what he did.

It is equally clear, from the plain language of ARPA, that "no person may purchase [or] transport, in interstate . . . commerce, any archaeological resource excavated [or] removed . . . in violation of any provision, rule, regulation, ordinance or permit in effect under State or local law." Title 16, United State Code, Section 470ee(c). What, then is the basis for Gerber's principal interpretive assault on the statute as applied to him?

Gerber concedes that "subsection (c) is silent as to whether it applies to artifacts removed from non-public, non-Indian lands." Brief of Appellant, at 16. Depicting this "silence" as a gap the statutory framework, Gerber asks this Court to engraft a limitation onto the prohibition set forth in subsection (c). He argues that despite the absence of any such language in subsection (c), that prohibition was only intended to apply to the interstate trafficking of archaeological resources removed from *public lands or Indian lands.* Because his illegal excavations occurred on private land, he argues, ARPA should not be applied to his interstate trafficking in stolen artifacts.

What Gerber's framing of the issue omits, of course, is that the very "silence of this provision proclaims forth, in the clearest possible tones, the intended scope of this prohibition, and its applicability to his conduct."

As was described earlier, ARPA enacted three categories of prohibitions, the knowing violation of which constitute criminal offenses. First, at subsection (a), ARPA prohibits the excavation or removal of any archaeological resource *"located on public lands or Indian lands"* without a permit. Title 16, United States Code, Section 470ee(a) (emphasis added). Second, ARPA prohibits the purchase or transportation of any archaeological resource, *"if such resource was removed from public lands or Indian lands"* either without a permit, or in violation of "any provision, rule, regulation, ordinance, or permit in effect under any other provision of Federal law." Title 16, United States Code,

Section 470ee(b) (emphasis added). Finally, in the provision with which Gerber was charged, ARPA prohibits the purchase or transportation, *in interstate commerce,* of *any* archaeological resource excavated or removed "in violation of any provision, rule, regulation, ordinance or permit in effect under State or local law." Title 16, United State Code, Section 470ee(c) (emphasis added).

Clearly, in drafting this statute, the basis for federal jurisdiction over the first two prohibitions is that the matters described affect <u>lands</u> of the United States or of Indian tribes. The sole jurisdictional requirement for the prohibition at subsection (c) is that the archaeological resources move in *interstate or foreign commerce.* There is no requirement under subsections (a) and (b) that the items move in interstate commerce; conversely, there is no requirement set forth under subsection (c) that the items have been removed from public or Indian lands. The two distinct groups of prohibitions arise from two independent bases for federal jurisdiction—the Property Clause and the Commerce Clause—each one sufficient by itself.

Viewed in isolation, then, subsection (c) certainly applies to Gerber's conduct. But that subsection also applies to Gerber's conduct when examined in light of the statute "as a whole," as Gerber himself urges. Brief of Appellant, at 15. The present case is not one in which, arguing by analogy and citing to other congressional enactments using similar terminology, one must contend that Congress knew how to express itself when it meant to proscribe only conduct involving "public lands or Indian lands." In this case, within the very *same section* of the *same statute,* Congress did express itself in specific terms when it intended its prohibitions to cover only "public lands or Indian lands," and omitted that same phrase when it did not so intend. Ascertaining the meaning of this particular subsection by reference to its context only strengthens the conviction that ARPA applies to interstate trafficking in unlawfully excavated artifacts, regardless of whether they came from private or public lands.

Under subsection (c), the categories of property and the contexts of archaeological resources to be protected will be delimited in the first instance by the states and localities; federal jurisdiction is triggered solely by the entry of state-protected or locally protected material into interstate commerce.

In this respect, subsection (c) or ARPA can be thought of as an archaeological Lacey Act. That Act, in terms strikingly similar to those outlined in ARPA's subsection (c), makes it unlawful for "any person . . . to import, export, transport, sell, receive, acquire, or purchase in interstate or foreign commerce . . . any fish or wildlife taken, possessed, transported, or sold in violation of any law or regulation of any state." Title 16, United States Code, Section 3372. Subsection (c) of ARPA is to archaeological resources what the Lacey Act is to wildlife protection: "a federal tool to aid states in enforcing their own laws," *United States v. Taylor,* 585 F. Supp. 393, 394 n.3 (D. Me. 1984), *rev'd on other grounds,* 752 F.2d 757 (1st Cir. 1985), <u>citing</u> S. Rep. No. 97-123, 97th Cong., 1st Sess. *reprinted in* 1981 U.S. Code Cong. & Ad. News 1748, 1749, regardless of whether the law or permit violations occurred on federal lands. It would be absurd to suppose that

Congress intended to limit that layer of support for state and local laws to federal and Indian lands.

Gerber's proposed limitation upon the scope of ARPA's interstate trafficking provision, moreover, engenders serious questions that Gerber is simply unable to answer. First, if federal jurisdiction were already established by the excavation of artifacts from public or Indian <u>lands</u> in violation of state or local law, why would Congress require the additional jurisdictional prerequisite of interstate trafficking? How would such a requirement—clearly unnecessary as a jurisdictional matter in light of the source of the artifacts—further the goal of protecting resources on the public lands?

Second, and even more perplexing, examine the language of subsections (b) and

(c). Subsection (b) applies to resources excavated or removed:

> in violation of . . . any provision, rule, regulation, ordinance, or permit in effect under any other provision of Federal law.

Title 16, United States Code, Section 470ee(b). Subsection (c) applies to resources excavated or removed:

> in violation of . . . any provision, rule, regulation, ordinance, or permit in effect under State or local law.

Title 16, United States Code, Section 470ee(c). The language is identical, save for the substitution of "State or local law" for "other provision of Federal law." If subsection (c) were intended, like subsection (b), to be limited to resources that had been removed from public or Indian lands, why would any legislative draftsman not simply have written subsection (b) to apply to resources excavated or removed:

> in violation of . . . any provision, rule, regulation, ordinance, or permit in effect *under State or local law,* or under any other provision of Federal law.

An example of how, once one's position is presented, arguments are presented designed to discredit that position.

With the simple addition of only the six underlined words, the drafter would have legislated everything Gerber claims for the sweep of subsection (c). Instead, the drafters created an entirely separate subsection, using parallel wording but omitting the requirement of public or Indian lands. Must they not have intended to create an entirely separate crime based not on lands, but on commerce in unlawfully excavated artifacts, whatever their source?

Moreover, if subsection (c) were intended to be limited to state or local law violations occurring on public or Indian lands, then one would suppose that some significant share of these cases would arise on Indian lands. Yet subsection (c) describes archaeological resources excavated and removed in violation of "local" laws, permits and ordinances. Give the intent ascribed to Congress by Gerber—an intent solely to police resources on public and Indian lands—why would subsection (c) omit any reference to archaeological resources removed in violation of "trivial" laws, permits and ordinances?

C. The Other APRA Provisions Cited by Gerber Do No Alter the Plain Meaning of Subsection 470ee(c).

Undaunted by the plain language of subsection (c) read both alone and in context, Gerber sweeps in ever-widening circles in search of some shred of support for his position. He believes he has found it in the following ARPA "saving provision" (Brief of Appellant, at 22-23):

> Nothing in this chapter shall be construed to affect any land other than public land or Indian land *or* to affect the *lawful* recovery, collection, or sale of archaeological resources *from land other than public land or Indian land.*

Title 16, United States Code, Section 470kk(c) (emphasis added).

Far from affording support for Gerber's position, however, the savings provision serves further to confirm the applicability of subsection 470ee(c) to resources removed from other than public or Indian land. Were the entire scope of ARPA restricted solely to public or Indian lands, the savings provision would simply say that ARPA "does not affect any lands other than public and Indian lands." There would be no reason to add a second clause to the effect that ARPA does not affect "the *lawful* collection of resources from *other than public land or Indian land.*"

As described above, only subsections (a) and (b) "affect land," in the sense that the full-blown regulatory and permitting scheme enacted by ARPA applies to public and Indian land. The only thing "affected" by subsection (c), as that term is being used in ARPA, is *commerce* in artifacts unlawfully removed, not the land from which they were removed.

Finding no support for his position in the savings clause, Gerber grasps for the broad policy statements contained in the congressional "Findings and Purpose" section of ARPA [16 U.S.C. § 470aa], claiming for them a significance that "cannot be overstated." Brief of Appellant, at 17. In that broadly worded preamble to ARPA, Congress sets forth its "finding" that "archaeological resources on public lands and Indian lands are . . . increasingly endangered because of their commercial attractiveness," and that present federal laws are inadequate to prevent their destruction. Title 16, United States Code, Section 470aa(a). Because the preamble refers to the need to protect public and Indian lands, without explicit mention of protecting resources on "non-public, non-Indian lands," Gerber argues that ARPA's interstate trafficking prohibition should be limited to archaeological resources removed only from public or Indian lands.

As a matter of broad public policy—which is the sole thrust of section 470aa—the prohibition of interstate trafficking in artifacts illegally removed from state or private land is entirely consistent with Congress's desire to protect resources that are located on public land. One of Congress's principal concerns in enacting this legislation was the spiralling "commercial attractiveness" of prehistoric American artifacts, 16 U.S.C. § 470aa(a) (2), which created such substantial economic incentives to looters of all prehistoric sites, public and private. These incentives had overwhelmed existing enforcement mechanisms, and overridden the paltry monetary fines which could be levied under the Antiquities Act. *See* H. Rep. 96-311, 1979 U.S. Code Cong. & Ad. News. at 1710; Collins & Michel, *Preserving the Past: Origins of the Archaeological Resources Protection Act of 1979,* in 5-2 AMER. ARCHAEOLOGY (1985), at 84, 85.

The prohibition of interstate trafficking in artifacts removed in violation of State or local law, whether the provenance of those specific items is publicly or privately owned lands, is complementary to the goal of keeping looters away from public and Indian lands. Many such looters no doubt do not discriminate; those looting public and non-public lands will often be the same people, in search of attractive "collection pieces" or a fast dollar. The legislation, being designed to have a chilling effect on the commerce in illegally excavated Indian artifacts, could thereby penetrate the private "museums" scattered throughout small western and midwestern towns, and the rented hotel exhibition halls of dealers such as Arthur Gerber.

Even assuming, *arguendo,* that the statement of policy contained in the preamble to the statute is incompatible with the plain meaning of subsection 470ee(c), an established principle of statutory construction holds that where the language of a statute is plain, a court may not resort to the preamble to ascertain its meaning. *See, e.g., Coosaw Mining Co. v. South Carolina,* 144 U.S. 550 (1892); *Yazoo & M. Valley Ry. Co. v. Thomas,* 132 U.S. 174 (1889).

D. As Interpreted by the Appellants, Subsection 470ee(c) of ARPA Would be Rendered Superfluous.

Gerber's next angle of attack insists that the sole basis for the district court's denial of his motion to dismiss the indictment was its conclusion that ARPA's interstate trafficking provision, if limited to public and Indian lands, would be rendered "superfluous." Brief of Appellant, at 18 n.5 27, 31-32.

This characterization of the district court's opinion utterly ignores that court's simple but important ruling that the statute is "unambiguous" in its applicability to Gerber's conduct in this case. (O.R. 7, at 3-4). The district court further noted that the "savings provision" cited by Gerber "does not create an ambiguity in the statute." *Id.*[11]

---

[11]   The district court made a similar observation in its eight-page written opinion on this issue in the related case of *United States v. Way,* No. EV 90-32-CR, an opinion which it explicitly reincorporated into its ruling in the present case. *See* O.R. 7, at 6. After emphasizing the presence of clauses specifying "public lands and Indian lands" in subsections (a) and (b) of § 470ee, the court noted that "to reach the defendant's position [limiting the scope of subsection (c) to public and Indian lands], the Court would have to ignore the remainder of the statute." Order, *United States v. Way,* No. EV 90-32-CR, at 4, in Brief of Appellant, Appendix, at 36.

Contrary to the hypothetical examples put forth by Gerber—based upon imagined state resource protection laws criminalizing "mere possession" or creating strict liability offenses (Brief of Appellant, at 29-30)—the terms of ARPA will in every case require a "knowing" violation, together with some act (transportation, purchase, sale) beyond mere possession. *See* Title 16, United States Code, § 470ee.

In light of Congress's explicit consideration and rejection of both "mere possession," and of a formulation of *mens rea* other than "knowing" violations as bases for criminal liability under ARPA, *see, e.g.,* H.R. No. 96-311, *reprinted in* 1979 U.S. Code Cong. & Ad. News at 1723, 1728, Gerber's proposed examples of non-duplicative applications of state laws on federal lands would certainly be preempted by congressional choices in defining archaeological resource violations on federal land. Put another way, it is inconceivable that any state or locality could prohibit, on federal land, what the comprehensive federal permitting scheme would permit. *See California Coastal Comm'n v. Granite Rock Co.,* 480 U.S. 572, 580 (1987); *Kleppe v. New Mexico,* 426 U.S. 529, 543 (1976) (absent cession, a State retains jurisdiction over federal lands within its territory; however, Congress retains power to legislate respecting conduct on those lands, and state legislation must not conflict).

Gerber's elaborate hypothetical proposing a person who removes resources from federal lands in violations of state (but not federal) law *before* the effective date of ARPA, and traffics in interstate commerce *after* the effective date of ARPA, affords the only example of how his narrowed interpretation of subsection (c) could even arguably apply to anything outside the scope of subsections (a) and (b). One is left to wonder, however, whether an interpretation of subsection (c) that renders it trivial is more plausible than an interpretation which renders it superfluous. More fundamentally, the articulation of a single set of facts whereby Gerber's interpretation of subsection (c) *could* be applied without duplication on federal land does not advance his proposition that subsection (c) may *only* be applied on federal land.

In sum, the district court's observation that Gerber's proposed limiting interpretation would renter ARPA's subsection (c) duplicative of other ARPA provisions and therefore superfluous is, as a practical matter, correct.

E. The Opinions of Commentators Support the Application of ARPA to Trafficking in Archaeological Resources Unlawfully Removed from Private land.

Gerber maintains, quite incorrectly, that "it is the uniform consensus of the commentators that ARPA is inapplicable to non-federal lands." Brief of Appellant, at 32, 38. Gerber fails to cite, for example, the following observations by Annetta Cheek, Federal Preservation Officer with the Office of Surface Mining Reclamation and Enforcement:

Here, the United States counters Gerber's claims that scholarly opinion supports his position by invoking other commentary favorable to its own position. Note how sources favorable to the United States are presented before attacking Gerber's use of secondary authorities.

ARPA contained a number of important new provisions . . . . It even imposed penalties on interstate commerce in such artifacts when removed in violation of ARPA or in violation of *any* state or local ordinance. This last provision essentially makes it an ARPA violation to transport across state lines any artifacts stolen from a state park *or even in private land.*

Cheek, *Protection of Archaeological Resources on Public Lands: History of the Archaeological Resources Protection Act,* in PROTECTING THE PAST x, 33, 35 (G. Smith & J. Ehrenhard eds. 1991) (emphasis in original and added).

To similar effect are the following comments of Arizona Superior Court Judge Sherry Hutt, Senior Instructor at the Federal Law Enforcement Training Academy Elwood W. Jones, and Forest Service consulting archaeological Martin McAllister:

In subsection (c), ARPA protects private lands where the owners' rights have been violated and state or local public lands that would not otherwise come under ARPA.

* * * *

[Subsection (c)] concerns excavation and theft of archaeological materials that do not occur on federal or Indian land but on state or private land without the permission of the land owner. This protects archaeological resources when one acts in violation of a nonfederal law and then places the illegally acquired materials in interstate commerce.

S. Hutt, E. Jones & M. McCallister, ARCHAEOLOGICAL RESOURCES PROTECTION 9, 35-36, 42 (1992).

In arriving at his hasty conclusion that the commentators unite in supporting his view, Gerber also overlooked the following published remarks of one of ARPA's original drafters, dating to 1980:

Subsection (c) enlists Federal assistance in enforcing state and local antiquities laws . . . . For example, one would be prohibited in the new Act from traveling from Arizona to New Mexico to bulldoze a site *on private land* without a permit, or to loot a site on state land in violation of the New Mexico law and return to Arizona with the artifacts before the local sheriff's office can move to prevent him.

Collins, *The Meaning Behind ARPA: How the Act is Meant to Work,* Cultural Resources Report No. 32 (USDA Forest Service, Southwest Region, July, 1980), at 5; *see also* Collins & Michel, *supra.*

In citing the very commentary that Gerber finds "most telling" (Brief of Appellant, at 32), at "technical brief" issued by the Department of the Interior, Gerber fails to note that the publication he cites was quickly superseded—within three months of its issuance and more than a year ago. The current version, at the same passage quoted by Gerber (Brief of Appellant, at 32-33), correctly reads as follows:

ARPA *felony* criminal prosecutions now require four elements of proof:

(1)   that defendant did knowingly excavate, remove, damage, alter, or deface an archeological resource, or attempted to do so;

(2)   that said resource was located on public or Indian lands, *or obtained illegally and transported across state lines;*

(3)   that the defendant acted without a permit; and

(4)   that the archeological or commercial value and cost of restoration and repair exceeded $500.

C. Carnett, *Legal Background of Archeological Resources Protection* (U.S. Dept. of Interior Technical Brief No. 11) (June 1991, revised September 1991), at 10 (emphasis in original and added).

While Gerber does find scholarly opinion that "impliedly" supports his position, those excerpts are not all that they appear. Gerber cites a remark in one article, for example, that the "ARPA does not address whether a person may be successfully charged under this section if he excavated on public property under the mistaken belief that the property was privately owned." Brief of Appellant, at 35. Gerber assumes that this hypothetical would not have been posed unless the author thought that ARPA was "inapplicable" to private property. *Id.* The hypothetical makes perfect sense, however, under the alternate assumption that ARPA does apply to *interstate trafficking* in artifacts unlawfully removed from private property. Under that assumption, the hypothetical merely poses the case of a person caught in the act of "excavating" on public land without a permit (no proof of interstate trafficking), and poses the question of whether he must "know" that he was on public land to make out a violation under subsection (a).

The foregoing tangle of dueling assumptions urges one back to the bedrock notion that it is the clear and simple language of the statute at issue, not the ruminations of commentators, that ultimately must govern this case. And citations to "implied" support aside, there exists ample recognition of the correctness of the government's position among those commentators who have given the matter direct thought and explicit voice.

2.   THE LEGISLATIVE HISTORY OF THE ARCHAEOLOGICAL RESOURCES PROTECTION ACT [16 U.S.C. §§ 470aa *et seq.*] SUPPORTS THE CONCLUSION THAT THE STATUTE'S ANTI-TRAFFICKING PROVISION APPLES REGARDLESS OF WHETHER THE LAND FROM WHICH THE RESOURCES WERE UNLAWFULLY EXCAVATED WAS PUBLICLY OR *PRIVATELY OWNED*

The limitations of any one person's *a priori* comments about what a law means—divorced from any concrete application of that law as is required of courts—are equally apparent when that person happens to be a legislator rather than a commentator.[12] This concern underlies the familiar principal of statutory construction that where the resolution of a question of federal law turns on a statute and the intention of Congress, a court must look first to the statutory language, and then to the legislative history only if the statutory language is unclear. *Blum v. Stenson,* 465 U.S. 886, 896 (1984). If the statute's language is unambiguous, it is to be regarded as conclusive unless there is a clearly expressed legislative intent to the contrary. *United States v. Bucey,* 876 F.2d 1297, 1302, 1306 (7th Cir.), *cert. denied,* 493 U.S. 1004 (1989), *quoting Dickerson v. New Banner Institute, Inc.,* 460 U.S. 103, 110 (1983); *see also Indiana Port Commission v. Bethlehem Steel Corp.,* 835 F.2d 1207 (7th Cir. 1987).

Should this court elect to examine the legislative history of ARPA, despite the clarity of the statute's language, it will find impressive support for the government's position that the anti-trafficking provision was meant to apply regardless of whether the land from which the resources were unlawfully excavated was privately owned.

Even before the advent of ARPA, in 1977, archaeologists and others alarmed at widespread commercial looting in the Southwest persuaded the New Mexico legislature to enact a law making it a misdemeanor "for any person . . . to excavate with the use of mechanical earth moving equipment an archaeological site for the purpose of collecting or removing objects of antiquity when the archaeological site is *located on private land* in this state, unless the person has first obtained a permit." N.M.S.A. (1978) 18-6-11 (emphasis added); Collins & Michel, *supra,* at 85 (1985). New Mexico also had in place a statute, unique at the time, making it a misdemeanor "to remove, injure, or destroy registered cultural properties *situated on private lands or controlled by a private owner* without the owner's prior permission." Cultural Properties Act, N.M.S.A. (1978) 18-6-10(B).

Despite this early success in the New Mexico legislature, proponents of archaeological resource protection concluded that a new federal law was also needed, one wiht greatly increased penalties and a focus on the organizers and dealers in stolen antiquities, not on the "diggers," who tended to be impoverished workers trying to earn extra income. Collins & Michel, *supra,* at 85. As one of the original drafters describes it, the draft legislation that was "later to become the core of [ARPA]" was

> a comprehensive reform bill that repealed the criminal sections of the 1906 [Antiquities] Act and replaced them with an entirely new code. Looting was prohibited, as were selling, purchasing, bartering, trafficking in, transporting, or receiving looted artifacts from federal lands. Trafficking in interstate commerce was also banned if the violation of a state or local law was involved. *Id.* at 87.

---

[12]   This inherent deficiency of legislative debates prompted Mr. Justice Holmes to remark, on the subject of statutory interpretation, that "We do not inquire what the legislature meant; we ask only what the statute means." Holmes, "The Theory of Legal Interpretation," 12 <u>Harv. L. Rev.</u> 417, 419 (1898).

A legal memorandum accompanying the draft legislation recommended that federal law confine itself to the two discrete jurisdictional bases of federal lands and interstate commerce, since both of these areas were unquestionably within the purview of Congress. Id.

With the backdrop provided by New Mexico's legislation, the proposed federal act was taken up by Congress. Senator Pete Domenici, also of New Mexico, was a senate sponsor of S. 490, one of two companion pieces of legislation that were merged to become ARPA. *See id.* at 88. In supporting the passage of ARPA, Senator Domenici placed the following comment into the CONGRESSIONAL RECORD:

> This proposed federal act contains several features which make it a good law which both federal and state officials can use to protect archaeological sites.
>
> If enacted, the law would dovetail with existing state laws, *such as New Mexico's,* so that offenders could not skip to another state to void prosecution.

125 CONG. REC. S10, 834 (July 30, 1979) (emphasis added). By observing that ARPA's trafficking provision would "dovetail" with New Mexico's statute—a statute that clearly prohibis certain kinds of archaeological depredations on private land, *see supra,* at 42-43—Senator Domenici clearly acknowledged that ARPA could, indeed should, be applied to the interstate trafficking of archaeological resources removed from private land in violation of state law.

Senator Domenici's observation echoed the remarks of Senator DeConicini at a hearing on ARPA held three months earlier before a Senate subcommittee:

> It is my intent to sponsoring this legislation to provide a workable enforcement system to protect our resources from those who knowingly and willfully steal *from the public lands, or trade in stolen artifacts, for personal profit.*

Hearing before the subcommittee on Parks, Recreation, and Renewable Resources on S. 490 (Publication No. 96-26), 96th Cong., 1st Sess. (May 1, 1979), at 145 (emphasis added). Thus, the prohibited acts set forth in ARPA "extend beyond existing law (the Antiquities Act of 1906) to include persons who would deal in stolen artifacts." S. Rep. 96-179, 96th Cong., 1st Sess. (April 9, 1979), at 6.[13] Because Gerber has admitted to being just such a person, it should be of no surprise to him that ARPA was actually intended to punish the kinds of conduct with which he is charged.

Gerber's insistence that Congress intended to limit ARPA to public and Indian lands centers on the remark of Representative Udall that ARPA "does not affect any

---

[13] *See also* H. Rep. No. 96-311, *reprinted in* 1979 U.S. Code Cong. & Ad. News 1709, 1713: "[Section 470ee of ARPA] prohibits *on public or Indian lands* the excavation, removal, alteration or defacement of archaeological resources except in accordance with permits or exemptions; prohibits dealing in those resources which are excavated or removed illegally; *and* precludes the sale and transportation *in interstate or foreign commerce when the resources are involved in violations of State or local law*" (emphasis added).

lands other than the public lands of the United States and lands held in trust by the United States for Indian tribes or individual Indian allottees." Brief of Appellant, at 26, *quoting* 125 CONG. REC. 17, 393-94 (1979).

At bottom, however, this observation differs little from the statutory savings provision cited earlier, which provides that nothing in ARPA "shall be construed to affect any land other than public or Indian lands *or* to affect the *lawful* recovery . . . of archaeological resources from land *other* than public land or Indian land." Title 16, United States Code, Section 470kk(c) (emphasis added). For the reasons discussed at length *supra,* at pp. 27-28, the idea expressed by Representative Udall and by the savings provision in no way detracts from the proposition that subsection (c) affects *commerce* in artifacts excavated—regardless of where they were excavated—in violation of state or local law. Moreover, the statements and opinions of individual legislators should not be relied on as authority for the meaning of language contained in a statute. 73 AM. JUR. 2d Statutes § 173, 376. It is, after all, impossible to determine from such a remark what the legislative body as a whole "intended," whether those who did not speak may have disagreed with those who did, or indeed whether Senator Domenici and DeConcini would have disagreed with Representative Udall. *See id.* at 377.

Nor is it surprising that the legislative history of ARPA contains numerous references to that statute's enhanced protections for archaeological sites on public and Indian lands. See Brief of Appellant, at 24-27. Such commerce signal only a focus of interest among legislators from the Southwest on the problem of looting on federal lands in their districts, not an intended limitation on the scope of ARPA. Testifying before a Senate subcommittee considering ARPA, Professor Raymond H. Thompson made this very observation:

> For a long time the archaeological resources, particularly from the Eastern United States, suffered depredations, and many States like [Arkansas] and Ohio and Kentucky lost hundreds of important prehistoric mounds. As our Nation moved westward, the aesthetically attractive items in the Southwest came into play and we are now focusing upon those items as a primary source of evidence for our discussions, largely because there is so much Federal land in that area where these things are found.

Hearing, *supra,* at 86.

In sum, although the plain language of subsection 470ee(c) should preclude any resort to the legislative record, an examination of that record affords substantial for the application of AP.PA to the conduct admitted by Arthur Gerber in this case.

3.   THE ARCHAEOLOGICAL RESOURCES PROTECTION ACT [16 U.S.C. § 470aa *et seq.*] ON ITS FACE PLAINLY PROSCRIBES INTERSTATE TRAFFICKING IN RESOURCES REMOVED IN VIOLATION OF "ANY" PROVISION, RULE, REGULATION, ORDINANCES OR PERMIT IN EFFECT UNDER STATE OR LOCAL

LAW, REGARDLESS OF WHETHER SUCH PROVISION IS OF GENERAL APPLICATION OR SPECIFICALLY *DESIGNED TO PROMOTE "ARCHAEOLOGICAL RESOURCE PROTECTION."*

As subsection 470ee(c) makes clear, a person commits a federal ARPA violation when he knowingly transports, in interstate commerce, archaeological resources that have been excavated or removed in violation of "any" provision in effect under state or local laws, regulations or permits. Such predicate state law provisions may, therefore, include traditional property offenses (such as conversion or trespass), or they may include violations of statutory or regulatory schemes specifically designed to protect archaeological resources.

Despite the foregoing statutory language, Gerber insists that "any" cannot mean "any." Instead, he asks this Court once again to disregard the "apparent literal meaning" of the statute, Brief of Appellant, at 43, in favor of his view that only those state and local laws involving schemes designed to protect *archaeological resources* should be deemed to fall within the sweep of ARPA. It is easy to understand why Defendant Gerber would insist on such an unusual interpretation: no comprehensive archaeological resource protection scheme existed under Indiana law until 1989, several months after the excavations charged in his own case.[14]

One of the predicate violations alleged in this case illustrates just one of the shortcomings of defendant's proposed gloss on the statute. The present indictment charges as a predicate, among others, the violation of provisions incorporated into an Indiana Department of Highways permit, providing that if "archaeological artifacts are encountered during excavation operations, the Contractor shall cease operations in the immediate vicinity and notify the Engineer." (O.R. 2, at ¶5). Gerber does not favor us wiht an interpretation whether, under his amorphous limiting interpretation of ARPA, he would include this provision as one implicating "resource protection," and therefore eligible for use as an ARPA predicate. Nonetheless, the defendant would have the government pick and choose (at its peril) which state and local laws sufficiently implicate "archaeological resource protection" concerns to qualify as ARPA predicates.

The simplest approach to limiting the scope of the statute—if that had been Congress's intent—would have been simply to define its limitations. That is precisely what Congress did in the closely analogous provisions of the Lacey Act, which outlaw interstate trafficking in wildlife taken in violation of state laws or regulations. The pertinent provision of the Lacey Act reads as follows:

---

[14] Prior to January 1, 1989, Indiana's principal provision affecting archaeological resources as such was I.C. § 14-3-3. 4-7, which proscribed excavations without a permit only "within the boundaries of property owned or leased by the state . . .". After that date, a more comprehensive state law came into effect which required, *inter alia,* permits to conduct excavations of certain archaeological sites on private property as well. The excavations and removals of artifacts charged in this Indictment are alleged to have occurred on private property during June, July and August, 1988.

It is unlawful for any person—

(2) to import, export, transport, sell, receive, acquire, or purchase in interstate or foreign commerce—

(A) any fish or wildlife taken, possessed, transported, or sold *in violation of any law or regulation of any state* . . . .

16 U.S.C. § 3372 (as amended, 1981) (emphasis added). The Lacey Act then elaborates its definition of "law or regulation" as follows:

The terms "law," "treaty," "regulation," and "Indian tribal law" mean law, treaties, regulations or Indian tribal laws *which regulate the taking, possession, importation, exportation, transportation, or sale of fish or wildlife or plants.*

16 U.S.C. § 3371(d) ("Definitions") (emphasis added).

ARPA, at Section 470aa of Title 16, United States Code, sets forth a number of definitions of terms used throughout its stautory scheme. Nowhere among those terms, however—or anywhere else—does there appear any parallel to the restrictive definition of "provisions in effect under state or local law" that Congress chose to employ in the Lacey Act. The limiting language used in the Lacey Act was simple, and Congress by that Act demonstrated that it knew how to employ it where such was its intent. Congress employed no such language, and harbored no such intent, with regard to ARPA.

Despite the utter lack of support for his interpretation, Gerber argues—again by hypothetical example—the "absurdities" that would result from the plainest interpretation of the statute's terms. Brief of Appellant, at 45-46. But the only thing "absurd" about Gerber's parade of *de minimis* "horribles" is that none of them states an ARPA violation. He argues, for example, that one who, in the course of selling an artifact in one state to someone in another state, makes a fraudulent misrepresentation in violation of civil law, violates ARPA by "sell[ing]" an archaeological resource "sold" in violation of sate law. *Id.* at 46. These facts fail to establish an "absurd" application of ARPA, because they fail to state any application of ARPA at all. As the statute's plain language indicates, to violate the Act one must sell archaeological resources that have already been excavated, removed, or sold in volation of state law. *See United Staes v. Carpenter,* 933 F.2d 748 (9th Cir. 1991) (in Lacey Act prosecutions, it is unlawful only for a person to acquire wildlife that has "already been 'taken or possessed'" in violation of state law; the very act of wrongfully shooting a bird does not fall within the scope of the Act).

The predicate acts which Gerber committed and aided (conversion, trespass, violation of construction permits regarding archaeological resources) involved the very means by which these archaeological resources were taken, and implicated ARPA's central concerns: the unauthorized violation of property rights and destruction of archaeological resources for commercial gain. The "absurdities" proffered by Gerber described violations wholly unrelated to the archaeological depredation itself—concerns regarding consumer fraud, uninsured motorists, highway safety, and motor carrier registration. Thus, one would be guilty of committing the "uninsured motorist" violation regardless of whether archaeological resources happened to be in the car or not; one commits conversion involving archaeological resources only by converting those resources.

The mere ability to imagine "clever" examples of "absurd results," a mental exercise that could no doubt be applied more successfully to any number of statues more broadly worded than ARPA,[15] can have no bearing upon the straightfoward application of statutory terms to facts clearly within the heartland of the defined offense. The predicate violations of Indiana's criminal trespass and criminal conversion statutes, as well as the state highway permit, satisfied ARPA's requirement of a violation of "any" provision or permit in effect under state law, and the indictment was therefore sufficient.

4. THE ARCHAEOLOGICAL RESOURCES PROTECTION ACT [16 U.S.C. §§ 470aa *et seq.*] IS NEITHER UNCONSTITUTIONALLY *VAGUE NOR OVERBROAD.*

Based exclusively on his previous arguments that the meaning of subsection 470ee(c) is unclear in its application to archaeological resources unlawfully removed from private lands, Gerber urges that ARPA is "at a minimum" constitutionally deficient on vagueness grounds. Brief of Appellant, at 38. His constitutional attack is nothing more than a re-framing or the arguments he advances with regard to statutory interpretation—that the legislative history and the "uniform consensus of commentators" creates ambiguity, and that therefore the statute is "vague." *Id.* His re-christened argument falls short for the same reasons his previous arguments did; he simply fails to create ambiguity or to advance a plausible alternative interpretation of subsection 470ee(c).

As a matter of constitutional analysis, the "void-for-vagueness" doctrine requires only that a penal statute defines the criminal offense with sufficient definiteness that ordinary people can understand what conduct is prohibited, and in a manner that does not encourage arbitrary and discriminatory enforcement. *Kolender v. Lawson,* 461 U.S. 352, 357 (1983). The courts' traditional concerns in vagueness cases have been with statutes containing terms of degree, that create no cognizable "standard" for what may or may not be prohibited.

These concerns are echoed in a long line of vagueness cases dating back many decades. In *United State v. Cohen Grocery,* 255 U.S. 81 (1921), for example, the Supreme Court invalidated a federal statute imposing a criminal penalty upon any person "who should make any unjust or unreasonable rate or charge in handling or dealing with any necessaries." The Court held that the terms "unjust" and "unreasonable" were insufficient to set standards for violation of a criminal statute. The California criminal

---

[15] The criminal provisions of the Clean Water Act, 13 U.S.C. § 1311, might arguably be applied to one who discharges a pollutant to a water of the United States, without an NPDES permit, by urinating into a creek.

statute struck down in *Kolender, supra,* relied upon by Gerber, required persons "who loiter or wander on the streets" to provide "credible and reliable" identification. The Court could find no cognizable standard for what could be considered "credible and reliable," and suspected that the statute could be used to vest complete discretion in the hands of the police—discretion that could be used to abridge First Amendment liberties such as freedom of movement. *Id.* at 358.

Examples of successful vagueness challenges, each involving standardless terminology susceptible to distinctions of degree—and most touching constitutionally protected conduct such as the right to move and to speak freely—could be multiplied to the same effect. *See, e.g., Gentile v. State Bar of Nevada,* 115 L. Ed. 2d 888, 906 (1991); *Cox v. Louisiana,* 379 U.S. 536 (1965). None of these characteristics are shared by the present case. The prohibitions contained in ARPA are binary and knowable. The statute asks only the question whether the artifacts were—or were not—excavated or removed in violation of provisions or permits in effect under state and local law.

In *United States v. Bryant,* 716 F.2d 1091, 1095 (6th Cir. 1983), *cert. denied,* 465 U.S. 1009 (1984), a Lacey Act defendant claimed that the analogous provisions of that Act were "vague" because the predicate conduct being punished could vary with the "whim" of fifty state legislatures. The Court rejected this challenge, holding that as long as the underlying state statutes were themselves constitutionally sound, a federal statute incorporating them would also withstand a vagueness challenge. The underlying provisions in this case—trespass, conversion, and highway regulations concerning protection of archaeological sites—are themselves sufficiently clear to place the defendant on notice of what conduct (combined with interstate trafficking) was prohibited. Indeed, the defendant in this case makes no challenge to the constitutional soundness of those state provisions. Therefore, the federal statute incorporating those provisions must also be upheld.

Amici in support of the appellant also raise an overbreadth challenge, contending that ARPA would chill academic freedom in the pursuit of archaeological information. The same argument was raised and rejected in both *United States v. Smyer,* 596 F.2d 939, 941 (10th Cir.), *cert. denied,* 444 U.S. 843 (1979), and *United States v. Austin,* 902 F.2d 743 (9th Cir.), *cert. denied,* 111 S.Ct. 200 (1990); both courts held that the excavation of native American archaeological sites is not of such constitutional stature as to trigger "strict scrutiny" of statutes designed to regulate such conduct. And viewing constitutionality "in the light of the conduct with which the defendant is charged," *see Smyer, supra,* at 941, one can hardly contend that Gerber had any cognizable liberty interest in invading the property of another in order to trespass and unlawfully convert prehistoric artifacts for commercial gain.

Note how the brief concludes by urging the court to adopt the view of another circuit which had little difficulty in rejecting claims similar to those made by Gerber.

The Ninth Circuit Court of Appeals had no difficulty in upholding the constitutionality of ARPA against vagueness and overbreadth challenges similar to those raised by *Gerber* and *amici. See Austin, supra.* That Court found that the statute "provided fair notice that it prohibited the [unlawful excavation] activities for which Austin was convicted," and further that the statute did not impermissibly reach constitutionally protected conduct. *Id.*, 902 F.2d at 745. Defendant's constitutional challenge in this case should meet a similar fate.

For all of the foregoing reasons, the United States respectfully submits that the district court's denial of defendant-appellant Gerber's motion to dismiss the indictment in this case should be affirmed.

Respectfully submitted,
DEBORAH J. DANIELS
UNITED STATES ATTORNEY
Southern District of Indiana

By: SCOTT C. NEWMAN
Assistant United States Attorney

By: LARRY A. MACKEY
Chief, Criminal Division

CERTIFICATE OF SERVICE

This is to certify that a copy of the foregoing BRIEF OF PLAINTIFF-APPELLEE had been served upon counsel of record, by placing same in the United States Mail, First-Class Postage prepaid and addressed to Jeffery L. Lantz, Attorney at Law, P.O. Box 1087, 525 Sycamore, Evansville, Indiana 47706, and to Harvey M. Silets and Kenneth M. Kliebard, Katten Muchin & Zavis, 525 West Monroe Street, Suite 1600, Chicago, Illinois 60661-3693, this _____ day of _____ , 1992.

_____
SCOTT C. NEWMAN
Assistant United States Attorney
Office of the United States Attorney
5th Floor, United States Courthouse
46 East Ohio Street
Indianapolis, Indiana 46204
Telephone: 317-226-6333

UNITED STATES of America, Plaintiff-Appellee,
v.
Arthur J. GERBER, Defendant-Appellant.

No. 92-2741.

United States Court of Appeals,
Seventh Circuit.

Argued June 3, 1993.

Decided July 20, 1993.

Larry A. Mackey (argued), Scott C. Newman, Asst. U.S. Attys., Indianapolis, IN, for U.S.

Harvey M. Silets (argued), Kenneth M. Kliebard, Katten, Muchin & Zavis, Chicago, IL, Jeffery L. Lantz, Evansville, IN, for Arthur J. Gerber.

Steven R. Dowell, Newport, KY, for Society for Documentation of Prehistoric America amicus curiae and Three Rivers Archaeological Soc., amicus curiae.

Steven R. Dowell, Newport, KY, E. Dean Singleton, Owensville, IN, C. Dean Higginbotham, Princeton, IN, for Indiana Archaeological Soc., amicus curiae.

E. Dean Singleton, Owensville, IN, C. Dean Higginbotham, Princeton, IN, for Council for Conservation of Indiana Archaeology, amicus curiae, Wabash Valley Archaeological Soc., amicus curiae, Society of American Archaeology, amicus curiae, Society of Professional Archaeologists, amicus curiae, Illinois Archaeological Survey, amicus curiae, Kentucky Organization of Professional Archaeologists, amicus curiae, Archaeological Society of Indianapolis, amicus curiae and National Trust for Historic Preservation in the U.S., amicus curiae.

Before POSNER, RIPPLE, and ROVNER, Circuit Judges.

POSNER, Circuit Judge.

Arthur Joseph Gerber pleaded guilty to misdemeanor violations of the Archaeological Resources Protection Act of 1979, 16 U.S.C. §§ 470aa et seq., and was sentenced to twelve months in prison, reserving however his right to appeal on the ground that the Act is inapplicable to his offense. What he had done was to transport in interstate commerce Indian artifacts[1] that he had stolen from a burial mound on privately owned land in violation of Indiana's criminal laws of trespass and conversion. The section of the

---

[1]   We are mindful that "Native American" is the term preferred by most members of the American Indian community. Since, however, the statute and both of the parties use the term "Indian," we have decided to do likewise.

Archaeological Resources Protection Act under which he was convicted provides that "no person may sell, purchase, exchange, transport, receive, or offer to sell, purchase, or exchange, in interstate or foreign commerce, any archaeological resource excavated, removed, sold, purchased, exchanged, transported, or received in violation of any provision, rule, regulation, ordinance, or permit in effect under State or local law." 16 U.S.C. § 470ee(c). Gerber argues that despite the references in this section to state and local law, the Act is inapplicable to archaeological objects removed from lands not owned either by the federal government or by Indian tribes. His back-up argument is that the provisions, rules, regulations, and so forth of state or local law to which the Act refers are limited to provisions expressly protecting archaeological objects or sites, as distinct from laws of general application such as those forbidding trespass and theft. The issues are novel because this is the first prosecution under the Act of someone who trafficked in archaeological objects removed from lands other than either federal or Indian lands.

More than fifteen hundred years ago in the American midwest Indians built a series of large earthen mounds over prepared mound floors containing human remains plus numerous ceremonial artifacts and grave goods made of silver, copper, wood, cloth, leather, obsidian, flint, mica, quartz, pearl, shells, and drilled, carved, or inlaid human and bear teeth. This mound culture, the product of a civilization that included the beginnings of settled agriculture, an elaborate ceremonialism, and far-flung trading networks, has been dubbed the "Hopewell phenomenon." N'omi B. Greber & Katharine C. Ruhl, *The Hopewell Site: A Contemporary Analysis Based on the Work of Charles C. Willoughby* (1989); Warren K. Moorehead, *The Hopewell Mound Group of Ohio (Field Museum of Natural History*, Publication No. 211, 1922). In 1985 farmers sold General Electric a piece of untillable land in southwestern Indiana adjacent to one of its factories. The land contained a prominent knob on top of a ridge. Unbeknownst to anyone this knob was a Hopewell burial mound some 400 feet long, 175 feet wide, and 20 feet high. The mound and its contents (which included two human skeletons) were intact—even the perishable materials such as wood and leather artifacts were well preserved—and when discovered it would prove to be one of the five largest Hopewell burial mounds known.

A highway was planned to run through the ridge on which the knob was located. In the course of construction, in 1988, earth was removed from the knob to stabilize the roadbed. Workmen engaged in this removal discovered in the knob curious objects—turtleback-shaped rocks—which they showed to a heavy-equipment operator on the project, named Bill Way, who happened to be a collector of Indian artifacts. Recognizing the significance of the find, Way nosed his bulldozer into the knob and quickly discovered hundreds of artifacts, including copper axeheads, inlaid bear canines, and tooled leather. He loaded these items into his pickup truck and covered up the excavation he had made. An acquaintance put him in touch with Arthur Joseph Gerber, a well-known collector of Indian artifacts and promoter of annual Indian "relic shows." Gerber paid Way $6,000 for the artifacts and for revealing to Gerber the location of the mound. Way took Gerber to the site the same night, encountering other people digging for Indian artifacts.

Gerber returned to the site several more times, excavating and removing hundreds of additional artifacts, including silver earspools, copper axeheads, pieces of worked leather, and rare silver musical instruments, some with the original reeds preserved. On Gerber's last visit to the site he was detected by a General Electric security guard and ejected. Shortly afterward Gerber sold some of the artifacts at his annual "Indian Relic Show of Shows" in Kentucky. He acknowledges that in entering upon General Electric's land without the company's permission and in removing, again without its permission, Indian artifacts buried there, he committed criminal trespass and conversion in violation of Indiana law. He also acknowledges having transported some of the stolen artifacts in interstate commerce.

The preamble of the Archaeological Resources Protection Act of 1979 states that "archaeological resources on public lands [defined elsewhere in the Act as federal public lands] and Indian lands are an accessible and irreplaceable part of the Nation's heritage" and that the purpose of the Act is "to secure, for the present and future benefit of the American people, the protection of archaeological resources and sites which are on public lands and Indian lands." 16 U.S.C. §§ 470aa(a)(1), (b). Consistent with this preamble, most of the Act is given over to the regulation, in the form of civil and criminal penalties, permit requirements, forfeiture provisions, and other regulatory devices, of archaeological activities on federal and Indian lands. The criminal penalties are for archaeological activities conducted on those lands without a permit and for trafficking in archaeological objects that have been removed from them in violation either of the Act's permit requirements or of any other federal law. §§ 470ee(a), (b). Gerber did not remove Indian artifacts from federal or Indian lands, however, and was therefore prosecuted under the third criminal provision (§ 470ee(c), quoted earlier), which is not in terms limited to such lands.

The omission of any reference in subsection (c) to federal and Indian lands was, Gerber argues, inadvertent. Not only the preamble of the Act, but its legislative history, shows that all that Congress was concerned with was protecting archaeological sites and objects on federal and Indian lands. This is indeed all that the preamble mentions; and a principal sponsor of the Act said that "it does not affect any lands other than the public lands of the United States and [Indian] lands." 125 CONG.REC. 17,394 (1979) (remarks of Congressman Udall). The legislative history contains no reference to archaeological sites or objects on state or private lands. The Act superseded the Antiquities Act of 1906, 16 U.S.C. §§ 431-33, which had been expressly limited to federal lands. And if the Act applies to nonfederal, non-Indian lands, its provisions are at once overinclusive and underinclusive: overinclusive because the Act authorizes the federal court in which a defendant is prosecuted to order, in its discretion, the forfeiture of the archaeological objects involved in the violation to the United States (unless they were removed from Indian lands), §§ 470gg(b), (c); underinclusive because the provisions authorizing civil penalties and the payment of rewards to informers out of fines collected in criminal prosecutions under the Act are administered by officials who lack jurisdiction over nonfederal, non-Indian lands. §§ 470bb(2), 470ff, 470gg(a). (The artifacts stolen by Gerber were recovered and are being held by the United States as evidence in this case, but they have not been ordered forfeited.) Most scholarly commentators on the Act assume that it is limited to federal and Indian lands. E.g., Kristine Olson Rogers, *Visigoths Revisited: The Prosecution of Archaeological Resource Thieves, Traffickers, and Vandals,* 2 J. ENVIRONMENTAL LAW & LITIGATION 47, 72 (1987). Gerber reminds us of the rule of lenity in interpreting criminal statutes and of the implied constitutional prohibition against excessively vague criminal statutes. He adds that subsection (c) of section 470ee would not be a nullity if the Act were held to be limited to sites and objects on federal and Indian lands. A number of state laws prohibit trafficking in stolen Indian artifacts regardless of their origin, and it has not been suggested that these statutes are preempted by the federal Act even with respect to artifacts stolen from federal or Indian lands. A person who trafficked in Indian artifacts in violation of state law would be subject to federal prosecution only under subsection (c) even if the artifacts had been removed from federal or Indian lands, if the removal happened not to violate federal law.

We are not persuaded by these arguments. That the statute, the scholarly commentary, and the legislative history are all focused on federal and Indian lands may simply reflect the fact that the vast majority of Indian sites—and virtually all archaeological sites in the Western Hemisphere are Indian—are located either in Indian reservations or on the vast federal public lands of the West. Subsection (c) appears to be a catch-all provision designed to back up state and local laws protecting archaeological sites and objects wherever located. It resembles the Mann Act, the Lindbergh Law, the Hobbs Act, and a host of other federal statutes that affix federal criminal penalties to state crimes that, when committed in interstate commerce, are difficult for individual states to punish or prevent because coordinating the law enforcement efforts of different states is difficult. The reference to interstate commerce would be superfluous if the subsection were limited to artifacts taken from federal or Indian lands, since either source would establish federal jurisdiction with no need to require proof that the artifacts were transported in interstate commerce. Probably the subsection was added as an afterthought, so one is not surprised that it does not jibe perfectly with the surrounding provisions; but that does not make it invalid, and it certainly is not vague. And we cannot see how the purposes of the Act would be undermined by our giving subsection (c) the interpretation that its words invite.

An amicus brief filed by several associations of amateur archaeologists claims that such an interpretation will infringe their liberty to seek to enlarge archaeological knowledge by excavating private lands. But there is no right to go upon another person's land, without his permission, to look for valuable objects buried in the land and take them if you find them. At common law General Electric would have been the owner of the mound and its contents regardless of the fact that it was unaware of them. *Elwes v. Brigg Gas Co.*, 33 Ch. D. 562 (1886); *South Staffordshire Water Co. v. Sharman*, [1896] 2 Q.B. 44. The modern American law is the same. *Klein v. Unidentified Wrecked & Abandoned Sailing Vessel*, 758 F.2d 1511, 1514 (11th Cir. 1985); *Ritz v. Selma United Methodist Church*, 467 N.W.2d 266, 269 (Ia. 1991); *Favorite v. Miller*, 176 Conn. 310,

407 A.2d 974, 978 (1978); *Bishop v. Ellsworth*, 91 Ill.App.2d 386, 234 N.E.2d 49 (1968); *Allred v. Biegel*, 240 Mo.App. 818, 219 S.W.2d 665 (1949); *Chance v. Certain Artifacts Found & Salvaged*, 606 F.Supp. 801, 806-08 (S.D.Ga.1984). Allred actually involved an Indian artifact. Although we have found no Indiana cases, we are given no reason to suppose that the Indiana courts would adopt a different rule. It would make no difference if they would. Whatever the rightful ownership of the mound and its contents under current American law, no one suggests that Way or Gerber obtained any rights to the artifacts in question. No doubt, theft is at the root of many titles; and priceless archaeological artifacts obtained in violation of local law are to be found in reputable museums all over the world. But it is almost inconceivable that Congress would have wanted to encourage amateur archaeologists to violate state laws in order to amass valuable collections of Indian artifacts, especially as many of these amateurs do not appreciate the importance to scholarship of leaving an archaeological site intact and undisturbed until the location of each object in it has been carefully mapped to enable inferences concerning the design, layout, size, and age of the site, and the practices and culture of the inhabitants, to be drawn. It is also unlikely that a Congress sufficiently interested in archaeology to impose substantial criminal penalties for the violation of archaeological regulations (the maximum criminal penalty under the Act is five years in prison plus a $100,000 fine, § 470ee(d)) would be so parochial as to confine its interests to archaeological sites and artifacts on federal and Indian lands merely because that is where most of them are.

We conclude that section 470ee(c) is not limited to objects removed from federal and Indian lands, but we must consider Gerber's alternative argument, that the section is limited to removals in violation of state and local laws explicitly concerned with the protection of archaeological sites or objects. Gerber argues that if it is not so limited all sorts of anomalies are created. Suppose he had bought an Indian artifact from its rightful owner but had failed to pay the applicable state sales tax, and had transported the artifact across state lines. Then he would, he tells us, be transporting in interstate commerce an archaeological object purchased in violation of state law. And likewise if he transported such an object in interstate commerce in a vehicle that exceeded the weight limitations imposed by state law.

These are poor examples. It is unlikely in either case that the state would consider the transportation of a good to be in violation of state law merely because sales tax had not been paid or an overweight vehicle had been used. But we agree with the general point, that the Act is limited to cases in which the violation of state law is related to the protection of archaeological sites or objects. A broader interpretation would carry the Act far beyond the objectives of its framers and create pitfalls for the unwary. But we do not think that to be deemed related to the protection of archaeological resources a state or local law must be limited to that protection. A law that forbade the theft of Indian artifacts "and any other objects having historical or artistic value" could not reasonably be thought a law unrelated to the protection of such artifacts merely because it had broader objectives. That is essentially what Indiana's laws forbidding trespass and conversion have: objectives that include but are not exhausted in the protection of Indian artifacts and other antiquities. A law that comprehensively protects the owner of land from unauthorized incursions, spoliations, and theft could well be thought to give all the protection to buried antiquities that they need, making the passage of a law specially protecting buried antiquities redundant—and the passage of new laws is never costless and rarely easy. The interpretation urged by Gerber would if accepted compel states desiring federal assistance in protecting Indian artifacts in nonfederal, non-Indian lands within their borders to pass laws that might duplicate protections already adequate conferred on landowners sitting atop undiscovered archaeological sites by existing laws of general applicability. Granted, all fifty states have laws expressly protecting their archaeological sites; and in 1989, too late for this case, Indiana amended its law to forbid—redundantly—what Gerber had done. So the interpretation for which he contends might not actually impose a significant burden on the states. But Indiana may not have amended its law earlier because it thought its general criminal laws of trespass and conversion adequate—for all we know, it amended the law in response to Gerber's contention that the federal Act contains a loophole through which he and others like him might be able to squeeze.

We conclude that Gerber's conduct was forbidden by the Act. We commend counsel, Harvey Silets for the defendant and Larry Mackey for the government, for the exceptional quality of their briefs and argument. We have not hesitated to criticize counsel who fall below minimum professional standards for lawyers practicing in this court; equally, counsel whose performance exceeds those standards by a generous margin deserve our public recognition and thanks.

AFFIRMED.

CHICAGO ACORN v. METROPOLITAN PIER AND EXPOSITION AUTHORITY

Nos. 98-1939 and 98-1977 (Consol.)

IN THE UNITED STATES COURT OF APPEALS
FOR THE SEVENTH CIRCUIT

CHICAGO ACORN, SEIU LOCAL NO. 880, AND TED THOMAS,	)))	Appeal from the United States District
Plaintiffs-Appellees, Cross-Appellants,	)))	Court of the Northern District of Illinois
v.	))	No. 96 C 4997
METROPOLITAN PIER AND EXPOSITION AUTHORITY,	)))	Hon. Blanche N. Manning,
Defendant-Appellant, Cross-Appellee.	))	*Judge Presiding*

OPENING BRIEF OF DEFENDANT-APPELLANT
METROPOLITAN PIER & EXPOSITION AUTHORITY

Renee Benjamin
Metropolitan Pier and
Exposition Authority
2301 South Prairie Avenue
Chicago, Illinois 60616
(312) 791-6265

Dated: May 11, 1998

Michele Odorizzi
Hugh R. McCombs
Gary S. Feinerman
Daniel G. Hildebrand
MAYER, BROWN & PLATT
190 South LaSalle Street
Chicago, Illinois 60603
(312) 782-0600

Nos. 98-1939 and 98-1977 (Consol.)

IN THE UNITED STATES COURT OF APPEALS
FOR THE SEVENTH CIRCUIT

CHICAGO ACORN, SEIU LOCAL NO. 880, AND TED THOMAS,	)))	Appeal from the United States District
Plaintiffs-Appellees, Cross-Appellants,	))))	Court of the Northern District of Illinois
v.	))	No. 96 C 4997
METROPOLITAN PIER AND EXPOSITION AUTHORITY,	)))	Hon. Blanche N. Manning,
Defendant-Appellant, Cross-Appellee.	))	*Judge Presiding*

CERTIFICATE OF INTEREST

The undersigned, counsel of record for defendant-appellant, furnishes the following list in compliance with Circuit Rule 26.1:

1. Metropolitan Pier and Exposition Authority.

2. N/A

3. Mayer, Brown & Platt.

_____
Michele Odorizzi

Dated: May 11, 1998

TABLE OF CONTENTS

TABLE OF AUTHORITIES

JURISDICTIONAL STATEMENT

This is an appeal from the district court's entry of a permanent injunction enjoining the Metropolitan Pier and Exposition Authority (the "MPEA" or Authority") from enforcing its existing policy with respect to public expression at Navy Pier and compelling the Authority to draft a new policy treating large portions of the Pier as public forums for political speech, protest and debate. The district court had federal question jurisdiction over this matter pursuant to 28 U.S.C. §1331 because plaintiffs alleged violations of federal statutes, 42 U.S.C. §§ 1983 and 1988 and 28 U.S.C. § 2201, and the United States Constitution.

This Court has jurisdiction over the MPEA's appeal from the entry of a permanent injunction pursuant to 28 U.S.C. § 1292(a)(1). The district court issued its opinion and permanent injunction order on April 1, 1998. The MPEA filed a timely notice of appeal on April 14, 1998. R103.[1] Plaintiffs filed a timely cross-appeal on April 17, 1998. R108.

The district court denied the MPEA's motion for a stay pending appeal on April 14, 1998. A34-35. The MPEA then sought a stay in this Court, which denied the motion on May 1, 1998, but granted the MPEA's motion for an expedited appeal. Because the injunction has not been stayed, the MPEA is complying with the district court's order to draft a new policy on public expression in accordance with the forum designations in the court's April 1st opinion. The MPEA anticipates that there will be further litigation in the district court concerning, among other things, the time, place and manner restrictions that will be set forth in that revised policy.

ISSUES PRESENTED FOR REVIEW

Whether the district court erred in enjoining the MPEA's existing policy on expression and requiring it to write a new policy treating large portions of Navy Pier as traditional or designated public forums, which must be made available to plaintiffs and other partisan groups for protests, leafleting and other similar types of expressive activity.

STATEMENT OF THE CASE

Note how the statement of the case begins with the key element in the client's position—the special nature of Navy Pier.

Plaintiffs are an advocacy group, a local union and an individual who wish to protest, leaflet and otherwise express their views in support of a higher minimum wage ordinance on Navy Pier. A4. The MPEA is limited-purpose governmental entity that owns Navy Pier and operates it as a commercial entertainment facility. 70 ILCS §§ 210/3-4. Although the Pier is open to public and dedicated to public entertainment, the MPEA has never allowed the kinds of protest activities plaintiffs wish to engage in on the Pier itself. Tr. 219, 232; App. 76-83. Instead, the MPEA has consistently limited such

---

[1]   Citations to the required appendix bound with this brief are to "A_." Citations to the separately bound appendix are to "App._." the transcript of the evidentiary hearing before Magistrate Judge Keys is cited as "Tr._," and exhibits are cited as "PX_" or "DX_." Citations to the clerk's record are "R_."

activities to Gateway Park, which is located across from the Pier, and the sidewalks abutting the entrances to the Pier. *Id.*

Plaintiffs filed their original complaint in this action on August 13, 1996, seeking an injunction allowing them to protest on the Pier during certain private functions held there in connection with the Democratic National Convention in August 1996. R1, ¶¶ 13-19. After an evidentiary hearing, the district court entered a preliminary injunction allowing plaintiffs limited access to the Pier during those particular functions. App. 1-23. The MPEA appealed the Preliminary injunction, but this Court dismissed the appeal as moot because "the events that were the subject of the appealed-from other [had] already taken place." App. 25.

After the Convention, in October 1996, plaintiffs filed an amended complaint that alleged, among other things, that the Pier was a public forum, that plaintiffs had a First Amendment right to engage in protest activities on the Pier, and that the Authority's policy was respect to expressive activities on the Pier was selectively applied and unconstitutional. R37, ¶ 51. In January of 1997, there was three-day evidentiary hearing on plaintiffs' motion for a permanent injunction before Magistrate Judge Arlander Keys. On February 27, 1997, Magistrate Judge Keys issued a Report and Recommendation, concluding that Navy Pier was not a public forum and that the MPEA had consistently and properly applied its licensing policy to promote the Pier's commercial interests. App. 54-57. Although he agreed with most of the MPEA's arguments, Magistrate Judge Key recommended the entry of a limited injunction requiring the Authority (i) to allow leafleting in designated areas of the Pier and (ii) to revise its existing policies to require permit and license applications to be acted upon within a specific period of time and to give disappointed applicants a right to appeal. App. 74-75.

Both sides filed objections to the magistrate judge's report.[2] R77-78. After reviewing the parties' briefs and the record, but without taking any additional evidence, the district court issued a Memorandum Opinion and Order on April 1, 1998, rejecting the magistrate judge's conclusions of law and holding that large areas of Navy Pier are either traditional or designated public forums. A5, A18. The district court entered a permanent injunction ordering the MPEA to write a new policy on expressive activity consistent with the court's forum designations. A33.

On April 10, 1998, the Authority filed a motion seeking clarification of the scope of the injunction and a stay pending appeal. R105. A few days later, plaintiffs filed a motion for a restraining order compelling the Authority to allow them to demonstrate on the Pier on April 16th. R106-07. After a hearing on April 14th, the district court issued an order stating that its April 1st order not only compelled the Authority to write a new

---

[2] The Authority disagreed with the magistrate judge's recommendation that it be required to permit leafleting on the Pier. It also argued that its licensing policy for the licensed spaces at the Pier-as opposed to its policy with respect to granting permits for expressive activity-was not at issue in the case and therefore should not be the subject of any injunctive order. R77.

policy, but also enjoined it from enforcing its existing policy. A35. The court declined to stay that order pending appeal. *Id*. Although it acknowledged that "[r]easonable minds could disagree as to what portions of the Pier are not public forums" and that "the MPEA has an arguable likelihood of success on the merits," the court denied the stay on the ground that the MPEA had not shown a likelihood of irreparable harm as a result of the planned April 16th demonstration. *Id*. With respect to that demonstration, the court substantially accepted the MPEA's proposal that plaintiffs be limited to protest zones and not allowed to march up and down South Dock, as they had demanded. *Id*. The court expressly state, however, that its ruling did not resolve the question of what time, place and manner restrictions the MPEA could impose in its new policy, but rather was "an interim solution to address the exigencies presented by" the April 16th protest. *Id*.

STATEMENT OF FACTS

The Parties

The MPEA is a limited-purpose governmental entity created by statute for the sole purpose of developing and managing McCormick Place and Navy Pier. R67, ¶3. It is run by a chairman, chief executive and a board appointed by the Mayor of Chicago and the Governor of Illinois. *Id*.

Plaintiff Chicago ACORN ("ACORN") is the local branch of a national advocacy group that represents the interests of low and moderate income people. Amended Complt., R37, ¶4. Plaintiff Ted Thomas is President of ACORN's board. Tr. 118. Plaintiff SEIU Local 880 ("Local 880") is the Chicago chapter of the Service Employees International Union. Tr. 138-9. Among other things, plaintiffs seek passage of a "Living Wage" ordinance in Chicago that would require contractors working on City projects to pay workers at least $7.60 an hour. R37, ¶8.

Note the emphasis on the possible disruptive nature of the activities planned by the ACORN group.

ACORN advocates the use of "direct action" to draw attention to its demands. Tr. 24, 123, 142. According to ACORN's handbook, its tactics include "demonstrations, pickets, sit-ins, squattings, street blockings, etcetera, usually leading to negotiations on demand." Tr. 28; DX 53. ACORN sometimes decides that having people arrested at demonstrations is the most effective way to communicate its message. Tr. 123. If permitted to do so, plaintiffs would hold demonstrations on Navy Pier involving 200, 250, or even as many as 1000 protestors. Tr. 120-22. Plaintiffs want to be free to circulate in all of the Pier's public areas to ask for contributions and signatures on petitions. Tr. 35-36. They also want to be able to use bullhorns and megaphones, engage in singing and chanting, and march and carry banners and signs. Tr. 43, 125, 145. The MPEA denied plaintiff's request for a "license" to engage in leafleting and solicitation on South Dock, but informed them that such activities were allowed, pursuant to the Pier's policy on public expression, in Gateway Park and on the sidewalks abutting the Pier's entrances. PX 9-10.

History And Redevelopment of Navy Pier.

Navy Pier was built in 1916. App. 46-47; R67, ¶2. It was originally known as Municipal Pier and served "largely as a freight, passenger boat and ship port" until World War II. *Id.* During both World Wars, the Navy used it as a training facility. *Id.* After World War II, until 1965, the University of Illinois used the Pier as its Chicago campus. *Id.* Thereafter, until it was conveyed to the MPEA, the Pier was occasionally used for festivals such as Taste of Chicago, but largely fell into disuse and neglect. PX 11, pp. 51-59.

Here the special nature of Navy Pier is emphasized by relating the history of its development. This information dies not appear in the opposing brief.

In 1989, the Illinois General Assembly granted the MPEA the authority to redevelop the Pier as a recreational, commercial and cultural facility for the enjoyment of the public. 70 ILCS § 210/4; Tr. 160. Shortly thereafter, the City of Chicago conveyed the Pier to the MPEA for $10. App. 22.[3] The magistrate judge found that "the City's primary purpose in transferring [Navy Pier] to MPEA was revitalize a portion of the downtown area," and that "Navy Pier is clearly an indispensable part of the City's and the State's [economic] plan." App. 37. The funds used to redevelop the Pier were raised through taxes, State of Illinois bonds and MPEA bonds. R67, ¶4. The General Assembly did not provide any public funds for the operation of Navy Pier; rather, the MPEA must manage the Pier so that leasing, licensing and parking fees cover all Pier operating costs. R67, ¶5; Tr. 160.

Prior to the MPEA's redevelopment work, the Pier proper and the so-called Headlands area immediately west of the Pier bore little resemblance to what a visitor sees today. Tr. 156-157. The Headlands consisted largely of parking lots surrounded by a chain link fence. Tr. 156. On the Pier itself, the lakeside wall of South Dock was breaking down, Tr. 157, and the various structures were, as the magistrate judge stated, "a rundown, rusty set of buildings at risk of sinking into Lake Michigan." App. 47.

In 1989, the MPEA began a massive, $200 million renovation of the entire Pier and Headlands. Tr. 159; R67, ¶4. New structures were built and old ones were gutted and reconstructed. Tr. 158. North Dock was built 50 feet out from the existing Pier wall, and

---

[3]   The MPEA's enabling legislation, 210 ILCS § 210/4, states:

It shall be the duty of the Authority: (a) to promote, operate and maintain fairs, expositions, meetings, and conventions from time to time in the metropolitan area, to arrange, finance, operate, maintain and otherwise provide for industrial, commercial, cultural, educations, trade, and scientific exhibits and events, and to construct, equip, and maintain grounds, buildings and facilities for those purposes . . . . (b) To carry out or otherwise provide for the recreational, cultural, commercial, or residential development of Navy Pier . . .

The City of Chicago Ordinance containing the "Plan of Development" for Navy Pier, PX 7, states that the Pier was developed to serve "public, cultural, recreational, business and commercial uses." PX 7 at NP000615. While the Pier was dedicated to public use, it was in the context of an overall economic development plan to operate the Pier as a commercially self-supporting facility for public entertainment, conventions, and cultural events. Tr. 160, 333.

South Dock was stripped, resurfaced, and fitted with performance stages, pavilions, landscaping, planters and benches. *Id*. The Headlands area was also completely transformed. In place of the old parking lots, the MPEA constructed Gateway Park, which included landscaping and a fountain, new roadways and entrances to the Pier, and a bus stop. Tr. 157.

The renovation was completed in July 1995. *Id*., ¶4. Today, the Pier's facilities include the Family Pavilion, the Crystal Gardens, the Skyline Stage, Festival Hall, and the Shelter and Terminal buildings (all in one continuous building), as well as the South Dock, North Dock, East End plaza, and the central area known as "Pier Park" that contains the Ferris wheel, carrousel and skating rink. *Id*., ¶8; Tr. 62. The MPEA's hearing exhibits include a videotape "tour" of the Pier that depicts most of its facilities. Tr. 189-193; DX 14 (videotape). They are also shown in a graphic, DX 18 (reproduced at App. 84).

The MPEA's Operation Of Navy Pier

At the hearing before Magistrate Judge Keys, the Pier's CEO, James Reilly, described the Pier as "a business owned by the public" that "has to make enough money in order to pay its operating costs and, therefore, continue to provide free entertainment" and other services to its visitors. Tr. 340. The Pier's core sources of income are leases and licensee agreements. *Id*. The Pier uses leases for permanent tenants such as restaurants, stores and boat operators. *Id*.; Tr. 350. It uses license agreements to rent temporary space at the Pier for concerts, meetings, banquets and the like. *Id*.

The Pier's leasing income derives largely from businesses in the Family Pavilion, which contains over 40,000 square feet of retail space, four full service restaurants, a food court, 15 retail tenants, the IMAX® theater, the Children's Museum, and the studios of WBEZ, a radio station. Tr. 162; R67, ¶14. Portions of South Dock are also subject to lease, with a number of restaurants having outdoor seating there. Tr. 163, 170; R67, ¶10. South Dock is also used by boat cruise operators who license permanent docking spaces and operate ticket booths adjacent to their spaces. Tr. 173. Finally, the Pier earns revenue from short-term agreements with pushcart vendors who operate throughout the Pier in both indoor and outdoor public areas. R67, ¶38; Tr. 164.

Pursuant to its standard lease agreement, the MPEA receives not only rent and building maintenance charges, but also a percentage of its tenants' sales over a certain "break point." R67, ¶37. As a result, the Pier has a significant financial interest in attracting patrons for its tenants. Tr. 216. As General Manager John Clay testified, "the success of our tenants is extremely important to the success of the Pier." *Id*. In 1996, Pier tenants had $54 million in sales, a significant percentage of which was paid to the Authority. *Id*.

The MPEA also earns licensing income by renting spaces such as Festival Hall, the Grand Ballroom or the Skyline Stage for special events on a short-term basis. R67, ¶44; Tr. 178, 180. When not in use, these areas are not open to the public. Tr. 62, 178-

79, 181. The MPEA licenses the Skyline Stage for a wide range of concerts and the-atrical productions. R67, ¶¶ 11, 22; Tr. 171, 177. The MPEA's main goal in operating the Stage is to minimize its own financial risk and increase its revenue by leasing it to pri-vate parties. Tr. 178. The MPEA has, on occasion, sponsored its own free concerts on the stage. Tr. 66, 178.

Festival Hall, the Grand Ballroom and the other East End buildings are licensed primarily for trade shows, consumer shows that are open to the public, large meetings, and banquets. Tr. 180. In these areas, the MPEA earns revenue not only from licensing fees, but also from food and beverage fees and other service charges, which in some cases greatly exceed the license fees. Tr. 180, 341, 362; R65, ¶¶ 29-30. As with other activities on the Pier, the MPEA also earns revenue from parking fees paid by people who attend these events. Tr. 167.

Another important revenue source for the MPEA is Pier Park, which is also called the "Entertainment Zone." Tr. 62, 236. This area, located above the parking garage between the Family Pavilion and Festival Hall, contains the Ferris wheel, the carrousel, and the reflecting pond. Tr. 62. It is generally open to the public. *Id.* In winter months the pond becomes a skating rink, and the MPEA rents out skates. Tr. 176. Together with the skating concession, the rides in Pier Park are the best net revenue sources on the Pier. Tr. 176-77.[4]

The Crystal Gardens also provide revenue for the Authority. Although this area is usually open to the public, a portion is leased by a restaurant that has the right, subject to Pier approval and payment for various fees, to close the entire area for private events. Tr. 62, 174-75.

South Dock, North Dock, the hallways and lobbies in the Family Pavilion, the South Arcade and Lower Terraces A and B are all open to the public during the Pier's hours of operation, subject to the rights of lessees and licensees in and abutting those areas.[5] Tr. 61. These public areas of the Pier, which are neither leased nor licensed, provide access to the various shops, restaurants and entertainment venues located throughout the Pier.

The MPEA's Policy On Expression By Tenants And Licensees.

The MPEA has always imposed certain restrictions on the expressive activities of its tenants and licensees. Tenants are not allowed to engage in any expressive activity outside their allotted spaces. Tr. 186-87, 299-300. For example, although boat operators

---

[4]   Pier CEO Reilly testified that Gateway Park, outside the Pier, was designed to function as a tra-ditional public park, an open place "with largely passive activities." Tr. 300. Pier Park, on the other hand, is designed for "active uses" like the Ferris wheel and carrousel and operates as "one of [the Pier's] biggest profit centers." *Id.*

[5]   After operating hours, all three entrances to the Pier are secured and the public is prohibited from entering any part of the Pier. App. 48-49; A21.

are allowed to hand out leaflets in the area adjacent to their ticket booths, they are prohibited from doing so in other areas of the Pier. Tr. 186.

The MPEA also controls tenants' expression within their leased premises. Its standard lease forms require that all tenant signage and leaflets must receive the prior approval of Pier management, which reviews them for content, size design, color and the like. R67, ¶ 41; Tr. 63-64. The MPEA has the right to control what films are shown at the IMAX® theater in the Family Pavilion. Tr. 165. Pier management also exercises control over the merchandise sold by and the appearance of the pushcarts to ensure that they are well-kept and attractive to Pier visitors. Tr. 164-165.

Similar rules apply to licensees. Licensees are not allowed to engage in expressive activity outside their licensed premises. Tr. 181. The Authority also exercises some control over the content of the expressive activity within the licensed spaces. Plaintiffs concede that the MPEA has not opened venues to all comers who agree to pay the fees. R37, ¶¶ 28, 36. Rather, the MPEA reserves the right to ensure that the activities at licensed events will not detract from the nature of the Pier as a family-oriented entertainment venue. *Id*. In addition, the Authority seeks to maximize the revenue- generating potential of the licensed areas by taking into account the nature and content of planned events in those areas. Tr. 182-83. For example, the MPEA tries to avoid creating conflicts with McCormick Place events and does not schedule similar events too close together, in order to maximize the turn-out for each individual even at the Pier. *Id*.

The MPEA's Policy On Public Expression.

Here, the client's position is supported by a positive portrayal of the management's access policies.

In October 1996, the Authority adopted a written policy formalizing its practice of prohibiting any and all demonstrations, marches, handbilling or solicitation in the unleased and unlicensed areas of the Pier that are open to the public. Tr. 219; R67, ¶57; App. 76-83. The MPEA's policy provides that "public assemblies, meetings, gatherings, demonstrations, parades, solicitation, handbilling, and other forms of public expression of views are not permitted at any time in any area east of the main entrances to Navy Pier. . . except pursuant to a valid lease or license agreement granted by the Authority." App. 77-78. The policy states that such activities are allowed in Gateway Park, which is located directly across from the Pier entrance, without a license or permit. App. 78. Demonstrations and the like are also allowed on the sidewalk areas abutting the Pier entrances so long as a permit is obtained from the MPEA. *Id*. The policy states that permits for the sidewalks areas outside the Pier's entrances shall be granted or denied without regard to the content of the message, on a first-come, first-served basis, subject to reasonable time, place and manner restrictions. *Id*.

General Manager Clay testified that the Pier's consistent policy, both before and after its adoption of the written policy described above, has been to confine the kinds of activities plaintiffs sought to engage in here—demonstrations, leafleting and the like—to Gateway Park and the sidewalk outside the Pier. Tr. 219-220. Although political groups (including plaintiffs, PX 10) are allowed to rent space for private fundraisers and similar events (R67, ¶ 46), the MPEA has never allowed any partisan group to engage in expressive activity on the Pier that is directed toward the general public visiting the Pier. Tr. 219-220; 232-33.[6]

The MPEA's policy on public expression contains "Factual Findings" explaining why the MPEA believes that limiting protests to Gateway Park and the sidewalk outside the entrances to the Pier strikes an "appropriate balance" between the interests of those who wish to engage in such activities and the "Authority's interest in the Pier's continued viability as a commercial venture and the health and safety of Navy Pier visitors." App. 76-77. These Findings explain that MPEA's primary goal in operating the Pier is to "create [a] desirable venue [] which successfully compete[s] in the international market for conventions, tradeshows and exhibitions; attract[s] visitors to Chicago and Illinois; and generate[s] economic activity with consequent jobs and business opportunities for State and local residents." App. 77. The Findings note that the "legislature provided no public operating funds, intending that MPEA manage Navy Pier so that . . . lease, licensing and parking fees and other charges for event services cover all operating expenses," and that "the continued viability of Nay Pier as a commercial venture is of paramount interest to the Authority and the State." *Id.*

Expressive Activities On Navy Pier

In their Amended Complaint, plaintiffs alleged that the MPEA had effectively opened up the Pier to all types of expressive activity by licensing particular events; plaintiffs also accused the Authority of applying its licensing policy in a selective and unconstitutional manner. R37, ¶ 51. Evidence was introduced at the hearing before Magistrate Judge Keys concerning a variety of different kinds of events. These events fall into three general categories; speech by the MPEA itself; speech by tenants or licensees in leased or licensed areas of the Pier, such the Skyline Stage or Grand Ballroom; and speech occurring in the outdoor, public areas of the Pier such as South Dock and Pier Park. These are addressed in turn below.

a.   *Expressive Activities Sponsored By The MPEA.*

The MPEA hires entertainers, including musicians, singers, jugglers, clowns, stilt walkers, mimes, a jazz band, and others who perform on South Dock. R67, ¶¶ 11, 22, 31, 35; Tr. 67, 168-69. Pier management hires these performers "for the enjoyment of visitors, and to promote their . . . having a good time," which in turn encourages "return visits which are important to the future success of the Pier." Tr. 171. For the same reason, the MPEA sponsors free concerts on the Skyline Stage, South Dock stages and other public areas of the Pier. Tr. 66, 178.

---

[6]   The district court placed a great deal of emphasis on the fact that the MPEA rented out the entire Pier during the Democratic National Convention to DNC supporters for a media party. A12-14. The party, however, was private, with only invited guests permitted to attend. App. 2.

On occasion, the MPEA has placed sculptures and artwork in unleased, unlicensed areas of the Pier to make it more attractive to visitors. R67, ¶ 34. In connection with a New Year's Eve event put on by the Pier, for example, the MPEA sponsored a "resolution sculpture" by a local artist, on which patrons placed postcards with their New Year's resolutions. Pier management then used those postcards to compile a mailing list. R67, ¶ 30. In a Veteran's Day ceremony in 1995, the MPEA dedicated an anchor at the east end of the Pier in memory of sailors who served in World War II and trained on the Pier. R49, ¶ 33. The MPEA also sponsored a Memorial Day veterans ceremony in 1996 at the east end of the Pier. R67, ¶ 33.

The Pier co-produced events related to Black History month that took place in the Crystal Gardens. These included a performance by the Black Ensemble Theater called "Great Women in Gospel"; a Black Newspaper exhibit; a Chicago Blues museum exhibit; and two forums hosted by radio station WVON and moderated by former alderman Cliff Kelly. R67, ¶ 25. The Pier's General Manager testified that this event "was [the MPEA's] idea" and that the Authority wanted to do it because it "would be enjoyable," it "would be good publicity," and it would "drive attendance" during the typically slow month of February. Tr. 258, 306.

On other occasions, the MPEA sponsored an appearance of Disney characters, Tr. 200, R67, ¶ 22, and a procession of guests along the Pier led by Ronald McDonald in connection with a family-oriented New Year's Eve party. Tr. 201, R67, ¶ 29.

b.   *Expressive Activities In Leased Or Licensed Areas Of The Pier.*

Subject to the restrictions outlined above, the MPEA allows its tenants and licensees to engage in a wide variety of expressive activities within leased or licensed spaces such as the Skyline Stage or Grand Ballroom. Most of this activity is not at issue in this case. The testimony at the hearing focused largely on instances where the MPEA licensed the Skyline Stage or Grand Ballroom or other facility without charging its standard fee. Plaintiffs argued that these charitable or civic events were sponsored by the Mayor or his wife, and that the Pier's fee waivers showed content discrimination and inconsistent application of Pier policies. The MPEA, on the other hand, argued—and the magistrate judge found—that its decisions regarding fee waivers were business decisions, made based on the potential of the event in question to draw patrons to the Pier, to provide revenue through food and beverage charges, or to provide an in-kind benefit (such as free entertainment or publicity) to the Pier. App. 54-57.

The event plaintiffs rely most heavily on is the licensing of the entire Pier for $1 to Chicago '96, a host of the 1996 Democratic National Convention, for a "media party" attended by members of the media, DNC delegates and national political figures. Tr. 209. The party was not open to the public, but rather was limited to invited guests. App. 2. Both Mr. Reilly and Mr. Clay testified at length about the benefits of having the media party at the Pier. Mr. Clay testified that the publicity afforded by this event was "absolutely unique" and a "once in a lifetime" opportunity. Tr. 209. He explained that the positive world-wide television coverage the Pier received was "just priceless," *id.*, and that "[t]here were going to be reporters and press there from all over the world seeing our facility at its best." Tr. 314. Mr. Reilly concurred, describing the party as having had a "tremendous economic impact" on the Pier:

> [T]he media party is The Event. It's the biggest event during the convention . . . . [O]nce it was publicized that we had been picked as the site of the media party, we booked hundreds of thousands of dollars worth of business. Our caterer in the month of August alone . . . did something like $1.1 million gross. But on top of that, even if none of that had happened . . . there were 20,000 media people there from all over the world. We would have paid them [to come] . . . . [T]his is a business dream to have that kind of press corps there with television cameras going, with the pictures being taken, with the stories in the New York Times and London papers and so on.

Tr. 349-50. For Mr. Reilly, the non-partisan business benefits of this event were confirmed by the fact that Republican businessmen, as well as the Republican governor and state legislature, gave millions of dollars to sponsor the convention in Chicago: "This was a great civic event." Tr. 348-49.

Plaintiffs also pointed out that the MPEA granted a free license for a "Celebrate Chicago" fundraising event held in the Grand Ballroom in October 1992—years before the Pier's renovation was completed. R65, ¶ 16; Tr. 159, 211-12. That event, which was sponsored by the Chicago Convention and Tourism Bureau, was attended by prospective customers for Navy Pier's exhibition spaces. *Id.* Governor Edgar's and Mayor Daley's names appeared in the program as honorary chairs of the event, and Mayor Daley spoke. R65 (Gutierrez Declaration, ¶ 18). Mr. Clay testified that the fee waiver in that case was absolutely justified by the need to promote the as-yet unfinished Pier. Tr. 212.

Another "free license" event plaintiffs relied on was a May 1994 benefit concert supporting "Gallery 37," an arts-related summer job program administered by the City. R65, ¶ 9. This concert was held in connection with the May 1994 opening of the Skyline State, before renovations at the Pier were complete and over a year before the Pier's grand opening.[7] Tr. 159, 309. Mr. Clay testified that the Pier licensed this event for free because it assured the Pier of positive pre-event publicity for the opening night of the Skyline Stage. Tr. 211, 309.

On a summer weekend in 1995 and again in 1996, the MPEA licensed the Skyline Stage and almost every other entertainment stage at the Pier to the "Magic City Festival," without charging a licensing fee. R65, ¶¶ 10-13. Mr. Clay testified that the fee waivers were justified because the festival was a unique event featuring children in the performing arts, who provided entertainment throughout the Pier; it was promoted at no cost to the Pier; and it promised to draw significant crowds of families. Tr. 207.

---

[7]   The Pier opened in phases. The Skyline Stage opened in May 1994; Festival Hall opened in May 1995. In July 1995, the crystal Gardens and the Family Pavilion were put into full operation and the Pier held its "grand opening." Tr. 159.

The MPEA has also allowed Chicago Police Department and Fire Department graduations to be held in the Grand Ballroom free of charge. R67, ¶ 50; Tr. 210. Mr. Clay testified that allowing these events made good business sense because the graduations brought anywhere from 1000 to 1200 attendees to the Pier, including family members of all ages, at midmorning on weekdays when few people ordinarily come to the Pier. *Id.* The events created revenue because the attendees paid for parking and many ate lunch at the Pier to celebrate the occasion. Tr. 210.

The MPEA also licensed Skyline Stage free of charge in August 1996 for the City of Chicago's "Mayor's Student Finance Graduation." R67, ¶51. A representative of the City spoke and addressed the approximately 300 people who attended. *Id.* As with the Police and Fire Graduations, the MPEA allowed this event free of charge because it was held at a non-peak time. Tr. 210-11.[8]

Apart from these events, plaintiffs also pointed to the fact that charity and political fundraisers have been held in the licensed spaces at the Pier, as have a number of civic ceremonies. R67, ¶ 46. For example, fundraisers—which supporters presumably paid to attend—have been held in the Grand Ballroom or in meeting rooms for President Clinton, Aurelia Pucinski, Mayor Daley and Governor Edgar. *Id.*, ¶¶ 15, 23, 26, 31. Naturalization ceremonies were held in the Grand Ballroom in 1994 and 1996, sponsored by the United Neighborhood Organization and the City of Chicago Department of Immigrant Affairs. *Id.*, ¶¶ 21, 27. In 1994, a public ceremony was held on the Skyline Stage to launch the Americorps program. *Id.*, ¶ 19. Plaintiffs do not claim that fee waivers were granted in connection with any of these events. The parties stipulated that these events all provided an economic benefit to the Pier in the form of license or rental fees, food and beverage or other service charges, and parking fees. R67.

No evidence was presented that the MPEA has ever denied any political, charitable or civic organization a license to hold a fundraiser or other similar event at the Pier so long as it agreed to pay customary lease and other charges. In fact, when plaintiffs inquired about the possibility of holding a fundraiser at the Pier, the MPEA's general counsel wrote a letter stating that the Authority would be "pleased" to rent a hall or meeting room to plaintiffs for such an event. PX 10, Tr. 298. Plaintiffs never followed up with any formal requests for a license.

  c. *Expressive Activities Occurring In Public Areas Of The Pier.*

A third category of testimony at the hearing concerned expressive activity in the outdoor, public areas of the Pier such as South Dock and Pier Park. Again, plaintiffs

---

[8] The MPEA has a written policy concerning fee waivers which provides that it will "consider" fee waivers for events that are strongly related to the history of the city or state, reflect a major initiative of the city or state, are sponsored by a not-for-profit entity, and involve a charitable event or admit guests free of charge. R67, ¶49; PX 4. Mr. Clay agreed that "there [are] other considerations" besides the written policy "that might lead the Authority to waive the license fee." Tr. 286. In general, the MPEA "exercise[d] [its] business judgment . . . in deciding whether or not to waive fees or costs associated with events on Navy Pier." Tr. 308.

claimed that the MPEA's decision to allow non-fee paying expressive activities in these areas showed that the Pier was not applying its policy on public expression in an even-handed manner. Once again, the MPEA's response was that it decided to license the activities described below, free of charge, because the events provided free publicity or entertainment and thus conferred a significant economic benefit to the Pier.

For example, the Pier granted a license, without charge, for a corporate giveaway by Dove Bar on South Dock at which White Sox players appeared to autograph Dove Bar sticks, with donations going to charity. R65, ¶¶ 7-8; Tr. 202. Pier manager Clay testified that this event provided valuable free publicity for the Pier and drew visitors to the Pier. *Id.*

The Pier management also allowed CAUSES, an anti-child abuse group, to set up a table and a large inflatable duck on South Dock to solicit contributions for an "adopt-a-duck" charitable event. R67, ¶ 52. Navy Pier was featured in print and radio advertisements for the event. *Id.* Mr. Clay testified that the MPEA permitted this event free of charge because there was a tie-in to a well-promoted duck race scheduled to occur on the Chicago River a few weeks later; it appeared to be something families and children would be attracted to; and it afforded the Pier favorable free publicity. Tr. 205-06; 262.

In August 1996, the MPEA licensed two stages on South Dock to the Austrian Heritage Celebration free of charge. R65, ¶18. The Austrian general counsel spoke at this event. *Id.* The Pier waived its licensed fee because the event included musical entertainment "that you don't see every day," provided publicity at no cost to the Pier, and seemed likely to increase attendance on the Pier. *Id.*; Tr. 208. The event also saved the Pier the expense of hiring performers for the South Dock stages that day. *Id.*

Another event plaintiffs and the district court relied on was a marathon Ferris wheel ride sponsored by a radio station, 94.7 KICKS Country. The Authority granted the station a license, free of charge, to do a continuous broadcast from the Ferris wheel to solicit charitable contributions for the Special Olympics. R65, ¶ 14. Mr. Clay testified that the Pier approved this event because it provided four and a half hours of free air time for the Pier and 14 hours of "cut-ins" during the broadcast day, in which the disk jockeys urged people to come to Navy Pier. *Id.* He testified that the air time alone was worth $30,000, and the event was an excellent attendance draw. *Id.*; Tr. 208.

The MPEA has never granted any group of license to protest, demonstrate or engage in any other partisan political activity on the Pier. Nor has it ever allowed leafleting or solicitation of contributions by people walking at large throughout the public areas of the Pier. Tr. 186.[9]

---

[9]   As described above, licensees seeking charitable donations have occasionally been allowed to set up tables in public areas. Tenants and licensees are also permitted to distribute leaflets in and around their leased or licensed spaces. Tr. 186. But the MPEA has never allowed-free-roaming handbilling or solicitation. *Id.*

Impact of Protest Activities On The Pier

Several witnesses testified that allowing protests and demonstrations in general, and the types of activities proposed by the plaintiffs in particular, would have a negative impact on the Pier's success as an entertainment and commercial facility. General Manager Clay put it as follows:

> I firmly believe that [allowing] protestors or demonstrators . . . full access to the areas on the Pier for the kinds of activities that have been described would . . . have a very negative impact on the image of the Pier and the image that the visitors of the Pier would have. And I think it would end up discouraging visitors to attend. The obvious result of that is decreased attendance, decreased revenues, and expenses don't go down.

Tr. 222-23. Pier CEO Reilly testified that plaintiffs' desire to move around the Pier and confront patrons, as opposed to occupying a stationary site, was particularly problematic, because patrons would be less able to enjoy the Pier, and instead would be forced to "decide[] [if] they do or don't want to conduct a conversation" (Tr. 344):

> One of the things the Pier sells, if you will, one the things people like about the Pier, is that when they are on the Pier proper, they can move around. They can enjoy themselves. They can move from one spot to another . . . . all with a feeling that this is purely relaxation and enjoyment. Anything that interferes with that is going to have an impact on our business.

Tr. 345.

Larry Schwartz, a pushcart operator, testified that in his experience the fun ambiance of the Pier was critical to its commercial success: "Patrons come to be entertained first, and then the commercialism is second. Get them in a good mood, they like to have a good time, and they'll spend some money." Tr. 376. In the pushcart business, "you have got 2.5 to about 5 seconds to catch the customer's attention because they are not coming directly to see your cart. It's an impulse sale." Tr. 377. Schwartz believed that demonstrations and protest activity in the Pier's open areas would "pull [his] customers eyes away," thereby decreasing his chances of making a sale. Tr. 378. He also testified that protest activities would hurt business generally by detracting from visitors' ability "to have a good time." Tr. 379.

These views were corroborated by a survey directed by the MPEA's expert witness, David Taylor, the executive director of the Metro Chicago Information Center, a professional data-gathering and analysis group. Tr. 424-25. When Pier patrons were asked how they would react to plaintiffs' proposed activities—including large demonstrations, being approached by a protestor seeking to convey a message, and being solicited for donations—approximately half said that it would make them less willing to return to the Pier. Tr. 435; DX 59. Almost 60 percent of the Pier's target audience—people with two or more children—said that protest activities like those described by plaintiffs would make them less likely to return. *Id*. Mr. Taylor testified that because most Pier visitors go there at most only a few times a year, "even small changes in the pattern of repeat business can have very large implications for the success of the business undertakings that are going on there." Tr. 433.

Magistrate Judge Keys' Report and Recommendation

After holding a three-day evidentiary hearing, on February 27, 1997, Magistrate Judge Keys issued a 50-page Report and Recommendation recommending that plaintiffs' request for injunctive relief be denied, virtually in its entirety. In his opinion, Magistrate Judge Keys rejected plaintiffs' contention that Navy Pier was a public forum. He found that "Navy Pier's pre-1989 history does not support an argument that it is, or ever was, a traditional public forum." App. 47. The magistrate judge also found that the public areas of the Pier, such as South Dock, are not so similar to traditional city sidewalks and streets that they must be considered, by their very nature, a public forum. App. 48-49. Finally, the magistrate judge concluded that the MPEA had not designated any portions of the Pier as a public forum by allowing the events described above to take place on the Pier. App. 66. Instead, Magistrate Judge Keys found that the Authority's licensing decisions were consistently designed to promote the commercial interests of the Pier. App. 54-57. He also found that turning the Pier into a forum for public protests and public debate would "actually interfere with the forum's stated purposes"—to create an economically successful entertainment, shopping and dining center on the Pier. App. 66.

The District Court's Opinion

Both parties filed objections to the magistrate judge's report. R77-78. Approximately one year later, on April 1, 1998, the district court issued its Memorandum Opinion and Order, "reject[ing] Judge Keys' conclusions of law." A5. Contrary to the magistrate judge's recommendation, the district court held that the public, outdoor areas of the Pier—South Dock, North Dock, Pier Park and the "east end plaza"—were traditional public forums and that the areas available for license—including the Grand Ballroom, Skyline Stage, Festival Hall and Crystal Garden—were limited purpose or "designated" public forums. A18. The court agreed with the magistrate judge that the Family Pavilion and the South Arcade, which are largely dedicated to retail tenants, are non public forums. A19-A27.

The district court concluded that South Dock and the other public, outdoor areas of the Pier were traditional public forums because they are walkways and areas for people to congregate. A19. The court concluded that these areas were indistinguishable from public streets and sidewalks and therefore had to be opened up to expressive activity. A19. The court also relied on what is characterized as a "plethora of First Amendment activity" that had been allowed in these areas in the past, such as the Ferris wheel charity event described above, the children's festival, product give-aways, and the Memorial Day ceremony at the east end of the Pier. A20-21. As to the portions of the Pier available for short-term licenses, the district court found that the Authority had effectively designated these areas as public forums by licensing them for events involving expressive activity, such as charity fundraisers. A23.

With respect to the Family Pavilion and the South Arcade, the district court accepted the arguments the Authority had made with respect to the entire Pier. The court stated that "these two spaces are similar to a shopping mall: a commercial area occupied completely by private commercial lessees who operate pushcarts, restaurants, bars, and retail storefronts for profit." A25. Although charitable solicitations had twice been permitted at tables set up inside the Family Pavilion and an entertainment stage in that Pavilion provides family entertainment, the court held that this expressive activity was not enough to give rise to an inference that the Authority had opened these areas up to become a forum for public debate. A26. On the contrary, the court found that the "plaintiffs' proposed political and social message is incompatible with and would likely harm the commercial nature of the Family Pavilion and South Arcade." *Id*. The court also noted that the MPEA had consistently prohibited non-charitable solicitation, leafleting and public protests within these areas. *Id*. Because "[p]ermitting unbridled access to the Family Pavilion and South Arcade would destroy the financial livelihood of the Pier and jeopardize all activity equally," the court found that the MPEA had "exercised sound business judgment by maintaining these locales as nonpublic fora." A27.

In light of its forum analysis, the district court held that the MPEA had infringed plaintiffs' First Amendment rights "to the extent that" it had denied them "equal access" to public areas of the Pier, with the exception of the public areas in the Family Pavilion and South Arcade. A33. The court enjoined the MPEA from enforcing its existing policy on expressive activity[10] and ordered it to revise that policy to adopt "content-neutral time, place and manner regulation of expressive activity," allowing "speakers" access to all areas of the Pier except the Family Pavilion and South Arcade on an "equal basis as all other license or permit applicant for said fora." *Id*. The court also ordered the MPEA to establish clear guidelines for the appeal of any denial of a license or permit application and for the viewer of any customary fees charged in connection with a particular license. *Id*.

STANDARD OF REVIEW

The controlling issue in this appeal is whether the district court's forum analysis was correct. On that issue, the standard of review is de novo. "Whether [government] property [i]s a public forum is a mixed question of fact and law." *Brown v. Palmer*, 915 F.2d 1435, 1441 (10th Cir. 1990), *aff'd on rehearing en banc*, 944 F.2d 732 (1991). This Court "review[s] the underlying factual findings under a clearly erroneous standard, but [] reviews de novo the legal conclusion of whether those facts make [government property] a public forum." *Id. Accord, Doe v. Board of Education of Oak Park*, 115 F.3d 1273, 1276 (7th Cir. 1997) ("this Court reviews de novo" a "mixed question of law and fact").

---

[10]   The district court clarified its order on April 14, 1998, stating that it had enjoined the MPEA from enforcing its existing policy as of April 1, 1998, A34-35.

In this case, the magistrate judge made a series of fact findings after hearing three days of testimony. The MPEA believes that those fact findings were correct. The district court did not disagree with the magistrate judge's findings, but rather disagreed with his proposed conclusions of law. A5. Thus, on appeal, the key issue is a pure question of law—whether the district court properly applied the legal standards governing forum analysis to the essentially undisputed facts.

SUMMARY OF ARGUMENT

I.   The extent to which expressive activity can be regulated on government- owned property depends on the nature of the forum. In a traditional public forum, the government is typically limited to imposing reasonable time, place and manner restrictions. It has greater control over a

Note how the argument begins with the client's most important position—that Navy Pier is not a traditional public forum.

forum that it has voluntarily designated as a public forum. in a designated or "limited" public forum, the government can limit access to certain kinds of groups or certain subjects and can limit the types of activities allowed. Finally, in a nonpublic forum, the government can impose restrictions on speech so long as they are reasonable in light of the purpose the forum serves and are not an effort to suppress particular viewpoints. See *Air Line Pilots Ass'n Int'l v. Dep't of Aviation*, 45F.3d 1144, 1151 (7th Cir. 1995) ("*ALPA*").

The MPEA's existing policy on expressive activity, which the district court enjoined, assumes that the entire Pier is a nonpublic forum. The policy is designed to limit expressive activity to that which will promote the Pier's purpose as a commercial and entertainment venue. Protests, demonstrations and similar kinds of activity in the public areas of the Pier not only would be inconsistent with that purpose, but would threaten the economic viability of the entire enterprise. It is for that very reason that the MPEA has never permitted such activities on the Pier.

II.   The district court struck down the MPEA's policy based on a fundamental misunderstanding of proper forum analysis. The district court was wrong in concluding that the licensed and unleased areas of the Pier, such as South Dock, North Dock, Pier Park and the east end plaza, are traditional public forums. The Pier does not have the kind of long history of use as a forum for public debate that would justify treating any portion of it as a traditional public forum. Indeed, the renovated Pier by its very nature is *not* designed to provide a forum for public debate. Much like an amusement park or shopping mall, the Pier is designed to be a place where people come to be entertained, to eat, and to shop—not to be confronted by protesters seeking to convey a political or ideological message. The mere fact that the Pier has internal walkways does not open those particular areas up to public debate. While city sidewalks and streets are traditional public forums, walkways that lead only to shops and theaters in a closed-off area like the Pier are not.

Because they are not traditional public forums, South Dock and the other public areas of the Pier could be deemed public forums only if the MPEA had designated them for use as such. Whether or not a forum has been so designated depends on the intent of the governmental entity that owns it. In this case, the MPEA's intent is crystal clear: it has never in fact opened up any portion of the Pier as a forum for public debate, nor would such a use be consistent with the purpose of the Pier. That the MPEA has permitted certain kinds of expressive activity in the public areas of the Pier does not change the analysis. As the magistrate judge concluded, all of the activities allowed by the MPEA in those areas were designed to promote the Pier as a commercial and entertainment enterprise. None of those activities involved political protests or, indeed, any of the kinds of activities plaintiffs seek to engage in here.

III.   The district court also erred in concluding that the MPEA had designated the licensed areas of the Pier, such as the Grand Ballroom, the Crystal Gardens, Festival Hall and the Skyline Stage, as public forums. These areas have never been opened up to public debate. On the contrary, many of these spaces are used primarily for *private* events. Furthermore, to the extent these areas have been used for public events, they have never involved political speech by partisan or advocacy groups. Thus, plaintiffs cannot claim a constitutional right to access to any of these areas for purposes of engaging in advocacy directed at patrons of Navy Pier.

IV.   If the district court erred in its forum analysis, it necessarily follows that its injunction must be reversed and the MPEA's existing policy reinstated. In his Report and Recommendation, the magistrate judge recommended that the MPEA be required to revise that policy to allow leafleting. Give the unique nature and configuration of the Pier, however, the MPEA's decision to prohibit leafleting outside licensed areas is entirely reasonable. Like any other protest activity, leafleting in the public areas on a free-floating basis would be extremely disruptive and fundamentally inconsistent with the Pier's commercial and entertainment purposes.

ARGUMENT

I.   Navy Pier Is A Nonpublic Forum Under The Supreme Court's Three-Part Forum Analysis.

Note how the very first sentence makes a critical argument for the client—that the government ownership of Navy Pier does not guarantee public access, and how this statement is then supported by a series of quotes from Supreme Court opinions.

"The First Amendment does not guarantee access to property simply because it is owned or controlled by the government." *Cornelius v. NAACP Legal Defense & Education Fund, Inc.*, 473 U.S. 788, 803 (1985); *United States v. Kokinda*, 497 U.S. 720, 725 (1990) (plurality opinion) ("[t]he Government's ownership of property does not automatically open that property to the public"); *Greer v. Spock*, 424 U.S. 828, 836 (1976) (public access to property "owned or operated by the Government" does not convert property to "a 'public forum' for the purposes of the First Amendment"). Rather, publicly-owned property is a public forum only if it "has as a principal purpose promoting 'the free exchange of ideas.'" *International Society for Krishna Consciousness, Inc. v. Lee*, 505 U.S. 672 679 (1992) ("*ISKCon*") (quoting *Cornelius*, 473 U.S. at 800).

The Supreme Court has identified three different categories of forums. A traditional public forum is a place that "by long tradition or by government fiat has been devoted to assembly and debate." *Cornelius*, 473 U.S. at 797. City streets, parks, and sidewalks are typically considered traditional public forums. *Perry Education Ass'n v. Perry Local Educators' Ass'n*, 460 U.S. 37, 45 (1983). Government authority to regulate speech in a traditional public forum is limited. Speakers may be excluded based on content only if the government can demonstrate a compelling state interest. Although the government may impose reasonable time, place and manner restrictions on speech, those restrictions must be narrowly drawn to serve a "significant government interest, and leave open ample alternative channels of communication." *Perry*, 460 U.S. at 954.

The second category of public forum is a place designated as a forum for public expressive activity. The question of whether a forum has been designated a public forum depends on the "government's intent in establishing and maintaining the property." *ALPA*, 45 F.3d at 1152. As the Ninth Circuit observed, "[t]he government does not create a public forum through unconscious, unspoken practices or by permitting limited discourse, but 'only by intentionally opening a non-traditional forum for public discourse.'" *Monterey Count Democratic Central Committee v. United States Postal Service*, 812 F.2d 1194, 1196 (9th Cir. 1987) (quoting *Cornelius*, 473 U.S. at 801). A designated public forum is generally governed by the same basic rules as a traditional public forum. however, the government may limit the forum to particular groups and those of similar character. *ALPA*, 45 F.3d at 1151. For example, in *Monterey County Democratic Central Committee*, the Ninth Circuit held that even if the post office had created a limited public forum by allowing non-partisan groups to register voters on its premises, it could properly limit access to similar types of organizations; a partisan political group seeking to engage in the same activity did not have a constitutional right of access to the forum. 812 F.2d at 1196.

The third category is a nonpublic forum—that is, a place that does not have the characteristics of a traditional public forum and has not been opened up for use as a public forum. If the forum is nonpublic, the state has the right to "reserve [it] for its intended purposes, communicative or otherwise, as long as the regulation on speech is reasonable and not an effort to suppress expression merely because public officials oppose the speaker's view." *Perry*, 460 U.S. at 46.

The MPEA's existing policy on expressive activity is based on the assumption that Navy Pier is a nonpublic forum. Although many areas of the Pier are open to the public, no portion of the Pier has ever been devoted to "public assembly and debate." Instead, the Pier is a commercial and entertainment venue that is operated as a business. As such, it is indistinguishable from the airport terminal that the Supreme Court found to be a nonpublic forum in *ISKCon*. In that case, the Court noted that there is no long- standing tradition of expressive activity in airports—indeed, modern airports, with long corridors lined with shops and

The ISCKon opinion upheld leafletting in public areas of an airport, and can therefore be construed as adverse authority. Here, however, carefully selected portions of that opinion are utilized to support the client's position.

restaurants, are a relatively new phenomenon. Furthermore, airport operators never acquiesced in allowing their terminals to bused as areas for public debate. As "commercial establishments funded by user fees and designed to make a regulated profit," "airports must provide services attractive to the marketplace." 505 U.S. at 681. in light of that fact, the Court concluded that "it cannot fairly be said that an airport terminal has as a principal purpose promoting 'the free exchange of ideas.'" *Id.* On the contrary, the Court observed that its principal purpose was to facilitate travel. *Id.* at 682.

The same analysis applies to Navy Pier. Government entities have only recently become involved in building and managing commercial entertainment complexes like Navy Pier. Thus, there is no long tradition of using such complexes as public forums. As the evidence in this case demonstrates, the MPEA has never acquiesced in the use of the Pier as a public forum. And the purpose of the Pier is clearly to provide entertainment and convention-related services "attractive to the marketplace" and, in so doing, making the Pier a financially viable enterprise—not to promote the free exchange of ideas.

II.   The District Court Erred In Concluding That Certain Public Areas Of The Pier Are Traditional Public Forums.

The district court concluded that Navy Pier's North and South Dock, Pier Park and the eastern end of the Pier were all traditional public forums. A19-23. In reaching that conclusion, the court considered the historical uses of the Pier before it was renovated, the nature of the outdoor public areas of the Pier, and the types of activities the MPEA has permitted in those areas. *Id.* As demonstrated below, none of these factors supports the district court's characterization of the outdoor public areas as a traditional public forum.

A.   The Historical Uses Of The Pier Do Not Make It A Traditional Public Forum.

The evidence below reflected that Navy Pier has been used, over the years, for many things, but that it never had as "a principal purpose[,] . . . the free exchange of ideas." *ISKCon*, 505 U.S. at 679. Initially, the Pier was a shipping center, then a navel training facility and then a college campus. None of these activities made it a traditional public forum. Indeed, for much of the Pier's recent history, it has served no purpose at all and remained largely closed to the public, except during special events. Contrary to the district court's opinion, the mere fact that the Pier occasionally played "host to cultural, political, entertainment, and civic events that have been targeted at attracting the general public," A21, does not mean that the Pier ever had as a principal purpose the creation of a forum for public debate.[11]

---

[11]   The mere fact that demonstrations were held on the Pier when it was a college campus or that the Pier was the site of Mayor Washington's first election victory party, A8-A9, does not mean that the Pier must forever be regarded as a traditional public forum, with all that such a designation entails.

In any event, Navy Pier today bears little or no resemblance to the Pier as it was before the MPEA took it over. Beginning in 1989, Navy Pier was radically transformed from a run-down, rusty set of municipal buildings at risk of sinking into the Lake into a completely renovated commercial and entertainment destination. App. 47. Thus, regardless of its prior history, the Court must focus on the Pier as it stands today. As demonstrated above, a commercial entertainment complex is not a traditional public forum—even if it is owned by a governmental entity.

B. The Public Areas Of The Pier Are Not The Equivalent Of City Sidewalks Or Traditional Parks For Forum Analysis Purposes.

That "Dock Street is, in fact, a sidewalk" does not mean, as the district court concluded, that it is a traditional public forum. A19. It is "simply incorrect [to] assert [] that every public sidewalk is a public forum." *Kokinda*, 497 U.S. at 728 (plurality opinion). Although South Dock is available to the public as a walkway at designated times, "that fact alone does not establish that those areas must be treated as traditional public fora under the First Amendment." *Id*. at 729. In *Kokinda*, the plurality concluded that a sidewalk constructed by the Postal Service that was designed to provide access only between a parking lot and a post office was not a traditional public forum despite the fact that it was indistinguishable in many ways from the municipal sidewalk across the street. The key distinction was that, unlike the municipal sidewalk, the sidewalk outside the post office did not lead anywhere other than to the post office itself. Because it had a single, dedicated use that did not include providing a public forum, the Supreme Court concluded that the sidewalk could not be considered a traditional public forum. *Id*. at 730.

Other courts have agreed that walkways that are not part of the city's transportation system, but rather are designed solely to service government-owned property, should not be considered traditional public forums. See, *e.g., Jacobsen v. Bonine*, 123 F.3d 1272, 1273-74 (9th Cir. 1997) (perimeter walkways of interstate rest areas are not a public forum); *Sentinel Communications Co. v. Watts*, 936 F.2d 1189 (11th Cir. 1991) (same*); Hampton Int'l Communications v. Las Vegas Convention and Visitors Authority*, 913 F.Supp. 1402, 1410 (D. Nev. 1996) (ingress and egress walkways to and from convention center are not a traditional public forum); *Int'l Caucus of Labor Comm. v. Maryland Dep't of Transportation*, 745 F.Supp. 323, 327 (D. Md. 1990) (interior walkways serving government office are a nonpublic forum).

So too, in this case, the walkways and driveways on the Pier are not part of the City's transportation system; instead, South Dock and North Dock are designed solely to provide access to various areas of the Pier and are not part of the City's general transportation grid.[12] In addition, South Dock, Pier Park and the east of the Pier are themselves entertainment and commercial venues, particularly during the summer, with pushcart vendors, outdoor cafes, rides, boats, and entertainment. Thus, like the rest of

---

[12]   As Magistrate Judge Keys noted, South Dock "simply does not lead anywhere," and North Dock is essentially "no more than a driveway" providing access to the parking garage. App. 49.

the Pier, the principal purpose of these areas is to attract patrons to the Pier by providing entertainment and to make money through the commercial endeavors located there—not to provide a forum for the public exchange of ideas.

C.   The MPEA Never Designated The Public Areas Of The Pier As A Public Forum For Political Speech, Protests And Debate.

That the Authority has occasionally allowed groups to provide entertainment or product giveaways in the public areas of the Pier and allowed an occasional charitable event in those areas (such as the marathon Ferris wheel ride and the "adopt-a-duck" promotion) does not mean that the Authority has opened up the Pier generally to the kinds of activities in which plaintiffs wish to engage. The events that have been allowed in the public areas of the Pier were all completely consistent with its character as a commercial entertainment venue. Indeed, as the magistrate judge concluded, all of these events were permitted precisely because they provided entertainment and thus enhanced the Pier's revenue-generating potential by attracting more patrons to the Pier. App. 54-55. None of these events even remotely resembled the kinds of activities that could be deemed evidence of an intent to open the public areas of the Pier to the full range of First Amendment activities.[13] In fact, the activities allowed on South Dock are virtually indistinguishable from the entertainment and charitable activities that were allowed in the Family Pavilion. The district court correctly concluded that those activities did not render the Family Pavilion a public forum. A26. The same analysis applies to the outdoor areas of the Pier.

The flaw in the district court's reasoning is its assumption that allowing *any* expressive activity on the Pier necessarily means that the MPEA intended to throw open the public areas of the Pier to *all* types of expressive activity. The courts have consistently rejected such an analysis. Thus, for example, in *Kokinda*, the plurality rejected the argument that the plaintiff had a right to solicit contributions on the sidewalks because individuals and groups had been allowed to "leaflet, speak, and picket on postal premises"; Justice O'Connor concluded that "a practice of allowing some speech activities on postal property" "do[es] not add up to the dedication of postal property to speech activities." 497 U.S. at 730.

The Supreme Court reached the same result in *Greer v. Spock*, 424 U.S. 828, 838 n.10 (1976), where it concluded that the fact that a military commander had allowed a civilian lecture on drug abuse, a religious service and a rock concert on a military base did not mean that the commander was "powerless thereafter to prevent any civilian from entering Fort Dix to speak on any subject whatever." Accord, *Families Achieving Inde-*

---

[13]   The district court repeatedly referred to the fact that the Authority rented out the entire Pier to Chicago '96 for a party during the Democratic Convention. A3, A10-A14, A23. But the court ignored one critical fact: the party was not open to the public. Rather, the Pier was closed down and attendance at the party was by invitation only. App. 2. The private Chicago '96 party is hardly proof that the MPEA has opened up the Pier to *public* debate.

pendence and Respect v. Nebraska Dep't of Social Services, 111 F.3d 1408, 1420 (8th Cir. 1997) (en banc) (a welfare office did not create a designated public forum by opening up the lobby to organizations like Head Start that provided advice and information to welfare recipients; the government policy prohibiting advocacy groups from using the lobby was constitutional); *Brown v. Palmer*, 944 F.2d (10th Cir. 1991) (en banc) (a one-day open house at an Air Force base did not become a public forum simply because some expressive activity was allowed, because it was clear that the Air Force never intended the open house to become a forum for ideological or political debate); *Calash v. City of Bridgeport*, 788 F.2d 80, 83 (2d Cir. 1986) ("Selective access by civic, charitable and non-profit organizations cannot be equated with 'indiscriminate use by the general public'"); *Monterey County Democratic Central Committee*, 812 F.2d at 1197-98 (fact that post office property had been used by the Red Cross for blood drives and the Lions Club for fundraising did not mean that it became a public forum, because the evidence showed that "[a]t no time . . . did the Postal Service swing wide the doors to indiscriminate use by the public").

In this case, the MPEA never opened the public areas of the Pier to ideological or political debate or otherwise took any action to "swing wide the doors to indiscriminate use" by those wishing to engage in public debate. Plaintiffs point to various events involving expressive activity, both in the public areas of the Pier and in the licensed areas, that were sponsored by the MPEA itself or by the City of Chicago. But speech by the government on government-owned property does not open the forum up to advocacy by members of the public. As the Tenth Circuit noted, "[i]f the government's own speech could be used to support a claim that it has thereby caused its facilities to become a public forum, then 'display cases in public hospitals, libraries, office buildings, military compounds, and other public facilities immediately would become Hyde Parks open to every would-be pamphleteer and politician. This Constitution does not require.'" *Brown*, 944 F.2d at 738 (quoting *United States Postal Services v. Council of Greenburgh Civic Ass'ns*, 453 U.S. 114, 130 n. 6 (1981)).

Plaintiffs also pointed to the fact that the Authority has allowed political speech inside the license spaces on the Pier when it allowed political fundraisers. That the MPEA rented a hall (or the entire Pier, in the case of the DNC party) to a political group for a private party or fundraiser does not mean that it intended to convert the public areas of the Pier into a public forum for political debate. In deciding whether a particular area is a public forum, the court must focus on the "'access sought by the speaker.'" *ALPA*, 45 F.3d at 1151. In *ALPA*, this Court reversed the district court because it based its forum analysis on the entire airport, when plaintiffs sought access only to certain display cases. So too, in this case, the district court's decision that the *unlicensed* areas of the Pier constitute a forum for public debate cannot be supported on the ground that the MPEA allowed *private* political speech in *licensed* areas of the Pier.

In the end, as this Court recognized in *ALPA*, the question of whether a particular place has been designated as a public forum depends on the government property owner's *intent*. In order to determine that intent, the Court must consider two issues: the "policy and practice of the government with respect to the underlying property" and "the nature of the property and its compatibility with expressive activity." 45 F.3d at 1152. In this case, the policy and practice of the MPEA has consistently been to prohibit protest activities and other types of public advocacy in the public areas of the Pier. Furthermore, the events the Authority has allowed in the public areas of the Pier have all been licensed with one purpose in mind: to provide entertainment to Pier patrons and attract people to the Pier. The Authority's business decisions to permit these kinds of events cannot possibly give rise to an inference that it intended to open the Pier up to political protest and debate.

The nature of the property and its incompatibility with the kind of speech proposed by plaintiffs also confirm that the MPEA's intent was not to create a public forum. The Pier is a commercial entertainment complex that must make money in order to survive. As the testimony at the hearing demonstrated, allowing protest activities on the Pier would not only be consistent with its character as an entertainment venue, but would also imperil the commercial success of the venture. A large percentage of the people who come to Navy Pier simply do not want to be accosted by protesters or anyone advocating a political or ideological position. If they were, many would choose not to return. Because the economic success of the Pier depends on maintaining a fun-filled atmosphere throughout its public areas, it is simply irrational to assume that the Authority ever intended to designate those areas as a forum for public debate.

III.   The Licensed Areas Of The Pier Have Not Been Designated As A Public Forum.

It is not clear why the district court made any ruling at all with respect to the licensed areas of the Pier—the Grand Ballroom, Festival Hall, the Skyline Stage and the like. Plaintiff's complaint did not seek access to these areas. Thus, the court had no occasion to determine whether or not the MPEA intended to designate any of those areas as a public forum.

Although the issue was not properly before it, the district court ordered the MPEA to rewrite its licensing policy to permit access to these areas "on an equal basis" to all speakers wishing to use these spaces. A33. To the extent the district court intended to eliminate the MPEA's right to make business decisions based, in part, on the content of the event for which a license is sought, its ruling was plainly wrong.

Contrary to the district court's opinion, the Authority never designated its licensed spaces as public forums. The Authority has never offered those spaces to all comers, regardless of the nature of the event for which a license is sought. Instead, the Authority has consistently reserved the right to take content into account in order to make an appropriate business decision as to whether the event in question is likely to be profitable in and of itself, and whether it will contribute to or detract from the family-oriented atmosphere the MPEA has created at the Pier.

Moreover, many of the spaces the district court characterized as designated public forums are meetings rooms and halls typically used for *private* events. That some of those private events were political or charitable fundraisers or otherwise involved expressive activity does not mean that the areas in question have been thrown open to use as forums for *public* debate. Although concerts and other events that are open to the general public are held in areas like the Skyline Stage, none of them have involved political or ideological speech or advocacy. That the Skyline Stage was used for civic ceremony or a rock concert does not mean that the MPEA intended to open that area up as a forum for public debate. On the contrary, the primary purpose of the Skyline Stage and the other licensed areas of the Pier is plainly commercial: to draw patrons to the Pier and generate revenue for the Authority through license fees, service charges and the like. There is simply no basis for concluding that the Authority ever intended to throw those areas open to use as a free public forum.

Whatever the district court failed to recognize is that even where a designated public forum has been established, the government has the right to limit access to that forum to particular groups and particular subject matters. *ALPA*, 45 F.3d at 1151. Thus, the fact that charitable organizations have been allowed to use the Skyline Stage for benefit concerts does not mean that plaintiffs must be allowed in these areas; rather, it is whether plaintiffs have been excluded from using the forum in the same manner as other similar groups. See *Monterey County Democratic Central Committee*, 812 F.2d at 1196. Political and advocacy; instead, they have been allowed to use the licensed spaces only for fundraisers and similar private events. There was no evidence that plaintiffs or any other similar group have ever been denied access to a hall or meeting room at the Pier for such a purpose. On the contrary, the MPEA specifically offered to provide plaintiffs with a license to use one of its halls for a meeting or fundraiser.

The district court appears to have concluded that the Authority was not offering access to plaintiffs on an equal basis because it did not offer to waive it customary lease charges for their proposed event, as it did for the DNC media party. A12-14. But the decision to rent the Pier for $1 for the DNC party was, as the Pier manager and CEO testified, purely a business decision. Apart from the revenues earned from other events booked on account of the DNC party, the publicity value of the event was enormous. Other functions where fee waivers were granted (none of which involved a political group) also provided the Authority with free publicity or free entertainment or the prospect of drawing large numbers of patrons at times that otherwise might be slow. Plaintiffs do not claim that their fundraisers would have provided the Authority with any similar benefits. Thus, they can hardly claim that they too were somehow entitled to use a licensed area without paying any license fee.

In any event, even if there had been something wrong with the Authority's exercise of its business judgment to grant fee waivers in certain situations, the proper solution would not be to declare all of the licensed spaces on the Pier a designated public forum. Instead, to the extent plaintiffs had standing to raise the issue at all, the court should have ordered the Authority simply to clarify its fee waiver policy.[14]

IV.   Because Navy Pier Is A Nonpublic Forum, The District Court Erred In Enjoining Its Existing Policy With Respect To Expressive Activity.

The district court struck down the MPEA's existing policy in reliance on its erroneous forum analysis. When the Pier as a whole is viewed as a nonpublic forum, it becomes clear that the restrictions in the existing policy are permissible. As described above, government restrictions on speech in a nonpublic forum must be upheld so long as they are reasonable in light of the forum's purpose and not a pretext for disfavoring particular speakers or viewpoints. In this case, the district court agreed that the MPEA's policy was constitutional with respect to the areas it found to be a nonpublic forum (the Family Pavilion and the South Arcade). A24-A27. The magistrate judge, who agreed that the entire Pier was a nonpublic forum, also substantially upheld the MPEA's existing policy. App. 66, 70-71. However, the magistrate judge recommended that the Authority be required to rewrite it policy, among other things, to allow leafleting in certain areas, subject to reasonable time, place and manner restrictions. App. 75.

Here is an example of dealing with adverse authority by denigrating its precedential value.

The magistrate judge's recommendation that the leafleting be allowed in the public areas of the Pier is based on the Supreme Court's companion decision in the *ISKCon* case. *International Society for Krishna Consciousness, Inc. v. Lee*, 505 U.S. 685 (1992) ("*ISKCon II*"). In that case, Justice O'Connor, who had supplied the fifth vote holding the airport to be a nonpublic forum, took the position that the airport was nevertheless required to allow leafleting (though not soliciting). *Id*. at 690-92. Given the way the Court split, the precedential value of that decision is weak.[15] In any event, Justice O'Connor's opinion does not purport to establish any bright-line rule requiring governments to open up even nonpublic forums to leafleting. Instead, in each and every case, the question is the reasonableness of the prohibition in light of the purpose of the forum.

---

[14]   Even if, as a result of the fee waivers, the MPEA somehow, in some unknown way, inadvertently created a limited public forum, it would have a right to "de-designate" the forum by changing its waiver policy to make it consistent with a nonpublic forum. See *Knolls Action Project v. Knolls Atomic Power Laboratory*, 771 F.2d 46 (2d Cir. 1985) (citing Perry, 460 U.S. at 46, for the proposition that a government owner that has created a designated forum need not "indefinitely retain" that character and holding that a government owned nuclear research facility could choose to close down an area it had previously allowed protestors to use).

[15]   The other four justices who joined Justice O'Connor in the second *ISKCon* decision did so on the ground that the airport was a public forum. The four other justices who believed that the airport was a nonpublic forum dissented from the result in ISKCon II, on the ground that the airport authority could properly ban both solicitation and leafleting. Thus, Justice O'Connor was the only justice who believed the two types of activity should be treated differently.

In this case, it was reasonable for the Authority to prohibit leafleting in the public areas of the Pier. The Authority does not allow leaflets to be distributed anywhere on the Pier except in and around licensed spaces, such as the ticket booths for the tour boats on South Dock.[16] Given the peculiar configuration of the public spaces at the Pier-which are narrow and often (particularly in the summer) extremely crowded-leafleting would be inherently disruptive. In *ISKCon II*, Justice O'Connor suggested that people who receive leaflets are less likely to stop or be disturbed as they hurry through airport terminals than people who are stopped and asked for money, since it is possible just to take a leaflet and keep walking. 505 U.s. at 690. But in a crowded area like South Dock, where people are strolling, rather than hurrying to a destination, patrons might not find it so easy to escape the attentions of a persistent leafleter. More importantly, unlike air travelers who have no choice but to walk through a terminal, Pier patrons who are annoyed by such activities do have a choice as to whether or not to come back to the Pier. The Pier has a real an substantial economic interest in preventing any activities, including leafleting, that could discourage patrons form returning to the Pier.

The record evidence demonstrates that allowing any kind of protest activity on Navy Pier, whether it be marching, soliciting signatures on a petition or donations, chanting, or leafleting, is likely to be disruptive and unpleasant to patrons who come to the Pier to be entertained or simply to relax. If plaintiffs are allowed to leaflet on the Pier, then the Authority would be required to let other advocacy groups do the same (subject, of course, to reasonable time, place and manner restrictions). As the record demonstrates, the prospect of being accosted by all manner of protestors handing out leaflets-members of the Ku Klux Klan or the Nazi Party, representatives of pro- or anti-abortion groups, or anyone else advocating a hundred other controversial viewpoints-would be daunting for people who come with their children to the Pier simple to partake in the family entertainment offered there. Many would simply choose to spend their entertainment dollars elsewhere.

The MPEA should be able to limit Navy Pier to the purpose for which it spent more than $200 million reconstructing it-creating a unique, commercially viable entertainment destination in downtown Chicago. The MPEA has never opened up the Pier as a forum for public debate. Plaintiffs' First Amendment rights are adequately protected by the policy allowing them to engage in the full range of expressive activity in Gateway Park and the sidewalks in front of the Pier entrances.

---

[16] In its opinion, the district court accused the MPEA of being "less then accurate" when it represented in the preliminary injunction hearing that leafleting was not allowed because of the physical characteristics of the Pier. A14. The court pointed to the fact that at the DNC event a man dressed up as "Uncle Sam" handed out leaflets at the entrance to the Pier. *Id*. Any suggestion that the MPEA was misleading the court dissolves, however, in light of the fact that the event took place *after* the representation was made at the preliminary injunction hearing. Moreover, as noted above, the leafleting occurred at a private party in which the entire Pier was licensed to a single licensee. App. 2; Tr. 209. That one event says nothing about the reasonableness of allowing leafleting on an ongoing basis.

CONCLUSION

For the foregoing reasons, the decision below should be reversed, the permanent injunction should be vacated, and the district court should be directed on remand to enter judgment in favor of the MPEA.

Respectfully submitted,

_____

One of the attorneys for Defendant-Appellee
Metropolitan Pier and Exposition Authority

Renee Benjamin
Metropolitan Pier and
Exposition Authority
2301 South Prairie Avenue
Chicago, Illinois 60616
(312) 791-6265

Michele Odorizzi
Hugh R. McCombs
Gary S. Feinerman
Daniel G. Hildebrand
MAYER, BROWN & PLATT
190 South LaSalle Street
Chicago, Illinois 60603
(312) 782-0600

Dated: May 11, 1998

IN THE
UNITED STATES COURT OF APPEALS
FOR THE SEVENTH CIRCUIT

No. 98-1939
No. 98-1977

CHICAGO ACORN, SEIU LOCAL NO. 880, and TED THOMAS,	)))	
Plaintiffs-Appellees, Cross-Appellants,	))))	On appeal from the United States District Court for the Northern District of Illinois, Eastern Division
v.	))	
	)	No. 96 C 4997
METROPOLITAN PIER AND EXPOSITION AUTHORITY,	)))	
Defendant-Appellant, Cross-Appellee.	)))	The Honorable Blanche M. Manning District Court Judge

BRIEF OF PLAINTIFFS-APPELLEES AND CROSS-APPELLANTS

Paul Strauss
Miner, Barnhill & Galland
14 W. Erie St.
Chicago, IL 60610
(312) 751-1170

Date: May 22, 1998

TABLE OF CONTENTS

TABLE OF AUTHORITIES

JURISDICTIONAL STATEMENT

The jurisdictional statement of the Metropolitan Pier and Exposition Authority (the "MPEA" or "Pier Authority") is complete and correct. R109.[1]

ISSUES PRESENTED FOR REVIEW

1.   Did the district court properly enjoin application of policies used to prohibit political dissent on public grounds at Navy Pier?

2.   Did the district court err in holding that the MPEA may restrict all expressive activities in the Family Pavilion and South Arcade buildings on Navy Pier, in order to promote shopping?

3.   After it held the MPEA's speech restrictions unconstitutional, did the district court err in allowing the MPEA to continue to limit plaintiffs' speech on the South Dock of Navy Pier?

STATEMENT OF THE CASE

This is a First Amendment case. Since August, 1996 plaintiffs have sought injunctive relief to prohibit the MPEA from interfering with political speech by the plaintiffs on public grounds at Navy Pier.

In August, 1996, after an evidentiary hearing before Judge Manning, the district court granted in part and denied in part plaintiffs' motion for preliminary injunctive relief. Op1.

After the events that were the subject of the district court's order were concluded, the MPEA filed a notice of appeal from the district court's order. Plaintiffs cross-appealed to preserve their rights, but moved to dismiss for lack of jurisdiction. That motion was granted. R72.

A second evidentiary hearing was held before Magistrate Judge Keys in January, 1997. He issued a report and recommendation in February, 1997. R73. In April, 1998, the district court rejected the Magistrate Judge's recommended findings, granting a declaratory judgment and partial injunctive relief. Op2. Plaintiff's moved for additional relief from the district court and the MPEA moved for a stay pending appeal. R105-107. The district court denied the MPEA's motion for a stay and held in a minute order that it had enjoined continued used of the MPEA's policies. R102. Nonetheless, the district court held that when plaintiffs appeared at the South Dock on Navy Pier on April 16, 1998, the MPEA could require plaintiffs to remain confined to three stationary "protest zones." R102.

[1]   Citations to the clerk's record are to "R__." The district court's opinion of August 22, 1996, R20, is cited as "Op1, __." The district court's opinion of April 1, 1998, R97, is cited as "Op2, __." The transcript of the hearing before judge Manning in August, 1996 is cited as "Tr. 8/96, __." The transcript of the evidentiary hearing before Magistrate Judge Keys in January, 1997 is cited as "Tr. 1/97, __." Exhibits from the January, 1997 hearing are cited as "PX __ or "DX __." The appendix to this brief is cited as "A__."

The MPEA and plaintiffs filed notices of appeal on April 14 and 17, respectively. R103, 108. The MPEA moved for a stay pending appeal, which this Court denied on May 1, 1998.

STATEMENT OF FACTS

The MPEA's statement of facts is inadequate. It leaves out many of the undisputed facts relied on by the district court and refers to recommended findings of the magistrate judge, rather than factual findings of the district court itself. A counter-statement of facts is required as a consequence.

Note how the recitation of the facts attempts to bolster the client's case by stressing the public nature of the various areas of Navy Pier. It also pictures the Pier management as a group guilty of past political favoritism, and which is permitted overbroad discretion in granting access to Pier facilities.

Plaintiff's request for access to Navy Pier.

Plaintiffs are supporters of a proposed "Living Wage" Ordinance, opposed by Chicago's Mayor Richard M. Daley. Op1, 1; R5, Talbott dec. ¶¶1 and 3-9. In August, 1996, Mayor Daley was scheduled to attend two events at Navy Pier connected with the Democratic Party's national convention: a "media party" for delegates during the evening of Saturday, August 24, and a luncheon for mayors on Tuesday, August 27. Plaintiffs sought to appear at Navy Pier during those events, pass out information about the proposed ordinance and the Mayor's refusal to support it, carry signs, and demonstrate against the Mayor. Op1, 2-3; Talbott dec. and 8/07/96 letter, in R5.

When the MPEA failed to answer plaintiffs' request for permission to appear at the Pier, plaintiffs filed a complaint and motion for a restraining order on August 13. R1, R4, and Op1, 3-4; R5 and Talbott dec., ¶¶25-26 and 8/07/96 letter. On August 20, Judge Manning held an evidentiary hearing, taking testimony from six witnesses. Tr. 8/96.

At the time, the MPEA had written policies providing that:

Distribution of flyers, handbills of any free publications is prohibited without the written permission of Navy Pier Management. Upon approval, distribution of these materials will occur at the time, place and manner designated by management.

* * *

Public demonstrations are prohibited unless there is a permit granted by Navy Pier Management. Upon approval, the demonstration may occur only at the time, place, and manner authorized by management.

Op1, 3, 15; DX 7; R67, ¶¶54-55. While these policies suggested that demonstrations and distribution of literature could be permitted on the grounds of Navy Pier, MPEA management testified that its practice is to allow plaintiffs and other similar groups to assemble only in a small "protest zone" south of the entrance to Navy Pier's Dock Street, or across the street from Navy Pier, in an area known as Gateway Park. The MPEA's CEO testified that the MPEA would prohibit groups like the plaintiffs from handing out fliers or engaging in any demonstration of Navy Pier itself. It would keep plaintiffs off Navy Pier regardless of any security concerns. Tr. 8/96, 94-95, 105.

The MPEA's practice is to deny "permits" for groups like the plaintiffs to engage in political speech on the grounds of Navy Pier, while providing some groups a free "license" to conduct political fundraisers, ceremonies, and benefit concerts on Navy Pier. Op1, 10-11. For example, after the Democratic National Committee's "media party" was held at Navy Pier on August 24, plaintiffs learned that the MPEA provided all of Navy Pier's facilities to the Democrats for $1.00. The MPEA donated facilities and services worth approximately $245,200.00. It did not even ask the Democrats to pay rent for use of the Pier. Op1, 10-11; PX 20, 23; Tr. 1/97, 291-96. Other recipients of license fee waivers include charities associated with Maggie Daley, the Mayor's wife, and events such as "Mayor Daley's Summer Jobs Program" and the Mayor's Student Finance Graduation." Op2, 11; Tr. 1/97, 282.

None of this was revealed to plaintiffs or the court in August, 1996, when plaintiffs sought access to the Pier. When plaintiffs contacted Pier management in August, 1996, they were not told that the Pier Authority might waive the license fee to use Navy Pier, or would do so for certain groups. Talbott dec., ¶¶23, 26 in R5. During the proceedings before the court in August, MPEA CEO James Reilly represented that groups can engage in political speech at Navy Pier only within the confines of space that they lease and pay for. Tr. 8/96, 88-89, 98.

Judge Manning ruled on plaintiffs' motion for injunctive relief on August 22, 1996. Based on the evidence before the court at that time, Judge Manning concluded that Navy Pier was properly characterized as a designated public forum, Op1, 11; wrote that the MPEA's management exercised unwarranted discretion in controlling speech at the Pier, Op1, 16; and held that the Pier Authority's restrictions on plaintiffs' speech were not proper time, place, and manner restrictions, Op1, 17-21. The court ordered the MPEA to allow plaintiffs to assemble on August 24 and 27 in stationary groups on the sidewalk in front of Navy Pier and at vehicle drop-off points on the North Dock. The court provided, however, that the MPEA could restrict plaintiffs from appearing at locations on Navy Pier such as the South Dock and could limit plaintiffs' movement and activities on both August 24 and August 27, particularly because of heightened security concerns during the Democratic convention. Op1, 18-23; Op2, 2. Plaintiffs appeared peacefully at Navy Pier on the 24th and 27th, confined to small areas. Tr. 1/97, 14-22, 53-55.

In October, 1996, plaintiffs filed an amended complaint renewing their request for preliminary and permanent injunctive relief. R39. The case was referred to Magistrate Judge Keys. R40, R48.

Plaintiffs formally asked the MPEA for access to Navy Pier again. In October, 1996, plaintiffs requested permission to appear at Navy Pier on November 23, 1996 inside the Family Pavilion area and on Dock Street, to hand out fliers in support of the Living Wage Ordinance, solicit members of the public to fill out postcards to Chicago aldermen, and seek petition signatures. PX 1. The MPEA's counsel wrote in response that the MPEA had adopted a new policy, pursuant to which it claimed that "public assemblies, gatherings, demonstrations, parades, solicitation, handbilling, and other forms of public expression of views [on Navy Pier] are not permitted at any time. . .except pursuant to a valid lease or license agreement. . . ." PX 2, 3, p. 3; Op2, 8-9, n.2.

On October 29, 1996 plaintiffs filed a new motion for a preliminary injunction, asking the court to enjoin the MPEA from interfering with leafleting, soliciting the public, carrying signs and other activities by plaintiffs on the Dock Street area of Navy Pier, in the Family Pavilion, and in the other internal mall areas and sidewalks open to the general public on Navy Pier. R42. The parties stipulated to a discovery schedule followed by a single hearing before Judge Keys. R45. The MPEA stipulated that plaintiffs had exhausted all requirements that they apply for a permit to appear at Navy Pier, that the MPEA would not grant a permit to plaintiffs, that the case was ripe for adjudication, and that plaintiffs did not lack standing because they had not applied for a lease or license. R45.

Plaintiffs took additional steps to ensure that they exhausted any requirements that they apply for a license. On November 11, 1996, plaintiffs asked the MPEA for a license to engage in three sets of activities:

(1)   leafleting and soliciting funds in support of the Living Wage Ordinance on South Dock (two people) and in the Family Pavilion (three people) on November 23, 1996 from 10:00 a.m. to 1:00 p.m.;

(2)   marching on South Pier, carrying signs and placards in support of the Living Wage Ordinance, on Saturday, January 25, 199[7], between 1:30 and 3:30 p.m. (20 people); and

(3)   conducting a fundraising dinner on Saturday, May 17, 199[7] from 8:00 p.m. to 2:00 a.m. in the Grand Ballroom, Crystal Garden, or a Terrace Room overlooking the water.

PX 9. Plaintiffs asked that any license agreement be provided at a nominal charge (*e.g.,* $1.00). PX 9.

The MPEA responded in a letter of November 21, 1996. PX 10. The MPEA denied plaintiffs' first and second requests, claiming that they were inconsistent with the MPEA's license policies. PX 10. With respect to the plaintiffs' request for space for a fundraising dinner, defendant said it would "consider" giving a license for a fundraiser, "provided that your clients can satisfy all the conditions of Navy Pier's standard form of license. . . as well as applicable minimum requirements for food and beverage consumption." That is, the MPEA might give a license for a fundraising dinner if plaintiffs paid $3,000.00-$7,000.00 in license fees for the space, hired the Pier's caterer for the event, and bought a $2 million liability insurance policy. PX 10. And see PX 5, R67, ¶44, and DX 2, p. 5. Since this was not an agreement to provide space at a nominal charge, as plaintiffs requested, and since the MPEA had already stipulated that plaintiffs did not lack standing because they had not applied for a license, plaintiffs did not submit any further application for a license for a fundraising dinner.

Plaintiffs filed a proposed preliminary and permanent injunction in early December, 1996. R54. Plaintiffs asked for an injunction prohibiting the MPEA from interfering with plaintiffs' access to all areas at Navy Pier open to the public without charge for admission, including the exterior sidewalks and walkways on the Pier, the exterior Pier Park area, and the interior areas in the Family Pavilion, the South Arcade, and the Crystal Gardens. R54.

The magistrate judge conducted an evidentiary hearing in January, 1997, and issued a report and recommendation in February. R73. Judge Keys concluded that there are no traditional parks, streets, or sidewalks on Navy Pier and accepted the MPEA's argument that it should be able to restrict speech at the Pier because it did not intend space at Navy Pier to be used for protest. R73, 24, 37. At the same time, the magistrate judge concluded that the MPEA's restrictions on leafleting are unreasonable, even if the Pier is characterized as a nonpublic forum, and concluded that the Pier Authority's permit and license procedures give unwarranted discretion to Pier managers. R73, 45-46. He recommended entry of an injunction requiring the MPEA to adopt new policies governing permit and license applications and allow leafleting within unspecified areas of Navy Pier. R73, 49-50.

On April 1, 1998, Judge Manning issued a memorandum opinion and order rejecting the magistrate judge's conclusions. Based on the testimony she heard in August, 1996 and the evidentiary record compiled before Judge Keys, Judge Manning found that Navy Pier "is intended to serve multiple purposes and functions"; the MPEA is required by law "to use Navy Pier for public parks, gardens, and gathering places"; and "commercial uses are required to be ancillary to the established public use." Op2, 7. The district court found that the MPEA maintains areas such as the South Dock as park space and public promenades. Op2, 7, 17-18. Judge Manning wrote that she approached the MPEA's representations about the facts "with a healthy dose of skepticism," based on her conclusion, from the testimony she heard, "that the MPEA's past representations to this court have been less than accurate." Op2, 12.

Here, the opinion of the court below is invoked to cast doubt on the veracity of the Pier management. Note also the next paragraph works the client's argument into the statement of facts by declaring the lower court properly categorized the Pier as a traditional public forum.

The district court held that the North Dock, South Dock, east end plaza, and Pier Park areas of Navy Pier are properly categorized as traditional public fora. Op2, 17-21. The district court held that internal spaces at the Pier used and licensed for entertainment, cultural, and political events, including the Grand Ballroom, Skyline Stage, Festival Hall, and Crystal Gardens, are designated public fora. Op2, 21-22. The court held that the internal space in the Family Pavilion and South Arcade are nonpublic fora. Op2, 22-25. The court held that the MPEA licensing and permit systems are defective with respect to the traditional and designated public fora on the Pier, but held that the MPEA may properly restrict all expressive activity, including leafleting, in the Family Pavilion and South Arcade. The district court entered a declaratory judgment for plaintiffs and enjoined the MPEA to revise its policies regarding speech at Navy Pier. Op2, 29-31.

On April 7, 1998 plaintiffs informed the MPEA that plaintiffs intended to bring 20-50 people to Navy Pier on April 16, 1998 to conduct a procession on the South Dock, handing out leaflets and carrying signs to solicit support for an increase in the national minimum wage. R106 and letter of 4/07/98 attached thereto. Treating plaintiffs' letter as a request for a permit, Navy Pier's general manager wrote that the request was denied. R106 and letter of 4/09/98 attached thereto.

Again, plaintiffs sought injunctive relief from the district court. R106, R107. Simultaneously, the MPEA moved for a stay of the district court's order pending appeal. R105. The district court denied the MPEA's motion for a stay and entered a minute order holding that the court had enjoined the continued use of the MPEA's policies. R102. But the court held that on April 16, the MPEA could confine plaintiffs to three stationary "protest zones," on the South Dock, with no more than 15 people in any one area. R102.

Plaintiffs appeared at Navy Pier on April 16, briefly and peacefully. To attract people at the Pier to come and engage them in the small areas to which they were confined, plaintiffs brought a mime to perform on the South Dock and sought to hand out balloons. R118.

The MPEA is required by law to operate Navy Pier as a public space *in which commercial interests are subordinated to the public's right of access.*

The MPEA has a legal duty to use Navy Pier for public parks, gardens, and gathering places, walkways, bicycle paths, and ramps. Op2, 7; PX 7, NP616.

By statute, 70 ILCS 210/5, the MPEA is required to comply with the provisions of the Chicago Zoning Ordinance and the Lake Michigan and Chicago Lakefront Protection Ordinance. To comply with those ordinances, the MPEA's redevelopment of Navy Pier required an amendment to the Chicago Zoning Ordinance, proposed by the MPEA itself and passed by the Chicago City Council in 1992. See PX 6 and 7; Tr. 1/97, 324-25; R65, ¶1; R67, ¶1.

The zoning ordinance describes the official government policy with respect to Navy Pier. It says:

> All of the Property shall remain public places for the use and enjoyment of the public. Any limitations on the public use and any private uses shall be subordinate and ancillary as well as complementary to the predominantly public character of the Property.

PX 7, NP 616. The "Navy Pier Recommendations, Policies and Standards," contained din the zoning ordinance, says that the redevelopment plan would "[c]onvert the one-half mile long south dock of Navy Pier to a major public lakefront promenade and open space." PX 7, NP681.

Many sections of the zoning ordinance emphasize that space at the Pier must be held open for free public access and assembly. Thus, for instance, the zoning ordinance provides that the South Dock area of Navy Pier is intended to be a "pedestrian-oriented public way." PX 7, NP672. The ordinance says that the Crystal Gardens and "On-Pier Park" sections of Navy Pier:

> shall be designed, constructed and maintained as public spaces to provide areas for passive activities and public gathering and, except as provided herein, at no charge or cost to public users. . . .

Id., at 619-20. The zoning ordinance provides that "[p]ublic pedestrian and bicycle passage during operating hours over all exterior areas depicted on the Exhibits as pedestrian walks, paths or ways, including the south dock and the north dock, shall not be unreasonably restricted." PX 7, NP618-19. It provides that any Kiosks placed on the South Dock "shall not unreasonably interfere with public pedestrian passage or with public access to the water or the lake front vista." PX 7, NP619.

In May, 1992, when the MPEA presented plans for redevelopment of Navy Pier to the Chicago Plan Commission, it emphasized that Navy Pier would not become a shopping mall. The MPEA chairman testified: "We said we wanted some retail activity, not to make the Pier into a commercial mall." PX 132, 12. When plans for redevelopment of Navy Pier were reviewed in June, 1992, a representative of the Chicago Planning Commission emphasized that the plans called for maintaining Navy Pier as an area open to the public, with "an outdoor park," "public spaces," and a "continuous pedestrian and bicycle promenade." PX 130, 14-20. Under the redevelopment plans, "[p]articular emphasis is placed upon the open and accessible nature of all pedestrian areas." *Id.,* at 27-28.

Description of the public sidewalks, plazas, and buildings on Navy Pier.

Navy Pier contains outdoor plazas, sidewalks, and park areas and a variety of buildings and rooms used for exhibitions, concerts, public assemblies, displays, and stores. Op2, 5-8, 17-18, 21-22. The Pier is over half a mile long and is designed to accommodate up to 50,000 people. Op2, 5; Tr. 1/97, 67. There is no charge for admission to the public grounds and buildings on the Pier, such as the South Dock, the Family Pavilion, and the Crystal Gardens. Tr. 1/97, 61-62; PX 7, NP619-20.

Photographs of the Pier are included in a book published by the MPEA: Navy Pier: A Chicago Landmark, by Douglas Bukowski, PX 11. The front and back covers of the Bukowski book provide a useful view of the Pier as a whole. A diagram of the Pier and its major components is included at p. 86 of the Bukowski book and in the MPEA's appendix, p. 84.

Photographs of individual parts of the Pier are attached to this brief as an appendix, A1-A15. These photographs were taken on a weekday in January, 1997, between

10:00 a.m. and noon. Tr. 1/97, 302. They show uncrowded areas—what the Pier typically looks like on a weekday morning in winter. Tri 1/97, 242-43, 246-47, 249-50. Photographs of the Pier at warmer times are included in the Bukowski book, PX 11, particularly at pp. 76-78, and in DX 12 A-I. Tr. 1/97, 237/38, 249/50.

The **South Dock** of Navy Pier (or "Dock Street") contains park benches, trees, and bike racks and is open to the public for walking, jogging, bicycling, and enjoying the view of Lake Michigan. Op2, 7, 17; Tr. 8/96, 135. Photographs of the Sough Dock are included in A4 and the Bukowski book, PX 11, at 78. Tr. 1/97, 241-42, 252. The South Dock and other sidewalks and walkways on the Pier are directly connected to surrounding municipal sidewalks. See A1-3 and DX 12C. Tr. 1/97, 252-53. In May, 1992, when the MPEA presented its plan for redevelopment of Navy Pier to the Chicago Plan commission, the MPEA's CEO said:

> [A]ll the way around, the whole south promenade, the great plaza area out at the end, all of this will be available for all kinds of public activities ranging from walking and biking to sitting and having a hot dog or a glass of wine or whatever your choice may be in the summertime.

PX 132, 27-28

The **North Dock** of Navy Pier includes a sidewalk that runs along the lake, with park benches and planters. Op2, 5; R67, ¶12. In this litigation the MPEA has resisted calling this sidewalk more than a "pedestrian walkway." But the Pier's manager testified at trial, "In everyday language I'd call it a sidewalk." Tr. 1/97, 240.

There is a large outdoor **plaza at the east end of Navy Pier**, shown on the cover of the Bukowski book, PX 11, and in DX 12A. This plaza connects with the South Dock and sidewalk on the North Dock to form a continuous promenade along the lake.

Pier Park is an outdoor park near the Ferris wheel at the center of Navy Pier. As shown in A5 and A6 and in the Bukowski book, PX 11, at p. 77, Pier Park contains grass, trees, park benches, and sidewalks. Tr. 1/97, 236, 240; and Op2, 17-18. It has been referred to repeatedly by the MPEA as a park, both in MPEA documents and in the zoning ordinance controlling the redevelopment of Navy Pier. PX 7, NP619-620, NP637; Tr. 8/96, 69; PX 126, NP1205; PX 55, NP1102. When the MPEA presented its plan for Navy Pier in May, 1992, the chairman and the CEO described this area as a "park" and "central park-like area." PX 132, 14, 17, 20, 24, 25. In the June, 1992 hearing before the Chicago Planning Commission, in which the plan for redevelopment of Navy Pier was described, Chicago's deputy planning commissioner said that this area "will be an outdoor park, which is intended to accommodate a variety of uses, including ice-skating area and outdoor performance area, a cafe and passive recreational uses." PX 130, 17.

The interior of **Crystal Gardens** is shown in the photographs marked as A11 and in the Bukowski book, PX 11, at 76. Tr. 1/97, 249-50. The Crystal Gardens is a large, light, glass building filled with warm-weather trees, plants, and wrought-iron tables and chairs. It is designed to be a winter garden or indoor park, available to the public when the weather outside is cold. The area is sometimes referred to by the MPEA as the "Crystal Gardens Indoor Botanical Park." PX 55, NP1102. In presenting the plan for redevelopment of the Pier, the MPEA's CEO said, "We really want it to have the feel of an indoor park." PX 132, 23. "It will be a space where we will have music events, just a space for passive activities like walking." *Id.,* at 24. Mr. Reilly pointed out that the Crystal Gardens and Pier Park would be interconnected on the second level. "So you literally walk at grade between the winter garden and the park on the Pier, the outdoor park on the Pier." *Id.*

The **Grand Ballroom, Skyline Stage, Festival Hall, and Terrace Rooms** on Navy Pier are used for political and charitable fundraisers, graduation ceremonies, concerts, cultural events, banquets, conventions, tradeshows, and meetings. *See, e.g.,* R65 ¶¶15-17, 19-30, 33, 35; R67 ¶¶22, 51; PX 126; PX 127. Pictures of these areas are included in PX 11, at 79, 80, 82.

The **Family Pavilion** is contained in the building at the west end of Navy Pier— at the "front" of the Pier, shown in A1-2, and in the PX 11 at 66. The Family Pavilion includes common areas, the Chicago Children's Museum, an IMAX theater, and retail stores and restaurants. Tr. 244-474; R67, ¶14. The interior of the Family Pavilion is shown in the photographs marked as A9-10, 14-15; Tr. 1/97, 244-47; and in PX 11, 77. As shown in these photographs, there are times when the common space in the Family Pavilion is virtually empty.

The **South Arcade** is an indoor sidewalk, lined with small shops and pushcarts, connecting the Family Pavilion to other buildings on the eastern end of the Pier. R67, ¶13; Op2, 5. A12 shows the South Arcade on a typical morning in the winter. Tr. 242-43. There is almost no one there.

The "**protest zone**" to which the MPEA seeks to confine plaintiffs cannot be seen in any of these areas, or in any of the photographs described above. It is a small area outside the Pier itself, **behind** an information booth, south of the entrance to the South Dock. Tr. 1/97, 262-70, 14-22, 53-55.

<u>The MPEA regulates speech at Navy Pier pursuant to a discretion-rich licensing system, in which preference is given to speech by City and State officials.</u>

The MPEA maintains a written "License Fee Waiver Policy," PX 4, which provides that the MPEA will consider waiving the license fee for use of space at Navy Pier in connection with events of "special importance" to the City and State. This policy provides that these events must meet the following criteria:

A.   Strongly related to the history of the City of Chicago or the State of Illinois;

B.   Reflects a major initiative of the City of Chicago or the State of Illinois;

C.   Has not-for-profit status;

D.   Is held for a charitable cause or admits all guests free of charge.

Op2, 10, n. 4; R67, ¶49.

Pier managers interpret this policy in unexpected ways. Pier Manager Jon Clay testified that license fee waivers properly are given for graduations of the Chicago Police Department academy because those events are "strongly related to the history of the City of Chicago and the State of Illinois." Tr. 1/97, 283. He testified that a party for Democratic National Convention volunteers, after the convention, "reflect[ed] a major initiative of the City of Chicago and the State of Illinois." Tr. 1/97, 284-85.

Under the MPEA's licensing system, the MPEA's managers have virtually unbounded discretion to determine the speech that will be allowed at the Pier. Tr. 1/97, 260-61. MPEA management makes personal judgments about whether a speaker will be good for business at the Pier, Tr. 1/97, 308; which events will be "fun and enjoyable," Tr. 1/97, 171, 201; whether a speaker is "a citizen in good standing," Tr. 1/97, 259; and whether an event is of "special importance" to the City and State, Tr. 1/97, 282-85. The Pier Authority can charge whatever it wants for use of space at the Pier and does not have to charge anything. Tr. 1/97, 274. Everything is negotiable. Tr. 1/97, 289-90, 291. Plaintiffs' exh. 4—the Pier Authority's only written policy governing the waiver of license fees, Tr. 1/97, 276—is not publicized in any way; the policy does not describe all the reasons why the Pier Authority may waive license fees; the Authority does not have to follow the policy; and, in fact, the Authority often does not follow it. Tr. 276-78, 283, 284-86, 288, 293-94, 296.

The discretion given to MPEA's managers to pick and choose between speakers was demonstrated in the testimony of the Pier's general manager. Mr. Clay testified that under the MPEA's policy, space might be provided to the Mayor, without charge, to hold a press conference describing the Mayor's accomplishments in office. "[I] could imagine that it could fit" under the policy, he testified. Tr. 1/97, 420. In contrast, Mr. Clay thought it was unlikely that the Pier Authority would provide space without charge to aldermen who want to hold a press conference, describing why they support the proposed Living Wage Ordinance. He testified, "Again, we'd have to know all the details, but just on the face of what you're describing, I'd have a hard time imagining it fit." Tr. 1/97, 420-21. See Op2, 27-28.

Pursuant to the MPEA's licensing policies, a series of groups related to the Mayor and the Governor have been given space at the Pier for free. See Op2, at 10-11. For example: (1) Gallery 37, a summer jobs program administered by the Chicago Department of Cultural Affairs, was allowed to use the Grand Ballroom at Navy Pier in 1994 for a benefit concert, without charge. Mayor Daley's wife chaired the program and the Mayor spoke at the event. R65, ¶9; R65, ¶37; Gutierrez dec., no. 17. (2) In 1995 and 1996, the Magic City Festival, a children's arts festival, was given space on the Skyline Stage to host fundraising performances. The Mayor's wife served on the steering committee of the Festival. The Festival netted $29,728.46 in 1995 and $14,843.72 in 1996, because it was not charged for use of Pier space. R65, ¶¶10-13; PX 64-71. (3) In August,

1996 the MPEA allowed the City to use the Skyline Stage for a program referred to as the Mayor's Student Finance Graduation. Members of the Mayor's staff were scheduled to speak at the ceremony. The MPEA did not charge for rent or expenses incurred in connection with the program. R67; PX 62. (4) In October, 1992 the Chicago Convention and Tourism Bureau held a fundraising dinner in the Grand Ballroom. The MPEA allowed the space to be used without charge for rent, labor, or its other expenses. Mayor Daley and Governor Edgar were named as honorary chairmen. Mayor Daley attended the event and addressed the crowd. R5, ¶¶16, 37 and Gutierrez dec. no. 18, attached thereto; PX 90-102. (5) The Chicago Police and Fire Departments have been allowed to use the Grand Ballroom repeatedly for graduation ceremonies. Mayor Daley has often attended and spoken at those ceremonies. Tr. 1/97, 282; R67, ¶50; R65, ¶37; and Gutierrez dec. nos. 3, 4, and 13.

<u>Navy Pier has been used for an enormous variety of assemblies, ceremonies, festivals, and political fundraisers.</u>

In the written policies the MPEA applied before this litigation began, it noted that "[t]he Pier's East End. . .was originally a public recreation and entertainment complex." DX 7 at 1. According to MPEA chief executive officer James Reilly, "There have been political fundraisers in the ball room for 50 years." Tr. 8/96, 97.

Since its redevelopment, the public spaces at Navy Pier have been used for a wide variety of assemblies and displays. For example, a Memorial Day ceremony was held in May, 1996 on the plaza at the east end of the Pier. A representative of the Mayor's office spoke at the ceremony and it was held in conjunction with a march in Gateway Park, organized by the Mayor's office and a veterans' group. R67, ¶¶33 and 53; PX 45-48. The MPEA has sponsored public forums on Black History month (hosted by former Chicago alderman Cliff Kelly) in the Crystal Gardens and exhibits on the redevelopment of Chicago neighborhoods. R67, ¶25, and PX 116-17, 124; R67, ¶22 and PX 126, NP1206. It has sponsored public concerts and fireworks. R67, ¶22. In a Veterans Day ceremony in 1995 the MPEA dedicated an anchor at the east end of the Pier as a reminder of those who served in World War II. R49, ¶33; PX 11, 74. The MPEA promoted a celebration of Chicago's ethnic neighborhoods at the Pier, R67, ¶22; PX 121; it displayed a sculpture in the shape of a peace dove inside the Family Pavilion, PX 53, NP1161; R67 ¶30; and it sponsored a parade for children on the Pier led by "Ronald McDonald." R67, ¶29; PX 53, NP1161-62.

A diverse array of groups has paid to use space at the Pier for political meetings and charitable balls. Space in the Grand Ballroom, Crystal Gardens, and Terrace Rooms have been used for fundraisers for Mayor Daley, Aurelis Pucinski, Governor Edgar, and President Clinton. R65, ¶¶15, 23, 26, 31; PX 72. Naturalization ceremonies were held at the Grand Ballroom in 1994 and 1996, sponsored by the United Neighborhood Organization and the Chicago Department of Immigrant Affairs, respectively. R65, ¶¶21, 27. A public ceremony marking the launch of the Americorps program was held on the Skyline Stage in 1994, with appearances by the Mayor and Secretary of Transportation.

R65, ¶19. The Terrace Rooms and Grand Ballroom have been used by groups like the National Bar Association, PX 106, and for events like an "American Indian Pow Wow." PX 125, NP1158; R65, ¶25.

Other speakers and groups have been allowed to solicit funds, hang signs, hand out promotional materials, and stage festivals on the Pier without being charged for space. A group called CAUSES (Child Abuse Unit for Studies, Education, and Service) was allowed to set up a table in the South Arcade and solicit contributions in September, 1995. R67, ¶52; PX 44. In August, 1996, the makers of the Dove Bar ice cream bar were allowed to use Dock Street to solicit money for charity. R65, ¶8. In June, 1996 a radio station was allowed to broadcast from Pier Park, hang signs and banners, hand out promotional materials, and solicit money for charity, without being charged for use of Pier space. R65, ¶14; PX 48-52. The MPEA allowed the Navy to dock a guided missile frigate at the Pier and offer free public tours in 1996. R49, ¶33; PX 120, 127. An Austrian Heritage Group was allowed to stage a festival on Dock Street, without charge, at which the Austrian General Consul addressed the crowd. R65, ¶18.

While the MPEA will license many groups to speak at the Pier and it may give space without charge to groups associated with the City and State, the MPEA will not allow speech on the Pier by "activists" like the plaintiffs. R84, 23. The MPEA'a explanation is that it intends to prohibit speech that "is likely to cause controversy and ill will." R84, 28.

STANDARD OF REVIEW

The Court of Appeals "may reverse a decision to grant a permanent injunction only if we are convinced that the district court abused its discretion in deciding that the circumstances of the case justified injunctive relief." *Winkler v. Eli Lilly & Co.,* 101 F.3d 1196, 1203 (7th Cir. 1996). "[A] district court would abuse its discretion if it applied an incorrect legal standard or based its injunction on a clearly erroneous finding of fact." *Id.,* 101 F.3d at 1204.

The MPEA argues that Judge Manning adopted all the proposed factual findings of the magistrate judge and made no findings of fact of her own. Relying on this assertion, the MPEA suggests that the Court should review the district court's decision *de novo,* relying on the factual conclusions of the magistrate judge and taking those findings as undisputed. MPEA brief, 27-28.

This argument is incorrect. The district court did not adopt the proposed findings of the magistrate judge. From small points to large ones, Judge Manning made findings of her own, substantially different from those of the magistrate judge. For instance, the magistrate judge ignored the zoning ordinance that describes the intended use of Navy Pier, accepting the MPEA's claims that Navy Pier is intended to be only a center for commerce and entertainment. R73. Judge Manning, in contrast, made findings about the zoning ordinance and relied on them, concluding as a matter of fact that Navy Pier "is intended to server multiple purposes and functions." Op2, 7. Judge Keys found that there was no public easement for access to the South Dock. R73, 23. Judge Manning, in contrast, noted that the zoning ordinance requires the MPEA to maintain the South Dock for public access. Op2, 20. Magistrate Judge Keys concluded that "[t]the North Dock is no more than a driveway." R73,24. This proposed finding was contrary to the parties' stipulation, R67, ¶12, and was not adopted by Judge Manning. Op2, 5. Unlike the magistrate judge, Judge Manning was skeptical about the MPEA's credibility and representations, based on her experience in the hearing held before her in August, 1996. Op2, 12. Judge Manning was respectful to the magistrate judge, but reached her own conclusions about the facts.

A district court is required to review recommended findings of a magistrate judge *de novo* and has "broad discretion to accept, reject, or modify the magistrate's proposed findings." 28 U.S.C. §636(b)(1); Fed.R.Civ.P. 72(b). The Court of Appeals reviews the actual findings of the district court, not the recommended findings of the magistrate judge. *LaPreferida v. Cerveceria Modeal, S.A. de C.V.,* 914 F.2d 900, 905, n. 6 (7th Cir. 1990). The MPEA has not argued that any of the district court's findings are clearly erroneous.

SUMMARY OF ARGUMENT

The district court correctly concluded that the sidewalks, the plaza at the east end of the Pier, and Pier Park are traditional public fora. These areas are intended to be used for general, unrestricted public access, not for any special, limited purpose.

The district court correctly described the Grand Ballroom, Skyline Stage, Festival Hall, and Crystal Gardens areas of the Pier as designated public fora. These areas are used for political fundraisers, public ceremonies, charitable balls, concerts, displays, and other forms of public expression. They have been dedicated by the government to be used for public assembly and expression and are similar to the municipal auditorium at issue in *Southeastern Promotions, Ltd. v. Conrad,* 420 U.S. 546 (1975).

The district court properly enjoined continued application of the MPEA's policies restricting speech at the Pier. The MPEA does not dispute that its restrictions on speech are impermissible in a public forum. The MPEA restricts speech based on viewpoint, a practice that is unconstitutional in any forum.

The district court erred, however, in holding that the MPEA's desire to promote shopping justifies suppression of all unlicensed expressive activity in common areas of the Family Pavilion and South Arcade. To our knowledge, no federal court previously has held that the government may establish a shopping mall and then prohibit criticism of the government on the grounds of the mall. In reaching its decision, the district court misread Supreme Court precedent on speech in airport terminals and erred in holding that speech by the plaintiffs may be prohibited because of "plaintiffs' proposed political and social message." Op2, 24. Even in nonpublic fora, restrictions on speech are valid only if they are "reasonable" and not based on the speaker's point of view.

Finally, the district court erred in allowing the MPEA to confine plaintiffs to stationary "protest zones" on the South Dock on Navy Pier, after holding that the MPEA's speech restrictions are unconstitutional. There was no significant government interest that required confinement of plaintiffs to fixed locations on the South Dock on April 16, 1998.

ARGUMENT

I. **The district court properly enjoined the MPEA from <u>continuing to apply its speech restrictions at Navy Pier.</u>**

Note how the argument begins with what is the client's key argument—that the public areas of the Pier are "traditional public fora."

A. <u>The district court correctly described the outdoor sidewalks, plazas, and parkland on Navy Pier as traditional public fora.</u>

The district court properly characterized the outdoor sidewalks, plazas, and park areas on Navy Piers as traditional public fora. Op2, 17-21. *United States v. Grace,* 461 U.S. 171, 178 (1983); *Air Line Pilots Ass'n Int'l v. Dept. of Aviation of Chicago,* 45 F.3d 1144, 1151 (7th Cir. 1995).

The sidewalks, plazas, and park on Navy Pier are properly described as traditional public fora because they are maintained for general, unrestricted use by the public, not for any special, limited government purpose. By the terms of the zoning ordinance amendment that the MPEA itself proposed, the MPEA is required to hold these spaces at the Pier open to the public as "areas for passive activities and public gathering," "an outdoor park," and a "public way" open for "public pedestrian and bicycle passage." These public spaces at Navy Pier were not built to serve a single, commercial purpose.

The public sidewalks, plazas, and park space on the Pier do not lose their public forum status because they are close to commercial businesses that operate on the Pier. "The mere fact that a sidewalk abuts a property dedicated to purposes other than free speech is not enough to strip it of its public forum status." *Henderson v. Lujan,* 964 F.2d 1179, 1182 (D.C. Cir. 1992) (National Park Service could not prohibit leafleting on sidewalks near the Vietnam Veterans Memorial to promote tranquil mood at Memorial wall). Thus, the Supreme Court held in *Grace,* 461 U.S. at 181, that the government's interest in preserving tranquility near the Supreme Court did not convert sidewalks around the Court into a nonpublic forum. *See also Gerritsen v. City of Los Angeles,* 994 F.2d 570 (9th Cir.), *cert. denied,* 510 U.S. 915 (1993) (city could not ban leafleting from area of park commemorating Mexican-American heritage, that housed commercial stores and Mexican consulate, despite city's claim that it had an interest in preserving calm, secure environment for the consulate and its visitors).

The right to speak in traditional public fora may not be denied by pointing to other areas that might be used for speech.

> Freedom of expression would not truly exist if the right could be exercised only in an area that a benevolent government has provided as a safe haven for crackpots. . . . [W]e do not confine the permissible exercise of First Amendment rights to a telephone booth or the four corners of a pamphlet, or to supervised and ordained discussion in a classroom.

Tinker v. Des Moines Independent Community School Dist., 393 U.S. 503, 513 (1969). *See also National People's Action v. Village of Wilmette,* 914 F.2d 1008, 1013 (7th Cir. 1990), *cert. denied,* 499 U.S. 921 (1991) (Village of Wilmette could not defend restrictions on solicitation by arguing that plaintiffs could solicit in other villages); *Collin v. Chicago Park Dist.,* 460 F.2d 746 (7th Cir. 1972) (park district could not justify denial of permit for public meeting by arguing that free speech areas were available in other parks without a permit).

The MPEA makes four arguments to support its claim that the district court erred in describing the sidewalks, plazas, and park on Navy Pier as traditional public fora. Each is incorrect.

An example of distinguishing adverse authority on the facts.

First, the MPEA relies on cases holding that sidewalks on government property dedicated to a limited purpose need not be treated as public fora. The Supreme Court has held, for instance, that the sidewalks used for access to a post office and on a military base are not traditional public fora. *United States v. Kokinda,* 497 U.S. 720, 728 (1990); *Greer v. Spock,* 424 U.S. 828 (1976). The sidewalk at issue in *Kokinda* was not a public forum because it "was constructed solely to provide for the passage of individuals engaged in postal business." *Id.* The sidewalks in *Greer v. Spock* were not a public forum because they were located on an enclosed military base—an area built for limited and special purposes, if there ever was one.

The MPEA argues that the sidewalks, outdoor plazas, and Pier Park on Navy Pier are like the sidewalks in *Kokinda* and *Greer* because, it claims, Navy Pier was built for a single, limited purpose, like the post office in *Kokinda* and the military base in *Greer.* According to the MPEA, "the purpose of the Pier is clearly to provide entertainment and convention related services." MPEA brief, 33. It characterizes Navy Pier as a "commercial entertainment complex," *id.,* at 35, and claims that the sidewalks, plazas, and park space on the Pier are designed solely to provide access to the commercial businesses on the Pier. *Id.,* at 36.

These arguments are flatly contradicted by the findings of the district court, however. The district court found that Navy Pier is not intended to be used only, or even primarily, as a "commercial entertainment complex." The district court found:

> In its most recent incarnation, Navy Pier is intended to serve multiple purposes and functions. An Intergovernmental Cooperation Agreement (cooperation agreement) executed with the city and state imposes a legal duty upon the MPEA to use Navy Pier for public parks, gardens and gathering

places; walkways, bicycle paths and ramps. Navy Pier's commercial uses are required to be ancillary to the established public use. In accordance with its legal obligations, the MPEA maintains the South Dock in a manner similar to a public promenade or plaza. There is a main pedestrian walkway called "Dock Street," along which patrons are provided park benches, trees, bike racks, and open spaces to walk, congregate, or simply enjoy the view of Lake Michigan.

Op1, 7. The MPEA does not and cannot argue that these findings are clearly erroneous. It pretends they do not exist. Its argument is based on unwarranted representations about the facts, contradicted by the district court's findings.

Next, the MPEA argues that the history of the Pier supports the MPEA's claim that Navy Pier is intended to be used only for limited commercial purposes, not held open for general use by the public. Again, in making this argument, the MPEA ignores the findings of the district court: "the Pier's overall history reveals an intent for the Pier to remain open to the public." Op2, 6.

But it is not necessary in any event to rely on the history of the Pier to find that the Pier's public spaces are traditional public fora. Sidewalks, streets, and parks are not traditional public fora because a particular sidewalk, or a particular street, has a long history of being used as a forum for public expression. Rather, this type of property is described as a traditional public forum because historically (that is, "traditionally") this *category* of property has been held open for public assembly and expression. *Hague v. Committee for Indus. Org.,* 307 U.S. 496, 515 (1939). Supreme Court decisions (and other court decisions) analyzing whether sidewalks or parks are traditional public fora do not describe the historical use of the particular sidewalk or park at issue. For instance, the Supreme Court in *United States v. Grace* held that the sidewalks around the Supreme Court were traditional public fora even though the property "has not been traditionally held open for the use of the public for expressive activities." 461 U.S. at 179.

Third, the MPEA argues that the sidewalks, plazas, and park on the Pier are not traditional public fora because they "are not part of the City's general transportation grid." MPEA brief, 36. That argument makes no sense, however. Parks are public fora and they are not part of the "transportation system." Traditional public fora are areas that open for general public assembly and recreation—"'a place where people [can] enjoy the open air or the company of friends in a relaxed environment.'" *Kokinda,* 497 U.S. at 728 (1990) (quoting form *Heffron v. Int'l Society for Krishna Consciousness, Inc.,* 452 U.S. 640, 651 (1981)). The open, outdoor areas on Navy Pier are traditional public fora because they were built and are maintained for public recreation and relaxation, giving members of the public free access to a space where they can meet and congregate. It is not necessary to show that Navy Pier is part of the "transportation system" to establish that its open, public areas are traditional public fora.

Finally, the MPEA argues that the sidewalks, public plazas, and park on Navy Pier are not traditional public fora because the MPEA does not intend that they be used for the public exchange of ideas. MPEA brief, 36-37. The government's desire to restrict speech on sidewalks and in parks does not convert them into nonpublic fora, however. Areas open to the public for general use and assembly may be used for the exchange of ideas. Whether or not the government wants that to happen. In *Grace,* for instance, the government clearly did not intend for the sidewalks around the Supreme Court to be used for public expression—long-standing government statutes prohibited demonstrations on those sidewalks. The Supreme Court held that the sidewalks were public fora, nonetheless. 461 U.S. at 179-81. The Court wrote that the government: "'may not by its own *ipse dixit* destroy the 'public forum' status of streets and parks which have historically been public forums.'" Id., 461 U.S. at 181 (citation omitted). *See also Henderson v. Lujan, supra,* 964 F.2d 1179, 1183 (D.C. Cir. 1992). The government may not treat public sidewalks and parks as nonpublic fora simply because it wants to regulate speech.

B.   The district court properly described space at the Pier used for entertainment, cultural, and political events as designated public fora.

The district court properly categorized the Grand Ballroom, Skyline State, Festival Hall, and Crystal Gardens as designated public fora. As described by this Court, designated public fora

are areas that the government has dedicated to use by the public as places for expressive activity. . . . They may be opened generally for all expressive activity. . . . Or they may be designated for more limited purposes such as use by certain groups . . . or discussion of certain subjects. . . .

Air Line Pilots, 45 F.3d at 1151 (7th Cir. 1995) (citations omitted).

Determining whether space has been set aside by for expressive activity, and therefore is a designated public forum, is resolved by examining two sets of facts: (1) how the property been used, in fact; and (2) the nature of the property and its compatibility with expressive activity. *Id.,* 45 F.3d at 1152. Past practice and policy are determinative—not a policy that defendant's managers assert during the litigation. *Id.*

Applying these standards, it is clear that the district court properly described these areas as designated public fora. The Grand Ballroom, Skyline Stage, Festival Hall, and Crystal Gardens have been used for political fundraisers, public ceremonies, charitable balls, concerts, displays, and other forms of public expression. Op2, 21. The areas found by the district court to be designated public fora are used in a fashion almost identical to the municipal auditorium in *Southeastern Promotions, Ltd. V. Conrad,* 420 U.S. 546 (1975)—an area that was a designated public forum. *Id.,* 420 U.S. at 555, 95 S.Ct. at 1245; *Air Line Pilots, supra,* 45 F.3d at 1151 (7th Cir. 1995). *See also Widmar v. Vincent,* 454 U.S. 263 (1981) (university facilities available for use by student groups were a designated public forum).

Note that this argument was rejected by the court.

These spaces are compatible with expressive activity. Stages, festival halls, and areas like the Grand Ballroom are *designed* for expressive activity. These are not properties intended to support some other function, like sidewalks next to a highway rest stop.

The sidewalks, park space, and plazas at Navy Pier also would be properly characterized as designated public fora, if not described as traditional public fora. These areas must be held open for free public access and have been used for a wide variety of ceremonies and festivals. Public expression is compatible with the intended use of these areas. As the MPEA notes itself, the open spaces on the Pier are not intended to serve a major transportation function. These are plazas and sidewalks along the lake, not airport terminals, intended primarily to promote air travel, or sidewalks on a military base, intended to promote movement of the military. *Compare Heffron,* 452 U.S. 640 (1981) (state fair was a public forum); *Paulsen v. County of Nassau,* 925 F.2d 65 (2nd Cir. 1991) (grounds of county coliseum used for "boisterous recreational activity," including parades, political rallies, speeches, religious weddings, and circuses, was a designated public forum).

Accordingly, the Grand Ballroom, Skyline Stage, Festival Hall, and Crystal Gardens, as well as the public sidewalks, plazas, and park on Navy Pier, are properly characterized as designated public fora because (1) they have been used, in fact, for public assembly and expression; and (2) the property, by its nature, is compatible with expressive activity.

C.   Areas on Navy Pier made available for public expression, including political speech, are designated public fora, despite the MPEA's desire to exclude "activist" groups with a "protest" message.

The MPEA resists admitting that any portion of the Pier is a designated public forum. It has to take this position. As we show in Part D, if space at the Pier is properly described as a designated public forum, the MPEA loses.

The MPEA tacitly concedes that it has allowed space at the Pier to be used for public expression, but argues that it is entitled to prohibit "disruptive" speech at the Pier, nonetheless. The MPEA writes, "[T]he district court failed to recognize. . .that even where a designated public forum has been established, the government has the right to limit access to the forum to particular groups and particular subject matters." MPEA brief, 43. The MPEA argues that it has created a forum that is open for public expression, but is not a designated public forum, because it is closed to "activist" groups with a "protest" message. The MPEA seeks to create a new category: government-owned property in which space is available for public expression, including political speech, but where criticism of the government is not allowed.

As we know in this section, the MPEA's forum argument is incorrect. The spaces at Navy Pier which are used for public expression *are* designated public fora. We show in Part D that the MPEA's licensing system and speed restrictions are unconstitutional, given the nature of the forum.

The MPEA offers four arguments to support its claim that no part of Navy Pier is a designated public forum. Each is incorrect.

First, the MPEA argues that use of space at the Pier for public expression does not make the Pier a designated public forum, because the Pier is intended to be only a "commercial entertainment" venue—a limited purpose that makes Navy Pier comparable to a military base, welfare office, or post office. (MPEA brief, 38-39.) In making this argument the MPEA ignores the district court's findings of fact, the Navy Pier "is intended to serve multiple purposes and functions," including provision of "multi-purpose exhibition, meeting, and reception facilities" and "public parks, gardens and gathering places," at which "commercial uses are required to be ancillary to the established public use." Op2, 7. Before this litigation began, the MPEA's managers and other government officials repeatedly promised that the Pier would be used for public purposes, above all others, and would not be operated like a commercial shopping mall. The MPEA has not addressed this evidence. It offers only an after-the-fact rationale for its actions, contrary to this Court's warning that a "post-hoc policy formulation" should be relied on in characterizing the forum. *Air Line Pilots, supra,* 45 F.3d at 1153.

To support its claim that Navy Pier is operated only as a commercial and entertainment facility, like a privately-owned business, the MPEA argues that all of its licensing decisions are made purely for business reasons. MPEA brief, 42-44, 16-19. But this argument ignores the MPEA's own policy, which provides that special consideration will be given to groups associated with the City and State. After the fact, the MPEA attempts to explain each instance in which it gave space at the Pier to groups without charge, arguing that the MPEA gained free advertising and the benefit of the crowds that were drawn to the events. But as the district court noted, other groups that provide entertainment and draw crowds to the Pier, unrelated to the Mayor or Governor, are not given space for free. Op2, 11.

For example, the Illinois Federation for Human Rights, a gay and lesbian rights organization, leased and paid to use the Skyline Stage to hold fundraising benefits concerts in 1994 and 1996. The Human Rights Federation brought "name talent" to the Pier; promoted the events at not cost to the MPEA; and the events were sold out. It is undisputed that the Human Rights Federation's events were good for the commercial business that operate on Navy Pier. R65, ¶20; Tr. 1/97, 291. Nonetheless, the Human Rights Federation was charged for the space at the Pier, unlike groups associated with the Mayor. There is no evidence of a commercial justification for this disparity in treatment. Op2, 11 Tr. 1/97, 291. Navy Pier is not intended to be operated like a private shopping center and licensing decisions at the Pier are not made for business reasons alone.

Note another argument rejected by the court.

Next, the MPEA argues that the ballroom, festival hall, winter garden, and stage at Navy Pier, as well as the sidewalks and plazas on the Navy Pier, are not designated public fora because a "protest" message from groups like the plaintiffs would be incompatible with the "fun-filled," "family-orientated" complex the MPEA wants to maintain at Navy Pier. MPEA brief, 41-42. These space are not intended for public expression, the MPEA claims, because it wants to exclude, and has excluded, groups like the plaintiffs, who have a dissenting point of view.

This argument is wrong as a matter of law. In determining whether portions of Navy Pier are designated public fora, the issue is whether these areas have been set aside for expressive activity—not whether they have been set aside for controversial public expression. The government may not argue that a forum open for meetings and expression is not a public forum because of the government wants to limit speech to accord with a particular point of view.

For example, the municipal auditorium in *Southeastern Promotions, Ltd. v. Conrad, supra,* 420 U.S. 546 (1975), was a dedicated public forum, even though the municipal defendant in that case intended to limit speech in the theater to "clean, healthful, entertainment which will make for the upbuilding for better citizenship." 420 U.S. at 551 and n. 4. That is, the government's intent to limit discussion to a particular point of view did not alter the nature of the forum.

This issue was discussed in detail in *Air Line Pilots,* 45 F.3d at 1157-58 (7th Cir. 1995). In that case, the City argued that display cases at O'Hare Airport were not designated public forum, and the City could properly deny space for an advertisement criticizing United Airlines, because the City did not intend to allow advertising that would undermine the commercial interest of its tenants. The Court rejected that claim, holding that the City's desire to prohibit "disruptive" speech did not control how the forum should be characterized. "The City (or more pointedly, United) doubtless objects to the proposed message. Nevertheless, such an objection is not a permissible basis for avoiding public forum status." 45 F.3d at 1158.

Third, the MPEA argues that there are no designated public fora on the Pier, because "[p]olitical and advocacy groups have never been permitted to use any areas of the Pier for purposes of public advocacy." MPEA brief, 43. That is flatly untrue. Groups allowed to hold "political functions on behalf of Mayor Daley, Governor Jim Egar, and other local and statewide politicians" were engaged in public advocacy. Op2, 8. The Democratic Party is a political advocacy group.

This case is not like *Cornelius v. NAACP Legal Defense and Education Fund, Inc.,* 473 U.S. 788 (1995). In *Cornelius,* the government claimed that it had a policy of excluding all political advocacy groups from a non-partisan charity drive directed at federal employees. The MPEA, in contrast, does not exclude partisan speakers from using space at the Pier and does not refuse to license space to political advocacy groups.

Finally, the MPEA argues that there are no designated public fora on the Pier because it has allowed only "speech by the government on government-owned property." It suggests that Navy Pier property has a been used like an office directory in a government building, or a display case in a public library. MPEA brief, 39. That does not describe what has happened here, however. The speech allowed at Navy Pier is not only speech by the MPEA and is not only speech about the MPEA's activities. For example, meetings of the National Bar Association, a fundraiser for Prentice Hospital, Op2 at 21, and a speech by a representative of the Mayor at the east end of the Pier do not constitute speech by the MPEA.

Given the facts, it is hard to see how the Grand Ballroom, Skyline Stage, Festival Hall, and Crystal Gardens, as well as the sidewalks, plazas, and park areas of Navy Pier, could be categorized as anything other than public fora. These are government-owned properties, made available to be used for public meetings and expression.

D.   The MPEA's systems for regulating speech at Navy Pier are unconstitutional.

Note how in this section, each paragraph begins with a positive statement supporting the client's position.

The MPEA relies entirely on the argument that the district court erred in characterizing portions of Navy Pier as traditional and designated public fora. It does not even attempt to argue that its speech restrictions can survive if the district court's conclusions about the nature of the fora are upheld.

The MPEA's speech regulations are much too restrictive for application to a traditional or designated public forum.

In both traditional and designated public fora, the government may only enforce content-based exclusions of speech if there is a showing that the restriction is necessary to serve a compelling state interest and if the exclusions are narrowly drawn to achieve that end.

Air Line Pilots, 45 F.3d at 1151. *See also Boos v. Barry,* 485 U.S. 312, 322 (1988), and *Grossbaum v. Indianapolis-Marion County Bldg. Authority,* 63 F.3d 581, 87 (7th Cir. 1995) ("*Grossbaum I*"). The MPEA cannot satisfy those requirements and does not even attempt to do so.

As the district court correctly concluded, the interests asserted by the MPEA are not "compelling." Op2, 27. The risk that shoppers may be disturbed by controversy is not a compelling state interest, sufficient to justify suppression of political speech. *Compare, e.g. Texas v. Johnson,* 491 U.S. 397 (1989) (flag-burning case).

The MPEA's total ban on unlicensed expressive activity at Navy Pier also is not necessary to serve the MPEA's business interest. "Necessary" in the constitutional analysis means more than just "related to" or "would promote." *R.A.V. v. City of St. Paul, Minn.,* 505 U.S. 377, 396-97 (1992) (ban on hate speech was not reasonably necessary to ensure rights of minorities living in community). The MPEA may adapt neutral time, place, and manner restrictions to control crowds and traffic flow at Navy Pier. But a total ban on political dissent is not required to protect those interest.

Furthermore, a complete and total prohibition on unlicensed expression is not narrowly tailored to preserving the Pier as a center for commercial activity. The MPEA has made no attempt, for instance, to limit the effect of its rules to areas in which there is commercial activity. There are no commercial enterprises on the plaza at the east of the Pier, or on the sidewalk on the North Dock. Nonetheless, the MPEA policies prohibit the plaintiffs from going to those locations to carry a single sign, or even talk to anyone about the Living Wage Ordinance that plaintiffs support.

The MPEA has not defended and cannot defend the licensing system it uses to regulate speech at the Pier. It argues that the district court should have not considered the MPEA's policies with respect to licensing areas such as the Grand Ballroom, Festival Hall, and Skyline Stage, claiming that plaintiffs did not seek a license for access to those areas. MPEA brief, 41. This argument ignores the findings of the district court. Op2, 21. See also Op2, 11, 15 and PX 9. Furthermore, as a matter of law, plaintiffs may pursue a facial challenge to the overly broad discretion allowed under the MPEA's licensing system, whether or not they applied for a license. *FW/PBS, Inc. v. City of Dallas,* 493 U.S. 215, 224 (1990).

The Supreme Court wrote in *Forsyth County, Ga. v. Nationalist Movement,* 505 U.S. 123 (1992):

> "[A] law subjecting the exercise of First Amendment freedoms to the prior restraint of a license must contain "narrow, objective, and definitive standards to guide the licensing authority." [Citations omitted.] The reasoning is simple: If the permit scheme "involves appraisal of facts, the exercise if judgment, and the formation of an opinion," *Cantwell v. Connecticut,* 310 U.S. 296, 305, 60 S. Ct. 900, 904, 84 L.Ed.2d 1213 (1940), by the licensing authority, "the danger of censorship and of abridgment of our precious First Amendment freedoms is too great" to be permitted. [Citation omitted.]

505 U.S. at 132. In addition to controlling the exercise of discretion in license decisions, the time during which a license application will be considered must be limited, *FW/PBS, supra,* 493 U.S. at 227; "expeditious judicial review of [the] decision must be available," *id.,* 493 U.S. at 229; and "the censor must bear the burden of going to court to suppress the speech and must bear the burden of proof once in court." *Id.*

The MPEA's license system does not meet any of these standards. Defendant's managers exercise discretion that is not bounded by "narrow, objective, and definitive standards." There is no time limit during which the Pier Authority has to respond to a license request. There are no rules that the Pier Authority ever has to respond to such a request. Tr. 1/97, 278. The Pier Authority is not obligated to give reasons for the denial of a license, Tr. 1/97, 278-79; there is no procedure for internal appeal, Tr. 1/97, 279-80; and there is no procedure that requires the MPEA to bring a court action to justify denial of a license. Tr. 1/97, 280. This is a licensing system in which no attempt has been made to satisfy the relevant constitutional requirements.

Finally, the MPEA's practices are unconstitutional because the MPEA regulates speech at the Pier Based on viewpoint. Op2, 26. In *any* forum, the government may not prohibit or burden speech because of the viewpoint expressed. *Grossbaum I, supra,* 63 F. 3d at 586-87 (government could not prohibit display of menorah in public building, a nonpublic forum, where other groups were allowed to put up displays); *Grossbaum v. Indianapolis-Marion County Bldg.,* 100 F.3d 1287, 1297 (7th Cir. 1996) ("*Grossbaum II*") (even "nonpublic forum regulations must be viewpoint neutral"), *cert. denied,* 117 S. Ct. 1822 (1997).

The MPEA does not deny that it regulates speech at the Pier based on viewpoint. The MPEA writes that its policy is to allow speech that will create a "friendly, welcoming, non-controversial image." R84, 28. The MPEA will allow speech and events that are "attractive," "family-oriented,' and "entertaining." MPEA brief, 42; R84, 22, 23, 24. But the MPEA will not allow protest speech—speech by "activists," R84, 23, that "is likely to cause controversy and ill will." R84, 28. The MPEA has given the Mayor and city administration space at Navy Pier to promote programs that have good public relations value for the Mayor. It may waive fees for speakers associated with the City and State. But the MPEA will not provide space at the Pier to groups like the plaintiffs, who seek to criticize the local government. Pro-administration speech is subsidized, while anti-administration speech is prohibited. The MPEA clearly is regulating speech based on viewpoint, *Air Line Pilots,* 45 F.3d at 1157, in violation of the Constitution. *Turner Broadcasting System, Inc. v. F.C.C.,* 512 U.S. 622, 643 (1994) (government may not "suppress, disadvantage, or impose differential burdens upon speech" because of viewpoint). *See Lamb's Chapel v. Center Moriches Union Free School District,* 508 U.S. 384 (1993) (without classifying the forum, Supreme Court held that defendant improperly denied plaintiffs access to school property to speak on family issues from a religious perspective, where other groups were given access to the property to speak on social, civic, and recreational topics).

For all of these reasons, the MPEA's speech restrictions violate the First Amendment and were properly enjoined by the district court.

II.   The district court erred in holding that the MPEA may completely ban all leafleting, solicitation, and other expressive activities in the Family Pavilion and South Arcade buildings on Navy Pier.

The district court held that the MPEA may prohibit all unlicensed expressive activity in the Family Pavilion and South Arcade buildings. These areas constitute a government-owned shopping center, the court held. Activities such as leafleting and solicitation of funds by the plaintiffs may be prohibited in the common areas inside these buildings, the court held, because "plaintiffs' proposed political and social message" would be likely to offend customers. Op2, 24. To our knowledge, this is the first time any federal court has held that the government may prohibit all forms of expression on government-owned property to promote shopping.

Access to the interior Family Pavilion and South Arcade areas on Navy Pier is important to groups like the plaintiffs for a simple reason: it gets cold in Chicago in the winter. It is not very helpful in January to be given access only to areas like South Dock, or the "protest zone" estab-

This section utilizes the device of stressing the undesirable results connected with a ruling against the client's position.

lished by the MPEA. The people who come to Navy Pier are not there. They go inside, into areas like the Family Pavilion. The district court's holding gives plaintiffs the right to stand in the cold, dark, and rain, offering leaflets to sea gulls.

Plaintiffs seek at least some access into the Family Pavilion and the South Arcade areas, shown in A9-12 and A14-15. The MPEA controls common space in these areas that is not leased to commercial tenants. The MPEA sponsors shows, performances, and other activities in the rotunda area of the Family Pavilion, Op2, 24, Tr. 1/97, 245, 304-05; R67, ¶30; R65, ¶3; and PX 125; it puts up a Christmas tree there in the winter, Tr. 1/97, 245; and it has used the area to screen short films by Chicago filmmakers, for a magic show with an anti-drug message, and for theatrical performances. PX 53. The MPEA has allowed charitable solicitation in these areas by a group opposing child abuse, Op2, 24-25; Tr. 1/97, 262; and has allowed a group associated with AIDS Ride Chicago to set up a table in the Family Pavilion to advertise their cause. PX 60.

Detailed analysis is not required to conclude that the MPEA's total restriction on unlicensed expression in these areas is unconstitutional on its face. The Supreme Court

An example of an argument accepted by the court.

considered a similar rule in *Board of Airport Commissioners v. Jews for Jesus, Inc.*, 482 U.S. 569 (1987). In that case, the Los Angeles Airport issued a rule like the MPEA's, purporting to prohibit all First Amendment activity in the airport. In a unanimous opinion, the Supreme Court held that rule unconstitutional. The Court held that it was not necessary to determine whether or not the airport was a public forum. "We think it obvious that such a ban cannot be justified even if LAX were a nonpublic forum because no conceivable governmental interest would justify such an absolute prohibition on speech." *Id.*, 482 U.S. at 576.

We do not doubt that defendant's restrictions might reasonable be adopted by a private shopping center. But some practices that are reasonable for a private business are not reasonable for a branch of the government. In holding that the government may totally prohibit all forms of protest against the government in an area that it operates like a shopping mall, the district court erred.

In 1992, the Supreme Court considered whether solicitation of funds and distribution of handbills could be prohibited in airport terminals operated by the New York Port Authority. *Int'l. Society for Krishna Consciousness, Inc. v. Lee*, 505 U.S. 672 (1992); and *Lee v. Int'l Society for Krishna Consciousness, Inc.*, 505 U.S. 830 (1992). In a pair of 5-4 rulings, the Court held that the airports were not a public fora because they were built and established to facilitate air travel, rather than public assembly and speech. The Court held that face-to-face solicitation of money could be banned in the airports, but distribution of leaflets in the airports could not. Even in a space that is not a public forum, the Court held, a total ban on the distribution of literature was not reasonable and violated the First Amendment. Justice O'Connor wrote:

> [W]e have consistently stated that restrictions on speech in nonpublic fora are valid only if they are "reasonable" and "not an effort to suppress expression merely because public officials oppose the speaker's view." [Citation omitted.]

505 U.S at 688.

In airport case, the government authority argued that leafleting was incompatible with the purpose of the airports, facilitation of air travel. Justice O'Connor, however, noted that the government has created a space that served more than that single purpose.

> Not only has the Port Authority chosen *not* to limit access to the airports under its control, it has created a huge complex open to travelers and non-travelers alike. The airports and house restaurants, cafeterias, snack bars, coffee shops, cocktail lounges, post offices, banks, telegraph offices, clothing shops, drug stores, food stores, nurseries, barber shops, currency exchanges, art exhibits, commercial advertising displays, bookstores, newsstands, dental offices and private clubs. . . . The International Arrivals Building at JFK Airport even has two branches of Bloomingdale's.

Id., at 689.

> The Port Authority. . .contends that it. . .has dedicated its airports to a single purpose—facilitating air travel—and that the speech it seeks to prohibit is not consistent with that purpose. But the wide range of activities promoted by the Port Authority is no more directly related to facilitating air travel than are the types of activities in which ISKCON wishes to engage. See *Jews for Jesus, supra,* 482 U.S. at 576, 107 S.Ct., at 2573 ("The line between airport-related speech and non airport-related speech is, at best, murky"). In my view, the Port Authority is operating a shopping mall as well as an airport. The reasonableness inquiry, therefore, is not whether the restrictions on speech are "consistent with. . .preserving the property" for air travel. *Perry, supra,* 460 U.S. at 50-51, 103 S.Ct., at 958 (internal quotation marks and citation omitted), but whether they are reasonably related to maintaining the multipurpose environment that the Port Authority has deliberately created.

Id., 505 U.S. at 688-89. This case is like the airport cases, where the Port Authority was "operating a shopping mall as well as an airport." In a government-owned and operated shopping mall, it is not reasonable to ban all forms of unlicensed expression, including leafleting.

In concluding that the MPEA may restrict speech in the Family Pavilion and South Arcade, the district court made a clear error of law. The district court understood these cases to hold that "restriction on leafleting in the airport is permissible so long as the government provides alternative channels of communication." Op2, 24. That is not what the Supreme court held.

Where the government has created a forum intended to attract crowds, it cannot reasonably ban all leafleting and solicitation. In *Jews for Jesus, Inc. v. Massachusetts Bay Transportation Authority,* 984 F.2d 1319 (1st Cir. 1993), the Court held that leafleting and solicitation of petition signatures could not be prohibited in mass transit stations. The Court wrote:

> The MBTA deliberately has invited into the subway system a range of expressive activities that can produce problems similar to those it attributes to leafleting. The condoned presence of these activities indicates that the subway system can accommodate peaceful leafleting.

Id., at 1325 (footnote omitted). And the Court wrote, "[W]e do not see how peaceful solicitation of signatures clashes with the multipurpose environment of the subway system. . . ." *Id.*

Plaintiffs have sought only very limited access to the Family Pavilion and South Arcade. Plaintiffs asked for leave to bring three people into the Family Pavilion to leaflet and solicit funds on a weekday morning in November, between 10:00 a.m. and 1:00 p.m., PX 1—not the massive demonstration involving hundreds of people described by the MPEA. MPEA brief, 5-6. A total prohibition on leafleting and solicitation in these areas is not required to promote pedestrian traffic flow or ensure safety. On a mid-week morning in the winter, these areas are virtually empty. A9-10, A14-15; Tr. 1/97, 244-47; PX 145; Tr. 242-43.

This effort to show the reasonableness of the client's position was accepted by the court.

The MPEA argues that it is reasonable to prohibit all communications by the plaintiffs inside the Family Pavilion and South Arcade because, it claims, massive demonstrations would drive customers away from Navy Pier. MPEA brief, 23-24. The MPEA relies particularly on a survey performed by Garth Taylor, in which patrons at Navy Pier were asked how they would react to demonstrations at the Pier. Four people from Mr. Taylor's company were stationed in the Family Pavilion and South Arcade to "intercept" patrons at the Pier—go up to people and ask if they would like to be interviewed. Tr. 1/97, 440, 441; DX 51, 1. Mr. Taylor reported that about half of the people who were surveyed said they would be less likely to return to Navy Pier if they were subjected to the combined effects of a demonstration involving several hundred people, loudspeakers, banners, picket signs, solicitations for signatures, solicitations for money, and other approaches. Tr. 1/97, 438-39; DX 64; DX 59, 7.

That result does not support the MPEA's argument, however, and does not address the issues in this case. The MPEA has not only banned mass marches on the Pier. It purports to ban *all* expressive activity on the Pier. Plaintiffs did not ask the MPEA for permission to conduct an intrusive demonstration, of the kind described in Mr. Taylor's survey. Mr. Taylor presented no measure of the possible effect of activities plaintiffs have actually sought to engage in. Tr. 1/97, 439.

Contrary to the district court's conclusions, Mr. Taylor's activities show that many First Amendment activities would *not* disrupt people at Navy Pier. Under the district court's order, the MPEA may prohibit a single representative of the plaintiffs from approaching people in the Family Pavilion, telling them about the Living Wage Ordinance, and asking for their opinion. But Mr. Taylor testified that people enjoy being asked for their opinions. Tr. 1/97, 429. Mr. Taylor's employees themselves intercepted people within the buildings at Navy Pier and asked them to stop, talk, and answer questions. They did not detect that anyone was annoyed. Mr. Taylor does not believe that these action cost the Pier anything in return visits to the Pier. Tr. 1/97, 442. (The MPEA clearly does not think this kind of activity is harmful to Pier operation—it has hired Mr. Taylor's company to approach, stop, and talk to people at the Pier on at least four occasions. Tr. 1/97, 441-42.) When Mr. Taylor was asked if people at the Pier would mind being asked about Living Wage and the Mayor's opposition to it he testified, "I—I don't know. I mean, I think people are flattered that people care about their opinions." Tr. 1/97, 439-40. That testimony simply does not support the conclusion that activities like asking petition signatures would damage commercial operations in the Family Pavilion and South Arcade.

The MPEA's claims about the likely effect of activities such as leafleting are not creditable. The district court found that the MPEA's past representations to the court "have been less than accurate," Op2, 12, because the MPEA claimed in August, 1996 that plaintiffs would block traffic and threaten public safety if they were allowed to distribute leaflets near the entrance to the South Dock, Tr. 8/96, 48, 85, 87, 103, 125-45— but then the MPEA allowed leaflets to be handed out in the entrance to the South Dock by a man on stilts. R97, 12; Tr. 1/97, 18-19. The MPEA claims that a complete prohibition on leafleting everywhere on the Pier is necessary to ensure the Pier's financial survival. But the Pier's managers do not really believe that themselves. Pier Manager Jon Clay testified that it was not clear to him that peaceful leafleting by two or three people on the south dock of the Pier would cause any harm to the Pier's operations. Tr. 1/97, 273.

It is not plaintiffs' proposed activities that the MPEA claim are incompatible with the Family Pavilion and South Arcade. Rather, the MPEA objects to plaintiffs' "protest" message. The MPEA argues that its operations will be harmed if shoppers are exposed to leaflets that express "controversial viewpoints." MPEA brief, 47. And it is plaintiffs' message—not their proposed activities—that the district court held was objectionable. The district court held that the MPEA may exclude plaintiffs from these areas because "[t]he plaintiffs' proposed political and social message is incompatible with and would likely harm the commercial nature of the Family Pavilion and South Arcade." Op2, 24.

In holding that plaintiffs' speech can be restricted in the Family Pavilion and South Arcade because of the "political and social message" that plaintiffs wish to convey, the district court erred as a matter of law. In May, 1998, the Supreme Court stated again, "To be consistent with the First Amendment, the exclusion of a speaker from a nonpublic forum must not be based on the speaker's viewpoint and must otherwise be reasonable in light of the purpose of the property." *Arkansas Educational Television Comm'n v. Forbes,* ___ U.S. ___, 1998 WL 244196, *10 (1998).

The district court's decision that the MPEA may prohibit all unlicensed expression in the Family Pavilion and South Arcade, including leafleting and solicitation, should be reversed. Complete prohibition of all unlicensed expression in the common grounds of a government-owned shopping area, to avoid disturbance of shoppers, is not a reasonable use of government power.

III. After it held the MPEA's policies unconstitutional, the district court erred by allowing the MPEA to continue to restrict plaintiffs' speech.

On April 1, 1998 the district court held that the MPEA has unconstitutionally restricted plaintiffs' speech in the public fora on Navy Pier. But when plaintiffs and the MPEA appeared before the court in mid-April, the district court held that the MPEA still was entitled to confine and limit plaintiffs' access to the South Dock. Without hearing any additional evidence the district court held that on April 16 the MPEA could require plaintiffs to remain stationary within three small areas on the South Dock, in groups of no more than 15 people. R102.

There was no basis for the district court's order and it was clearly wrong, as a matter of law. The South Dock is a traditional public forum. The MPEA presented no evidence suggesting that there was any event on the South Dock on April 16 that justified restricting plaintiffs to small protest zones. Plaintiffs were not subject to these restrictions pursuant to any narrowly-tailored regulations. And defendant's licensing and permit system did not meet constitutional requirements. It was the same system that the court had already found unconstitutional.

Note the clear statement that the court below was wrong, supported by the client's argument in the following paragraphs.

First Amendment violations are supposed to be addressed with prompt, effective injunctive relief. "The loss of the First Amendment freedoms, for even minimal periods of time, unquestionably constitutes irreparable injury." *Elrod v. Burns,* 427 U.S. 347 (1976). "The timeliness of political speech is particularly important." *Id.,* 427 U.S. at 374, and n. 29. But the district court's orders have allowed the MPEA to continue to restrict plaintiffs' speech, without any constitutional basis.

The district court's first job, after it found that the MPEA was unconstitutionally interfering with the plaintiffs' speech, was to enjoin the MPEA from interfering with plaintiffs' speech in the future. The court should not have attempted to write its own time, place, and manner regulations for the MPEA. *Association of Community Organization for Reform Now (ACORN) v. Edgar,* 56 F.3d 791 (7th Cir. 1995) (district court should enjoin state but should not attempt to write regulations dictating how state is to comply with the law); *Jenkins v. Bowling,* 691 F.2d 1225, 1234 (7th Cir. 1982).

The district court enjoined the MPEA to write new regulations, but did not enjoin the MPEA from interfering with plaintiffs in the interim. The court did not require the MPEA to write new regulations within any set period of time; did not require that the MPEA's new regulations be approved by the Court; and did not order the MPEA to refrain from interfering with plaintiffs' speech after entry of the court's orders. Pursuant to the district court's orders, the MPEA may write new regulations that, like the old ones, fail to satisfy the Constitution, and may continue to restrict plaintiffs' First Amendment rights, leaving the burden on plaintiffs to seek relief from the court. The district court gave plaintiffs a victory in principle, but failed to provide the restraining orders needed to give plaintiffs relief in fact.

On remand, the district court should be directed to enjoin the MPEA to refrain from interfering with the plaintiffs' speech on the traditional public fora at Navy Pier and in areas of the Pier open to the public without charge, that are not subject to private licenses, unless and until the MPEA satisfies the court that it has adopted constitutional, neutral, time, place, and manner restrictions on speech. If the MPEA acts reasonably to comply with the Constitution the MPEA should be able immediately to put in place regulations that protect its legitimate interests.

CONCLUSION

For the reasons set forth above, the district court's decision should be affirmed in part and reversed in part.

The district court's declaratory judgment and decision enjoining the MPEA from continuing to apply its restrictions on speech at Navy Pier should be affirmed. The district court's description of the outdoor sidewalks on the Pier, the plaza at the Pier's east end, and Pier Park as traditional public fora should be upheld. The court's description of the Grand Ballroom, Skyline Stage, Festival Hall, and Crystal Garden as designated public fora and the court's decision to enjoin application of the MPEA's licensing practices should be affirmed.

The district court's holding that the MPEA may prohibit all unlicensed, expressive activity Family Pavilion and South Arcade should be reversed. The district court's decision, allowing the MPEA to restrict plaintiffs to confined spaces on the South Dock on April 16, 1998, should be reversed. On remand, the district court should be directed to enjoin the MPEA to refrain from interfering with plaintiffs' speech on the traditional public fora at Navy Pier and in areas of the Pier open to the public without charge, that are not subject to private licenses, unless and until the MPEA satisfies the court that it had adopted constitutional, neutral time, place, and manner restrictions on speech.

The case should be remanded to the district court for future proceedings in conformity with this Court's opinion.

Respectfully submitted,

_____

Paul Strauss
One of the Attorneys for
Plaintiffs-Appellees and
Cross-Appellants
Miner, Barnhill & Galland
14 W. Erie St.
Chicago, IL 60610
(312) 751-1170

**CHICAGO ACORN, SEIU Local No. 880, and Ted Thomas,
Plaintiffs-Appellees, Cross-Appellants,**

v.

**METROPOLITAN PIER AND EXPOSITION AUTHORITY,
Defendant-Appellant, Cross-Appellee.**

Nos. 98-1939, 98-1977.

United States Court of Appeals,

Seventh Circuit.

Argued June 5, 1998.

Decided July 21, 1998.

Paul Strauss (argued), Miner, Barnhill & Galland, Chicago, IL, for Plaintiffs-Appellees.

Michele Odorizzi (argued), Mayer, Brown & Platt, Renee Benjamin, Metropolitan Pier and Exposition Authority, Chicago, IL, for Metropolitan Pier & Exposition Authority.

Before POSNER, Chief Judge, and BAUER and KANNE, Circuit Judges.

POSNER, Chief Judge.

We have an appeal and a cross-appeal from an injunction that restricts the right of the Metropolitan Pier and Exposition Authority (MPEA)—the Illinois governmental unit that owns Navy Pier in Chicago—to limit the exercise of free speech by people who frequent the pier. The plaintiffs want to engage in a range of expressive activities there—leafletting, soliciting signatures on petitions, carrying signs and banners, wearing clothing festooned with symbols and slogans,chanting,speechifying—all to the end of advocating an increase in the minimum wage. They wanted to do these things during the Democratic National Convention in 1996, when the MPEA rented the entire pier to the Democrats for $1 for a party, and they were turned away, and brought this suit.

Navy Pier, in downtown Chicago, juts out 3,000 feet into Lake Michigan and is more than 400 feet wide at its widest point. Formerly a naval facility, by the 1980s it was little used and in 1989 the Illinois legislature handed it over to the MPEA (at the time known as the Metropolitan Fair and Exposition Authority) and appropriated $200 million for the pier's renovation. The pier was to be transformed into a recreational and commercial center—part park, part meeting and exhibition facility, part shopping emporium, part amusement park. The reconstruction was completed in 1995.

The stylized map at the end of this opinion will give the reader a rough sense of the pier's current design. For our purposes, the design has four elements. The first consists of outdoor strolling areas, mainly sidewalks. The principal sidewalk—the pier's thoroughfare—is Dock Street (misnamed—it is not a street; except for parking, the pier is closed to vehicles other than service vehicles). It runs the length of the pier on its south side. It is broad, abuts the lake, and is more like a boardwalk than a conventional sidewalk. Tourist boats are moored on the lake side of the street, and the other side is lined with shops (the Arcade Shops) and restaurants. Dock Street ends, at the eastern end of the pier, in a plaza in which sculpture is sometimes exhibited. There is a sidewalk on the north side of the pier as well, between the lake and the service street, but it is narrow and little used. The district court treated what we are calling the first design element as a traditional public forum, which means (as we shall see) that the MPEA must open it up to the full range of First Amendment expressive activities, subject however to reasonable restrictions as to the time, place, and manner of expression.

The second design element is a tiny amusement park, consisting of a ferris wheel, carousel, reflecting pool, and small indoor park, called Crystal Gardens, which has fountains that squirt columns of water to each other, surmounted by a glass dome. The second element, too, the district judge deemed a traditional public forum. The third element, consisting mainly of the Family Pavilion at the western end of the pier and the Arcade Shops, which lead off from the Family Pavilion, is an indoor shopping mall. The district judge treated this as a nonpublic forum in which the plaintiffs have no right to engage in expressive activity. The fourth element, which includes the Grand Ballroom and Festival Hall, consists of large meeting rooms suitable for trade and other conventions (such as the trade association of candy manufacturers, which held its annual convention recently in Festival Hall), weddings and other parties (in the Grand Ballroom), and exhibitions (for example the annual Chicago Art Fair, which is also held in the Grand Ballroom). The fourth element the district judge held was a designated public forum, which she equated to a traditional public forum.

The sidewalk, park, and mall sections of the pier are open to the public without charge, except that they are closed from 2 a.m. to 6 a.m., the same hours that the parks owned by the Chicago Park District are closed. The MPEA's suggestion that only a facility that is open 24 hours a day can be classified as a public forum for First Amendment purposes does not merit discussion.

The injunction entered by the district court (and in this court challenged by both sides) gives the plaintiffs no rights in the indoor shopping mall but full First Amendment rights in the rest of the pier, though subject to reasonable time, place, and manner restrictions.

All the buildings on the pier, as well as the pier itself, are owned by the MPEA; and because the legislature has appropriated no operating funds for the pier, the MPEA must defray the cost of running the pier out of the lease rentals that it receives from the shops and other concessions and the fees that it receives for renting out the meeting rooms. Since Navy Pier is, thus, essentially a commercial enterprise, the MPEA is naturally highly sensitive to the spillover effects, whether positive or negative, of each activity on the pier on every other activity on the pier. The positive effects are illustrated by the

MPEA's sponsorship of fireworks displays for which there is no charge. The displays are a form of advertising; they publicize the pier and attract people who buy goods or services from the shops and restaurants on the pier. So while the displays generate no revenue directly, their cost is recouped in the greater sales that they generate for the MPEA's lessees. The act of largesse that set off this suit—the rental of the entire pier to the Democratic Party for $1—was motivated, we are assured by the MPEA, not by any fealty to the Democrats but by the enormous and on the whole favorable publicity that the event was expected to generate for the pier. When we asked the MPEA's lawyer at argument whether her client would rent the pier to the American Nazi Party for $1, we received an emphatic negative answer; there would be enormous publicity, but of the wrong kind. The MPEA refuses to waive fees for the plaintiffs, who like to hold a rally in the Grand Ballroom in support of their proposal for a higher minimum wage.

If the MPEA were a private entity, it would have a free hand in deciding whom to admit to its property and on what terms, provided that it did not violate certain antidiscrimination laws that are of no moment to this suit. The pier if privately owned would not fall within the "company town" exception of *Marsh v. Alabama*, 326 U.S. 501, 66 S.Ct. 276, 90 L.Ed. 265 (1946), to the rule that the First Amendment constrains only governmental action; it is not a town. *Lloyd Corp. v. Tanner*, 407 U.S. 551, 92 S.Ct. 2219, 33 L.Ed.2d 131 (1972); compare *Petersen v. Talisman Sugar Corp.*, 478 F.2d 73, 82 (5th Cir.1972). But it is publicly owned, and so its owner, the MPEA, is subject to the First Amendment and as a result its discretion is curtailed. Clearly, it is not permitted to pick and choose among the users of its facilities on political grounds: to waive fees for the Democratic Party because the mayor of Chicago is a Democrat and wanted to avoid in 1996 any repetition of the disastrous events that attended the 1968 Democratic National Convention, the last to be held in Chicago, but not to waive fees for Chicago Acorn and the other plaintiffs because the mayor opposes the increase in the minimum wage that they advocate. *Arkansas Educational Television Comm'n v. Forbes*, _____ U.S. _____, _____, 118 S.Ct. 1633, 1640, 140 L.Ed.2d 875 (1998); *Rosenberger v. Rector*, 515 U.S. 819, 828-29, 115 S.Ct. 2510, 132 L.Ed.2d 700 (1995); *May v. Evansville-Vanderburgh School Corp.*, 787 F.2d 1105, 1113 (7th Cir.1986). The MPEA denies that its decisions are politically motivated, and the record contains no direct evidence that they are. There is favoritism for events associated with Chicago's mayor, who is a Democrat; but the MPEA contends that the motivation for this favoritism is purely economic; its policy is to waive fees for users who will generate large favorable publicity. A policy so motivated is likely, however, to favor the political establishment. As applied to political applicants for fee waivers, a favorable-publicity criterion is especially likely to have political consequences, since the only political users of the pier who will generate large amounts of favorable publicity are respectable, popular politicians and respected, well-established political groups; pariahs need not apply.

We doubt that the MPEA has to allow its meeting rooms to be used for political events at all, for we disagree with the district judge's ruling that these rooms constitute a public forum. Unlike public streets or the speakers' corner in London's Hyde Park, the exhibition, convention, and meeting facilities of Navy Pier are not traditional sites for public assembly, demonstrations, or debate. They thus are not what in the jargon of free-speech law are called "traditional public forums." *United States v. Grace*, 461 U.S. 171, 179-80, 103 S.Ct. 1702, 75 L.Ed.2d 736 (1983); *Perry Education Ass'n v. Perry Local Educators' Ass'n*, 460 U.S. 37, 45, 103 S.Ct. 948, 74 L.Ed.2d 794 (1983). Nor are they nontraditional such sites (that is, not public streets, public sidewalks, or public parks) which the government by throwing open to the public for a range of expressive purposes has dedicated as a public forum ("designated public forums," id.), though unlike traditional public forums the dedication of a designated public forum to the public can be revoked, *id.* at 46, 103 S.Ct. 948, and its subject- matter can be limited in accordance with the character of the forum. *City of Madison Joint School District No. 8 v. Wisconsin Employment Relations Comm'n*, 429 U.S. 167, 175 n. 8, 97 S.Ct. 421, 50 L.Ed.2d 376 (1976); *see, e.g., Widmar v. Vincent*, 454 U.S. 263, 267-68 and n. 5, 102 S.Ct. 269, 70 L.Ed.2d 440 (1981) (university facilities held to be public forum for students but not nonstudents); *Southeastern Promotions, Ltd. v. Conrad*, 420 U.S. 546, 555, 95 S.Ct. 1239, 43 L.Ed.2d 448 (1975) (publicly owned theater held permissibly limited to theatrical performances); *Piarowski v. Illinois Community College Dist.* 515, 759 F.2d 625, 628-29 (7th Cir.1985) (public college's exhibition area limited to members of college community); *Church on the Rock v. City of Albuquerque*, 84 F.3d 1273, 1278 (10th Cir.1996) (senior citizens' center open to the public but only for discussion of subjects of interest to the elderly). The meeting facilities at Navy Pier fall into the residual category of "nonpublic forums." *Perry Education Ass'n v. Perry Local Educators' Ass'n, supra*, 460 U.S. at 46, 103 S.Ct. 948. These are facilities that are not open to the general public although they are sites usable and sometimes used for discussion and other expressive activities. See *May v. Evansville-Vanderburgh School Corp., supra*, 787 F.2d at 1113.

Navy Pier's meeting rooms are rented to organizations for use by their members and guests rather than by the public at large unless the lessee decides to admit the public. In deciding whom to rent to and at what price, the MPEA seeks to maximize positive spillovers and minimize negative ones, since as we have said the spillovers affect the MPEA's revenues from its other customers. It's not as if the MPEA owned a theater at which any member of the public was welcome who could pay the admission price, as in the Southeastern Promotions case. Selectivity and restriction are of the essence of the commercial strategy that informs the MPEA's management of the pier. *Cf. Lehman v. City of Shaker Heights*, 418 U.S. 298, 303-04, 94 S.Ct. 2714, 41 L.Ed.2d 770 (1974). These features mark it as a nonpublic facility within the meaning of the First Amendment precedents. *See, e.g., Arkansas Educational Television Comm'n v. Forbes, supra*, 118 S.Ct. at 1642; *Cornelius v. NAACP Legal Defense & Educational Fund*, 473 U.S. 788, 799-806, 105 S.Ct. 3439, 87 L.Ed.2d 567 (1985).

The MPEA could, therefore, as the *Lehman* and *Cornelius* cases make clear, adopt a blanket rule barring the use of its meeting rooms for political events, if it reasonably believed that such events, because of their controversiality, would drive customers from the pier and reduce the MPEA's revenues. Government is not required to subsidize the market in ideas and opinions by throwing open its nonpublic meeting facilities to politicians. And by the same token, if it does allow such facilities to be used for such events, it does not have to waive its normal fee just because a particular applicant can't afford the fee; that is, it does not have to subsidize marginal or unpopular political causes. The recent *Forbes* case makes this clear (more on *Forbes* shortly), as do *Stonewall Union v. City of Columbus*, 931 F.2d 1130, 1137-38 (6th Cir.1991), and the cases which hold that government is not required to exempt expressive activities from general taxes, *e.g.*, *Leathers v. Medlock*, 499 U.S. 439, 447-48, 111 S.Ct. 1438, 113 L.Ed.2d 494 (1991); *Regan v. Taxation with Representation of Washington*, 461 U.S. 540, 545-46, 103 S.Ct. 1997, 76 L.Ed.2d 129 (1983); *Cammarano v. United States*, 358 U.S. 498, 513, 79 S.Ct. 524, 3 L.Ed.2d 462 (1959), and nondiscriminatory fees. *Cox v. New Hampshire*, 312 U.S. 569, 577, 61 S.Ct. 762, 85 L.Ed. 1049 (1941); *Northeast Ohio Coalition for the Homeless v. City of Cleveland*, 105 F.3d 1107, 1109-10 (6th Cir.1997); *National Awareness Foundation v. Abrams*, 50 F.3d 1159, 1165 (2d Cir.1995). What the MPEA may not do is to employ political criteria to decide who may use its facilities and on what terms, even if they are not public forums in even the most limited sense. *Cornelius v. NAACP Legal Defense & Educational Fund*, supra, 473 U.S. at 806, 105 S.Ct. 3439; *Grossbaum v. Indianapolis-Marion County Building Authority*, 63 F.3d 581, 587 (7th Cir.1995); *cf. Police Department v. Mosley*, 408 U.S. 92, 95-96, 92 S.Ct. 2286, 33 L.Ed.2d 212 (1972).

It is only a small step to the conclusion that the MPEA may not discriminate in the terms of access to these facilities in favor of established parties and popular politicians on the ground that, being established, being popular, they generate favorable publicity. Such a policy would be a form of the heckler's veto; it would be the equivalent of charging a higher permit fee for a march or other demonstration by an unpopular group on the ground that the onlookers are likely to be hostile, thus necessitating increased security; and that is forbidden. *Forsyth County v. Nationalist Movement*, 505 U.S. 123, 133-35, 112 S.Ct. 2395, 120 L.Ed.2d 101 (1992), and cases cited there. The motive is innocent, but the discriminatory effect too great to be permitted. Although the principle barring discrimination in favor of popular politicians may make it more difficult for the MPEA to maximize its profits from the management of Navy Pier (which is why its motive may indeed be innocently commercial rather than invidiously political), nowhere is it written that government, when it embarks on essentially commercial ventures, is entitled to the same freedom of action as private venturers. It is not as if the ownership of shopping malls and convention centers were at the core of the American concept of government.

At argument the MPEA pressed on us the Supreme Court's recent decision in *Arkansas Educational Television Commission v. Forbes*, supra, which holds that a publicly owned television station may use "editorial discretion" to exclude an independent candidate who has little public support from a debate among the candidates for a public office. *Forbes* might be read to endorse the same form of heckler's veto to which the MPEA is appealing in this case. But to read *Forbes* so broadly would be to place it on a collision course with *Forsyth*, which *Forbes* did not even cite and we doubt meant to overrule. A debate cannot be staged without deciding who may participate in it, and given the inescapable need to choose, the criterion of choice that the television station used was as good as any. Speech values were on both sides of the equation in Forbes. If, to avoid restricting speech, the station invited all the candidates to participate in the debate, the time available to the frontrunners would be curtailed, yet what frontrunners have to say is probably more valuable to the audience than what the fringe candidates have to say—probably, not certainly. Major parties can originate as fringe parties, and fringe parties can contribute ideas that are later picked up by major parties. Still, restricting the speech opportunity of the fringe candidates may increase the speech benefits of the debate overall. No such necessity of making tradeoffs faced the MPEA when asked to waive fees for the plaintiffs, having done so for the Democrats. It's not as if the plaintiffs had wanted to crash the Democrats' party, in the way that Forbes wanted to crash the debate of the frontrunners.

Forbes may, however, rest on a broader ground. Whenever the government is in the business of speech, whether it is producing television programs or operating a museum or making grants or running schools, the exercise of editorial judgment is inescapable. If there is any political or ideological resonance to the expressive activity involved, the good-faith exercise of that judgment may have unavoidable political or ideological consequences; and so (because they are unavoidable) these consequences do not condemn the judgment. *See, e.g., National Endowment for the Arts v. Finley*, ___ U.S. ____, 118 S.Ct. 2168, 2177-80, 141 L.Ed.2d 500 (1998). A publicly owned art gallery, which has to decide which pictures to hang where, is not constitutionally debarred from placing the most offensive pictures in the least conspicuous exhibition area. *Piarowski v. Illinois Community College Dist.* 515, *supra*, 759 F.2d at 630-31. But Navy Pier is not a producer of speech; it is a renter of premises to speakers. It need not make any editorial judgments about the content of the speech in its meeting rooms, any more than the telecommunications carriers that transmitted the television debate in the Forbes case to viewers' homes had to exercise an editorial judgment about the debate.

What we have said so far shows that the district judge was right to require the MPEA to formulate criteria for the renting out of the Grand Ballroom and other meeting facilities that will prevent the direct or indirect use of politics to determine whether to waive the normal fees. If the MPEA waives fees for one political group, it must waive fees for other political groups, without favoritism.

We must next decide whether the district judge was also right to classify the sidewalks, the plaza, and Crystal Gardens as traditional public forums. *Capitol Square Review & Advisory Board v. Pinette*, 515 U.S. 753, 761, 115 S.Ct. 2440, 132 L.Ed.2d 650 (1995); *Perry Education Ass'n v. Perry Local Educators' Ass'n, supra*, 460 U.S. at 45, 103 S.Ct. 948; *Grossbaum v. Indianapolis-Marion County Building Authority*, 100 F.3d 1287, 1296-97 (7th Cir.1996). Clearly these are not designated public forums. The MPEA has not thrown them open for assembly, debate, demonstrations, or other forms of mass expressive activity. They are not traditional public forums either. The sidewalks are not through routes; they lead only to the pier facilities themselves. The plaintiffs' lawyer told us at argument that the sidewalks contain bike lanes that are part of a bike path that runs along the Chicago lakefront from far to the south of the pier to far to the north of it. This is not accurate. There are no bike lanes on the pier, though some bicycling is permitted; the lakefront bike path crosses the base of the pier rather than running into it. Rather than being part of the city's automotive, pedestrian, or bicyclists' transportation grid, the sidewalks on the pier and the service street on its north side are internal to the pier, like the sidewalks, streets, and parking lots in Disney World or McCormick Place (Chicago's major convention center, also owned by the MPEA). *Cf. United States v. Kokinda*, 497 U.S. 720, 727, 110 S.Ct. 3115, 111 L.Ed.2d 571 (1990) (plurality opinion). The pier itself is a discrete, outlying segment or projection of Chicago rather than a right of way. It is its own little world of delights and in this respect it is something like a major airport, which the Supreme Court in *International Society for Krishna Consciousness, Inc. v. Lee (ISKCON)*, 505 U.S. 672, 112 S.Ct. 2701, 120 L.Ed.2d 541 (1992), refused to classify as a public forum. A major airport is both a transportation facility and a shopping mall; Navy Pier is an amusement park and a meeting and entertainment center. Whatever one calls such a complex—there doesn't seem to be a compendious term for it— neither it nor the concourses within it are a public forum as the cases use the term. Navy Pier's being classified as a public forum is also not indispensable to the health of the market in ideas and opinions; there are plenty of other areas in Chicago for demonstrations in support of a higher minimum wage or other political objectives.

Yet while holding that the airport was not a traditional public forum, the Court also held that the Krishnas were entitled to hand out leaflets in the public areas of the airport. *See International Society for Krishna Consciousness, Inc. v. Lee, supra*, 505 U.S. at 689-93, 112 S.Ct. 2701 (O'Connor, J., concurring); *Lee v. International Society for Krishna Consciousness, Inc.*, 505 U.S. 830, 112 S.Ct. 2709, 120 L.Ed.2d 669 (1992) (per curiam). Actually, this was only Justice O'Connor's view; but it is the lowest common denominator of the Court's fractured decisions invalidating the airport authority's ban on leafletting while upholding its ban on soliciting and is therefore the holding that binds us. The holding is decisive in favor of so much of the district judge's order as commands the MPEA to rescind its ban against leafletting on the sidewalks and in the other open areas. But it is equally decisive against any suggestion that the plaintiffs have a right to picket, stage marches, hold demonstrations, wave posters, shout through bullhorns or public-address systems, solicit passersby for money or signatures, or harangue them from soapboxes, as they could do (subject of course to reasonable restrictions) on Michigan Avenue, on the plaza outside the Daley Center, on the sidewalks outside the federal courthouse on Dearborn Avenue, or at the other familiar Chicago sites for political expression. Because the MPEA owns the buildings on Navy Pier and depends for the upkeep of the pier on the commercial revenues that those buildings generate, it has a legitimate and substantial interest in preventing activities that could kill those revenues. It has a greater interest than the City of Chicago itself has in the prosperity of the shops along State Street. Even that interest is not negligible, because the amount of tax that the

City can extract from merchants and their customers depends on the merchants' revenues. But it is a lesser interest than the MPEA's corresponding interest in the commercial health of Navy Pier and therefore it does not justify equivalent restrictions on political expression. This may be why State Street is a traditional public forum and Navy Pier is not.

Not only are the costs of intrusive, noisy, or menacing demonstrations greater on Navy Pier than on State Street, but the benefits in dissemination of ideas and opinions are less because of the geography of the pier. It is rather out of the way, and is so configured that everyone entering it either on foot or by car must enter through a narrow bottleneck, appropriately named Gateway Park, which the MPEA also controls and which it concedes is a traditional public forum. By demonstrating in Gateway Park, persons wishing to exercise their First Amendment right of expression can communicate with every single person who enters Navy Pier. *Cf. International Society for Krishna Consciousness, Inc. v. Lee, supra*, 505 U.S. at 684-85, 112 S.Ct. 2701 (O'Connor, J., concurring). The plaintiffs complain that the MPEA has confined expressive activities in Gateway Park to a tiny, almost invisible corner; if so, this may be an independent violation of the First Amendment, but that issue is not before us.

We do not quite know, and need not at this stage of the litigation decide, just how broadly or narrowly the right of leafletting carved in ISKCON should be interpreted in the setting of Navy Pier. What is particularly interesting about Justice O'Connor's swing opinion is that it blurs the line between the public and nonpublic forum, suggesting a sliding- scale approach—a standard versus a rule or categories—in which the benefits and costs of free speech are balanced in particular settings. *See also Heffron v. International Society for Krishna Consciousness, Inc.*, 452 U.S. 640, 650-51, 101 S.Ct. 2559, 69 L.Ed.2d 298 (1981). Between marches, bullhorns, soliciting, and the like, on the one hand, and leafletting on the other may be forms of advocacy that would not interfere with the commercial objectives of the MPEA. The plaintiffs are perfectly free to wear T-shirts, hats, and other articles of clothing on which they display slogans or symbols, provided the slogans are not obscene. If the plaintiffs wanted to hand out T- shirts that display their message, *cf. Ayres v. City of Chicago*, 125 F.3d 1010 (7th Cir.1997), this wouldn't be any more disruptive than handing out leaflets, and indeed the T-shirt could be considered a leaflet in another medium-cloth rather than paper. But as we are vacating the part of the injunction relating to the open areas of the pier because they are not traditional public forums, it would be premature for us to try to decide exactly what restrictions the MPEA can be permitted to impose on the use of them for political expression.

We come last to the plaintiffs' cross-appeal, which attacks the district judge's ruling that the indoor mall areas of Navy Pier are nonpublic forums so that the MPEA is free to exclude all expressive activity from them. If, to repeat an earlier point, these were private shopping malls, the owner could impose such a ban; and this would be equally true of O'Hare Airport if it were privately owned. But as Navy Pier is publicly owned, it seems to us to come within the rule of the *ISKCON* case, and leafletting must be allowed, just as the First Circuit held, in reliance on *ISKCON*, with reference to the Boston subway in *Jews for Jesus, Inc. v. Massachusetts Bay Transportation Authority*, 984 F.2d 1319, 1324-25 (1st Cir.1993). There is no relevant difference between the sidewalks on Navy Pier and the public areas of the indoor shopping malls. Both types of pathway are pedestrian walkways leading mainly to shops. The fact that one type has a roof over it and the other does not cannot make as large a difference as the district judge (who, remember, classified the sidewalks as a traditional public forum and the interior walkways as a totally nonpublic forum) thought. What is true is that some of the interior walkways are rather narrow, compared to Dock Street. The plaintiffs should not be permitted to hand out leaflets in places where pedestrian traffic will be obstructed.

To summarize, although we agree with the district judge that the MPEA has violated the First Amendment rights of these plaintiffs and should be enjoined, we think that the injunction that she entered must be vacated. It is at once too broad in treating the open areas, the amusement park, and the meeting rooms as public forums, and too narrow in denying ISKCON status to the interior walkways. But it is correct in requiring that fee waivers for the meeting rooms not be granted on discriminatory terms, though this is not because, as the district judge believed, the rooms are public forums; they are not; but government may not discriminate on political grounds in the terms of access to the nonpublic forums that it owns. The case must be remanded for the drafting and entry of a new injunction in conformity with the analysis in this opinion.

We are guardedly optimistic that on remand the parties will be able to agree on an appropriate injunction, for we sensed by the close of the oral argument that they are not as far apart as their briefs had suggested. We doubt that the plaintiffs want to destroy the amenities or impair the commercial viability of Navy Pier. What good would it do them? It would accelerate what is now a nationwide trend toward the privatization of public property. If the First Amendment handcuffs the effective exploitation of commercially valuable public property, the government will have an incentive to sell it to a private company, which will not be cabined by the First Amendment. We doubt that a private owner of Navy Pier would allow the plaintiffs even the limited rights of expression that we hold the Constitution entitles them to engage in there.

We wish in closing to commend the counsel for both parties for their excellent briefs and oral arguments.

VACATED AND REMANDED WITH INSTRUCTIONS.

UNITED STATES v. MULHEREN

90-1691
To be Argued by Andrew L. Frey

IN THE
UNITED STATES COURT OF APPEALS
FOR THE SECOND CIRCUIT

UNITED STATES OF AMERICA,
Appellee,

v.

JOHN A. MULHEREN, JR.,
Appellant.
———

**On Appeal from a Judgment of the United States
District Court for the Southern District of New York**

———

BRIEF OF APPELLANT

———

ANDREW L. FREY
WENDY E. ACKERMAN
MAYER, BROWN & PLATT
2000 PENNSYLVANIA AVENUE, N.W.
WASHINGTON, DC 20006
(202) 778-0602

THOMAS P. PUCCIO
MILBANK, TWEED, HADLEY & MCCLOY
ONE CHASE MANHATTAN PLAZA
NEW YORK, NY 10005
(212) 530-5000
Counsel for Appellant

TABLE OF CONTENTS

IN THE

United States Court of Appeals

FOR THE SECOND CIRCUIT

———

No. 90-1691

———

UNITED STATES OF AMERICA

Appellee,

v.

JOHN A. MULHEREN, JR.,

Appellant.

On Appeal from a Judgment of the United States District Court for the Southern District of New York

———

BRIEF OF APPELLANT

———

PRELIMINARY STATEMENT

John A. Mulheren appeals from his convictions in the United States District Court for the Southern District of New York (Judge Cedarbaum). Mulheren was convicted on three counts, growing out of a single incident, of manipulating the stock of Gulf & Western Industries Inc., in violation of Section 10(b) of the Securities Exchange Act, 15 U.S.C. § 78j (b) and Rule 10b-5, 17 C.F.R. § 240.10b-5, and one count of conspiring to engage in such manipulation, in violation of 18 U.S.C. § 371.

ISSUES PRESENTED FOR APPEAL

1.   Whether the evidence was sufficient to establish beyond a reasonable doubt that Mulheren purchased Gulf & Western stock for the purpose of inflating its price.

2.   Whether the government satisfied, and whether the jury was properly instructed on, the elements of securities fraud under Section 10(b) and Rule 10b-5, specifically, (a) a misrepresentation or breach of a duty of disclosure; (b) materiality; and (c) scienter.

3.   Whether evidence that Mulheren had refused on other occasions to engage in similar acts of securities fraud should have been admitted on the issue of his intent under Fed. R. Evid. 404 (b).

4.   Whether expert testimony on the symptoms of manic depression and the bearing of that illness on Mulheren's demeanor and credibility should have been admitted under Fed. R. Evid. 702.

5.   Whether the fine was based on an erroneous calculation of loss under the alternative fine statute, 18 U.S.C. § 3571(d).

STATEMENT OF THE CASE

On June 14, 1989, John Mulheren was charged in a 42-count indictment alleging securities and mail fraud. Only the first four counts are involved in this appeal. Count One charged that Mulheren conspired with Ivan Boesky and others to commit the substantive offenses charged in the indictment. Counts Two through Four charged Mulheren with violating Section 10(b) of the Securities Exchange Act and Rule 10b-5 by "manipulating" the market for Gulf & Western common stock. The alleged manipulation consisted of causing Jamie Securities Co.-an investment firm of which Mulheren was a general partner and for which he acted as chief trader-to purchase 75,000 shares of Gulf & Western stock on the floor of the New York Stock Exchange on October 17, 1985 in order to increase its price.[1]

Accepting the government's evidence as true, it showed the following. In September 1985, Ivan Boesky and Carl Icahn each held slightly less than 5% of the stock of Gulf & Western. J.A. 117-118. On September 5, 1985, and again on October 1, 1985, Boesky and Icahn met with Martin Davis, chief executive officer of Gulf & Western. J.A. 49-51, 119. At these meetings, Boesky expressed interest in acquiring the company, but his proposals were rejected. J.A. 49-52, 117, 119-120. Boesky then decided to sell his shares back to Gulf & Western at $45 per share and directed a representative to attempt to sell the stock for that price. J.A. 53-54. That representative then met with Davis and conveyed to him Boesky's offer to sell at $45 per share. J.A. 54-55. Thereafter, late in the day on October 16, 1985, Boesky again told Davis that he would be willing to sell his stock back to the company at $45 per share. J.A. 55- 56, 130-131. (The stock had traded at $45 earlier that day. J.A. 370 (NYSE Daily Stock Price Record)). Davis responded that he would be willing to buy back Boesky's shares the next day but would not pay more than the price at which they traded on the New York Stock Exchange at the time. J.A. 55-56, 131-132.

Either late on October 16 or early on October 17, Boesky and Mulheren spoke with each other on the telephone. J.A. 56. As he had on previous occasions (see J.A. 44-45), Mulheren asked Boesky if he liked Gulf & Western on that particular day, and Boesky said yes, he "still liked it" (J.A. 57). According to Boesky, he told Mulheren that he

---

[1]   The remaining counts charged fraud and record-keeping violations relating to stock "parking" allegedly performed by Mulheren as an accommodation to Ivan Boesky between July 2 and November 1, 1985. Counts 29 through 39 were dismissed at the close of the government's case, and Count 41 was dismissed before trial. The jury hung and mistrial was declared as to the rest of the Counts.

"would not pay more than 45 for it and it would be great if it traded at 45." Mulheren replied that he "understood." *Ibid*.[2]

On the morning of October 17, acting pursuant to Boesky's recommendation, Mulheren caused Jamie Securities to place an order for 50,000 shares of Gulf & Western stock with a floor broker, Oliver Ihasz, at the market price. J.A. 74. At 11:04 a.m., in response to Jamie's order, Ihasz bought 16,100 shares at $44.75 (Count II); from 11:05 to 11:08 a.m., Ihasz bought an additional 33,900 shares at $44.875 (Count III). J.A. 75-82, 92-93. Mulheren then placed an order for 25,000 shares at no more than $45, which Ihasz executed at 11:10 a.m. at that price (Count IV). J.A. 82-88, 94. At 11:16 a.m., Icahn and Boesky sold their positions in Gulf & Western stock back to the company. J.A. 128. *There is no evidence that Mulheren knew this was going to occur.* In fact, Boesky testified unequivocally that he never told Mulheren of his dealings with Gulf & Western or its willingness to pay $45 for his stock if the market price reached that level on October 17, 1985. J.A. 58-59.

On June 30, 1990, following six weeks of trial, most of which was focused on the "parking" charges, the case was sent to the jury. On July 10, 1990, after six days of deliberations, the jury returned, and the court accepted, a partial verdict finding Mulheren guilty of stock manipulation under Section 10(b) and Rule 10b-5 (Counts Two through Four) and of conspiracy to commit such manipulation (Count One).[3] On July 12, concluding that the jury was irrevocably deadlocked, the court declared a mistrial on the remaining counts.

On November 14, 1990, the district court denied Mulheren's motion for judgment of acquittal or, in the alternative, a new trial. J.A. 343-344. On that same day, it sentenced Mulheren to concurrent terms of imprisonment for one year and one day on each count and to a fine of $1,681,700. J.A. 345-346.

INTRODUCTION AND SUMMARY OF ARGUMENT

This case revolves around the desire of Ivan Boesky to sell several million shares of Gulf & Western stock back to the company at a price of $45 per share in October of 1985. On October 16, 1985, Boesky was told by Gulf & Western's chief executive officer, Martin Davis, that the company would be willing to purchase his shares at that price but only if that was the market price at the time of the sale. At the close of trading on October 16, the price of Gulf & Western stock was $44.75, although it had traded at $45 earlier in the day. Presumably in order to cause an increase in the publicly-traded price—and therefore to be able to consummate the sale to Gulf & Western—Boesky induced Mulheren to purchase Gulf & Western on the market at a price of up to $45. It

---

[2] Mulheren testified that what he "understood" by this conversation was that Boesky reputed at the time to be a brilliant arbitrageur—recommended Gulf & Western as a good investment up to the price of $45. J.A. 188-189.

[3] By special verdict, the jury indicated that the sole conspiracy object on which it could agree was the manipulation.

was disputed at trial whether Mulheren was aware of the existence or extent of Boesky's ownership of Gulf & Western stock, but there was no suggestion that Mulheren was apprised of Boesky's intention to sell his stock or of the terms on which Gulf & Western was willing to buy it.

On the morning of October 17, Mulheren placed orders to buy 75,000 shares of Gulf & Western, causing its price to rise to $45 per share. At that point, unbeknownst to Mulheren, Boesky and Carl Icahn, who also owned a large block of Gulf & Western stock, sold their shares to Gulf & Western at the $45 price. Because Boesky and Icahn had acquired the stock at a far lower price, they made many millions of dollars in profit on their Gulf & Western holdings. Gulf & Western too fared well from this transaction, as the price of the stock, after dropping initially in response to the Boesky/Icahn transaction, rose steadily in the ensuing months and years. See Dow Jones Historical Stock Quote Reporter Service (1985-1989) (Dow Jones News/Retrieval). Only Mulheren's firm lost; its Gulf & Western holdings declined in value by about $64,000 by the end of that day. J.A. 365. Ironically, only John Mulheren was criminally prosecuted for these events.

At the end of the day, this prosecution is based on a shaky factual foundation and on an effort to extend the scope of the prohibition on securities fraud to conduct far removed from that which has underlain previous manipulation cases. But the government's reach far exceeds its grasp.

I

Note how the facts highly favorable to the client's position are incorporated here.

It is essential to the government's case, under any legal theory, that Mulheren acted for the deliberate purpose of inflating the price of Gulf & Western stock and did not possess any bona fide investment purpose. The only evidence the government can point to in support of such a conclusion is a few cryptic fragments of a brief conversation between Boesky and Mulheren. We respectfully submit that, far from excluding an investment motive, this conversation is most naturally understood to embody an investment recommendation by Boesky, who said in response to Mulheren's inquiry that he "still liked" the stock but "would not pay more than 45 for it." Only rank speculation can transform Boesky's further statement that "it would be great if it traded at 45" and Mulheren's reply that "I understand" into an agreement to pump up the price of the stock, rather than a confirmation of the price at which Gulf & Western would be a "great" buy (arbitrageurs like Boesky and Mulheren were presumably not interested in making trades that were unlikely to be "great").

It is difficult to escape the conclusion that Mulheren was simply duped by an investment recommendation into acting in a way that (unbeknownst to him) advanced Boesky's interests. Certainly, the government never showed why Mulheren would willingly make himself a sitting duck by buying 75,000 shares of stock that he knew were about to decline significantly in market value. Although this Court must view the record in the light most favorable to the government, where, as here, a jury's verdict is based on nothing more than pure speculation and conjecture, this Court has a duty to overturn the defendant's convictions.

II

The government never put forth a coherent explanation of its theory of securities fraud in this case. As the case went to the jury, the theory of the prosecution was that Mulheren committed a fraud on the "market" if he did nothing more than purchase Gulf & Western stock for the purpose of raising its price. But the proof did not show, and the jury was erroneously instructed with respect to, the essential elements of Section 10(b) and Rule 10b-5, specifically, (A) a misrepresentation or a breach of a duty to disclose; (B) materiality; and (C) a purpose to deceive others.

A.   It is untenable to hold, as the district court instructed the jury, that the mere act of purchasing a stock carries with it an implied representation that the buyer believes he is paying a price reflecting the operation of "legitimate market forces" (J.A. 323). The only statement a buyer makes to the market is that he wishes to purchase a particular stock and is willing to pay a particular price for it.

In this section, the client's position is bolstered by the use of effective phraseology. It is states that a "coherent explanation" of the government's position was never offered. The lower court's reasoning is characterized as "untenable," and the term "rank speculation" is applied to allegations that the client's actions impacted on trading decisions. In fact, in the concluding paragraph of its opinion, the court states that "the jury must have engaged . . . in rank speculation."

The only even arguable theory, therefore, is that Mulheren breached a duty of disclosure by not revealing his motives for purchasing the stock. But the Supreme Court has made it quite clear that the mere fact of participation in a securities transaction does not give rise to such a duty—reversing this Court on precisely that point in *Chiarella v. United States*, 445 U.S. 222, 228-229 (1980). Rather, there must be an insider or fiduciary relationship to trigger a disclosure duty. Moreover, any obligation of disclosure would not extend to Mulheren's subjective motivations for making a stock purchase on the open market.

B.   By instructing the jury that "misstatements or omissions concerning the price of a security are material" (J.A. 324), the district court erroneously pretermitted jury determination of the issue of materiality. This would require reversal even if there were ample evidence of materiality. Here however, it is rank speculation to suppose that disclosure of Mulheren's alleged improper motives in making the purchases and causing a small movement in the stock price would have caused the average investor—or Gulf & Western—to alter any trading decisions.

C.   Finally, the government's theory effectively dispenses with any requirement that Mulheren be found to have acted with scienter. That requirement cannot be satisfied by showing merely that the defendant engaged in purchases or sales on the open market in order to affect price. In virtually every other manipulation case, the defendants were shown to have employed some or all of a broad range of deceptive artifices or strategems to create a substantially false impression of value, and to have done so for the purpose of deceiving investors to engage in purchases or sales of securities in reliance on the impression thus created. There is simply no basis in this case for inferring a similar motive for Mulheren's actions.

III

Reversal is also required because the district court erroneously excluded two important items of evidence offered by the defendant. First, the court excluded evidence that Mulheren had refused to engage in other acts of securities fraud. Such evidence should have been admitted under Fed. R. Evid. 404(b) because it tended to demonstrate Mulheren's lack of criminal intent to commit securities fraud under Section 10(b). Because the government's evidence of Mulheren's intent in this case was extremely weak, the exclusion of this evidence was highly prejudicial. The district court also erred in refusing to admit under Fed. R. Evid. 702 expert testimony on the bearing of the disease of manic depression on Mulheren's credibility and demeanor. Because such testimony would have been extremely helpful to the jury on the crucial question of Mulheren's credibility, its exclusion was highly prejudicial and requires reversal.

Finally, the $1,681,700 fine was not authorized by the alternative fine statute because it is based upon an erroneous calculation of Gulf & Western's loss. Mulheren's motive in buying the stock was material only if its disclosure would have caused Gulf & Western to refrain from purchasing the stock. But in that case Gulf & Western, which profited because the price of its stock subsequently increased, would have been *worse* off. It therefore suffered no loss from its reliance on Mulheren's supposed "misrepresentation." The fine calculation also rests on the erroneous assumption that, but for Mulheren's actions, Gulf & Western could have consummated the Boesky/Icahn transaction at $44.75. But the evidence before the district court suggested that Boesky was unwilling to sell below $45. It was therefore error to measure Gulf & Western's loss by the difference between $44.75 and $45.

ARGUMENT

I.   THE GOVERNMENT FAILED TO PROVE THAT MULHEREN PURCHASED GULF & WESTERN STOCK FOR THE PURPOSE OF RAISING ITS PRICE AND NOT AS AN INVESTMENT

This section is an example of effectively leading with one's strongest argument. In its opinion, the court ruled in favor of Mulheren entirely on the basis of the arguments presented in this part of the brief.

It is essential to the government's case that Mulheren's motive in purchasing the stock was merely to inflate its price and that he was not making a bona fide investment. As we now show, there is no proof—much less proof beyond a reasonable doubt—to establish that crucial fact.

The thread by which the government's case hangs is the following testimony by Ivan Boesky:

Q.   [BY MR. GILBERT] Subsequent to your conversation with Martin Davis, did you have any discussion with John Mulheren concerning Gulf & Western?

A.   Yes.

Q.   Was that in person or by telephone?

A.   By telephone.

* * * *

Q.   To the best of your recollection, Mr. Boesky, when did this conversation occur?

A.   It was either on the 16 or the 17 of October.

Q.   And in that conversation, Mr. Boesky, would you tell us what you said to John Mulheren and what Mr. Mulheren said to you.

A.   Mr. Mulheren asked me if I liked the stock on that particular day, and I said yes, I still liked it. At that time it was trading at 44 3/4. I said I liked; however, I would not pay more than 45 for it and it would be great if it traded at 45. The design of the comment—

MR. PUCCIO: Objection to the "design of the comment." I would ask only for the conversation.

Q.   What if anything did he say to you?

A.   I understand.

Q.   Is there anything else that you recall that was said in that conversation?

A.   Nothing else.

J.A. 56-57.

On cross-examination, Boesky added that Mulheren was not present at any of the meetings Boesky had with Martin Davis of Gulf & Western, that those meetings were "very confidential," and that Boesky did not impart to Mulheren the subject or content of the meetings and telephone conversations relating to the proposed sale of Boesky's stock to Gulf & Western. J.A. 58-59.

Beyond this one conversation, the government showed only that Mulheren purchased 75,000 shares of Gulf & Western common stock on the floor of the New York Stock Exchange between 11:04 and 11:10 a.m. on October 17, 1985. *See* J.A. 60-109.

The government's evidence is woefully inadequate to establish that Mulheren purchased the Gulf & Western stock for the purpose of raising its price. To begin with, Mulheren had no knowledge of the discussions regarding Gulf & Western's possible purchase of Boesky's stock, or of its unwillingness to pay more than the market price, as Boesky explicitly acknowledged on cross-examination. J.A. 59.[4] Moreover, the conversation itself afforded no basis for finding that Mulheren knew that Boesky wanted him to raise the price of Gulf & Western stock. The government's support for such a conclusion boils down to two fragments taken out of context: Boesky's comment that "it would be great if it traded at 45" and Mulheren's answer that "I understand." To infer from these two fragments that Mulheren's subsequent purchases were motivated by a desire to increase the price of Gulf & Western stock is pure conjecture.

According to Boesky's own testimony, the Gulf & Western conversation was initiated by Mulheren—not Boesky—and it was Mulheren who asked whether Boesky "liked the stock on that particular day." J.A. 57.[5] The most natural understanding of Boesky's answer to this question—that he "liked it; however, I would not pay more than 45 for it and it would be great if it traded at 45" (*ibid.*)—is that he recommend the stock for investment up to a price of $45 and that it would be a "great" buy up to that point. Indeed, from Mulheren's perspective (not knowing of the prior dealings between Boesky and Gulf & Western regarding a sale at the $45 price), Boesky's statement that he "wouldn't pay higher than $45" was quite inconsistent with a desire to jack up the price.[6] Thus, one cannot reasonably infer from the mere fact that Boesky said the stock "would be great" up to a price of $45 and that Mulheren said he "understood" that Mulheren knew that Boesky wanted him to raise the price of Gulf & Western stock.[7]

What is more, the evidence affirmatively demonstrates that Mulheren did act for investment purposes in purchasing the Gulf & Western stock. As testified by the floor broker, Oliver Ihasz, Mulheren's first order was for 50,000 shares at the market. J.A. 74. His second order, made after the price had risen from $44.75 to $44.875, was for 25,000 shares at a limit price of $45. J.A. 83. This is wholly consistent with the actions to be expected from a large-scale trader such as Mulheren who believed that Gulf & Western represented a good value at $45 per share or less. On the other hand, if Mulheren's sole

---

[4]   Even if Mulheren knew or suspected that Boesky had a substantial position in Gulf & Western stock, that fact would not support a reliable inference that he bought the stock for the purpose of increasing its price, as opposed to investment. To the contrary, if Boesky—reputed to be a brilliant arbitrageur—had a personal stake in the stock and "still liked it," that would be all the more reason for Mulheren to invest in it. At most, any suspicion that Boesky had substantial holdings in Gulf & Western would support an inference that Mulheren had reason to believe that his purchases might inure to Boesky's benefit. That, however, is a far cry from proof that Mulheren's *purpose* in buying the stock was to help Boesky out.

[5]   Such a request was not unusual. Mulheren had on several previous occasions asked Boesky what he thought of Gulf & Western stock. *See* J.A. 44-45.

[6]   By contrast, the fact that Mulheren imposed a limit price of $45 on his purchases in no way demonstrates that his purpose was not investment-related. That price made sense because it was the price recommended by Boesky and because, as Mulheren testified, it was a strike price of Gulf & Western options. See J.A. 193 ("I think I told him at one point that the stock was, you know, up a lot the day before and I didn't think I would pay higher than 45. I would look to 45 for one reason, that's the strike price of the option, and he said, 'I wouldn't pay higher than 45 either,' something like that.").

[7]   The government has never suggested that Boesky's conversation with Mulheren was in some sort of code, in which the words used did not have their usual meaning.

purpose in buying the stock was to increase its price to $45, there was no reason to place the last order for a quantity as large as 25,000 shares. As the Gulf & Western specialist testified, Mulheren would have needed to purchase only a "couple of thousand shares" to have increased the price from $44.875 to $45. J.A. 165.[8]

Accordingly, there is no basis for concluding that Mulheren purchased the Gulf & Western stock for any reason other than that Boesky—a noted securities expert—had recommended it as a good value up to $45 a share. Even after indulging every reasonable inference in favor of the verdict, we respectfully submit that no rational jury could have rejected the possibility—indeed, likelihood—that Mulheren was simply used as an innocent pawn in Boesky's scheme to sell his stock at $45. By recommending the stock up to the price of $45 to an individual who in the past had relied on his advice, Boesky obtained what he wanted from Mulheren without having to implicate Mulheren in questionable activities. Indeed, no reason readily suggests itself why Boesky would have wanted to let Mulheren in on his scheme if that was not necessary to get him to buy the stock.

Not only did the government fail to demonstrate that Mulheren lacked an investment purpose in buying the Gulf & Western stock, but it could show none of the traditional surreptitious devices courts look for as signs of market manipulation. Mulheren did not seek to unload artificially inflated securities on an unwary public, dominate the market, control the supply of the stock, purchase through nominees, engage in "wash" sales or "matched" orders, spread misleading information to induce purchases by others, make fictional quotes, pay touts to recommend the stock, or engage in any of the myr-

---

[8]   In his testimony, Mulheren recounted the critical conversation much as Boesky had described it. Mulheren fleshed the subject out by relating his understanding of the exchange and his reasons for acting as he did. He testified that he purchased the Gulf & Western stock for investment purposes, explaining that he bought the 75,000 shares because he "had a real smart guy telling me not to be short the stock, be[ ] long in it." J.A. 188-189. Mulheren further testified that he had no idea that Boesky was planning to sell stock back to Gulf & Western, and that when he learned about the sale he felt "taken." J.A. 193-194. "[I]f somebody is going to be talking to you on a basis that they are your friend and giving you ideas, and we are doing all this, and he's using you to mark a stock so he can put a print on [it], you feel pretty pissed off when that happens. He ought to give you the choice whether you want to be involved with something like that." J.A. 194-195.

Mulheren's co-defendant on the parking charges, Leonard DeStefano, who was employed by Jamie Securities as an options trader and clerk and who was acquitted by the jury, would have told a similar account at trial but for his invocation of his Fifth Amendment privilege not to testify. According to DeStefano, "[a] few minutes after John told me to execute the trades, the Jamie Securities' trading room watched a 6,702,600 share trade in Gulf & Western go across the tape. Right after the trade went across the tape, John Mulheren exclaimed in the trading room to the effect, 'Boesky screwed us.' He immediately told me to enter more orders to sell Gulf & Western call options to protect against the negative effect the 6,702,600 trade was about to have on our [investment]." J.A. 430 (Affidavit of Leonard DeStefano ¶ 4 (Nov. 9, 1990) (submitted in support of Mulheren's Motion for a New Trial)).

iad other deceptive activities identified in cases where unlawful manipulation has been found.[9]

Here, by contrast, there is no evidence that Mulheren sought to deceive the market for Gulf & Western stock. To the contrary, he merely undertook open purchases of securities on a national securities exchange. It is perfectly lawful to purchase large blocks of stock on the open market, even though the predictable effect is to drive up the stock's price. *See Chris-Craft Indus., Inc. v. Piper Aircraft Corp.*, 480 F.2d 341, 383 (2d Cir.), *cert. denied,* 414 U.S. 910 (1973); *Ray v. Lehman Bros. Kuhn Loeb, Inc.*, 624 F. Supp. 16, 22 (N.D. Ga. 1984); *Trane Co. v. O'Connor Sec.*, 561 F. Supp. 301, 304-305 (S.D.N.Y.), *appeal dismissed as moot,* 718 F.2d 26 (2d Cir. 1983). This is true even when the purpose of the purchases is to extract greenmail (*see Pin v. Texaco, Inc.*, 793 F. 2d 1448, 1452 (5th Cir. 1986)) or to stimulate further market activity (*see Trane*, 561 F. Supp. at 306).

Significantly, the government never demonstrated by comparison to purchases on other days, or through testimony, that Mulheren's purchase of 75,000 shares constituted anything out of the ordinary. The amount constituted only a tiny fraction of the 70.2 million shares then issued and outstanding. J.A. 122. And the floor broker, Oliver Ihasz, testified that there was nothing unusual about his being asked to buy 75,000 shares of stock. J.A. 102. Nor was the price to which the stock rose unusual: it had traded at $45 the previous day and earlier in October and rose well above $45 in the months following the Gulf & Western transaction. *See* J.A. 370.

In determining whether sufficient evidence of manipulation exists, courts have relied heavily on whether the defendant stood to gain personally from his conduct. *Baum*

---

[9] Nearly all the cases that have found sufficient evidence of manipulation under Section 10(b) have involved some form of deceptive conduct aimed at misleading the public. *See, e.g., Crane Co. v. Westinghouse Air Brake Co.*, 419 F.2d 787, 792-798 (2d Cir. 1969) (in an attempt to block a takeover by a third party of a company with which it wished to merge, the defendant made massive purchases of the company's stock, driving the price above what it would have otherwise been, while simultaneously selling those securities at lower prices for a substantial loss in secret and unreported sales), *cert. denied,* 400 U.S. 822 (1970); *United States v. Scop*, 846 F.2d 135, 137 (defendants, seeking to promote public offering of new stock, engaged in matched orders through fictitious nominees), *modified on other grounds,* 856 F.2d 5 (2d Cir. 1988); *United States v. Gilbert*, 668 F.2d 94, 95 (2d Cir. 1981) (defendant "manipulated the price increase through an elaborate series of wash sales and matched orders" to make profits for himself and the accounts he controlled), *cert. denied,* 456 U.S. 946 (1982); *SEC v. Resch-Cassin & Co.*, 362 F. Supp. 964, 978 (S.D.N.Y. 1973) (defendants paid brokers to quote the security and manipulated the supply of the stock).

Deceptive conduct is also the hallmark of manipulation cases under Section 9(a)(2) of the Securities Exchange Act, 15 U.S.C. § 78i(a)(2). *See, eg., United States v. Projansky*, 465 F.2d 123 (2d Cir.) (promoters of stock paid brokers to recommend and to buy the stock for their customers), *cert. denied,* 409 U.S. 1006 (1972); *United States v. Stein*, 456 F.2d 844 (2d Cir.) (defendants offered brokers secret compensation to induce them to promote sales of the stock), *cert. denied,* 408 U.S. 922 (1972); *United States v. Minuse*, 114 F.2d 36, 38 (2d Cir. 1940) (market manipulated by use of dummy accounts, guaranteeing purchasers against loss, using wash and matched sales, making payments to brokers to advise customers to purchase the stock, and disseminating misleadingly bullish literature); *R.J. Koeppe & Co. v. SEC*, 95 F.2d 550, 552 (7th Cir. 1938) (company compensated an individual to "tout" the stock).

v. Phillips, Appel & Walden, Inc., 648 F. Supp. 1518, 1531 (S.D.N.Y. 1986) ("there is no evidence that either [defendant] stood to gain anything from artificially driving the price of [the company] down"), *aff'd,* 867 F.2d 776 (2d Cir.), *cert. denied,* 110 S.Ct 114 (1989); *Ray*, 624 F. Supp. at 22 (in finding insufficient proof to establish market manipulation, court stressed lack of evidence that the defendant "intended to profit from the alleged artificial price" of the stock).[10] Here, there is no evidence that Mulheren was rewarded in any way by Boesky for his help. To the contrary, the evidence indicated that Jamie Securities—of which Mulheren was general partner—suffered a loss of over $64,000 on October 17 on its Gulf & Western investment. *See* J.A. 365. The absence of proof of gain is particularly telling in this case, because it forces the government to depend on the theory that Mulheren willingly made himself a sitting duck by buying stock that he knew was not a good investment.

The missing manipulative purpose cannot be demonstrated merely by showing that Boesky and Mulheren had shared information in the past. There is nothing either uncommon or illegal about two arbitrageurs sharing their views on the valuation of particular stocks or disclosing their respective positions in various stocks. Indeed, Mulheren shared information with a number of other individuals in the business. J.A. 183. And there is no evidence that Mulheren received any information specifically in return for his purchase of the Gulf & Western stock. To infer that Mulheren acted unlawfully merely from the combination of the fact that it was natural in the course of Mulheren's business to exchange information with fellow traders like Boesky and the fact that he purchased Gulf & Western on Boesky's recommendation is to cross the line from sustainable inference to pure speculation.

In sum, even when the evidence is viewed in the light most favorable to the government, it was grossly insufficient for a rational jury to find beyond a reasonable doubt that Mulheren purchased Gulf & Western stock with the intent to increase its price, rather than for investment purposes. This Court should accordingly reverse Mulheren's convictions and order judgments of acquittal.

II. THE ELEMENTS OF SECURITIES FRAUD UNDER SECTION 10(B) WERE NOT ESTABLISHED IN THIS CASE

Even if the Court rejects the foregoing argument and finds the evidence sufficient to support the conclusion that Mulheren acted for the purpose of affecting the market price and not for bona fide investment reasons, the government's case still fails. The gov-

---

[10] *See* also *SEC v. Commonwealth Chem. Sec., Inc.*, 410 F. Supp. 1002, 1013 (S.D.N.Y. 1976) (in finding manipulation, court emphasized that "there can be no question that [the defendants] misused their dominant market position to manipulate trading and inflate the price of [the] securities artificially for their own gain"); *Resch-Cassin*, 362 F. Supp. at 977 (in finding manipulation, court stressed that defendants, distributors of the company's stock, "had an obvious incentive to artificially influence the market price of the security in order to facilitate its distribution or increase its profitability"); *United States v. Charnay*, 537 F.2d 341, 348 (9th Cir.) (defining fraud under Section 10(b) as the "manipulation of securities prices for personal gain"), *cert. denied,* 429 U.S. 1000 (1976).

ernment's theory at trial was that such activity violated Section 10(b) and Rule 10b-5 by defrauding general market participants. The only other theory that suggests itself is that Mulheren intended to defraud Gulf & Western in particular. The government, however, never asserted that theory below, presumably because of its view that the mere purchase of stock for the purpose of raising its price—without the intent to deceive anyone—violates Section 10(b) and Rule 10b-5.

As we show in the argument that follows, the government's case founders under any theory of what constitutes fraudulent manipulation because of the failure to satisfy any of the three essential elements of securities fraud under Section 10(b) and Rule 10b-5: (A) that the defendant made a misrepresentation or failed to disclose a fact that he was under a duty to disclose; (B) that the undisclosed fact was material to others in connection with their purchase or sale of a security; and (C) that the defendant acted in order to deceive such purchasers or sellers.

A.   Mulheren Neither Misrepresented Any Fact Nor Failed To Disclose Any Fact That He Was Under A Duty To Disclose In Connection With His Purchases Of Gulf & Western Stock

Section 10(b) prohibits "any manipulative or deceptive device or contrivance in contravention of [SEC rules]." As SEC Rule 10b-5 (17 C.F.R. § 240.10b-5) makes clear, devices are "manipulative or deceptive" under that provision only if they are part of a scheme to defraud others.[11] Thus, it is well settled that these provisions are not violated unless the defendant has engaged in some form of deception. *See Schreiber v. Burlington Northern, Inc.*, 472 U.S. 1, 7-8, 12 (1985); *Chiarella v. United States*, 445 U.S. 222, 225-235 (1980); *Affiliated Ute Citizens v. United States*, 406 U.S. 128, 154 (1972); *Maldonado v. Flynn*, 597 F.2d 789, 793 (2d Cir. 1979); *Panter v. Marshall Field & Co.*, 646 F.2d 271, 287 (7th Cir.), *cert. denied*, 454 U.S. 1092 (1981). Deception, in turn, requires that the defendant either misrepresented a material fact or failed to disclose a material fact that he was under a duty to disclose in connection with the purchase or sale of securities. *See Schreiber*, 472 U.S. at 7-8, 12; *Affiliated Ute Citizens*, 406 U.S. at 154.[12]

---

[11]   Specifically, Rule 10b-5 provides:

It shall be unlawful for any person, directly or indirectly, by the use of any means or instrumentality of interstate commerce, or of the mails or of any facility of any national securities exchange,

   (a) To employ any device, scheme, or artifice to defraud,
   (b) To make any untrue statement of a material fact or to omit to state a material fact necessary in order to make the statements made, in the light of the circumstances under which they were made, not misleading, or
   (c) To engage in any act, practice, or course of business which operates or would operate as a fraud or deceit upon any person, in connection with the purchase or sale of any security.

[12]   Accord, *Stephenson v. Paine Webber Jackson & Curtis, Inc.*, 839 F.2d 1095, 1098 (5th Cir.), *cert. denied*, 488 U.S. 926 (1988); *Pin v. Texaco, Inc.*, 793 F.2d at 1451-1452 & n.7; *Straub v. Vaisman & Co.*,

This misrepresentation or non-disclosure requirement applies to price manipulation with the same force as it does to other species of fraud. That is, a manipulation is not a violation of Rule 10b-5 unless it is effected by means of misrepresentations or culpable non-disclosures. The Supreme Court confirmed this view in *Schrieber*, 472 U.S. at 12-13, where it held that even if an activity affects the market price of a stock, it is not manipulation unless there is a misrepresentation or breach of a duty to disclose. *See ibid.* Although that case was decided under Section 14(e) of the Securities Exchange Act, the Court held that claims under both that provision and Section 10(b) require proof of a misrepresentation or violation of a duty of disclosure. The Court explained:

> [W]e have interpreted "manipulative" in [10b-5 cases] to require misrepresentation. . . . All three species of misconduct, *i.e.*, "fraudulent, deceptive, or manipulative," listed by Congress are directed at failures to disclose. The use of term "manipulative" provides emphasis and guidance to those who must determine which types of acts are reached by the statute; it does not suggest a deviation from the section's facial and primary concern with disclosure or congressional concern with disclosure which is the core of the Act.

Schreiber, 472 U.S. at 7-8 (footnote omitted).

Applying these principles to the facts of this case, it is clear that Mulheren's convictions must be reversed because he neither made any misrepresentation nor failed to disclose any material fact that he was under a duty to disclose in connection with a sale or purchase of securities. Moreover, the jury was wrongly instructed on this point. Over defense objection (*see* J.A. 269-299), the court instructed the jury (J.A. 423):

> In Counts Two through Four the government contends that the scheme to defraud consisted primarily of the employment of devices to manipulate the price of Gulf & Western common stock to an artificially high level by engaging in purchases of Gulf & Western stock for the purpose of raising the market price to $45 a share. Defendant Mulheren contends that he purchased Gulf & Western for investment purposes, and not to artificially manipulate the price.
>
> I charge you that when purchasers and sellers of stock negotiate a transaction at a particular price, or at the market price, they impliedly state that the price of the securities is the result of legitimate market forces rather than

---

540 F.2d 591, 596 (3rd Cir. 1976); *Village of Arlington Heights Police Pension Fund v. Poder*, 700 F. Supp. 405, 406 (N.D. Ill. 1988); *Kennedy v. Chomerics, Inc*, 669 F. Supp. 1157, 1160 (D. Mass. 1987); *O'Keefe v. Courtney*, 655 F.Supp.16, 19 (N.D. Ill. 1985); *Jaksich v. Thomson McKinnon Sec., Inc.*, 582 F. Supp. 485, 493 (S.D.N.Y. 1984). The only distinction among the three subparagraphs of Rule 10b-5 in this regard is that subparagraph (b) applies to situations in which the defendant told an untruth or a misleading half-truth, whereas subparagraphs (a) and (c) apply to situations, such as insider trading, in which the defendant did not disclose anything at all, although he was under a duty to do so. *See Affiliated Ute Citizens*, 406 U.S. at 153; *Village of Arlington Heights Police Pension Fund*, 700 F. Supp. at 406.

manipulation. Such implied representation is false, where, as the government contends here, the buyer has engaged in a scheme to manipulate the price of the stock.[13]

This theory is patently erroneous. As demonstrated above, Section 10(b) requires, and the jury must find, the existence of actual deception, *i.e.*, that the defendant made a misrepresentation or violated a duty of disclosure. That element was eliminated by the court's instruction that the mere purchase of stock with the intent to increase its price constitutes a misrepresentation. Even if, contrary to our argument in Point I, Mulheren did purchase Gulf & Western stock with such an intent, it is absurd to say that his *silence* constituted a false *representation*. Because Mulheren did not speak to anyone concerning his purchase of Gulf & Western stock except to specify quantity and price in placing the order, he can in no way be found to have made an affirmative misrepresentation.

At bottom, then, the government's theory must rest on the premise that Mulheren breached a duty of disclosure, *i.e.*, that he was obliged to disclose his subjective motivation in purchasing Gulf & Western stock. The law, however, does not support that premise. Given that Mulheren was neither an insider nor a fiduciary, it is clear that he had no duty to disclose any facts to others—even material ones. As the Supreme Court explained in *Chiarella* in holding that an employee of a financial printer had no duty to disclose material non-public information in his possession before making purchases based on that information:

> [O]ne who fails to disclose material information prior to the consummation of a transaction commits fraud only when he is under a duty to do so. And the duty to disclose arises when one party has information "that the other [party] is entitled to know because of a fiduciary or other similar relation of trust and confidence between them." . . . Accordingly, a purchaser of stock who has no duty to a prospective seller because he is neither an insider nor a fiduciary has been held to have no obligation to reveal material facts.

445 U.S. at 228-229 (footnotes and citations omitted). *Accord Dirks v. SEC*, 463 U.S. 646, 654- 655 (1983); *General Time Corp. v. Talley Indus., Inc.*, 403 F.2d 159, 164 (2d Cir. 1968), *cert. denied,* 393 U.S. 1026 (1969); *SEC v. Great American Indus., Inc.*, 407 F.2d 453, 460 (2d Cir. 1968), cert. denied, 395 U.S. 920 (1969); *Deutschman v. Beneficial Corp.*, 841 F.2d 502, 506 (3rd Cir. 1988) ("[m]arket participants who are

---

[13] When the jury requested clarification during its deliberations, manipulation was again defined (over defense objection, see J.A. 337-341) as simply the purchase of stock for the purpose of raising its price. J.A. 330, 342. In the same request, the jury asked for reinstruction on the meaning of the word "voluntarily" in the definition of "knowingly." *See* J.A. 330. Because Mulheren's free will was not at issue, the jury must have been uncertain as to the knowledge that was required to find Mulheren guilty. The court should not in these circumstances have rejected defense counsel's request to reinstruct in full on the crucial element of knowledge, as opposed to merely redefining voluntariness as "free choice."

neither insiders nor fiduciaries of another type need not disclose material facts"), *cert. denied,* 109 S. Ct. 3176 (1989); *Kohler v. Kohler Co.,* 319 F.2d 634, 637-638 (7th Cir. 1963).[14]

Moreover, even if Mulheren had a duty to disclose material facts to others, that duty would not extend to his motive in purchasing Gulf & Western stock. Numerous courts have held that there is no general duty to disclose one's subjective motivation for engaging in securities transactions. *See Field v. Trump,* 850 F.2d 938, 947 (2d Cir. 1988) (rejecting "[e]fforts to dress up [state-law claims] in a § 14(a) suit of clothes . . . [by] including allegations of . . . failure to disclose an alleged ulterior motive'") (citation omitted); *Ward v. Succession of Freeman,* 854 F.2d 780, 791 (5th Cir. 1988), *cert. denied,* 490 U.S. 1065 (1989); *Kas v. Financial Gen. Bankshares, Inc.,* 796 F.2d 508, 513-515 (D.C. Cir. 1986) (federal securities law do not impose any requirement that officers and directors or courts engage in public psychoanalysis about the real motives of corporation officers and directors); *Panter,* 646 F.2d at 288 ("the disclosure philosophy of the statute" does not "obligate[ ] defendants to reveal either the culpability of their activities, or their impure motives for entering the allegedly improper transaction"); *Alabama Farm Bureau Mut. Cas. Co. v. American Fidelity Life Ins. Co.,* 606 F.2d 602, 610 (5th Cir. 1979), *cert. denied,* 449 U.S. 820 (1980); *Golub v. PPD Corp.,* 576 F.2d 759, 765 (8th Cir. 1978) (federal law does not entitle shareholders to disclosure of the alleged "true motivation of . . . management in selling the assets of the company"); *Bucher v. Shumway,* [1979-80 Transfer Binder] Fed. Sec. L. Rep. (CCH) ¶97,142, at 96,300 (S.D.N.Y. 1979) ("The securities laws, while their central insistence is upon disclosure, were never intended to attempt any such measures of psychoanalysis or preported [*sic*] self-analysis'") (citation omitted), *aff'd,* 622 F.2d 572 (2d Cir.), *cert. denied,* 449 U.S. 841 (1980). *Cf. Roeder v. Alpha Indus., Inc.,* 814 F.2d 22, 26-27 (1st Cir. 1987) (no affirmative duty to disclose that corporate officers had paid bribes, even though information was material).[15]

---

[14] By contrast, most cases finding manipulation under Section 10(b) or Section 9(a)(2) involve representatives of the company or issuers of stock who do owe a special duty to investors. See, *e.g., Pagel, Inc. v. SEC,* 803 F.2d 942, 946 (8th Cir. 1986) (defendants were underwriters of the stock); *Alabama Farm Bureau Mut. Cas. Co. v. American Fidelity Life Ins. Co.,* 606 F.2d 602, 608 (5th Cir. 1979) (defendants were corporate directors and officers), *cert. denied,* 449 U.S. 820 (1980); *United States v. Projansky,* 465 F.2d 123 (defendants were promoters of the stock); *Mutual Shares Corp. v. Genesco, Inc.,* 384 F.2d 540, 546-547 (2d Cir. 1967) (majority stockholder manipulated stock to deceive minority shareholders); *United States v. Minuse,* 114 F.2d at 38 (defendant company manipulated market of its own stock); *R.J. Koeppe & Co.,* 95 F.2d at 552 (same); *Resch-Cassin,* 362 F. Supp. at 978 (defendants were distributors of new stock); *Davis v. Pennzoil Co.,* 264 A.2d 597, 603 (Pa. 1970) (company manipulated its own stock).

[15] If there were a duty to disclose subjective reasons for buying or selling a particular stock, it would seem to follow that the duty would extend to any reason that might be material to others trading in the stock. For example, investors might find it material that a large purchase of stock was based on mere speculation or on the application of an especially powerful new formula for measuring the likely price

The weakness of the government's theory is highlighted by its inability even to identify the parties to whom Mulheren owed a duty to disclose his subjective motivations. The only parties with whom he engaged in a purchase or sale of securities were those who sold him the stock; but Mulheren's alleged manipulative motivations were in no way material to their decision to sell. Moreover, he cannot be found to have violated any duty to Gulf & Western because there was no evidence that he knew about Boesky's plan to sell back his stock to Gulf & Western when the price reached $45. This case is thus significantly different from the situation condemned in a few old (and possibly outdated) cases in which an individual fails to disclose his prior manipulation to those to whom he *subsequently* sells the stock. *See SEC v. Barrett & Co.*, 9 SEC 319, 329 (1941) ("when a security is sold 'at the market,' the failure to disclose to purchasers the fact that the market price had been artificially inflated by the sellers manipulation is an omission to state a material fact and constitutes a fraud on the purchasers"). In such a case, if (a big if) there is any violation of Section 10(b), it is the *selling* of the stock without disclosing the *fact* that the price is the result of manipulation. But in a case such as this, where there was no sale by Mulheren at an artificially inflated price, it is clear that no material nondisclosure can be found to have occurred. *Cf. Murphy v. McDonnell & Co.*, 553 F.2d 292, 295 (2d Cir. 1977) (because defendant stock exchange did not participate in the fraudulent transaction, it could not be found liable merely for its failure to disclose material facts to investors at large).[16]

Tellingly, we have located no prior reported case basing a finding of manipulation solely upon open market purchases by a defendant in his own name done to raise the market price. Use of the criminal sanction to enforce such a rule is particularly troublesome, given that the imposition of criminal liability for a buyer's failure to disclose his mere subjective desire that his purchases will increase the stock's price not only finds no support in Section 10(b), but would subject any party who engaged in large purchases of stock to a substantial and unfair risk of criminal punishment. Given that the difference between *knowing* that a purchase will increase the stock's price and acting for the *purpose* of bringing about such a result is often a marginal one, purchasers could never be

---

movement of a security. Indeed, there is no limit to the reasons for past purchases or sales of stock that subsequent investors might find it useful to know in assessing the value of the stock. There is simply no basis in law or policy, however, for imposing a duty to disclose these subjective motivations.

[16]   Given that Mulheren did not engage in (or knowingly aid and abet) any particular transaction that was itself fraudulent, the government's theory is apparently that Mulheren committed a "fraud on the market" by causing investors in Gulf & Western to pay more for the stock than it was worth. The fraud on the market theory, however, is completely inapposite in this context. That "theory has nothing to do with an affirmative duty to disclose material information." *Roeder*, 814 F.2d at 27. To the contrary, "[i]t only addresses the 'unreasonable and irrelevant evidentiary burden' of requiring plaintiffs in non-disclosure cases to prove reliance.... [It] does not dispense with the requirement that there must be a duty to disclose before there can be liability." *Ibid.* (citation omitted). Thus, the fraud on the market theory provides no support whatsoever for the conclusion that Mulheren had a duty to disclose his subjective motivation to the general public.

certain that a jury would find the former, rather than the latter. Indeed, a purchaser could easily have both an investment purpose and a purpose of raising the price. This Court should reject the government's attempt to make criminal liability turn on so fine a line. *Cf. Dirks*, 463 U.S. at 658 n.17 (rejecting an expansive interpretation of the securities laws that would be "inherently imprecise, [because] imprecision prevents parties from ordering their actions in accord with legal requirements"); *Pinter v. Dahl*, 486 U.S. 622, 654 n.29 (1988) (warning against the "risks [of] over-deterring activities related to lawful securities sales" as a result of judicial creation of open-ended legal standards that "produce[ ] unpredictable results").

In sum, because the government failed to prove, and the jury was not required to find, that Mulheren misrepresented any fact, or omitted to disclose any fact that under the circumstances he had a duty to disclose, this Court should reverse his convictions for violating, and conspiring to violate, Section 10(b) and Rule 10b-5.

B.   The Element of Materiality Was Not Satisfied In This Case

Even if Mulheren failed to disclose a fact that he was under a duty to disclose, Section 10(b) also requires proof that the fact was material. It is our submission that the evidence was insufficient to prove that Mulheren's subjective intent in purchasing Gulf & Western stock—the only "fact" that he is charged with having failed to disclose—was material. Even if this Court were to conclude otherwise, however, Mulheren is entitled to a new trial because the district court improperly removed the materiality issue from the jury.

> The test for materiality is an objective one, requiring a showing of substantial likelihood that, under all the circumstances, the omitted fact would have assumed actual significance in the deliberations of the reasonable shareholder. Put another way, there must be a substantial likelihood that the disclosure of the omitted fact would have been viewed by the reasonable investor as having significantly altered the "total mix" of information made available.

TSC Indus., Inc. v. Northway, Inc., 426 U.S. 438, 449(1976). *See also Basic Inc.* v. *Levinson*, 485 U.S. 224, 232, 240 (1988) (adopting "the *TSC Industries* standard of materiality for the § 10(b) and Rule 10b-5 context" and stressing that "materiality depends on the significance the reasonable investor would place on the withheld or misrepresented information"); *Elkind v. Liggett & Myers, Inc.*, 635 F.2d 156, 166 (2d Cir. 1980) (applying *TSC Industries* standard and finding that negative information about corporation possessed by tippee was not material because it could not "be deemed 'reasonably certain to have a substantial effect on the market price of the security'") (citation omitted).[17]

---

[17]   Where, as here, the Section 10(b) violation takes place in an open-market context, the required showing of materiality is particularly demanding. *Thomas v. Duralite Co.*, 524 F.2d 577, 584 (3rd Cir. 1975).

Mulheren's subjective motivation for buying Gulf & Western stock is not material under this standard. To begin with, there is simply no sense in which that fact could have been material to those from whom Mulheren purchased the 75,000 shares of Gulf & Western stock. His motive for buying the stock could not have altered the sellers' decision to sell it to him, for they sold their stock at a *higher* price than they otherwise would have received. If anyone received a bad deal on the sale, it was Mulheren, who was stuck with 75,000 shares of what he knew (by the government's theory) was overvalued stock.

There is also no reason to think that Mulheren's subjective motivation for buying the stock would have been material to investors in the market. For example, the investor who bought the stock at $44.875 during the interval between the first Mulheren purchases and the Boesky/Icahn sale presumably had made a determination that the stock was worth that price. Because of Mulheren's purchases, that would have been the only price at which it was available. While it might have been of academic interest that the small increase in price was due to purchases made for the purpose of raising the price it is pure speculation to conclude that such knowledge would have caused that purchaser to refrain from buying the stock.

It is equally clear that materiality was not proven as to Gulf & Western. Plainly, when the company, with all its knowledge regarding its own circumstances, agreed to purchase more than 6.7 million shares of its own stock from Boesky and Icahn in an off-market transaction, it was not relying on the market price to establish the value of its stock. To paraphrase the court in *Burlington Indus., Inc. v. Edelman*, 666 F. Supp. 799, 807 (M.D.N.C. 1987): "As a practical matter, it is inconceivable that [Gulf & Western] would rely, in purchasing or selling its own stock, on any information defendants compiled. . . . [Gulf & Western] obviously has access to more detailed and current financial information, regarding its own stock, that defendant [] could ever hope to amass."

The likeliest explanation for Gulf & Western's refusal to pay more than the market price was its desire to avoid the appearance of paying greenmail to Boesky and Icahn by purchasing at a price in excess of that at which the stock was traded.[18] Given Gulf & Western's determination that its stock was worth Boesky's $45 asking price, it is virtually certain that knowledge that the price had reached that level because of purchases made at Boesky's behest would not have altered its investment judgment. Certainly, the government adduced no evidence—through testimony of Martin Davis or otherwise — that disclosure of Mulheren's alleged lack of an investment motivation would have affected the actions of one in Gulf & Western's position.

Even if the evidence on materiality were deemed sufficient, however, the convictions would still have to be reversed because the issue was taken away from the jury. It is well settled that materiality is a question of fact for the jury. *See Basic Inc.*, 485 U.S.

---

[18] Boesky himself testified that "Mr. Icahn told [him] that he felt that the company would be willing to buy back the shares at 45, however, [it] would not be willing to buy back the shares in a premium over the market, so that if the market were not 45, they would not pay 45." *See* J.A. 55.

at 250; *TSC Industries*, 426 U.S. at 450; *Goldman v. Belden*, 754 F.2d 1059, 1067 (2d Cir. 1985). Here, although the jury was told that materiality was an element of the offense, the court then stated that "[o]n the question of materiality, I instruct you that the price of the security is a material fact to those buying and selling the security, and therefore misstatements or omissions concerning the price of the security are material." J.A. 324. The instruction that "omissions concerning the price of the security are material" must have been understood by the jury to mean that if Mulheren was found to have intended to increase the price of Gulf & Western stock, his failure to disclose that intent was material as a matter of law.

This instruction violated not only the rule that materiality is a question of fact for the jury, but the constitutional requirement that the jury find each element of a criminal offense by proof beyond a reasonable doubt and that its consideration of the evidence may not be restricted by conclusive presumptions. *See Carella v. California*, 491 U.S. 263 (1989) ; *Francis v. Franklin*, 471 U.S. 307, 317 (1985); *Sandstrom v. Montana*, 442 U.S. 510, 524 (1979).

Accordingly, Mulheren's convictions should be reversed because of insufficient evidence to prove materiality, or because the court improperly removed that issue from the jury.

C. Mulheren Did Not Act For The Purpose Of Deceiving Others When He Purchased The Gulf & Western Stock

In addition to proving that the defendant made a material misrepresentation or violated a duty of disclosure under Rule 10b-5, the government must establish that the defendant took such action with the purpose of deceiving others. As the Supreme Court has stressed, "Section 10(b) is aptly described as a catchall provision, but what it catches must be *fraud.*" *Chiarella*, 445 U.S. at 234-235 (emphasis added). Similarly, the SEC's pronouncements at the time it adopted Rule 10b-5 make clear that the Rule was intended to prohibit "*fraud* by any person in connection with the purchase of securities. Securities Exchange Act of 1934 Release No. 3230 (May 21, 1942) (emphasis added).

In many securities fraud cases, evidence that establishes a material misrepresentation or violation of a duty of disclosure will at the same time show the presence of a purpose to deceive others in their purchases and sales of securities, but that is by no means always the case. Thus it is not sufficient that conduct causes harm to investors; there must be "intentional or willful conduct *designed to deceive or defraud* investors." *Ernst & Ernst v. Hochfelder*, 425 U.S. 185, 199 (1976) (emphasis added). *See also Dirks*, 463 U.S. at 663 n.23 (defendant's "motivation" is relevant to whether he had the requisite intent to deceive investors); *Chemical Bank v. Arthur Andersen & Co.,* 726 F.2d 930, 943 (2d Cir.), *cert. denied,* 469 U.S. 884 (1984); *Alabama Farm Bureau*, 606 F.2d at 612; *Schreiber*, 568 F. Supp. at 202. With respect to manipulation in particular, the Supreme Court has explained that manipulation refers narrowly to "practices, such as wash sales, matched orders, or rigged prices, that are intended to mislead investors by artificially affecting market activity." *Santa Fe Indus., Inc. v. Green*, 430 U.S. 462, 476 (1977).

In interpreting the scienter element under Section 10(b), it is helpful to consider Section 9(a)(2) of the Securities Exchange Act, a prohibition that is directly focused on manipulation. Because Congress enacted Section 9(a)(2) as the primary vehicle for proscribing manipulative practices, courts have looked to that provision for guidance in evaluating manipulation claims brought under Section 10(b).[19]

Section 9(a)(2) makes it unlawful for any person, by the use of interstate commerce or of the mails,

> [t]o effect, alone or with one or more other persons, a series of transactions in any security registered on a national securities exchange creating actual or apparent active trading in such security or raising or depressing the price of such security, *for the purpose of inducing the purchase or sale of such security by others.*

15 U.S.C. § 78i(a)(2) (emphasis added). Under this provision, then, it is not sufficient that a defendant engage in noninvestment-motivated trading that affects the price of a security; he must do so "for the purpose of inducing the purchase or sale of such security by others."[20] In interpreting this requirement, the courts have repeatedly stressed that "Section 9(a)(2) was aimed at preventing an individual from dominating the market in a stock for the purpose of conducting a one-sided market at an artificial level for its own benefit and to the detriment of the investing public." *Crane*, 419 F.2d at 794; *see also Trane*, 561 F. Supp. at 305; *Resch-Cassin*, 362 F. Supp. at 978.

The "purpose" requirement of Section 9(a)(2) is similar to the requirement of an intent to defraud under Section 10(b). That is, under Section 10 (b), it is not sufficient that a defendant intends to increase the price of a stock; he must intend to do so for the purpose of deceiving others, *i.e.*, inducing others to buy or sell securities at an artificial price. *Cf. Alabama Farm Bureau*, 606 F.2d at 612 (manipulation under Section 10(b)

---

[19]   *See, e.g., Santa Fe Industries*, 430 U.S. at 476; *Hundahl v. United Benefit Life Ins. Co.*, 465 F. Supp. 1349, 1361- 1362 (N.D.Tex. 1979) ("the scope of manipulation in section 9 sheds light on its scope under section 10(b)," and "[l]egislative history supports the even narrower view that the manipulative conduct prohibited in section 10(b) is limited to the devices which section 9 bars") (citation omitted); *SEC v. D'Onofrio*, [1975-76 Transfer Binder] Fed. Sec. L. Rep. (CCH) ¶ 95,201, at 98,017-98018 (S.D.N.Y. 1975) (applying definition of manipulation in Section 9(a)(2) to Section 10(b) claim) ; *Resch-Cassin*, 362 F. Supp. at 975.

[20]   As one noted commentator has explained, the "purpose" required by Section 9 (a) (2) might arise from the desire to exploit "an option to purchase a substantial amount of the security at a price above the current market, or a desire to obtain more than the current market price for a block of stock that the manipulator plans to distribute either as owner or as best-efforts underwriter or that is left in an underwriter's hands after a 'sticky' offering, or to get rid of a 'white elephant,' or to make more attractive a security pledged as collateral for a bank loan that the borrower is being pressed to repay or reduce, or to further or defeat a tender offer." L. Loss, *Fundamentals of Securities Regulation* 994 (1983) (footnotes omitted).

refers to conduct "used to induce investment in a company's stock" and to "[c]onduct designed to deter investment').

It is not difficult to apply the foregoing principles to this case. Even if, contrary to our arguments, a juror could fairly have inferred that Mulheren intended to raise the price of Gulf & Western stock, no rational juror could have concluded that his purpose was to deceive others, *i.e.*, to induce others to buy or sell securities at an artificial price. In order to establish such a purpose, the government was required to show that Mulheren sought to induce some person (or entity) or class of persons to buy or sell stock. There is simply no such thing as an intent to deceive in the air. As the court observed in *Klamberg v. Roth*, 473 F. Supp. 544 (S.D.N.Y. 1979), "[i]n 10b-5 cases, whether conduct may 'fairly be viewed as deceptive' will generally depend upon the circumstances of the particular person or class allegedly deceived, their knowledge and perceptive faculties. In other words, before the court can ask 'Was the conduct deceptive?', it must first ascertain 'To whom?'" *Id.* at 550. Here, there is no evidence that Mulheren had the purpose of deceiving any person or class of persons by his purchase of Gulf & Western stock.

To begin with, Mulheren could not be found to have intended to deceive Gulf & Western, since the government did not allege, the proof did not show, and the jury was not even asked to find that Mulheren knew of Boesky's stock-sale negotiations with Gulf & Western. As noted, Boesky testified that he never informed Mulheren about his discussion with Gulf & Western or the latter's offer to buy back his stock at the market price. J.A. 59. Since Mulheren is not claimed to have known of Boesky's purpose, the allegation that he acted pursuant to Boesky's request is of no moment. Thus, the manipulation convictions cannot be supported on the basis that Mulheren sought to deceive Gulf & Western.[21]

Second, it is inconceivable that Mulheren could be found to have intended to deceive the parties from whom he purchased Gulf & Western stock. As explained earlier, the sellers were in no way misled by Mulheren's purchases but were simply incidental *beneficiaries* of his actions.

Finally, there is no evidence that Mulheren sought to deceive, defraud or influence members of the general investing public by his open market purchases of Gulf & Western stock. To prove that a defendant engaged in manipulation for the purpose of deceiving the general public, the government must establish that he desired to mislead others by creating a false picture of the market. *See Crane*, 419 F.2d at 794 (conduct constitutes unlawful manipulation if performed " ' *to persuade the public* that activity in a security is the reflection of a genuine demand instead of a mirage'") (citation omitted) ; *Resch-Cassin*, 362 F. Supp. at 975 (same). Even if Mulheren bought the Gulf & Western stock with the intent of increasing its price, that does not *ipso facto* mean that his purpose was

---

[21] Although the indictment named the investors in Jamie Securities as the victims of Mulheren's alleged manipulation (*see* J.A. 22 (Indictment ¶ 19(f), (g))), the government expressly abandoned any contention that Jamie investors were defrauded by Mulheren's conduct. *See* J.A. 284-286.

to create a false picture of Gulf & Western stock for the purpose of influencing others' investment decisions. In fact, there is absolutely no basis here to suppose that Mulheren had any motive to deceive the general investing public by his purchases, as he neither intended to nor did engage in any subsequent transactions with them that would have been aided by his purchases on the market on October 17.

Note the attempt to characterize as absurd the United States' charges of wrongdoing against the client. This is followed up with a paragraph contrasting the client's situation to numerous other cases where fraud was actually found to have occurred.

The logic of the government's position is that if Mulheren awakened one morning and decided to attempt to raise the price of Gulf & Western common stock 1/4 point to $45 as a mater of whimsy, or because it was his wife's 45th birthday and Gulf & Western was her favorite stock, or because he wanted to stimulate corporate activity in the stock, or because he wanted to force a competitor to pay a high price for the stock, he would be guilty of securities fraud even though he did not seek to fool anyone and the only action he took was to purchase stock openly on the exchange. Although such activity may affect the price that investors must pay to acquire the stock, that does not *ipso facto* mean that those investors are deceived or were intended to be deceived. *See Dirks*, 463 U.S. at 663 n.23 ("[i]t is not enough that an insider's conduct results in harm to investors, rather a violation may be found only where there is 'intentional or willful conduct designed to deceive of defraud investors'") (citation omitted).

No case finding manipulation under either Section 10 (b) or Section 9 (a) comes close to holding this kind of activity to be unlawful. To the contrary, at the very heart of all the cases finding unlawful market manipulation is a demonstrated effort to deceive others. That is, every manipulation case has involved attempts by defendants to increase or decrease the price of stock *in order to* influence others' decisions to purchase or sell the stock. *See, e.g., United States v. Gilbert,* 668 F.2d 94,95 (2d Cir. 1981) (defendant "manipulated the price increase through an elaborate series of wash sales and matched orders" to make profits for himself and the accounts he controlled), *cert. denied,* 456 U.S. 946 (1982) ; *Alabama Farm Bureau,* 606 F.2d at 608 (defendant corporate directors and officers allegedly deceived shareholders by instituting a stock repurchase program to retain their position of control over the company; by inflating the market price, program would discourage others attempting to gain control of the company by acquiring its stock); *United States v. Charnay,* 537 F.2d 341. 344 (9th Cir.) (defendants secretly compensated individuals to sell shares to depress market price of stock in order to facilitate a takeover attempt), *cert. denied,* 429 U.S. 1000 (1976); *Schlick v. Penn-Dixie Cement Corp.,* 507 F.2d 374, 378-381 (2d Cir. 1974) (one party to a corporate merger allegedly caused the market price of its stock to increase artificially in order to obtain a more favorable exchange ratio), *cert. denied,* 421 U.S. 976 (1975); *Mutual Shares Corp. v. Genesco, Inc.,* 384 F.2d 540, 546-547 (2d Cir. 1967) (majority stockholder implemented scheme to reduce dividends in order to force down the market price of stock and cause minority shareholders to sell out at depressed values); *In re Delafield & Delafield,* [1967-69 Transfer Binder] Fed. Sec. L. Rep. (CCH) ¶ 77,648 (1968) (SEC found broker in violation of Rule 10b-5 for his activities in manipulating stock prices downward in order to induce a shareholder to sell his substantial holdings at a reduced price to the broker's customers); *Davis v. Pennzoil Co.*, 264 A.2d 597, 603 (Pa. 1970) (company attempted to inflate market price of its own stock so that it could expand by purchasing companies cheaply with stock of inflated value).[22]

An apt illustration of manipulation performed with the requisite intent to deceive others is found in *Crane Co. v. Westinghouse Air Brake Co.* There the court held that Rule 10b-5 was violated by a corporation's scheme to merge with, and prevent a third-party takeover of, another corporation by buying large blocks of shares of the target corporation at a price above the then market price, thus driving up the market price to ward off the takeover, while at the same time disposing of the newly acquired stock at a loss in secret and unreported sales. 419 F.2d at 795-796. The court found that the manipulation of prices violated Section 10(b) because the failure to disclose it operated as a fraud or deceit on the defeated tender offeror and on the shareholders of the target corporation, who were induced to reject the tender offer. *Ibid.*

Here, by contrast, there is no evidence, nor was the jury required to find, that Mulheren intended to defraud anyone, *i.e.*, to induce anyone to buy or sell stock at a higher price by his purchases of Gulf & Western stock.[23] All that the government alleged, and all that the jury was required to find, was that he purchased the stock on the open market with the hope that such inflation would result. This case is therefore similar to *Trane*, where the court found that the purchase of stock with the intent to stimulate investment interest in the company did not constitute unlawful manipulation under Section 9(a)(2) because the defendants did not intend "to induce public investment to its detriment." 561 F. Supp. at 304-305. The government's failure to establish the requisite element of an intent to deceive others requires reversal of Mulheren's convictions.[24]

---

[22] For cases under Section 9(a)(2) involving similar conduct, *see United States v. Stein*, 456 F.2d 844 (defendants attempted to inflate stock price so that company could unload stock at a profit) ; *Minuse*, 114 F.2d at 38 (in order to unload large block of stock at a profit, defendant company manipulated market by engaging in various deceptive activities); *R.J. Koeppe & Co.*, 95 F.2d at 552 (company attempted to inflate the price of its own stock in order to unload its large holdings upon the public).

[23] Indeed, it is not clear that this element was satisfied even with regard to Boesky. True, Boesky caused the increase in price in order to facilitate his sale to Gulf & Western at his desired price of $45, so that any "manipulation" at lease related to a purchase or sale of securities by Boesky. But there is no evidence that Boesky intended to deceive Gulf & Western, to whom, as noted above (*see* pages 28-29, *infra*), the reasons for the rise in price were unlikely to be material.

[24] Here again, the instructions to the jury were also deficient. To be sure, the district court instructed that Mulheren must be found to have intended to deceive others by his purchase of Gulf & Western stock. But the jury was clearly misled as to this element by the court's erroneous instruction that, as a matter of law, manipulation constitutes the mere purchase of stock for the purpose of raising its price. *See* J.A. 323-324, 337. From a reading of the entire instructions, it is clear that the jury must have understood this statement to mean that if a defendant intended to purchase stock for the purpose of raising its price, then as a matter of law he had the requisite intent to deceive.

III. THE DISTRICT COURT ERRED IN EXCLUDING EVIDENCE OF MULHEREN'S REFUSAL TO ENGAGE IN OTHER ACTS OF SECURITIES FRAUD

The district court also erred in excluding evidence that Mulheren had refused to engage in other proposed acts of securities fraud. Specifically, the defense sought to present testimony by witnesses—including Mulheren himself—that on several occasions Mulheren was approached by individuals proposing that he become involved in schemes to park stock and to participate in insider trading and that, in response, he flatly refused. *See* J.A. 166-180; *see also* Memorandum of Law in Support of Defendant John Mulheren's Motion to Admit Evidence Pursuant to Rules 404 and 405 of the Federal Rules of Evidence; Memorandum of Law in Support of Defendant Mulheren's Application to Testify Regarding Specific Honest Transactions. In particular, one witness, Mr. Santangelo, would have testified that he asked Mulheren to "park" stock for him by buying a large position in securities at no risk and that Mulheren would not buy the stock on those terms. J.A. 146-147, 168. Mulheren would have testified that he told Santangelo that he wouldn't do this for Ivan Boesky and therefore he would not do it for Santangelo. J.A. 176.

The evidence of Mulheren's refusal to engage in other acts of securities fraud should have been admitted under Fed. R. Evid. 404(b), which provides:

> Evidence of other crimes, wrongs, or acts is not admissible to prove the character of a person in order to show action in conformity therewith. It may, however, be admissible for other purposes, such as proof of motive, opportunity, *intent*, preparation, plan, knowledge, identity, or absence of mistake or accident.

(emphasis added). Because the evidence of Mulheren's refusal to engage in other violations of the securities laws would have tended to demonstrate that he lacked the requisite criminal intent to commit securities fraud, it fell within Rule 404(b). Such evidence would have lent substantial support to the defense's theory that Mulheren did not intend to manipulate the stock market, but rather was duped by Boesky into buying the Gulf & Western stock.

Numerous cases have permitted defendants to introduce evidence of refusals to engage in similar criminal conduct to demonstrate a lack of criminal intent. For example, in *United States v. Sternstein*, 596 F.2d 528 (2d Cir. 1979), a prosecution for the preparation of fraudulent tax returns, this Court held that evidence that a substantial number of returns prepared by the defendant were not fraudulent was admissible to show that the defendant had made innocent mistakes in the preparation of returns and thus lacked the requisite criminal intent in the case at bar. *Id.* at 530-531.

Other circuits have reached similar conclusions. For example, *United States v. Garvin*, 565 F.2d 519 (8th Cir. 1977), held that a defendant charged with mail fraud

based on numerous misstatements in insurance applications should have been permitted
to demonstrate his lack of criminal purpose by showing specific innocent acts:

> [The defendant] was not allowed to present proof of his truthful responses to
> similar questions on these and other insurance applications filed during the
> same period. We agree with the District Court that honesty in some trans-
> actions is usually relevant to the issue of fraud in a different transaction.
> However, the issue here is the existence of a criminal purpose to defraud
> and a scheme to defraud insurance companies by the use of the mails. On
> these issues we find it was error to exclude such testimony.

Id. at 521.[25]

Although it did not involve the defendant's own acts, this Court's decision in *United
States v. Aboumoussallem*, 726 F.2d 906 (2d Cir. 1984), illuminates a crucial factor supporting admission in a case such as this. The Court there observed that "the standard of
admissibility when a criminal defendant offers similar acts evidence as a shield need not
be as restrictive as when a prosecutor uses such evidence as a sword." *Id*. at 911. When
the government presents evidence of similar bad acts, there is always the danger that "an
innocent person [] may be convicted primarily because of the jury's willingness to
assume his present guilt from his prior misdeed." *Ibid*. When the defense offers similar
acts evidence, however, those concerns do not exist; rather "the only issue arising under
Rule 404(b) is whether the evidence is relevant to the existence or non-existence of
some fact pertinent to the defense." *Id*. at 912. *Accord, United States v. Cohen*, 888 F.2d
770, 776-777 (11th Cir. 1989) ; *United States v. McClure*, 546 F.2d 670, 673 (5th Cir.
1977); *People v. Flowers*, 644 P.2d 916, 919 (Colo.), *appeal dismissed,* 459 U.S. 803
(1982). Evidence that Mulheren adamantly refused to engage in other proposed acts of
securities fraud is unquestionably highly relevant to solving the riddle of his Delphic conversation with Boesky (particularly the meaning of his statement "I understand") and

---

[25]   *See also United States v. Bitter*, 374 F.2d 744, 747-748 (7th Cir.) ("[p]roof of otherwise similar
transactions which did not involve fraud might tend to show that the losses suffered in the instant cases were
accidental or incidental rather than the product of a designed scheme"), *rev'd on other grounds,* 389 U.S. 15
(1967); *United States v. Shavin*, 287 F.2d 647, 654 (7th Cir. 1961) (reversible error not to allow a defendant
charged with defrauding insurance carriers to introduce evidence of legitimate transactions to negate fraudulent intent) ; *Worthington v. United States*, 64 F.2d 936, 939-942 (7th Cir. 1933) (in mail fraud prosecution for selling worthless lot contracts, exclusion of testimony that other purchasers of contracts had not been
defrauded was reversible error; "[s]uch evidence, while not conclusively disproving the existence of a fraudulent scheme or purpose on appellant's part, would tend to refute the Government's evidence"). *Cf. United
States v. Manos*, 848 F.2d 1427, 1429-1430 (7th Cir. 1988) (observing that trial court had permitted code-
fendant, a city restaurant inspector accused of taking bribes from owners, to offer evidence of "honest inter-
actions" and "legitimate transactions"); *United States v. Giese*, 597 F.2d 1170, 1189 (9th Cir.) (defendant
charged with conspiracy to commit offenses against the United States by bombing two military recruiting
centers was permitted to produce books that he owned, sold or read that exemplified his non-revolutionary
views and to testify about his involvement in various peaceful political demonstrations, because evidence
tended to show that it "would have been inconceivable for him to have turned to violence in order to make
a political statement"), *cert. denied,* 444 U.S. 979 (1979).

determining whether he intended to commit unlawful stock manipulation. It therefore should have been admitted under the reasoning of *Aboumoussallem*.[26]

In sum, the district court erred in refusing to admit evidence of similar acts under Rule 404 (b) for the purpose of showing Mulheren's lack of criminal intent. Because the issue of intent was hotly contested, and because the government's proof on that issue was exceedingly weak, this Court should reverse his convictions and remand for a new trial. *See United States v. Detrich*, 865 F.2d 17, 21-22 (2d Cir. 1988) (exclusion of evidence relating to defendant's state of mind was reversible error, given its relevance to sole contested issue of defendant's *mens rea* and the lack of overwhelming evidence of guilt) ; *United States* v. *DiMaria*, 727 F.2d 265, 272 (2d Cir. 1984) (same).

IV.   THE DISTRICT COURT ERRED IN EXCLUDING EXPERT TESTIMONY ON THE BEARING OF MANIC DEPRESSION ON MULHEREN'S CREDIBILITY AND DEMEANOR

The district court also erred in refusing to admit expert testimony on the symptoms of manic depression and the bearing of that disease on Mulheren's credibility and demeanor. Although the jury heard evidence that Mulheren suffered from manic depression (*see* J.A. 181), the defense was never permitted to present psychiatric testimony explaining the effects of that disease.[27]

Specifically, the defense sought to introduce the testimony of Dr. Robert Sadoff, who had examined Mulheren and his medical records (J.A. 234) and who would have testified that manic depression is a recognized mental illness that

> manifests in [Mulheren's], primarily, manic activities, which includes racing thoughts, it includes grandiose ideas, it includes impaired judgment when he becomes very high, it includes behavior that is excessive and thinking that is expansive and grandiose. He, at times, when he wasn't taking his medicine,

---

[26] In *Aboumoussallem,* the defendant sought to support his defense that his cousins unwittingly "duped" him into transporting contraband by adducing evidence that, five months prior to his arrest, his cousins duped another person into transporting hashish from Lebanon to the United States. This evidence was offered under Rule 404(b) as similar acts evidencing a common plan to import narcotics from Lebanon using innocent dupes. 726 F.2d at 911. The Court noted that "[t]he proffered evidence satisfies the liberal relevancy standard of the Federal Rules of Evidence: It tends to make the existence of a consequential fact, [Aboumoussallem's] knowledge, less probable. . . . The existence of such a plan would lend some support to the inference that [Aboumoussallem] was duped and thereby bolster his defense of lack of knowledge." *Id.* at 912.

[27] As explained by one expert, Dr. Ross J. Baldessarini of Harvard Medical School, who wrote to oppose a term of incarceration for Mulheren, manic depression "is one of the most severe forms of mental disorder, typically affecting mood, but also having potentially profoundly disruptive effects on reasoning, judgment, and behavior." J.A. 420 (Sentencing Memorandum of John A. Mulheren, Jr. at 8).

As he does every day, Mulheren took lithium carbonate during his trial as a treatment for his disease. (Indeed, such treatment was made a condition of his bail.) According to Dr. Baldessarini, that drug "causes certain side effects which at a minimum cause physical discomfort (hand tremors, severe headaches, diarrhea, salt and fluid loss)." J.A. 427.

became psychotic, which means he was not in touch with reality. He has been depressed, at times, very depressed and had suicidal thoughts. That is—those are the basic characteristics of the bi-polar disorder [of manic depression].

J.A. 234-235. Dr. Sadoff further would have testified that

many manics . . . become irritable. Sometimes nasty with other people, and show behavior and attitude that appear arrogant and special or elitist, but that's part of the illness. . . . [S] sometimes people with this illness, when they became manic, and as they get higher and higher begin to feel very special, they feel as though they are vulnerable, and they look and appear on—for example, Mr. Mulheren would dress differently from other people, wouldn't follow the norm, and would often go out of his way to be different, and sometimes even a bit antagonist. . . . He often goes without a tie or coat in an atmosphere where people wear ties and coats, because that's his way.

J.A. 237-238.

Dr. Sadoff's explanation of the effects of manic depression clearly would have helped the jury to evaluate the demeanor or Mulheren, whose unusual attitudes and behavior under cross-examination (evident to anyone who reads the transcript of his testimony) might well have had a major impact on the jury's assessment of his credibility.[28] Accordingly, it should have been admitted under Fed. R. Evid. 702, which allows an expert to give an opinion when his specialized knowledge "will assist the trier of fact to understand the evidence or to determine a fact in issue." Because the credibility of a testifying defendant is "a fact in issue within the meaning of Rule 702," *State v. Kim*, 645 P.2d 1330, 1336 n.7 (Haw. 1982), and because Dr. Sadoff's testimony would have assisted the jury in evaluating that fact by addressing matters not within the ordinary understanding or knowledge of lay persons, his testimony came within the ambit of Rule 702. *See United States v. Altman*, 901 F.2d 1161, 1164-1165 (2d Cir. 1990) (error to exclude expert testimony on manic depression that would have aided the court's determination of willfulness and might have explained the defendant's otherwise inconsistent testimony).

This conclusion is supported by the well settled rule that psychiatric testimony is admissible to impeach the credibility of witnesses. As one court explained: "[t]he testimony of specialists or others with particular knowledge of the witness' mental or physical condition may provide invaluable assistance to the jury." *People v. Parks*, 390

---

[28] A specific example of an instance where such testimony could have been helpful concerns Mulheren's response to questions about his testimony under oath in two prior SEC depositions. In that testimony, Mulheren had stated, that he talked to Boesky "twenty times a day." When Mulheren was first confronted with this statement at trial, he said that he had lied; later, he explained that his testimony before the SEC was simply a "gross exaggeration." J.A. 197-200. Dr. Sadoff's testimony that manic depressives are prone to exaggeration clearly could have helped neutralize the damaging effect that this testimony may have had on Mulheren's credibility.

N.Y.S.2d 848, 857, 359 N.E.2d 358, 367 (1976). *See also, e.g., Barnes v. Jones*, 665 F.2d 427, 435 (2d Cir. 1981) ("evidence relevant to a complainant's mental condition may be admissible on the issue of credibility"), *rev'd on other grounds,* 463 U.S. 745 (1983); *People v. Russel*, 443 P.2d 794, 800 (Cal.) (expert testimony is relevant if it "show[s] the effect of a particular mental or emotional condition upon [a witness'] ability to tell the truth"), cert. denied, 393 U.S. 864 (1968).[29]

The reasoning behind this rule applies with as much force to testimony that supports credibility as to that which impeaches it, and accordingly courts have found supportive expert testimony admissible. In *Stout v. State*, 528 N.E.2d 476, 479 (Ind. 1988), for example, the court upheld the prosecution's introduction of psychiatric testimony regarding the victim's demeanor in the courtroom, including testimony that "there was nothing unusual in the victim's rather factual and unemotional rendition and that the victim just wanted to hurry up, tell her story, and not have to deal with it anymore." Similarly, in *State v. Davis*, 422 N.W.2d 296, 299 (Minn. Ct. App. 1988), the court held that psychiatric testimony regarding the common behavioral characteristics of sexually abused adolescents was admissible to provide the jury with "insight into the cause of some of [the victim's] peculiar behavior, and [to] assist [] the jury in evaluating her credibility." *See also People v. Scott*, 578 P.2d 123, 129 (Cal. 1978); *People v. Hamilton*, 415 N.W.2d 653, 655-656 (Mich. Ct. App. 1987) (error to reject murder defendant's request to introduce expert testimony regarding his psychological makeup that would have helped jury evaluate the credibility of his statements to the police; "[e]ven though defendant's statements were voluntary and no insanity defense is raised, such psychiatric testimony is admissible as it relates to the weight and credibility of defendant's statements").

If the government is allowed to introduce expert testimony supporting the credibility of prosecution witnesses, *a fortiori* the defendant should be permitted to introduce such testimony supporting his own credibility. As this Court stressed in *United States v. Wolfson*, 437 F.2d 862, 874 (2d Cir. 1970), "[i]n criminal cases especially, defense counsel should be given great latitude in adducing proof which might bear on credibility." This is especially true where, as here, the evidence related to the crucial testimony of the defendant himself. *See State v. Roberts*, 677 P.2d 280, 286-287 (Ariz. Ct. App. 1983) ("[w]here the testimony of a witness is so crucial in determining whether a defendant may or may not be imprisoned, . . . we feel the value to the jury of expert testimony far exceeds any confusion which might have been caused by the testimony).

---

[29]   *Accord United States v. Rosenberg*, 108 F. Supp. 798, 806 (S.D.N.Y.), *aff'd,* 200 F.2d 666 (2d Cir. 1952), *cert. denied,* 345 U.S. 965 (1953); *United States v. Hiss*, 88 F. Supp. 559 (S.D.N.Y. 1950); *People v. Schuemann*, 548 P.2d 911, 913 (Colo. 1976); *State v. Sinnott*, 132 A.2d 298, 306 (N.J. 1957); Taborsky v. State, 116 A.2d 433, 438 (Conn. 1955); *Ingalls v. Ingalls*, 59 So. 2d 898, 911 (Ala. 1952).

V.   MULHEREN'S FINE WAS BASED ON AN ERRONEOUS CALCU-LATION OF LOSS

In addition to a term of imprisonment of a year and a day, the district court sentenced Mulheren under the alternative fine statute, 18 U.S.C. § 3571(d), to a fine of $1,681,700. J.A. 343-344. That fine is substantially larger than the maximum otherwise available, under Section 3571 (b), of $250,000 per count.[30] The alternative fine statute

Unlike the previous sections that rely on the citation of authority, this part of the brief is an example of arguing a position entirely from the facts of the case.

permits a fine to be based on the gain derived from or loss caused by an offense. Here, the fine was based on the amount of loss that was purportedly caused by Mulheren's manipulation of Gulf & Western stock. Specifically, the court adopted the government's theory that the victims of Mulheren's crimes were those who purchased stock between the time of Mulheren's first purchases on October 17, 1985 and the time, 12 minutes later, when Boesky and Icahn sold their stock to Gulf & Western at $45 a share. The court measured the amount of the loss caused by Mulheren by computing the difference between the price of the stock before Mulheren's purchases ($44.75) and the amount paid by later purchasers to buy the stock. During the relevant period, 200 shares of stock were purchased on the open market at $44.875, resulting (under the government's theory) in a loss of $25, and 6,726,700 shares were purchased (by Gulf & Western from Boesky & Icahn) at $45, resulting (under the government's theory) in a loss of $1,681,675. See J.A. 416 (Gov't Sentencing Mem. at 13). Thus, the district court found that the total loss caused by Mulheren's offenses was $1,681,700, and that figure was selected as the amount of the fine.

The district court's calculation of loss is analytically flawed. The government's theory of liability is that Mulheren violated Section 10(b) solely by buying 75,000 shares of Gulf & Western stock without disclosing his intention to inflate the stock's price. Under this theory, Mulheren had a duty to disclose his intent because it would have been material to investors in deciding whether to purchase Gulf & Western stock. This theory thus does *not* rest on the premise that, but for Mulheren's violation, investors would have bought the stock at $44.75. To the contrary, it assumes that if investors had known that Mulheren had increased the price of the stock, they would not have bought the stock at all. Certainly, they could not have bought the stock for $44.75 because, after Mulheren's purchases, the stock was not available at that price. Thus, it was error for the district court to calculate the loss caused by Mulheren on the basis of the difference between $44.75 and $45.

To be sure, if those who purchased after Mulheren's trading had actually lost money as a result of their purchases of Gulf & Western stock, they could be found to

---

[30] We note that, should it become material, it is our position that the charged conduct, if a crime at all, amounted to no more than one substantive manipulation offense, so that the maximum allowable fine would be $500,000 (one substantive count and one conspiracy count). The issue presented at this stage, however, is confined to the lawfulness of the sentence based on the alternative fine statute.

have suffered a loss as a result of Mulheren's conduct. (In that case, Mulheren's conduct would at least have been a but-for cause of their loss.) The government, however, adduced no evidence of any such losses. While the price of the stock declined immediately following the Boesky/Icahn transaction, that was clearly due to the transaction itself, not to anything Mulheren did. Indeed, given that the price of the stock almost doubled in the following years, Gulf & Western itself certainly suffered no loss. *See* Dow Jones Historical Stock Quote Reporter Service (1985-1989) (Dow Jones News/Retrieval).[31] Accordingly, because the government has failed to establish that anyone suffered actual pecuniary loss as a result of their purchase of Gulf & Western stock after Mulheren's trading in the stock on October 17, 1985, the district court erred in imposing a fine against Mulheren on that basis.

Quite apart from the flaws in its theory for calculating loss, the district court erred in basing Mulheren's fine on the surmise that Gulf & Western in fact could and would have bought the 6,726,700 shares from Boesky and Icahn at a price below $45 per share. The government presented no proof that Boesky and Icahn would have sold their stock to Gulf & Western at any lower price. Indeed, the evidence at trial established just the opposite. Boesky testified quite explicitly that his price was $45. (J.A. 54, 56), and he never indicated to Davis any willingness to sell at a lower price (*see* J.A. 126, 131). The government's assumption that Boesky and Icahn would have sold their stock back to Gulf & Western for less than $45 is nothing more than rank speculation.

Moreover, there is every possibility that the market price of Gulf & Western stock would have reached $45 on October 17 even if Mulheren had not traded in the stock that day. After all, the stock had reached that price the previous day. *See* J.A. 145, 370. This possibility, combined with the likelihood that Boesky and Icahn would not have sold their stock to Gulf & Western for less than $45, renders the amount of harm suffered by Gulf & Western as a result of Mulheren's offenses entirely conjectural. Because the government failed to meet its burden of proving that Gulf & Western in fact could have bought the stock for less than $45, the district court should not have based Mulheren's fine on any loss suffered by Gulf & Western.

Accordingly, this Court should reverse Mulheren's fine on the ground that it was based on an erroneous calculation of loss and therefore constitutes an illegal sentence under Section 3571 (d). At the very least, this court should order the district court to hold a hearing on the matter and to make a specific finding, as opposed to a mere assumption, that Gulf & Western could and would have bought its stock from Boesky and Icahn for less than $45 but for Mulheren's action.[32]

---

[31]   That Gulf & Western did not suffer the very substantial loss attributed to it by the district court is strongly suggested by the fact that the company never attempted to sue Boesky or Mulheren for any damages incurred as a result of its purchase of Boesky's and Icahn's shares.

[32]   In the restitution area, courts have favored the practice of holding a hearing to determine the exact extent of the victim's loss. *See United States v. Cloud*, 872 F.2d 846, 855 (9th Cir.), cert. denied, 110 S. Ct. 561 (1989); *United States v. Duncan*, 870 F.2d 1532, 1539 (10th Cir.), *cert. denied,* 110 S. Ct. 264 (1989); *United States v. Watchman*, 749 F.2d 616, 619 (10th Cir. 1984) ; *United States v. Ciambrone*, 602 F. Supp. 563, 570 (S.D.N.Y. 1984).

2. CONCLUSION

The judgment of conviction should be reversed and judgments of acquittal should be ordered, or, in the alternative, a new trial.

Respectfully submitted,

ANDREW L. FREY
WENDY E. ACKERMAN
MAYER, BROWN & PLATT
2000 Pennsylvania Avenue, N.W.
Washington, D.C. 20006
(202) 778-0602

THOMAS P. PUCCIO
MILBANK, TWEED, HADLEY & McCLOY
One Chase Manhattan Plaza
New York, NY 10005
(212) 530-5000
Counsel for Appellant

Dated: February 15, 1991

UNITED STATES of America, Appellee,

v.

John A. MULHEREN, Jr., Defendant-Appellant.

No. 1557, Docket 90-1691.

United States Court of Appeals,
Second Circuit.

Argued May 20, 1991.

Decided July 10, 1991.

Andrew L. Frey, Washington, D.C. (Wendy E. Ackerman, Mayer, Brown & Platt, Washington, D.C., and Thomas P. Puccio, Milbank, Tweed, Hadley & McCloy, New York City, of counsel), for defendant-appellant.

E. Scott Gilbert, Asst. U.S. Atty. (Roger S. Hayes, Acting U.S. Atty., S.D.N.Y., Daniel C. Richman, of counsel), for appellee.

Before VAN GRAAFEILAND, MESKILL and McLAUGHLIN, Circuit Judges.

McLAUGHLIN, Circuit Judge:

In the late 1980's a wide prosecutorial net was cast upon Wall Street. Along with the usual flotsam and jetsam, the government's catch included some of Wall Street's biggest, brightest, and now infamous—Ivan Boesky, Dennis Levine, Michael Milken, Robert Freeman, Martin Siegel, Boyd L. Jeffries, and Paul A. Bilzerian—each of whom either pleaded guilty to or was convicted of crimes involving illicit trading scandals. Also caught in the government's net was defendant-appellant John A. Mulheren, Jr., the chief trader at and general partner of Jamie Securities Co. ("Jamie"), a registered broker-dealer.

Mulheren was charged in a 42-count indictment handed-up on June 13, 1989. The indictment alleged that he conspired to and did manipulate the price on the New York Stock Exchange (the "NYSE") of the common stock of Gulf & Western Industries, Inc. ("G & W" or the "company") in violation of 18 U.S.C. § 371, 15 U.S.C. § 78j(b) & 78ff and 18 U.S.C. § 2, by purchasing 75,000 shares of G & W common stock on October 17, 1985 for the purpose of raising the price thereof to $45 per share (Counts One through Four); that he engaged in "stock parking" transactions to assist the Seemala Corporation, a registered broker-dealer controlled by Boesky, in evading tax and other regulatory requirements in violation of 15 U.S.C. §§ 78j(b) & 78ff and 18 U.S.C. § 2 (Counts Five through Twenty-Four); that he committed mail fraud in connection with the stock parking transactions in violation of 18 U.S.C. §§ 1341 & 2 (Counts Twenty-Five through Thirty-Nine); and that Mulheren caused Jamie to make and keep false books and records in violation of 15 U.S.C. § 78ff & 78q(a) (Counts Forty through Forty-Two).

Count Forty-One was dismissed before trial on the government's motion. At the conclusion of the government's case, the district court dismissed Counts Twenty-Nine through Thirty-Nine pursuant to Fed.R.Crim.P. 29. Of the remaining thirty counts, the jury returned a partial verdict of guilty on Counts One through Four. A mistrial was declared by the district court when the jury could not reach a verdict on the other twenty-six counts. On Counts One through Four, Mulheren was sentenced to concurrent terms of one year and one day imprisonment, a $1,681,700 fine and a $200 special assessment.

This appeal thus focuses solely on the convictions concerning Mulheren's alleged manipulation of G & W common stock. The government sought to prove that on October 17, 1985, Mulheren purchased 75,000 shares of G & W common stock with the purpose and intent of driving the price of that stock to $45 per share. This, the government claimed, was a favor to Boesky, who wanted to sell his enormous block of G & W common stock back to the company at that price. Mulheren assails the convictions on several grounds.

First, Mulheren claims that the government failed to prove beyond a reasonable doubt that when he purchased the 75,000 shares of G & W common stock on October 17, 1985, he did it for the sole purpose of raising the price at which it traded on the NYSE, rather than for his own investment purposes. Second, Mulheren argues that even if his sole intent had been to raise the price of G & W stock, that would not have been a crime because, he claims, (1) he neither misrepresented any fact nor failed to disclose any fact that he was under a duty to disclose concerning his G & W purchases; (2) his subjective intent in purchasing G & W stock is not "material"; and (3) he did not act for the purpose of deceiving others. Finally, Mulheren cites various alleged evidentiary and sentencing errors that he believes entitle him to either a new trial or resentencing.

Although we harbor doubt about the government's theory of prosecution, we reverse on Mulheren's first stated ground because we are convinced that no rational trier of fact could have found the elements of the crimes charged here beyond a reasonable doubt.

BACKGROUND

Reviewing the evidence "in the light most favorable to the government, and construing all permissible inferences in its favor," *United States v. Puzzo*, 928 F.2d 1356, 1357 (2d Cir.1991) (citing *United States v. Diaz*, 878 F.2d 608, 610 (2d Cir.), *cert. denied* 493 U.S. 993, 110 S.Ct. 543, 107 L.Ed.2d 540 (1989)), the following facts were established at trial.

In 1985, at the suggestion of his long-time friend, Carl Icahn, a prominent arbitrageur and corporate raider, Ivan Boesky directed his companies to buy G & W stock, a security that both Icahn and Boesky believed to be "significantly undervalued." Between April and October 1985, Boesky's companies accumulated 3.4 million shares representing approximately 4.9 percent of the outstanding G & W shares. According to Boesky, Icahn also had a "position of magnitude."

On September 5, 1985, Boesky and Icahn met with Martin Davis, the chairman of G & W. At the meeting, Boesky expressed his interest in taking control of G & W through a leveraged buyout or, failing that, by increasing his position in G & W stock and securing seats on the G & W board of directors. Boesky told Davis that he held 4.9 percent of G & W's outstanding shares. Davis said he was not interested in Boesky's proposal, and he remained adamant in subsequent telephone calls and at a later meeting on October 1, 1985.

At the October 1, 1985 meeting, which Icahn also attended, Boesky added a new string to his bow: if Davis continued to reject Boesky's attempts at control, then G & W should buy-out his position at $45 per share. At that time, G & W was, indeed, reducing the number of its outstanding shares through a repurchase program, but, the stock was trading below $45 per share. Davis stated that, although he would consider buying Boesky's shares, he could not immediately agree to a price. Icahn, for his part, indicated that he was not yet sure whether he would sell his G & W stock.

During—and for sometime before—these negotiations, Mulheren and Boesky also maintained a relationship of confidence and trust. The two had often shared market information and given each other trading tips. At some point during the April-October period when Boesky was acquiring G & W stock, Mulheren asked Boesky what he thought of G & W and whether Icahn held a position in the stock. Boesky responded that he "thought well" of G & W stock and that he thought Icahn did indeed own G & W stock. Although Boesky told Mulheren that G & W stock was "a good purchase and worth owning," Boesky never told Mulheren about his meetings or telephone conversations with Davis because he considered the matter "very confidential." Speculation in the press, however, was abound. Reports in the August 19, 1985 issue of Business Week and the September 27, 1985 issue of the Wall Street Journal indicated that Boesky and Icahn each owned close to five percent of G & W and discussed the likelihood of a take-over of the company. Mulheren, however, testifying in his own behalf, denied reading these reports and denied knowing whether Boesky and Icahn held positions in G & W.

On October 3, 1985, two days after his meeting with Boesky and Icahn, Davis met with Mulheren. Mulheren stated that he had a group of investors interested in knowing whether G & W would join them in acquiring CBS. According to Davis, Mulheren also volunteered that he could be "very helpful in monitoring the activities of Ivan Boesky [in G & W stock;] [Mulheren] knew that [Davis] considered Mr. Boesky adversarial;" and Mulheren agreed with Davis' unflattering assessment of Boesky. In a telephone conversation sometime between this October 3 meeting and a subsequent meeting between the two on October 9, 1985, Mulheren told Davis that he believed that Boesky did not own any G & W securities. Mulheren also said that he did not own any G & W stock either. When Davis and Mulheren met again on October 9, they spoke only about Mulheren's CBS proposal.

In the meantime, Boesky continued to press Davis to accept his proposals to secure control of G & W. When Boesky called Davis after their October 1, 1985 meeting, Davis "told [Boesky] as clearly as [he] could again that [G & W] had no interest whatsoever in doing anything with [Boesky]." Boesky then decided to contact his representative at Goldman, Sachs & Co. to arrange the sale of his massive block of stock to G & W. Boesky advised Goldman, Sachs that G & W common stock was not trading at $45 per share at the time, "but that should it become 45," he wanted to sell. A Goldman, Sachs representative met with Davis shortly thereafter regarding the company's repurchase of Boesky's G & W shares.

Sometime after the close of the market on October 16, 1985, Boesky called Davis, offering to sell his block of shares back to G & W at $45 per share. NYSE trading had closed that day at $44 3/4 per share, although at one point during that day it had reached $45. Davis told Boesky that the company would buy his shares back, but only at the "last sale"—the price at which the stock traded on the NYSE at the time of the sale—and that Boesky should have his Goldman, Sachs representative contact Kidder Peabody & Co. to arrange the transaction.[1]

Shortly after 11:00 a.m. on October 17, 1985, Jamie (Mulheren's company) placed an order with Oliver Ihasz, a floor broker, to purchase 50,000 shares of G & W at the market price. Trading in G & W had been sluggish that morning (only 32,200 shares had traded between 9:30 a.m. and 11:03 a.m.), and the market price was holding steady at $44 3/4, the price at which it had closed the day before. At 11:04 a.m., Ihasz purchased 16,100 shares at $44 3/4 per share. Unable to fill the entire 50,000 share order at $44 3/4 , Ihasz purchased the remaining 33,900 shares between 11:05 a.m. and 11:08 a.m. at $44 7/8 per share.

At 11:09 a.m., Ihasz received another order from Jamie; this time, to purchase 25,000 shares of G & W for no more than $45 per share. After attempting to execute the trade at $44 7/8 , Ihasz executed the additional 25,000 share purchase at $45 per share at 11:10 a.m. In sum, between 11:04 a.m. and 11:10 a.m., Jamie purchased a total of

---

[1]   Around the same time, Mulheren received a call from a broker at another firm who had failed to execute an order that day to buy 25,000 shares of G & W for an institutional customer. The broker asked Mulheren if Mulheren would sell him the 25,000 shares he needed. Mulheren, who, at the time, did not own any shares of G & W, checked the stock, noted "it was up a dollar that day" and agreed to "short" the broker—sell what he did not own—25,000 shares. Obviously, Mulheren would soon be obligated to cover his short position, i.e. buy 25,000 shares of G & W.

After this conversation with Davis, but before 11:00 a.m. on October 17, 1985, Boesky called Mulheren. According to Boesky's testimony, the following, critical exchange took place:

> Boesky: Mr. Mulheren asked me if I liked the stock on that particular day, and I said yes, I still liked it. At the time it was trading at 44 3/4 . I said I liked it; however, I would not pay more than 45 for it and it would be great if it traded at 45. The design for the comment—

> DEFENSE COUNSEL MR. PUCCIO: Objection to the "design of the comment." I would ask ask only for the conversation.

> A.U.S.A. GILBERT: What if anything did he say to you?

> BOESKY: I understand.

75,000 shares of G & W common stock, causing the price at which it traded per share to rise from $44 3/4 to $45. At 11:17 a.m., Boesky and Icahn sold their G & W stock—6,715,700 shares between them—back to the company at $45 per share. Trading in G & W closed on the NYSE on October 17, 1985 at $43 5/8 per share. At the end of the day, Jamie's trading in G & W common stock at Mulheren's direction had caused it to lose $64,406.

DISCUSSION

A convicted defendant, of course, bears "a very heavy burden" to demonstrate that the evidence at trial was insufficient to prove his guilt beyond a reasonable doubt. *United States v. Carson*, 702 F.2d 351, 361 (2d Cir.), *cert. denied*, 462 U.S. 1108, 103 S.Ct. 2456, 2457, 77 L.Ed.2d 1335 (1983). "A jury's verdict will be sustained if there is substantial evidence, taking the view most favorable to the government, to support it." *United States v. Nersesian*, 824 F.2d 1294, 1324 (2d Cir.) (citing *Glasser v. United States,* 315 U.S. 60, 80, 62 S.Ct. 457, 469, 86 L.Ed. 680 (1942)), *cert. denied*, 484 U.S. 957, 108 S.Ct. 355, 98 L.Ed.2d 380 (1987) (emphasis added). Where "'any rational trier of fact could have found the essential elements of the crime,' the conviction must stand." *United States v. Badalamenti*, 794 F.2d 821, 828 (2d Cir.1986) (quoting *Jackson v. Virginia*, 443 U.S. 307, 319, 99 S.Ct. 2781, 2789, 61 L.Ed.2d 560 (1979)) (emphasis in original).

On this appeal, however, we are reminded that "in America we still respect the dignity of the individual, and [a defendant] . . . is not to be imprisoned except on definite proof of a specific crime." *United States v. Bufalino*, 285 F.2d 408, 420 (2d Cir.1960) (Clark, J., concurring). To that end, it is "imperative that we not rend the fabric of evidence and examine each shred in isolation; rather, the reviewing court 'must use its experience with people and events in weighing the chances that the evidence correctly points to guilt against the possibility of innocent or ambiguous inference.'" *United States v. Redwine*, 715 F.2d 315, 319 (7th Cir.1983) (quoting *United States v. Kwitek*, 467 F.2d 1222, 1226 (7th Cir.), *cert. denied*, 409 U.S. 1079, 93 S.Ct. 702, 34 L.Ed.2d 668 (1972)), *cert. denied*, 467 U.S. 1216, 104 S.Ct. 2661, 81 L.Ed.2d 367 (1984).

The government's theory of prosecution in this case is straightforward. In its view, when an investor, who is neither a fiduciary nor an insider, engages in securities transactions in the open market with the sole intent to affect the price of the security, the transaction is manipulative and violates Rule 10b-5.[2] Unlawful manipulation occurs, the argument goes, even though the investor has not acted for the "purpose of inducing the purchase or sale of such security by others," an element the government would have had

---

[2]   Although we have misgivings about the government's view of the law, we will assume, without deciding on this appeal, that an investor may lawfully be convicted under Rule 10b-5 where the purpose of his transaction is solely to affect the price of a security. The issue then becomes one of Mulheren's subjective intent. The government was obligated to prove beyond a reasonable doubt that when Mulheren purchased 75,000 shares of G & W common stock on October 17, 1985, he did it with the intent to raise its price, rather than with the intent to invest. We conclude that the government failed to carry this burden.

to prove had it chosen to proceed under the manipulation statute, § 9(a)(2). 15 U.S.C. § 78i(a)(2). Mulheren was not charged with violating § 9(a)(2). When the transaction is effected for an investment purpose, the theory continues, there is no manipulation, even if an increase or diminution in price was a foreseeable consequence of the investment.

In order to convict, the government had to demonstrate, in the first place, that Mulheren was aware that Boesky had a stake in G & W. In proof of knowledge, the government makes three arguments.

First, the government suggests that Boesky himself told Mulheren of his G & W positions. Boesky, however, never so testified; and the greatest puzzle in this record is why that critical question was never directly put to Boesky.[3]

Second, the government relies on the speculation reported in the media, specifically the *Wall Street Journal* and *Business Week*, and the rumors floating on Wall Street that Boesky and Icahn owned substantial positions in G & W. There was no evidence, however, that Mulheren read these articles or heard these rumors. On the contrary, Mulheren flatly denied knowing of their existence. Moreover, knowledge of a rumor, particularly one on Wall Street, can hardly substitute for knowledge of a fact.

Third, the government contends that Mulheren's knowledge of Boesky's position is evident in the October 3, 1985 meeting between Davis and Mulheren. In that meeting, Mulheren told Davis that he knew that Davis and Boesky had an "adversarial" relationship and Mulheren "understood" Davis' "position" and offered to help Davis "in any way he could" to "monitor" Boesky's G & W transactions. While this evidence, taken in isolation, might create an inference that Mulheren knew of Boesky's G & W holdings (as the source of the Boesky-Davis adversarial relationship), the rest of Davis' testimony casts a considerable shadow on the inference. Davis went on to testify that in a telephone conversation sometime between their October 3 and October 9 meetings Mulheren stated that he did not believe Boesky owned any G & W stock at all. By this time, of course, Boesky had already told Davis (at their September 5 meeting) that he owned 4.9 percent of G & W's outstanding shares. Given that Mulheren was at the time attempting to curry favor from Davis in connection with Mulheren's CBS proposal, it was hardly in Mulheren's best interest to lie to Davis by telling him that Boesky owned no shares, if in fact Mulheren knew that Boesky owned 3.4 million shares. In sum, the evidence of Mulheren's knowledge that Boesky had an interest in G & W rests on a very slender reed.

---

[3]   The closest Boesky came to testifying that he told Mulheren about his G & W holdings is the following exchange on direct examination concerning a telephone conversation between Mulheren and Boesky sometime in the period between April and the end of September 1985:

A.U.S.A. GILBERT: What in fact did you tell [Mulheren] about the stock?

BOESKY: As my position was being accumulated, I told him that's how I felt about it, that it was a good purchase and worth owning.

Even were we to conclude otherwise, however, the convictions still could not be sustained. Assuming that Mulheren knew that Boesky held a substantial position in G & W stock, the government nevertheless failed to prove that Mulheren agreed to and then purchased the 75,000 shares for the sole purpose of raising the price at which G & W common stock traded.

The strongest evidence supporting an inference that Mulheren harbored a manipulative intent, is the telephone conversation between Boesky and Mulheren that occurred either late in the day on October 16 or before 11:00 a.m. on October 17, 1985. In discussing the virtues of G & W stock, Boesky told Mulheren that he "would not pay more than 45 for it and it would be great if it traded at 45." To this Mulheren replied "I understand." The meaning of this cryptic conversation is, at best, ambiguous, and we reject the government's contention that this conversation "clearly conveyed Boesky's request that the price of the stock be pushed up to $45 . . . [and Mulheren's] agreement to help." Boesky never testified (again, he was not asked) what he meant by his words.[4]

We acknowledge that, construed as an innocent tip—i.e. G & W would be a "great" buy at a price of $45 or below—the conversation appears contradictory. It seems inconsistent for Boesky to advise, on one hand, that he would not pay more than $45, yet on the other to exclaim that it would be a bargain ("great") at $45. The conversation does not make any more sense, however, if construed as a request for illicit manipulation. That Boesky put a limit on the price he would pay for the stock ("I would not pay more than 45 for it") seems inconsistent with a request to drive up the price of the stock. If a conspiracy to manipulate for his own selfish benefit had been Boesky's intent, and if Davis were poised to repurchase the shares at the "last sale," Boesky would obviously have preferred to see Mulheren drive the trading in G & W stock to a price above $45. In this regard, it is noteworthy that there was no evidence whatever that Mulheren knew of Boesky's demand to get $45 per share from G & W. Moreover, during the four to six weeks preceding this conversation, Mulheren repeatedly asked Boesky what he thought of G & W—evincing Mulheren's predisposition (and Boesky's knowledge thereof) to invest in the company. In fact, Mulheren took a position in G & W when he shorted a broker 25,000 shares of G & W after the market closed on October 16.

Clearly, this case would be much less troubling had Boesky said "I want you to bring it up to 45" or, perhaps, even, "I'd like to see it trading at 45." But to hang a conviction on the threadbare phrase "it would be great if it traded at 45," particularly when the government does not suggest that the words were some sort of sinister code, defies reason and a sense of fair play. Any doubt about this is dispelled by the remaining evidence at trial.

---

[4] Defense counsel objected after Boesky testified "[t]he design of the comment. . . ." No ruling was made on the objection and the government—for reasons known only to itself—abandoned further inquiry into Boesky's state of mind.

First, and perhaps most telling, is that Jamie lost over $64,000 on Mulheren's October 17th transactions. This is hardly the result a market manipulator seeks to achieve. One of the hallmarks of manipulation is some profit or personal gain inuring to the alleged manipulator. *See, e.g., Baum v. Phillips, Appel & Walden, Inc.*, 648 F.Supp. 1518, 1531 (S.D.N.Y.1986), *aff'd per curiam*, 867 F.2d 776 (2d Cir.), *cert. denied*, 493 U.S. 835, 110 S.Ct. 114, 107 L.Ed.2d 75 (1989); *Walck v. American Stock Exchange, Inc.*, 565 F.Supp. 1051, 1065-66 (E.D.Pa.1981), *aff'd*, 687 F.2d 778 (3rd Cir.1982), *cert. denied*, 461 U.S. 942, 103 S.Ct. 2118, 77 L.Ed.2d 1300 (1983); *SEC v. Commonwealth Chemical Securities, Inc.*, 410 F.Supp. 1002, 1013 (S.D.N.Y.1976), *aff'd in part, modified on other grounds*, 574 F.2d 90 (2d Cir.1978).

Second, the unrebutted trial testimony of the G & W specialist demonstrated that if raising the price of G & W to $45 per share was Mulheren's sole intent, Mulheren purchased significantly more shares (and put Jamie in a position of greater risk) than necessary to achieve the result. The G & W specialist testified that at the time Jamie placed its second order, 5,000 shares would "definitely" have raised the trading price from $44 7/8 to $45 per share. Yet, Jamie bought 25,000 shares.

Although there was no evidence that Mulheren received a quid pro quo from Boesky for buying G & W stock, the government, nevertheless, claims that Mulheren had a "strong pecuniary interest" in accommodating Boesky in order to maintain the close and mutually profitable relationship they enjoyed. With this argument the government is hoist with its own petard. Precisely because of this past profitable relationship, the more reasonable conclusion is that Mulheren understood Boesky's comment as another tip—this time to buy G & W stock. Indeed, there was no evidence that Boesky had ever asked Mulheren to rig the price of a stock in the past.

None of the traditional badges of manipulation are present in this case. Mulheren conspicuously purchased the shares for Jamie's account in the open market. *Compare United States v. Scop*, 846 F.2d 135, 137 (matched orders through fictitious nominees), *modified on other grounds*, 856 F.2d 5 (2d Cir.1988); *United States v. Gilbert*, 668 F.2d 94, 95 (2d Cir.1981) (matched orders and wash sales), *cert. denied*, 456 U.S. 946, 102 S.Ct. 2014, 72 L.Ed.2d 469 (1982); *United States v. Minuse*, 114 F.2d 36, 38 (2d Cir.1940) (fictitious accounts, matched orders, wash sales, dissemination of false literature). The government argues that Mulheren's deceptive intent can be inferred from the fact that (1) he purchased the G & W shares through Ihasz, a floor broker whom the government claims was used only infrequently by Jamie; and (2) Ihasz never informed anyone that the purchases were made for Jamie. These arguments are factually flawed.[5]

---

[5] In a wash sale transaction, beneficial ownership of the stock does not change. A matched order involves the prearranged purchase and sale, usually through different brokers, of the same amount of securities at substantially the same price and time. Both practices give the appearance of legitimate market activity.

There was no evidence that there was anything unusual about Ihasz's execution of the trades. Oliver Ihasz testified that Jamie was a customer of his company. There was no testimony that his company was used infrequently, or that Mulheren's request was in any way out of the ordinary. Nor is there anything peculiar about the fact that Ihasz disclosed only the name of the clearing broker and not Jamie, as the purchaser, when he executed the trade. As Ihasz testified, in an open market transaction, the only information the floor broker provides to the seller is the name of the clearing broker, not the ultimate buyer. Jamie was conspicuously identified as the ultimate buyer of the G & W securities on Ihasz's order tickets, where it is supposed to appear.

The government also argues that manipulative intent can be inferred from the fact that Mulheren's purchase on October 17, 1985 comprised 70 percent of the trading in G & W common stock during the period between the opening of the market and 11:10 a.m. Such market domination, the government contends, is indicative of manipulation. While we agree, as a general proposition, that market domination is a factor that supports a manipulation charge, the extent to which an investor controls or dominates the market at any given period of time cannot be viewed in a vacuum. For example, if only ten shares of a stock are bought or sold in a given hour and only by one investor, that investor has created 100 percent of the activity in that stock in that hour. This alone, however, does not make the investor a manipulator. The percent of domination must be viewed in light of the time period involved and other indicia of manipulation. Taken in this context, the cases upon which the government relies, *United States v. Gilbert*, 668 F.2d 94 (2d Cir.1981), *cert. denied*, 456 U.S. 946, 102 S.Ct. 2014, 72 L.Ed.2d 469 (1982); *United States v. Stein*, 456 F.2d 844 (2d Cir.), *cert. denied*, 408 U.S. 922, 92 S.Ct. 2489, 33 L.Ed.2d 333 (1972); *In re Delafield & Delafield*, [1967-69 Transfer Binder] Fed.Sec.L.Rep. (CCH) ¶ 77, 648 (SEC 1969), are readily distinguishable.

Gilbert, for example, involved the manipulation of the shares of Conrac Corporation where, over a one-year period, the defendant's trading constituted more than 50 percent of the overall trading. *See United States v. Gilbert*, [1981-82 Transfer Binder] Fed.Sec.L.Rep. (CCH) ¶ 98, 244, at 91,602, 91,605, 1981 WL 1662 (S.D.N.Y.1981), *aff'd*, 668 F.2d at 95. In Stein, the manipulator's transactions accounted for 28.8 percent of the daily exchange volume of transactions in Buckeye Corporation stock over a four month period. *See Stein*, 456 F.2d at 846. When domination is sustained over such an extended period of time, evidence of manipulation is strong. But, if the percentage of control be measured in terms of minutes or hours, anyone could find himself labeled as a manipulator.

In re Delafield & Delafield is the only case that gives us pause. There, the respondents entered into a consent decree with the Securities and Exchange Commission concerning allegations that they had manipulated the Class A common stock of the Mary Carter Paint Company by selling 17,600 shares of the stock between 2:00 p.m. and the close of the market on January 9, 1968. Respondents' transactions represented 83 percent of the transactions in the stock during that period. Significantly, however, the sales "were effected in the name of two foreign banks to conceal the identity" of the true seller.

See In re Delafield & Delafield, ¶ 77,648 at 83,400. No such chicanery exists here. Thus, in the absence of other indicia of manipulation—and there are none—the fact that Mulheren dominated the market between 9:30 a.m. and 11:10 a.m. on October 17, 1985 (noting that Mulheren's purchases represented a small fraction of the total October 17th activity in G & W stock) carries little weight.

The government also urges that Mulheren's manipulative intent—as opposed to investment intent—can be inferred from certain of Mulheren's actions after his purchase of the G & W shares. For example, Mulheren sold G & W call options in the afternoon of October 17, 1985 that were designed to create a hedge in the event of a drop in the price of stock. Had Mulheren known, however, that Boesky and Icahn were going to unload 6.7 million shares of G & W stock—which had the inevitable effect of driving the price down—surely Mulheren would have had the foresight to write the options before Boesky and Icahn had a chance to sell. That Mulheren wrote the options in the afternoon suggests only that he was attempting to mitigate his losses.

Finally, the government contends that the fact that Mulheren continued to do favors for Boesky after G & W repurchased Boesky and Icahn's shares is inconsistent with his claim that he was "duped" by Boesky into purchasing the 75,000 G & W shares. We disagree. First, the evidence of "favors" rests largely on the unproven "stock parking" charges. Second, Mulheren's conduct after his G & W purchases is equally consistent with that of a sophisticated businessman who turns the other cheek after being slapped by the hand that usually feeds him.

We acknowledge that this case treads dangerously close to the line between legitimate inference and impermissible speculation. We are persuaded, however, that to come to the conclusion it did, "the jury must have engaged in false surmise and rank speculation." *United States v. Wiley*, 846 F.2d 150, 155 (2d Cir.1988) (citing *United States v. Starr*, 816 F.2d 94, 99 (2d Cir.1987)). At best, Mulheren's convictions are based on evidence that is "at least as consistent with innocence as with guilt," *United States v. Mankani*, 738 F.2d 538, 547 (2d Cir.1984), and "on inferences no more valid than others equally supported by reason and experience." *United States v. Bufalino*, 285 F.2d 408, 419 (2d Cir.1960). Accordingly, the judgments of conviction are reversed and Counts One through Four of the indictment are dismissed.

IN RE HOLTZMAN

To be argued by:
ROY L. REARDON
Time Requested: 30 minutes

Court of Appeals

In the Matter of
ELIZABETH HOLTZMAN,

Petitioner-Appellant,

for a Judgment under Article 78
of the Civil Practice Law and Rules

—against—

SHELDON OLIENSIS, SHIRLEY ADELSON SIEGEL, BENITO ROMANO, BRUCE A. GREEN,
and THE CITY OF NEW YORK CONFLICTS OF INTEREST BOARD,

Respondents-Respondents.

BRIEF FOR RESPONDENTS-RESPONDENTS
SHELDON OLIENSIS, *et al.*

ROY L. REARDON
425 Lexington Avenue
New York, New York 10017
(212) 455-2840

*Attorney for Respondents-Respondents
Sheldon Oliensis, et al.*

Of Counsel:
  Robert F. Cusumano
  Elizabeth A. Fuerstman
  Lynn K. Neuner
  David L. Lessing

Date Completed: February 20, 1998

REPRODUCED ON RECYCLED PAPER

TABLE OF CONTENTS

TABLE OF AUTHORITIES

PRELIMINARY STATEMENT

Elizabeth Holtzman ("Holtzman"), former Comptroller of the City of New York, challenges an order of the Appellate Division, First Department, denying her Article 78 petition to annul a decision of the City of New York Conflicts of Interest Board (the "Board") in which the Board held that Holtzman violated sections 2604(b)(2) and (b)(3) of the New York City Charter (the "Charter").

Note how in the second and third paragraphs, the Petitioner's position is effectively characterized as untenable.

By this appeal, Holtzman would have this Court declare the City legally powerless to regulate the conduct *in office* of its highest elected officials because a federal statute governs their conduct *outside of office*. Failing that, Holtzman would have this Court declare her conduct, which was obviously unethical and for which she has publicly apologized, to be perfectly proper and legal. Failing that, finally, Holtzman would have this Court declare her unethical conduct to be illegal only prospectively, because no one informed her with sufficient specificity that it was illegal before she did it.

These various positions slice and dice the ethical standards of public office into vanishingly small pieces. Were this Court to adopt them, it would signal the demise of effective local regulation designed to enhance the ethics and to assure the integrity of local government in the City of New York.

What Holtzman did wrong in this case is not nearly as complicated as her 72-page brief would suggest. Holtzman simply had a personal creditor hostage to the official power of her office. Having personally guaranteed a loan that later went into default—a loan large enough to bankrupt her were the creditor to collect on it—Holtzman (a) chose not to recuse herself from the exercise of her official responsibility to decide whether an affiliate of that same creditor would become a co-manager for a major City bond offering; (b) chose instead to recuse herself (and her campaign staff) from further negotiations with her creditor about the loan in default while the selection process was ongoing; (c) thus held substantial official power over her creditor concerning a specific official decision of major importance to that creditor, which she used, literally, to silence the creditor for months, and (d) ultimately selected her creditor for the City business, only to have this selection voided once this scandal broke. For this, the Board found a civil violation of the City's ethical rules and imposed a reasonable fine of $7,500.

Holtzman's primary argument on this appeal is federal preemption, albeit an aggressive brand of federal preemption that would strip the City of any ability to regulate the conduct in office of its officials who run for federal office. Holtzman continues to misunderstand the federal election laws as somehow regulating conduct in office, just as she continues to misapprehend her violation as being "the appearance of impropriety" allegedly created by the loan when the lender's affiliate sought City business. In fact, the Board has neither sought nor exercised jurisdiction over federal campaign financing and has no complaint with the loan *per se*. Federal candidates like Holtzman may go about their campaign financing activities without the least interference by the City or the Board. The City *must* however, continue to regulate the ethics of its officials *as they conduct their City business*. And the Board, as the City's ethical regulator, must have jurisdiction over officials and their acts in office.

Nothing in federal law purports to preempt local ethical regulation aimed at acts in office. Further, *it is simply irrelevant to this violation* that the loan-in-default that created the conflict of interest happened to be a campaign loan. Exactly the same purely local considerations would have led to exactly the same result had the conflict arisen from a mortgage loan, a car loan, or any other indebtedness in default. Federal candidates are free to raise money without local constraints; by the same token, local officials remain subject to local regulations that govern their actions in office. Here, Holtzman should have recused herself from involvement in a selection process that involved a creditor with whom she was then in negotiations. Instead, she retained the power of her office and used it to silence the negotiations.

Holtzman's remaining contentions are generally attempts to minimize her violations by attributing responsibility to others, by asserting that Holtzman's official duties exceeded her actual involvement in decisions, and by making very strained distinctions between "official" and "non-official" acts. Whether active or passive, explicit or implicit, fully intentional or merely negligent, however, it remains simply unethical for a Comptroller to preside (or to appear to preside) over the selection or rejection of her defaulted creditor for a major piece of City business. And it is no defense to the ethics violation to insist, as Holtzman does here, that she did not really favor the creditor, nor really exercise the authority she so dearly projected. It is the threat and the intimidation that matter, and it is the appearance of impropriety that is quite rightly proscribed by statute. Holding official authority over a decision affecting one's negotiating adversary is an unethical exertion of improper power. Here, that power was sufficient to shut down the negotiations entirely. The violation of ethics law is clear and is purely a matter of local concern. The Board's determination should not be annulled.

COUNTERSTATEMENT OF QUESTIONS INVOLVED

1.   Did the Board conclude arbitrarily and capriciously or without substantial evidence that Holtzman violated section 2604(b)(2) of the New York City Charter by participating in the selection of Fleet Securities as co-manager of a City bond offering while in default on a loan from its affiliate bank?

The Appellate Division answered in the negative.

2.   Did the Board conclude arbitrarily and capriciously or without substantial evidence that Holtzman violated section 2604(b)(3) of the New York City Charter by participating in the selection of Fleet Securities as co-manager of a City bond offering and prohibiting its affiliate bank from speaking to her regarding loan repayment during the selection process?

The Appellate Division answered in the negative.

3.   Does the Federal Election Campaign Act preempt the application of the ethical provisions of the New York City Charter to city officials based on their acts in office?

The Appellate Division answered in the negative.

4.   Did the Board arbitrarily and capriciously fail to follow its administrative policy or to provide proper notice to Holtzman with respect to the application of sections 2604(b)(2) and (b)(3)?

The Appellate Division answered in the negative.

COUNTERSTATEMENT OF FACTS

A. THE PARTIES

Elizabeth Holtzman served as the New York City Comptroller from January 1, 1990 through December 31, 1993. (A1997)[1] The Comptroller's Office includes the Bureau of Asset Management, which is responsible for managing the assets of five municipal pension systems (A2003-04), and the Bureau of Debt Management, which manages the City's debt financing program, issuing municipal bonds and notes to support the City's capital expenditures.

The fact pattern of this case is long and involved. Here, the facts are broken down into manageable segments through the use of headings. Further, the facts as related in the court's opinion are essentially an abridged version of events as presented here.

(A1795.) The Comptroller, jointly with the Mayor, selects a management team of senior managers and co-managers to underwrite the City's bonds and notes. (A2014, A1798.)

The Conflicts of Interest Board is an independent City agency consisting of five members. The Board derives its independence in part from its members' six-year staggered terms. Established under section 2602 of the New York City Charter to administer and enforce the City's Code of Ethics (Charter section 2603), the Board replaced the Board of Ethics, which was purely advisory and lacked enforcement powers.

B. FLEET PURSUES CITY BUSINESS

Fleet Financial Group, Inc. ("FFG") is a holding company based in Providence, Rhode Island. (A281).[2] FFG is the parent company of both Fleet Bank (the "Bank") and Fleet Securities, Inc. ("Fleet Securities") (collectively, "Fleet"). (A281, A652, 657-58.). Fleet Securities is FFG's bond trading and public finance unit. In the late 1980s, Fleet Securities adopted a corporate strategy to expand its public finance capabilities in New York. (A994, A1183-85.) In particular, Fleet Securities wanted to increase its business with the City of New York by becoming a manager of municipal bond offerings and pension funds. (A994, A1001-02, A1185-86, A1716.) Underwriters aggressively compete for positions on the City's management team because of the profits to be earned from bond sales and the management fees paid by the City.[3] (A1002-06, A1195-96, A1706-08.) In addition, New York City's management team has the prestige of underwriting debt for the largest issuer of municipal bonds in the nation. (A1706 08, A1850-52.)

---

[1] Citations in the form "A__" are to the Joint Appendix.

[2] FFG was foamed in 1988 as result of a merger between Fleet Financial Group and Norstar Bancorp. (A658). Between 1988 and 1992, FFG was known as Fleet/Norstar Financial Group, Inc. (A2477, A2478, A2524).

[3] The management team consists of both senior managers and co-managers. Senior managers run the books on the sale and are chosen for their ability to assist the City in structuring bond issues and advise the City on market conditions. Co-managers are selected primarily for their selling capabilities. Both senior and co-managers are contractually bound to the City to purchase a portion of the bonds issued by the City. (A1001-02, A1699-01, A1801-02).

As part of Fleet's efforts to pursue City business, FFG hired James Murphy as executive vice president in charge of government lobbying and inter-governmental relations. (A772-73, A997-99, A1188.) Murphy had extensive government contacts which he used to further Fleet's New York City initiatives. (A2881, A888, A997-99, A1188.) Starting in June 1990, Murphy sought meetings with senior members of Holtzman's staff to promote Fleet's abilities. (A2477, A2478, A778.) Through a friend in the Comptroller's office, Murphy was able to schedule a meeting on June 7, 1990 with Edward O'Malley, Holtzman's Senior Assistant Comptroller and Chief of Staff, who later served as the campaign manager for her Senate race. (A2477, A2478, A778, A1095-96.) Murphy explained Fleet Securities' expanding public finance division and sought further contact with the individuals in the Comptroller's Office handling that business, which O'Malley agreed to arrange. (A2477, A783, A1096-97.) Approximately one month later, Murphy met with members of the Comptroller's Bureau of Asset Management to discuss Fleet's desire to become involved in the City's investment activities. (A784-785, A2479-80.)

In February 1991, Murphy arranged for a meeting with Darcy Bradbury, Deputy Comptroller for Finance, to promote Fleet Securities' effort to become a co-manager on City bond issues. (A2515-16, A796-99, A1189-93, A1836-37). At this meeting, Murphy unequivocally expressed Fleet Securities' interest in achieving co-manager status. (A799-800, A1189-93, A1836-37). After the meeting, Fleet Securities' personnel wrote numerous letters to Bradbury and others describing Fleet Securities' record of selling the City's bonds and reiterating the company's desire to play an enhanced role in the City's negotiated sales. (A1183-87, A1196, A1213, A2515-16, A3121-32, A3246-48, A3258-61, A3263-65.)

As part of its strategy to obtain business from the Comptroller's Office, Fleet also began contributing funds to help Holtzman's political career. In November 1990, Murphy attended a fundraising dinner for Holtzman. (A795-96.) Later that month, Fleet's Political Action Committee ("PAC") made a $4,000 contribution to the Friends of Liz Holtzman, a campaign committee for Holtzman's Senate race. (A795-96, A2953-64.)

Fleet's efforts met with success. In August 1990, Fleet Securities was selected to participate in Project Home, a $50 million program administered by the Bureau of Asset Management.[4] (A2481-84, A2485-2511, A787.) In September 1990, Fleet Bank was selected to participate in the Small Business Loan Program, a $50 million program administered by the Comptroller's Bureau of Asset Management and sponsored by the Police Pension Fund. (A788.)[5] In August 1991, Fleet Securities applied to serve on the

---

[4] Holtzman is quoted in the press release announcing Fleet's selection (A2481-84), and Holtzman specifically commented on Fleet's participation in the program during a ceremony at City Hall. (A793-94). Murphy recalled that he was introduced to Holtzman at the ceremony as "Jim Murphy of Fleet Norstar." (A793.)

[5] Holtzman's office issued a press release on September 26, 1990 announcing Fleet Bank's (then Norstar Bank) participation in the Small Business Loan Program. (A2512-13, A787.)

management team for a Health and Hospitals Corporation bond initiative. (A2600-11, A2884-2952, A1007, A1193-94). In December 1991, in what Fleet personnel described as a "landmark," Fleet Securities was chosen to be a co-manager. (A2616, A1011, A1195.)

C. FLEET'S CAMPAIGN CONTRIBUTIONS

While these business and solicitation events were ongoing, Holtzman announced her formal candidacy for the United States Senate against incumbent Alfonse D'Amato in July 1991. (A2626-28.) Holtzman designated The Liz Holtzman for Senate Committee (the "Committee") as her principal campaign committee. (A2626-28, A1902.) O'Malley, Holtzman's Chief of Staff and long-time political advisor, took a leave of absence to become Holtzman's campaign manager. (A1076-79.) Holtzman named Sheila Levin as the Committee's Finance Director. (A1079, A1377).

Fleet personnel became increasingly involved with Holtzman's campaign. In October 1991, while Fleet's application for the Health and Hospitals Corporation bond initiative was pending, Holtzman and Levin met with Murphy and Terrence Murray, the President and Chief Executive Officer of FFG, to discuss Holtzman's Senate platform. (A2612, A803, A1383-84, 1389-92, A2043-44, A2100-03.) Holtzman admitted that she hoped this meeting would lead to financial support from Murray. (A1390-91, A2099-2100.) In the months that followed, Fleet's PAC and employees made significant contributions to Holtzman's Senate campaign. (A2953-64, A795-96, A812-13, A1020-21, A1230-32.) In addition, Murphy became a member of Holtzman's Campaign Finance Committee. (A2340-76, A2098.)

Fleet's participation in Holtzman's fundraising continued. In November 1991, Murphy attended another fundraising dinner for Holtzman's Senate campaign. (A808.) Following this event, Murphy invited Holtzman to a Fleet holiday party scheduled for December 9, 1991. (A2613-14, A2615, A808-09, A2042, 2100.) That same month, the Fleet PAC and Fleet Securities' executives made contributions to Holtzman's campaign. (A2953-64, A808.) In May 1992, Murphy co-hosted a fundraising event for Holtzman, which Holtzman attended along with various Fleet employees. (A2519-23, A808-810, A1257-58, A1099, A1394, A1751-54.) Holtzman later sent a letter to Murphy, addressing him as "Dear Jim" and thanking him for "hosting a wonderful fundraiser." (A2523.) Also in May, the Fleet PAC made another $4,000 contribution to Holtzman's Senate campaign. (A2953-64.)

---

[6] A Fleet representative testified that when arranging the breakfast meeting, he told Levin that Fleet Securities would make a $2,000 contribution to Holtzman's campaign. (A1200-02, A1059, A1397-98.) He stated that Fleet viewed the promised contribution as a way of "get[ting] [its] foot in the door with Ms. Holtzman" and of "eas[ing] [its] ability to have a meeting to make a case" as to Fleet's abilities. (A1021, A1222-23.)

In June 1992, Holtzman and Levin attended a private breakfast meeting with Fleet personnel, including John O'Brien, President of Fleet Securities. (A2527.) At the meeting, O'Brien made a case for why Fleet Securities should be selected as co-manager for the City's municipal bond offerings. (A2623, A1016-18, A1054-55.) At the time of the meeting, both Fleet and Holtzman were aware that the City would issue a new Request for Proposals ("RFP") in late 1992. (A2617-18, A1016-20.) A Fleet representative testified that Holtzman listened "attentively" to their presentations. (A1256.) After Holtzman left the meeting, one of the Fleet representatives handed an envelope to Levin; the envelope contained a number of checks from Fleet employees for Holtzman's Senate campaign. (A1020-21), A1057-59, A1200-02, A1230-32, A1401.)

D.   FLEET BANK LENDS THE HOLTZMAN CAMPAIGN $450,000

By early August 1992, Holtzman's Senate campaign was in trouble. Polls showed Holtzman running a distant third to Democratic candidates Geraldine Ferraro and Robert Abrams. (A1093.) Moreover, the Committee had only $80,000 available in primary eligible funds. (A3134-35, A311, A1405-06, A2111, A1093.) Holtzman decided that she needed to run a media campaign or else her bid for the Senate would fail "for sure." (A1092-93, A1420-21, A2111.) On August 11, 1992, the campaign's advertising company submitted a media plan to begin on August 27, 1992 - just two weeks away - with a projected cost of $450,000. (A2340-76, A1092, A1401-02.) The broadcasters, however, had to be paid before the campaign could begin. (A1081-82, A1402.) The Committee needed to obtain a significant loan quickly.

With Holtzman's approval, O'Malley called Murphy to ask whether Fleet would make a loan to the Committee. (A1094, A1099-1100, A1132-33, A1168-69, A1095, A2048-49, A2111-12.) Murphy had no credit experience or lending authority and was not an employee, officer or director of Fleet Bank. (A292, A586, A832.) Nevertheless, Murphy arranged for senior Fleet Bank loan officers to review the proposed loan. These officers expressed severe reservations about making the loan. (A826, A3086-94, A319-20, A590-602.) Not only did the Fleet Bank have no borrowing experience with Holtzman or the Committee, but the Fleet's Credit Policy Manual categorized loans for political purposes as "undesirable." (A587, A603, A560A.)

Faced with this reluctance, Murphy contacted John Robinson, the Executive Vice President of FFG in charge of Fleet Bank in New York State. (A3095-97, A672-77, A588-89, A831-32.) Murphy did not disclose to Robinson the "undesirable" nature of the loan, the disapproval of other Bank officers, or Murphy's own ties to the Holtzman campaign. (A672-77.) Moreover, Robinson, like Murphy, had no credit experience and no authority to approve loans made by Fleet Bank. (A654.) Nonetheless, Robinson told Murphy he could not offer any reason not to pursue the loan. (A677.) Murphy re-contacted Fleet Bank's most senior lending officer, Edward Fanning, with this news, and Fanning begrudgingly assigned Nancy O'Connor, a Senior Vice President at Fleet Bank, as the loan officer."[7] (A303, A58890, A846, A3086-94, A3095-97, A291, A590-92, A836.)

As a result of Murphy's efforts, O'Connor held a meeting with representatives of the Committee to discuss the loan on August 20, 1992. (A322, A847-48.) During the meeting, the Committee represented to O'Connor that it would repay the loan from the proceeds of a fundraising dinner at Tavern on the Green, scheduled for September 9, 1992. (A301-302.) At the time, the Committee had "commitments" for ticket sales totalling approximately $373,500 and a list of projections for additional sales. (A2316-30, A307, A850-51, A1118-19, A1420, A1592-1592A, A311-13, A1419-20.) The Bank advised the Committee that, "in order to proceed with any consideration [of] this loan, the Committee needed to be aware that it would require a personal guarantee from Ms. Holtzman"—an idea that the Committee, Holtzman, and their attorney, Joseph McDonald resisted. (A1590-91, A2116.) The meeting concluded with a request from O'Connor for additional information concerning the nature, amount and reliability of the ticket sales. (A352, A1417-18, A1593, 1597.)

The next day, the Committee submitted a list increasing the amount of allegedly confirmed pledges for the September 9 dinner from $373,500 to $548,500—an overnight increase of $175,000. (A2340-76, A322-33, A1383-84, A1420-21.) That same day, the Committee sent O'Connor a memorandum purporting to list "attendees" of two previous Holtzman fundraising dinners, a Finance Committee list, a balance sheet, ongoing expense projections, and the proposed media plan. (A2340-76, A322, 339, A598-99, A1420-21.) After reviewing these materials, O'Connor refused to approve the loan. (A3095-97, A290, A327, A340.) Among other things, O'Connor was concerned that the "loan could have a lot of internal exposure if it was not repaid." (A3091, A290, A327, A340.)

O'Connor nonetheless participated in a conference call later that day with Murphy and Fanning to discuss the loan. (A853-54, A314, A327, A598.) Fanning and O'Connor asked Murphy about the reliability of the pledges—the key to the Bank's agreement to provide a loan. (A320-21, A561, A59698.) Murphy told the Bank that Holtzman's supporters were "good for their pledges," even though he had only "glanced" at the original pledge list and had never seen the final list.[8] (A850, A852, A860-61, A871, A316-17, A337, A1417-19.) Relying on Murphy's recommendation, Fanning agreed to

---

[7]   Fanning felt that Murphy, whom Fanning viewed as "senior" to him in the FFG hierarchy, "applied great pressure, dropped names, [and] pushed [the] deal through." (A2970.) Fanning stated that he "would not have considered the loan" if Holtzman had come directly to him, without Murphy's and Robinson's involvement (A3097.)

[8]   Moreover, Murphy deemed the pledge list he saw reliable even though it included a projected commitment for three tickets from him—a "commitment" he knew he had never given the Committee. (A861, A1436-39.)

approve a $400,000 loan.[9] (A321, A333, A341, A473-74, A596-97, A860.) Murphy then asked whether the Bank would lend an additional $50,000 if the Committee could show that it would raise another $100,000 at the September 9 dinner. (A873, A334.)

Later that day—just one day after the first meeting between the Committee and Fleet Bank—Murphy and O'Connor notified O'Malley and Levin that the Bank would lend $400,000 against the information provided, and that if the Committee demonstrated additional pledges of $100,000, the Bank would lend an additional $50,000.[10] (A333-37, A862, A601-02, A1136-38.) The Committee did not submit documentation for the additional $100,000 in pledges until August 26, 1992, the same day it sent the Bank wire transfer instructions for the entire $450,000. (A2424, A3133, A1441-42, A1488).

On August 28, 1992, Holtzman entered into a letter agreement with Fleet Bank for the $450,000 loan to the Committee (the "Loan Agreement" or the "Agreement"). (A2425-2427, A371.)[11] Holtzman signed the required promissory note on behalf of the Committee and, in addition, executed a personal guaranty. (A2428-30, A2561-63, A372-73, A1598-99, A2159.) The Loan Agreement set forth that the loan was to be repaid on September 30, 1992, at an interest rate of prime plus one, with a $4,500 back-end fee. (A2425-27, A1562-64.) The Agreement further provided that the Committee would make daily deposits into a pledge account of the proceeds from the ticket sales to the September 9 dinner. (A2425-27, A371-72, A1603, A1606-07, A1915, A1918.) In addition, the Loan Agreement provided that, in the event of a shortfall from the Sep-

---

[9]   Even after approving the loan, Fanning continued to express doubts as to the validity of the pledge lists provided by the Committee. Fanning wrote on the draft loan proposal sent to him by O'Connor for his review, "How good are the pledge lists? Would they ever lie to us?" (A2298-2307, A327-28, A594-95.)

[10]   Fanning's formal approval of the loan on August 24 violated the Bank's internal policies in two respects. (A2420-23, A369, A613, A838.) Fleet required the signatures of two lending officers for loans over $250,000 and three signatures for "undesirable" loans over $250,000. (A3051-52.) However, Fanning was the only lending officer to approve the loan. Fleet's policy also dictated that only Fleet Bank officers could serve as "sponsoring officers." (A3056, A350-51, A865.) The "Sponsoring Officer" on the loan was listed as Murphy, who was neither a Fleet Bank officer nor an employee with any lending authority. (A2420-23, A369, A838, A350-51, A691, A832.) The New York State Banking Department and Board of Governors of the Federal Reserve later investigated the loan and concluded that the Bank had not complied with its established loan policies and procedures, including a lack of requisite authorized approvals and failure to exercise due diligence in the loan analysis. (A3079-81.)

[11]   The record demonstrates that Fleet Bank extended the loan in order to generate goodwill for Fleet with the Comptroller. Indeed, the draft loan proposal approving the loan indicated as follows:

James Murphy, EVP, FFG, has recommended this loan to meet the needs of Ms. Holtzman's campaign in order to support the bank's relationship with [Holtzman's] (accounts maintained at the Church Street Branch) and [with] New York City, via her position as City Comptroller.

(A2302; A343-44, A364-65.) On the advice of Fleet's attorney, this language was deleted from the final loan agreement. (A2409-16, A3076-78, A343-44, A364-65.)

tember 9 dinner the Bank, "in its sole discretion," could require the Committee to hold additional fundraisers to pay down the debt. (A 2426, A383.)

E.   HOLTZMAN AND THE COMMITTEE FAIL TO REPAY THE LOAN

On August 25, 1992, Holtzman released her media campaign which involved a negative attack on the front-runner, Geraldine Ferraro. The public reacted adversely to the advertisements, and as a result, Holtzman's ratings plummeted and her September 9 dinner was a "disaster." (A1443.) Instead of the expected $650,000 in revenues the Committee projected to Fleet Bank, the dinner generated approximately $200,000. (A2436-38, A376-77, A875-76, A1141-42, A1443-44, A2050.) The Bank in turn received less than half of these proceeds—about $91,000. (A2436-38, A2440-42, A377, A1462, A1758, 1934-35.)

In violation of the Loan Agreement, the Committee did not deposit all of the dinner proceeds into the pledge account, and in fact, at O'Malley's direction, spent approximately $48,000 of the proceeds on other campaign-related expenses. (A2631, A2632, A449, A1559-60, A1615-16, A1932-33). The Committee deliberately "diver[ted] . . . the Bank's funds" because the Committee "deemed it essential to its continued fundraising ability that [its] expenses be paid." (A3376-77, A4587, A1559-61, A1915-19, A1932-33.)

The New York Senate primary was held on September 15, 1992. Robert Abrams won; Holtzman ran fourth in a field of four. (A1142, A2050.) Fleet's Murphy attended the Holtzman party on the evening of the primary. (A1149.) Holtzman's Senate campaign was over.

1.   The Bank Requests a Schedule for Repayment of the Loan

On September 24, 1992, O'Connor and Murphy met with Levin and McDonald to discuss the Committee's plans to repay the loan. (A2440-42, A383, A877-79, A1452-55, A1612-14.) Because of the poor turnout at the September 9 dinner, it was clear the Committee would not be able to meet the September 30, 1992 due date for the loan. (A387-81, A876-77.) At the meeting, the Bank expressed concern about the Committee's diversion of funds from the fundraising dinner to pay campaign expenses, and the Committee's failure to provide a schedule for repayment of the debt. (A383-84, A877-79, A1613-14.) McDonald testified that the Bank was "upset" and described the meeting as very "recriminatory." (A1613, 1617-18.)

The Bank told Levin and McDonald that it expected the Committee to hold significant debt fundraisers to reduce the outstanding balance of the loan. (A385.) Despite its contractual obligation to do so, the Committee told the Bank it would not hold a debt fundraiser until after the general election on November 3, 1992, because Holtzman had promised her support to Robert Abrams. (A2436-38.)

2.   The Loan Goes Into Default And The Bank Grants Numerous Extensions

On September 30, 1992, the loan went into default. (A2428-30, A395, 2051, 2152A.) Prior and subsequent to this date, Holtzman and her staff engaged in negotiations with the Bank to extend the loan and to avoid payment on Holtzman's personal guaranty. Thus, on or about September 30, 1992, the Bank extended the loan until November 2, 1992 without requiring any consideration from Holtzman or the Committee.[12] (A2445-47, A395, A1624.) When the loan became due and payable on November 2, 1992, the Bank again agreed to extend the note through December 4, 1992. (A2451-53, A1624.)

Throughout the period that Holtzman was engaged in discussions with the Bank regarding the loan, Holtzman was well aware that Fleet was doing business with the City and eager to increase those business dealings. For example, on November 10, 1992, Holtzman received an electronic mail memorandum identifying Fleet Bank as a participant in the financing of a $4.5 million dollar housing project administered by the Comptroller's Office. (A2629.) Holtzman, of course, had also attended the June 12 breakfast meeting at which Fleet executives expressed their interest in obtaining City work in unmistakable terms. (A2044.) Holtzman nonetheless failed to disclose to appropriate City officers and employees her relationship with Fleet Bank and the delinquent status of the loan.

3.   The Bank Presses Holtzman For Repayment From Her Personal Assets

Growing increasingly concerned about Holtzman's failure to repay the loan, the Bank insisted upon a meeting on December 15, 1992. (A404, A1620.) While Jim Murphy did not attend, Holtzman was present for the meeting. (A1456, A2054.) The meeting was very "hostile" and "accusatory," with the Bank talking "tough" about repayment of the loan. (A165, A1491, A2158-59.) For the first time, the Bank informed Holtzman that it was considering requiring collateral for the loan or transferring the loan to Holtzman personally. (A2456-57, A408-09, A2055, A2159-60.) Holtzman became "visibly tense" about the Bank com[ing] after her personal assets." (A3093, A1455, A1491-92, A1622-24.) Holtzman later testified that she was worried about "losing her house" and that she found the Bank's conduct threatening, like a "police detective, open[ing] his or her jacket and showing a gun but not taking it out of the holster." (A2055, A1622-24, A2160.) The parties also discussed the fact that, if the guaranty were enforced, Holtzman could be forced into bankruptcy—a personal and professional disaster. (A1660, A1664-67.)

In spite of the Bank's threatening proposals, the Committee stated its refusal to hold additional debt fundraisers, as required by the Loan Agreement, until after the general election for Comptroller in November 1993—almost a year away. The Committee told the Bank that its "priority [was] to get Ms. Holtzman re-elected so she still

---

[12]   Fanning was the sole Fleet officer to approve the extension. This action entailed yet another violation of Fleet credit policies—the requirement that three loan officers approve such an extension. (A3055.)

has the ability to raise funds to reduce our debt." (A2457, A406, A410, A460-61, A1625-76, A2055-57.)

Based on its understanding that negotiations with the Committee would be ongoing, the Bank agreed to extend the loan until February 1, 1993. (A2459-69, A411-13, A1941, A2168.) The parties agreed that a follow-up meeting would be held in January to discuss repayment. (A2456-57, A411, A1624-27.) On December 29, 1992, in the midst of the holidays and New Year's vacation, Holtzman personally signed a replacement note with the February 1 date and had the note hand-delivered to the Bank. (A2459-69, A2643, A413-14, A885-86, A2057.)

F.   THE "QUIET PERIOD" SILENCES NEGOTIATIONS ABOUT THE DEFAULT; HOLTZMAN RETAINS AUTHORITY OVER SELECTION OF BOND MANAGERS

1.   Holtzman Remains Involved in Fleet's Competition to Become a Bond Manager

On December 22, 1992, the Office of the Comptroller and the Office of the Mayor issued an RFP to select a new management team to underwrite the City's general obligations bonds and New York City Water Authority revenue bonds. (A2528-44.) Fleet Securities responded to the RFP, applying for a co-manager position. (A2545-60.)

Pursuant to a delegation of authority executed on December 17, 1992—just two days after Holtzman's meeting with Fleet Bank where the potential for pursuing her personal assets was discussed—Holtzman designated Darcy Bradbury to exercise certain "powers and duties of the Comptroller," including the authority to oversee the RFP process. (A3234-35, A3280-81, A1796-97, A2020-21.) While this delegation gave Bradbury the power to act in Holtzman's place with regard to finance matters, it made no mention of, and did not purport to be, an effective recusal. Holtzman, moreover, retained the ultimate authority within the Comptroller's Office to designate senior managers and co-managers. Holtzman "always had the right to take back the authority [she] had given [Bradbury]." (A2086.) Holtzman did not disclose to Bradbury her personal obligation to Fleet Bank. (A3151-53, A1856, A2188.)

2.   Holtzman's "Quiet Period" Policy Avoids Repayment On (or Even Discussion of) the Guaranty

In mid to late January 1993, O'Malley, having resumed his position as Deputy Comptroller after the primary, had a telephone conversation with McDonald, Levin and Mary Kornman, the campaign's Treasurer, in which they indicated to O'Malley that they were planning to meet with the Bank regarding the loan. (A1107, A1469-70, A1633, A1772-73, A1942-46.) During that conversation, O'Malley said that "Fleet may have responded to this R.F.P., I'm not so sure you can meet with them, let me put you on hold, let me check with someone down in Finance and I'll get right back to you." (A1109.) After quickly confirming Fleet's response, O'Malley "went back to the conversation and said, listen, they responded and I don't believe you can meet with them during this period," and asked one of them to "convey this to the bank." (A1109, A1470-71, A1633-34, A1773, A1945.)

At the time of this conversation, O'Malley and the representatives of the Committee were well aware of the delinquent status of the loan and the Bank's pressure for repayment. (A2643, A1110-11, A1116-17, A1468, A1622-23, A1942.) They also knew that the loan deeply troubled Holtzman and that she was "not happy with the way the bank was pressing her." (A1146-49, A1468, A1492, A1541-44, A1940-41, A1622-23.) "O'Malley based his instructions not to communicate with Fleet Bank about the loan—an effective "quiet period"—upon what he believed was Holtzman's "personal" policy that there should be no communications with underwriting firms that respond to RFPs. (A1111-15, A1633-34, A1770-71, A2169-70, A1857-58.) This has been euphemistically referred to as the "quiet period."

Holtzman's own description of her personal "quiet period" leaves no question that, properly applied, it in no way barred communications with the Bank. As Holtzman testified:

> I had instituted a policy which during the period of time from the sending out of the R.F.P to the conclusion of the selection process for underwriters that we would not engage in campaign solicitations or discuss the [selection] process with the underwriters [which had responded to the RFP] except . . . [where] discussion of the [selection] process would be [had] under very controlled circumstances.

(A2169-70, A2176-77.) Indeed, upon reflection, O'Malley admitted that the "quiet period" did not prevent the Committee from discussing the loan with Fleet Bank. (A1105 (conceding that "maybe [Holtzman and the Committee] could" have discussed the loan with the Bank during the RFP process).) Thus, no personal policy of the Comptroller prevented the Committee from negotiating with the Bank about the loan in default.[13] Rather, the moratorium on loan discussions with the Bank was used solely for Holtzman's personal benefit to avoid repayment negotiations.[14] Holtzman admitted that she was responsible for O'Malley's imposition of the moratorium on discussions with the Bank, testifying that:

> In the end I am responsible as the Chief Executice in that office for the acts of everybody no matter what their title . . . . (A2196, A3229-32.)

---

[13] In addition, no City policy prevented the Committee from discussing the loan with the Bank or even discussing any non-RFP issues with the potential underwriters. Indeed, Bradbury admitted that such a policy "would be impossible because [the Comptroller's Office] need[s] to have ongoing business conversations with a variety of firms in order to keep up the City's business." (A1865-66).

[14] That this moratorium was used solely to benefit Holtzman is further demonstrated by the fact that it did not interfere with communications between Fleet and the Comptroller's Office that benfitted Holtzman. Thus, for example, Holtzman herself signed the last renewal note on the loan on December 29, 1992, during the period when communications with the Bank were allegedly prohibited. (A2507, A2168-69.)

On January 25 1993 Fleet's O'Connor telephoned McDonald to discuss the impending February 1st due date of the loan. (A2476, A416-17, A895-96, A1471, A1640.) As O'Malley had instructed, McDonald informed O'Connor that, because the Comptroller's Office had bids out to investment banks for bond underwriting, a City "rule or regulation" precluded Holtzman from having dealings with the Bank. (A2476, A417, A605-10, A895, A1646-47.)

O'Connor thought this purported policy was "outrageous" and "unconscionable." (A3093, A420, A478-79, A543.) When O'Connor told Fanning of the moratorium, Fanning did not even believe it was true, and asked O'Connor if the Committee was "pulling our legs." (A3093, A420, 478-79, A606, SA1-SA2.) Nevertheless, the Bank abided by this "quiet period" without asking for any details from the Committee or Holtzman, and without discussing it with its lawyers. (A420, A478-79, A607, SA1-SA2.)

The moratorium effectively lasted from the beginning of January through March 17, the day the Comptroller's Office announced the underwriters for the City's management team. During this lengthy reprieve, Holtzman testified that she did not *once* inquire about the loan, even though she knew the loan was due on Februay 1 and that she still owed approximately $250,000. (A2164-65, A903, A1737.) Holtzman's explanation for her alleged lack of interest in this enormous personal obligation was that "possibly psychologically I just wanted to push it away from me." (A2152-53, A2166.) By misusing the powers of her office, Holtzman accomplished just that; she did not have to discuss her quarter-of-a-million dollar debt to the Bank for over two-and-a-half months.

February 1 passed without repayment of the loan or any contact with Bank by the Committee or Holtzman. (A414-15, A1278.) On February 12, 1993, O'Connor advised McDonald by letter that the loan would be transferred to the Bank's workout group, known as the Managed Assets Department, as a result of the Bank's "inability to negotiate such a restructure until after March 1, 1993 *because of Ms. Holtzman's position as Comptroller and her involvement in choosing banks for city underwriting.*" (A2476, A442-43 (emphasis added).) McDonald admits receiving this letter. (A2276.) Holtzman also received a copy of this letter, but claims she did not read it because, although it was from the Bank that she owed $250,000 and which had the power to foreclose on her home and bankrupt her, she generally does not read mail which includes her only on the "cc" line. (A2476, A443, A1784, 2059-60, A2151-53, A2181 (conceding that Holtzman subscribed to the Sherlock Holmes-like notion that if mail "was important enough for [her] to see the sender would send it to 'her] directly").)

G.   FLEET SECURITIES IS PROMOTED TO CO-MANAGER ON THE RECOMMENDATION OF THE COMPTROLLER'S OFFICE

During the same period that Fleet decided to transfer the loan to its workout group, the offices of the Comptroller and the Mayor were in the final stages of selecting a new underwriting team for the City's bonds. Fleet Securities was among the applicants reviewed by the Comptroller's Office. (A1240-1241, A1715-1718, A1835-1846.)

Throughout this period, Deputy Comptroller Bradbury and Holtzman had significant contact concerning the RFP process. (A2633-36, A2644-46, A1886-92, A2182-85.) Holtzman reviewed and commented on the RFP before it went out and participated in the selection process leading to her Office's recommendation and selection of Fleet Securities to be co-manager. (A2021-23, A2182-85, A1825-28, A1713-15, A1735-37.) Holtzman and Bradbury recalled discussing the selection of senior managers on numerous occasions. (A1826-1827, A2021-2023.) In addition, Holtzman and Bradbury discussed the selection of certain co-managers. (A1827-28, A1854-56, A1885-87, A2022-23, A2182-84.) These discussions necessarily had an impact on Fleet's candidacy because, given that there was a finite offering of bonds, there was also a finite number of co-managers that could be selected.[15]

On or about March 10, 1993, a week prior to the announcement of the City's new underwriting team—and during the alleged "quiet period"—O'Malley called Murphy and told him that Fleet was "going to be getting good news" in the near future. (A458-459, A899-900, A1119, A1123-24.) Murphy understood that the "good news" was that Fleet Securities had been chosen as a co-manager. (A900.) Murphy immediately passed this good news on to Fleet's Robinson and O'Connor (even though O'Connor worked for the Bank, not Fleet Securities). (A458, A692-703, A900-901.)

At a meeting on March 16, 1993, Bradbury proposed to representatives of the Mayor's Office and others that Fleet Securities be chosen as co-manager. (A1715-1719, A1843-50.) The Mayor's Office agreed. *Id.* On March 17, 1993, the Offices of the Mayor and Comptroller announced the names of the financial institutions that would comprise the City's underwriting management team. (A903, A1737, A1841.) Fleet Securities was selected—for the first time—as co-manager on a New York City bond issue.

On April 1, 1993, Holtzman and the Mayor personally signed the public notice of the bond offering, or "tombstone," listing Fleet Securities as co-manager. (A2662-2852, A2080-082, A1731-32, A1812-20.) Holtzman admits to signing the tombstone, but claims not to have read it or looked at its cover. (A2018, A2080-82.)

H.   THE MAYOR REMOVES FLEET AS CO-MANAGER AS A RESULT OF FLEET'S LOAN TO HOLTZMAN

On April 23, 1993, the press reported that the Comptroller's Office had recommended Fleet Securities as a co-manager seven months after Holtzman's Senate campaign obtained a $450,000 loan from Fleet Bank. (A3345-48, A1740-41, A2066.) That same day, Holtzman "recused [herself] from any involvement in decisions of the [Comptroller's] Office regarding Fleet Bank and/or its affiliates." (A3297, A2066-2069.) Holtz-

---

[15]   Bradbury also kept O'Malley informed of the progress of the selection process and sought his advise on negotiations with the Mayor's Office. (A1119-1120, A1875-76, A1882-83.) Like Holtzman, O'Malley remained silent about Holtzman's massive debt to Fleet Bank.

man admitted that she should have recused herself from the process of selecting the successful firms:

> [I]n hindsight, I should have asked for the names of everyone who was applying to be co-manager and then I would have been advised about Fleet and I could have formally recused myself, advised everybody about the loan, and there would have been no appearance of impropriety.

(A3229-32.) Holtzman also admitted that her actions created "an appearance of conflict." (A3151-53, A3154 (Mayor Dinkins advised that Holtzman "greatly regrets any appearance of impropriety her actions may have caused").) In an interview televised on *New York 1 News* on May 6, 1993, Holtzman admitted to errors in judgment. Significantly, she acknowledged making a "mistake" by thinking that "there was no problem" because she was not directly involved in the RFP selection process. (A3229-32.) Holtzman further admitted that:

> Clearly, you know in hindsight I should have known . . . Clearly, I should have anticipated, and it was a mistake not to have anticipated the possibility that the bank could have sought to become a co-manager. And clearly I made a mistake in not envisioning that and therefore finding out about it and recusing myself right away.

Id. Although Holtzman denied the accuracy of these quotes from the television interview when they were referred to in a newspaper article (A2253-56), the videotape of this interview establishes without a doubt these admissions by Holtzman. (A3229-32.)

The Mayor appointed an *ad hoc* investigation committee consisting of Barry Sullivan, Deputy Mayor; Peter Sherwood, Corporation Counsel; George Daniels, Mayoral Counsel; Michael Geffrard, Director of the Mayor's Office of Public Finance; and Mark Page, General Counsel of the New York City Office of Management and Budget. (A3157.) On May 13, 1993, the committee recommended that Fleet Securities not be appointed co-manager because, *inter alia*, "the appearance of a favor is a serious matter that requires decisive action to safeguard the City's reputation of integrity." (A3150.) The committee stated that "as public servants we have an obligation not only to avoid conflicts of interest, but to avoid even the appearance of conflicts." (A3150.) That same day, Mayor Dinkins removed Fleet Securities as a co-manager on the bond issue. (A3154, A3155-60.)

PROCEDURAL HISTORY

A.   THE DOI INVESTIGATION

In May 1993, the Board ordered the Department of Investigation of the City of New York (the "DOI") to investigate whether Holtzman's participation in the appointment of Fleet Securities as co-manager violated the Charter. After a five-month investigation in which it reviewed more than 15,000 documents and interviewed more than 40 witnesses, the DOI issued a report to the Board, finding that:

- Fleet Bank's loan was made to generate goodwill for Fleet Securities (A161);

- In guaranteeing the loan, Holtzman "entered into a financial relationship" with Fleet which was "doing and actively seeking business with the Comptroller's Office." (A162);

- Holtzman "participated in the process leading to her Office's recommendation of Fleet Securities to be a co-manager." (A163);

- Holtzman knew that Fleet was "doing and seeking business with the Comptroller's Office." (A164); and

- Holtzman was "grossly negligent in failing to ascertain" whether Fleet was doing business with her Office before guaranteeing the loan and participating in the selection process. (A165).

The Board subsequently concluded that there was probable cause to believe Holtzman had violated the Charter's conflicts of interest provisions and filed a Petition dated December 29, 1993, charging Holtzman with violating sections 2604(b)(2),[16] 2604(b)(3),[17] 2604(b)(5)[18] and 2604(b)(13)[19] of the Charter.[20] (A168-90.)

B.   THE HEARING BEFORE ADMINISTRATIVE LAW JUDGE SPOONER

Pursuant to section 2603(h)(2) of the Charter, the Board directed that a hearing be held before a hearing officer. (A169.) In May and June 1994, Administrative Law Judge ("ALJ") John B. Spooner conducted an eleven day hearing in which testimony was

---

[16]   Section 2604(b)(2) provides:

No public servant shall engage in any business, transaction or private employment, or have any financial or other private interest, direct or indirect, which is in conflict with the proper discharge of his or her official duties.

[17]   Section 2604(b)(3) provides;

No public servant shall use or attempt to use his or her position as a public servant to obtain any financial gain, contract, license, privilege or other private or personal advantage, direct or indirect, for the public servant or any person or firm associated with the public servant.

[18]   Section 2604(b)(5) provides:

No public servant shall accept any valuable gift, as defined by rule of the board, from any person or firm which such public servant knows is or intends to become engaged in business dealings with the city . . . .

[19]   Section 2604(b)(13) provides:

No public servant shall receive compensation except from the city for performing any official duty or accept or receive any gratuity from any person whose interests may be affected by the public servant's official duties.

[20]   Sheldon Oliensis a member of the Board, recused himself from all Board deliberations concerning the Holtzman matter, including the determination that there was "probable cause" that Holtzman had violated the Charter. Jane Parver, who later became a Board member, also recused herself from this matter.

received from more than fifteen witnesses, 150 exhibits were entered into evidence, and 2,000 pages of testimony were taken. On November 23, 1994, Judge Spooner issued a Report and Recommendation. (A3784-52.)[21] As a threshold matter, Judge Spooner rejected Holtzman's claim that the City conflicts of interest rules were preempted by FECA or state laws, concluding the "FECA was not meant to preempt local regulation of the officials acts of a City official with regard to the selection of a lender for significant City business." (A3834.)[22]

Judge Spooner believed that, although Fleet had violated its internal procedures in granting Holtzman the loan, the Bank did not treat Holtzman more favorably after she defaulted than it would other bank customers. (A3838, A3840.) As a result, he found no basis for determining that Holtzman received a "gift" or "gratuity" as defined in sections 2604(b)(5) or 2604(b)(13) of the Charter.

Judge Spooner then found that, given the magnitude of the loan, Holtzman's personal guaranty and the default, Holtzman had a duty to learn of Fleet's application to be co-manager on a City bond offering. (A3848.) He wrote that "Ms. Holtzman had an obligation to determine whether Fleet was doing business with the City after the Fleet Bank loan went into default and her failure to do so and take steps to eliminate the conflict established a violation of section 2604(b)(2) of the Charter." (A3850.) Judge Spooner then found that, despite O'Malley's use of the "quiet period" to "deflect the pressure Fleet Bank was placing on the Committee for repayment of the loan and to gain additional time," Holtzman was not responsible for her subordinate's actions, and he thus recommended a finding that Holtzman did not violate section 2604(b)(3). While Judge Spooner believed that Holtzman did not violate this section, the forty-page factual summary contained in his Report includes all of the facts that overwhelmingly establish a violation and justify the fine imposed by the Board. Judge Spooner's recommendation with respect to section 2604(b)(3) disregards both the fact that Holtzman was on notice of the imposition of the quiet period and her admission of her responsibility for her staff's actions.

With regard to the appropriate penalty, Judge Spooner made a plea for leniency for Holtzman, suggesting that any fine levied should not be severe given his view that Holtzman was not "grossly negligent" and that the scrutiny given the loan had been a significant factor in her ultimate election loss. (A3851-52.)

---

[21]   Under the Board's Rules Section 2-04, 12 Rules of the City of New York, Title 53, the ALJ's recommendation is not final. It is subject to a complete review of the record and of the evidence, as well as the written comments of the parties, by the Board, which then issues its final findings of fact and conclusions of law.

[22]   Judge Spooner distinguished between Holtzman's acts in initially obtaining the loan, which he found to be preempted by FECA, and her acts following the default, which were not preempted. (A3835-36.)

C.   THE BOARD'S DECISION

The Board received all of the testimony before Judge Spooner, as well as all of the exhibits introduced during the trial. After reviewing these materials and Judge Spooner's recommendations, the Board concluded that Holtzman violated section 2604(b)(2), holding that Holtzman's "'private interest' in the bank loan in which her personal assets were at risk was 'in conflict with the proper discharge of . . . her official duties' in overseeing the bond underwriting selection process. . . ." (A3999.) In so holding, the Board noted that "a violation of Section 2604(b)(2) arises whenever, with knowledge of the private interest, the public servant retains the interest or fails to recuse himself or herself from the official duties with which the private interest may conflict." (A3994.)

The Board further observed that section 2604(b)(2) "applies whenever a private interest of a public servant may reasonably be viewed as potentially influencing an official act . . . . [A]n appearance of impropriety exists when the transaction in question 'suggest[s] that official actions were being taken as a result of a private benefit.'" *Id.* The Board noted the "particular importance of avoiding even the appearance of bias by high-ranking officials in departments considered to be especially sensitive," and observed that the Comptroller's Office is an especially sensitive department. (A3995.) In addition, the Board noted that "[w]hether an appearance of impropriety exists is to be determined from the perspective of the public at large." (A3995.) Thus, the Board held that "it is unnecessary for purposes of applying Section 2604(b)(2) for us to consider [Holtzman's] good faith or whether [Holtzman] had a subjective belief that her private interest was not in conflict with her official duties." *Id.* Finally, the Board concluded that a public official is charged with exercising "reasonable care in ascertaining all the relevant facts necessary for compliance with its ethics provisions." (A3996.)

The Board also found that Holtzman violated section 2604(b)(3) in two ways. First, the Board held that Holtzman's "exercise of authority over the decision to select Fleet Securities as co-manager of a City bond issue was reasonably likely to influence Fleet Bank to act favorably toward Respondent with respect to the Loan." (A4000.) Second, the Board held that Holtzman's "exercise of authority over the selection process foreseeably led to a further impermissible use of office in the form of the 'quiet period' which forestalled the Bank's efforts to compel repayment of the Loan." *Id.* The Board found that Holtzman was "on notice that her 'quiet period' policy—which technically applied only to communications regarding the selection process with underwriting firms that responded to the RFP—had in this case been applied to curtail communications with Fleet Bank regarding repayment of the delinquent loan." (A4001.)

Furthermore, the Board concluded that Holtzman "knew of the Loan and the need for on-going communications with Fleet Bank regarding the pending loan extension deadline of February 1, 1993" (A4002), and the "unexpected silence should have alerted [Holtzman] to the reason the Bank had stopped pressuring her, or at least should have caused her to ask Mr. McDonald or Ms. Levin if they could explain the silence." *Id.*

In reaching these conclusions, the Board construed section 2604(b)(3) in the following manner:

> Section 2604(b)(3) embodies a strong public policy that public authority is to be exercised solely for the public good. It is a violation of this section for a public servant knowingly to use or attempt to use his or her public office in any manner which is reasonably likely to result in a private gain, either to the public servant or to others having a specified relationship with the public servant. The prohibitions of Section 2604(b)(3) apply without regard to whether the public servant intended personally to benefit from the use of public office, or whether official authority is expressly invoked in a private transaction, or whether a benefit is actually conferred upon the public servant.

(A3999.)

The Board also concurred with Judge Spooner's rejection of Holtzman's claim that federal election laws prevented the enforcement of the Charter. The Board concluded that those laws are not intended to preclude "local government from disciplining its public servants for misusing their public office." (A4003.) The Board further held that its "exercise of jurisdiction over [Holtzman's] failure to recuse herself from the selection of co-managers for the City's bond issue, and over the use of a 'quiet period' to hold off her lender, is narrowly tailored to further New York's substantial, indeed compelling, governmental interest in protecting public confidence in the integrity of its municipal government." (A4005-06.)

Finally, the Board noted its authority to impose penalties up to $10,000 for violations of section 2604(b)(3), and assessed a $7,500 fine for Holtzman's improprieties. (A4007, A4009.) The Board held that either violation—the failure to recuse or the imposition of the "quiet period"—supported the $7,500 fine.

D.   THE APPELLATE DIVISION'S DECISION

Holtzman instituted an Article 78 proceeding challenging the factual and legal findings of the Board, and the matter was transferred on stipulation of the parties to the Appellate Division, First Department. After reviewing the entire record, which included trial exhibits and testimony, as well as the recommendations of Judge Spooner and the findings of the Board, the Appellate Division unanimously held that the Board's factual determinations were supported by substantial evidence and its legal conclusions were not affected by errors of law. (AA1-AA2.) The Court also rejected Holtzman's argument that the Charter was preempted by the FECA or similar state laws. *Id.* Significantly, the Appellate Division ruled that the Board's "interpretation of the relevant statutes and regulations" is "entitled to deference." *Id.*

ARGUMENT

I. THE APPELLATE DIVISION APPLIED THE APPROPRIATE STANDARD OF REVIEW

Section 7803 of the New York Civil Practice Law and Rules governs the standard of review applicable to Article 78 petitions. Pursuant to section 7803(3), where a determination has been made as a result of a hearing required by law, the question presented for review is whether, on the entire record, the determination is "supported by substantial evidence." N.Y. C.P.L.R. § 7803(3). Here the Board made a determination that Holtzman's conduct violated the ethics provisions of the Charter as a result of a required hearing held before Administrative Law Judge Spooner. *See* 68 N.Y.C. Charter § 2603(h)(2) (providing that Board shall hold hearing where there is probable cause to believe an ethics violation has occurred). Accordingly, the Board's factual findings must be upheld if they are supported by "substantial evidence." *Jennings v. N.Y.S. Office of Mental Health,* 90 N.Y.2d 227, 239, 660 N.Y.S.2d 352, 357 (1997); *Matter of Consolidated Edison Co. v. New York State Div. of Human Rights,* 77 N.Y.2d 411, 417, 568 N.Y.S.2d 569, 572 (1991) ("Substantial evidence 'means such relevant proof as a reasonable mind may accept as adequate to support a conclusion or ultimate fact.'"); *Nigro v. McCall,* 218 A.D.2d 846, 847, 629 N.Y.S.2d 866, 867-68 (3d Dep't 1995) (court neither "review[s] administrative findings of fact as to the weight of the evidence, nor substitutes [its] judgment for that of the administrative body").

Where, as part of such a petition, a party challenges the agency's legal conclusions, this Court has held that it will apply an "arbitrary and capricious" standard of review. *Jennings,* 90 N.Y.2d 227, 239, 660 N.Y.S.2d 352, 357 ("[w]hile factual findings made pursuant to a hearing required by law must be affirmed when supported by substantial evidence in the record, we have applied an arbitrary and capricious standard of review for challenges to an agency's interpretation or application of a statute or regulation") (citations omitted). *See also Chevron U.S.A., v. Natural Resources Defense Council, Inc.,* 467 U.S. 837, 844 (1984). Interpretations of statutes or regulations by agencies charged with administering them are entitled to "great deference," *see Gaines v. New York State Div. of Hous. & Community Renewal,* 646 N.Y.S.2d 106, 108 (1st Dep't 1996), and will be upheld so long as they are rational. *Jennings,* 90 N.Y.2d at 240, 660 N.Y.S.2d at 357.[23]

With respect to an administrative penalty, courts apply the most restrictive of reviewing standards. In *re John Paterno, Inc.,* 88 N.Y.2d 328, 645 N.Y.S.2d 424 (1996),

---

[23] Here, the Board is charged with the authority under the New York City Charter to enforce the conflicts of interest provisions under Chapter 68. The Charter expressly delegates to the Board the authority to "promulgate rules as are necessary to implement and interpret" the Charter's conflicts of interest provisions. *See* 68 N.Y.C. Charter § 2603(a). Under section 2603, the Board also has authority to issue advisory opinions and enforce the Charter.

this Court stated that "judicial review of an administrative punishment is guided by the 'abuse of discretion' standard, which translates into a circumscribed judicial inquiry: the administrative penalty must be upheld unless it 'shocks the judicial conscience.'" 88 N.Y.2d at 336, 645 N.Y.S.2d at 428. Finally, courts have held that administrative determinations will not be annulled where procedural irregularities or evidentiary decisions constitute "harmless error." *See Claffey v. Commissioner of Education*, 142 A.D.2d 845, 846, 530 N.Y.S.2d 710, 711 (3d Dep't 1988) (brief absence of administrative officer from hearing constitutes harmless error); *In re Dumpson*, 225 A.D.2d 809, 639 N.Y.S.2d 498, 500 (3d Dep't 1996) (hearing officer's failure to provide medical records and incident reports constitutes harmless error). Under this standard, agency determinations are upheld despite procedural errors where such determinations are supported by substantial evidence. *See, e.g., Bezuneh v. Urlacher*, 149 A.D.2d 944, 540 N.Y.S.2d 76, 77 (4th Dep't 1989) (substantial evidence supported revocation of license, despite erroneous admission of evidence).

II. THE APPELLATE DIVISION PROPERLY UPHELD THE BOARD'S DETERMINATION THAT HOLTZMAN VIOLATED SECTION 2604(b)(2) OF THE CHARTER

The Board found that Holtzman violated section 2604(b)(2) based on her ongoing participation in the selection process for the City bond managers at the same time she was working out a personal loan with one of the bidder's banking affiliates.

Note how the point headings in this section reiterate that the Board was correct each time it ruled against petitioner.

The Board concluded that Holtzman's "private interest" in the bank loan was "in conflict with the proper discharge of her official duties" and that her failure to recuse herself from the selection process consequently breached the Charter's conflict of interest provision. Holtzman's brief does not have a section dealing expressly with the (b)(2) violation, but her scattered response can be summarized as follows: (1) I did not know Fleet was involved in the manager competition and should not have been found liable on a "should have known" basis; (2) even if I was aware of Fleet's involvement, I did not really participate in the selection process and did not favor Fleet's application; and (3) even if I acted improperly, section 2604(b)(3) exempts my conduct from the strictures of 2604(b)(2). As we demonstrate below, these arguments do not stack up against the weight of the evidence and the Board's reasonable and consistent interpretation of the Charter's ethical provision.

A. The Board Properly Discounted Holtzman's Alleged Lack of Knowledge

Holtzman tries to justify her behavior by claiming that she did not know that Fleet Securities applied to be a co-manager. The Board properly found that Holtzman need not have had actual knowledge of her conflict of interest in order to have violated section

2604(b)(2).[24] By its plain terms, the Charter does not require the Board to prove that Holtzman had actual knowledge of the facts creating a conflict. *See* 68 N.Y.C. Charter § 2604(a)(6) ("a public servant shall be deemed to know of a business dealing with the city if such public servant *should have known* of such business dealing with the city") (emphasis added). In keeping with § 2604(a)(6), the Board has held that, if a public official should have known of a firm's business dealings with the City, she will be found to have violated the Charter. *See, e.g.,* Board Opinion No. 486 (Mar. 8, 1979) (employee who accepted loan from community advocate should have known of advocate's personal financial interest in community-related project); Board Opinion No. 92-30 (Nov. 16, 1992) (public servant may not have interest in a firm she knows or should have known is engaged in business dealings with her agency); Board Opinion No. 92-31 (No. 23, 1992) (same).

The "should have known" standard adopted by the Board is the standard generally applied under conflict of interest provisions. *See, e.g., Liljeberg v. Health Services Acquisition Corp.,* 486 U.S. 847, 867-68 (1988) (although judge had no actual knowledge of his private interest in the litigation, he "should have known" of it and recused himself from proceedings); *Gaynor- Stafford Indus., Inc. Water Pollution Control Auth.,* 474 A.2d 752, 759 n. 15 (Comm.) (public official has a "duty to apprise himself of all facts and circumstances surrounding the matter which might lead a reasonable disinterested person to question the public official's impartiality"), *cert. denied,* 469 U.S. 932 (1984); *Scott v. United States,* 559 A.2d 745, 754 (D.C. Cir. 1989) (endorsing the "should have known" standard for assessing violations of American Bar Association Code of Judicial Conduct). Applying the "should have known" standard here promotes the underlying objective of the Charter to ensure public confidence in the integrity of government decision-making. Otherwise, public officials could skirt the conflicts of interest laws by willfully or negligently closing their eyes to conflict situations. Given the Board's consistent interpretation in numerous cases, similar authority from other jurisdictions, and sound policy objectives, the Board's application of the "should have known" standard to Holtzman's case was not irrational.

Moreover, there was an abundance of evidence regarding Holtzman's knowledge of Fleet's business endeavors. Holtzman clearly knew that Fleet was doing business with the City and was eager to increase its business dealings. As detailed above, Holtzman's office had selected Fleet to participate in three different underwriting initiatives prior to the 1992 RFP. In June 1992, Holtzman personally attended a breakfast meeting with Fleet executives who expressed their desire to increase Fleet's business with the City and to become a co-manager of a City bond offering. *See supra* p. 9. At the time of this meeting, Holtzman knew that the City would issue a new RFP in late 1992. In addition,

---

[24] Holtzman's alleged lack of knowledge reaches astounding proportions. The same person who has held herself out as a professor to campaign law, the City's top financial officer, and a qualified candidate for the United States Senate also claims that it did not occur to her that Fleet Securities was connected to Fleet Bank. Holtzman Br. at 27.

Holtzman had ongoing contact with Jim Murphy, a key Fleet operative who repeatedly made the case for Fleet's abilities while at the same time supporting Holtzman's political ambitions. Ultimately, Holtzman's Office selected Fleet as co-manager and her own signature is on the offering "tombstone." (A2662-2852.) Based on these facts, the Board had more than ample authority to conclude that Holtzman knew or should have known of Fleet's application to be a co-manager in the 1992 FRFP.

B.   The Board Properly Concluded that Holtzman's Participation in the Manager Selection Process Was Improper

Holtzman claims that the section 2604(b)(2) violation finding is improper because she was not truly involved in the 1992 management selection process and she in no way favored Fleet's application. The Board rightly concluded after reviewing all of the evidence that Holtzman retained authority over the management selection and that her alleged mental impartiality toward Fleet did not resolve her conflict situation.

The evidence at trial made clear that Holtzman did not recuse herself from the manager selection process. Holtzman testified that prior to mid-December 1992, she knew that the City was preparing to issue an RFP for a new underwriting team for New York City bonds. (A2633-2636, A2106-2108.) On December 17, 1992, in a written delegation of authority, Holtzman designated Darcy Bradbury, Deputy Comptroller for Finance, to exercise certain powers and duties of the Comptroller. (A3234-3235, A3280-3281, A2096-2097, A2020-2021.) As part of this delegation, Bradbury received authority to oversee the RFP process involving the selection of co-managers and senior managers to underwrite City bonds. Holtzman, however, retained the ultimate authority to designate who would be the new senior managers and co-managers. (A2086.) Indeed, Holtzman conceded that she always had the right to revoke the authority delegated to Bradbury as well as the ability to exercise her own judgment whenever she wished to be involved in the RFP. *Id.*

In addition to reviewing and commenting on the RFP before it was issued, Holtzman met with Bradbury to discuss the selection process. *See supra* p.22-23. Holtzman had numerous discussion regarding the applications of senior managers and recalled discussing the particular status of at least one co-manager applicant. *See supra* p. 22. During this process but prior to a formal announcement, Holtzman's Deputy Comptroller personally called Fleet's Murphy to advise him of the "good news" of Fleet's selection. *See supra* p. 23. On April 1, 1993, Holtzman and the Mayor personally signed the public notice of the bond offering listing Fleet Securities as a co-manager. *See supra* p. 23. It was not until April 23, 1993, after the appointment of Fleet, when the press reported that the Comptroller's Office had recommended Fleet Securities as a co-manager, that Holtzman recused herself from any involvement in decisions regarding Fleet Bank, admitting that her actions created an "appearance of impropriety." *See supra* p. 24.

In short, the record provides overwhelming support for the conclusion that Holtzman participated in the selection process that resulted in the selection of Fleet as co-manager. Whether Holtzman flagrantly pressed for the selection of Fleet is immaterial.

Section 2604(b)(2) patrols the "appearance of impropriety" as well as the blatant swapping of favors. From the point of view of competing underwriters and the public at large, Holtzman had the opportunity to influence (and indeed retained ultimate authority over) the decision to award Fleet lucrative City business. Meanwhile, Fleet had loaned Holtzman nearly half a million dollars and retained authority over the decision to foreclose on her personal guaranty. Given this web of entanglement, the Board reasonably concluded that Holtzman's continued exercise of authority over the co-manager selection process violated the Charter's conflict of interest provision.

Holtzman's argument that she was not mentally engaged in the duties of her office is no defense. Government offices operate through the assignment of responsibility to officials which is not annulled by the official's delegation of responsibilities to staff personnel. Here, Holtzman delegated substantial authority to her personnel while retaining authority and responsibility, and the staff performed certain function while routinely reporting to her. In accordance with the explicit duties of her office, Holtzman ultimately signed the document appointing Fleet as a co-manager. If Holtzman can disclaim any responsibility for the duties performed by her Office, no official would ever be responsible for "acting" without an intense debate about her "management style." Here, Holtzman—the Comptroller of the City of New York—acted.

Moreover, the misuse of official power that is the "quiet period" cannot be passed off as someone else's doing. This was Holtzman's own policy applied to silence discussions about her personal financial guarantee. Holtzman's position as official decision maker, projected very clearly and directly to Fleet by her staff when the "quiet period" was initiated, certainly is official in nature and is exactly the kind of misuse of office that the ethical rules prohibit.

The Board, and its predecessor, the Board of Ethics,[25] have consistently applied the "appearance of impropriety" standard to determine violations of section 2604(b) of the Charter, including section 2604(b)(2). This rule of law promotes the Charter's overarching goals of preserving the trust placed in public servants of the City and ensuring that official decisions are made in the interests of the public at large. *See Golden v. Clark*, 76 N.E.2d 611, 617, 563 N.Y.S.2d 1, 7 (1990) (noting that Charter was designed to fulfill "the desire of [New York City's] electorate to restore public confidence in government"); Board Opinion No. 93-17 (June 9, 1993) ("maintaining public confidence in the integrity of government decision-making is one of the primary goals of Chapter 68"); Board Opinion No. 651 (May 17, 1989) (prohibiting the appearance of impropriety in order to promote the underlying purpose of the Charter).

In implementing the "appearance of impropriety" standard, the Board has concluded time and again that a public official who is in a conflict situation which might

---

[25] In 1990, the Charter was revised and the Board of Ethics was replaced by the Conflicts of Interest Board. Board Opinions cited to herein which do not include the year of the decision in the opinion number were written by the Board of Ethics.

tempt her to promote personal interests at the expense of the interests of the public at large will be found to have violated the Charter. Thus, known or unknown conflicts that "could give rise to an appearance of pressure, favoritism or unfair advantage in dealing with City agencies and officials" violate the Charter. Board Opinion No. 93-15 (May 20, 1993); *see also* Board Opinion No. 91-10 (Nov. 18, 1991) ("appearance of impropriety may be created if the nature of the official's involvement is perceived to be coercive or provides an inappropriate opportunity for access to such official"). By placing herself in a conflict situation, the official has violated the Charter, regardless of whether the conflict has affected the officials decisions or actions. *See, e.g.*, Board Opinion No. 651 ("We construe the statutory provisions to prohibit actions by City officers and employees that may result in or *create the appearance* of [impropriety]. . . .") (emphasis added); Board Opinion No. 210 ("We construe the statutory provisions to mean that *no City employee shall place himself in a position where his private interests may appear to or may actually conflict with his official duties . . . .*") (emphasis added); *see generally Town of Woodbury v. Taylor*, No. 104481, 1993 WL 544630, at *7 (Conn. Super. Ct., Dec. 28, 1993) ("[Public official]) must not be permitted to place himself in a position in which personal interest may conflict with his public duty. No room must be allowed for suspicion or dubiety."). Thus, whether or not Holtzman was somehow "above" being affected by this admitted conflict of interest, a citizen's faith in government should not turn on such high hopes. On the contrary, the conflict itself should be avoided.

For example, in Board Opinion No. 145 (June 9, 1970), the Board considered whether an official responsible for substantial purchases by the City and properly be a guest of a company at its home office and attend seminars regarding the company's products and operations. The Board noted that "[w]hile there may be occasions when trips of this kind are necessary in order to fulfill the requirements of public office, it is the opinion of the Board that in the absence of special circumstances City officials should not place themselves in the position of receiving gifts or favors, because their official actions should be free from even the appearance of impropriety." *Id.* There was no finding in that case that the public official was or would be influenced by the receipt of the gift. The existence of the conflict situation alone constituted a violation of the Charter. Indeed, the Board has invoked Charter section 2604 "to prohibit certain conduct which, *while well-intentioned*, could give rise to an appearance of pressure, favoritism or unfair advantage in dealing with City agencies and officials." Board Opinion No. 93-15 (May 20, 1993) (emphasis added).[26]

---

[26] The rule is the same in other jurisdictions. *Cf. Wyzykowski v. Rizas*, 626 A.2d 406, 413 (N.J. 1993) (to prove a violation of code governing conduct of state officials, "[a]n actual conflict of interest is not the decisive factor, nor is 'whether the public servant succumbs to the temptation,' but rather whether there is a potential for conflict") (citation omitted); *In re Beychok*, 495 So.2d 1278, 1283 (La. 1986) (Louisiana Code of Governmental Ethics imposes "objective" standard to determine ethical violation and "does not require that there be actual corruption on the part of the public servant or actual loss by the state.").

Moreover, the Board repeatedly has cautioned that high-level public officials must be particularly careful to avoid any appearance of impropriety due to the sensitive nature of their positions. *See* Board Opinion No. 90-5 (Apr. 16, 1990) ("high-level officials have a special obligation to avoid even the appearance of impropriety"); Board Opinion No. 495 (Apr. 11, 1979) ("the appearance of propriety in the field of ethics is so very important, especially for high City officials"). Thus, the "appearance of impropriety" standard is even more critical here, as Holtzman violated the Charter while serving as Comptroller of the City of New York, arguably the second-most powerful position in the New York City government. *See* 5 N.Y.C. Charter § 93.

Finally, the Board properly decided that Holtzman's conduct must be judged not by her own subjective beliefs regarding the propriety of her conduct, but by the objective standard of whether the public at large would find her conduct circumspect. See Board Opinion No. 93-15 (May 20, 1993) ("active fundraising" is prohibited because it could easily create a perception in "the public at large" that would undermine the public's confidence in the fairness of its officials). *See also In re Opinion No. 653 of the Advisory Comm.* on Professional Ethics, 623 A.2d 241, 244 (N.J. 1993) (violations of the conflicts of interest law occur when "ordinarily knowledgeable citizens" acquainted with the facts would conclude there is substantial risk of improper behavior); *Formal Opinion No.* 86-F6, 1986 N.Y. Op. Atty. Gen. 24 (Sept. 24, 1986) (issue is whether the "public reasonably [might] question [] whether the [subject persons carried out] their [public] responsibilities solely in the public interest"); *Gaynor-Stafford Indus., Inc v. Water Pollution Control Auth.,* 474 A.2d 752, 759 (Conn.) (to prove an appearance of impropriety a litigant must "show the existence of a fact or set of facts that might reasonably be viewed as having an improper influence on the public official"), *cert. Denied,* 469 U.S. 932 (1984). In implementing this standard the Board did not, as Holtzman suggests, react "with hindsight and in response to public opinion (whipped up by inaccurate reports by the media and the DOI)." Holtzman Br. At 71. To the contrary, in reaching its decision, the Board reviewed all of the available relevant evidence, including more than 2,000 pages of testimony and more than 150 exhibits. Accordingly, the Board's application of the "appearance of impropriety" standard from the public's perspective is reasonable and consistent with the Board's previous opinions, as well as the holdings of other courts in similar contexts.[27]

C.   Section 2604(c)(3) Does Not Exempt Holtzman From the Charter's Ethical Standards

When overcome by the facts of her situation, Holtzman ultimately falls back on the legal contention that any conduct associated with her loan is exempt from ethical review

---

[27] Ironically, while Holtzman suggests that erroneous news reports convinced the public she had acted improperly, (Holtzman Br. at 7), Holtzman helped shape the public perception of impropriety by confirming on television that she had made a mistake in not recusing herself from the decision on co-managers. Holtzman is now in the awkward position of asking this Court to conclude that it is unreasonable for the public to believe something she herself told them.

because of 2604(c)(3), which provides that the Charter shall not prohibit "a public servant from obtaining a loan from any financial institution upon terms and conditions available to members of the public." Holtzman would turn section 2604(c)(3) into a whale of an exemption capable of swallowing up an entire set of ethical rules for any conduct that is related to a loan.

By its terms, section 2604(c)(3) provides only that the conflicts law should not be used to prohibit an official from "*obtaining*" a loan. The section does not purport to regulate a public servant's post-loan conduct or the ethical administration of his or her duties. Here, the Board did not find that Holtzman violated the Charter by merely obtaining the loan from Fleet Bank, but by continuing to exercise official authority over a competitive bidding process involving her personal creditor in the context of a default. Holtzman's suggestion that this is a "strained interpretation," (Holtzman Br. at 62), overlooks the logical distinction between regulating one specific act and regulating other acts that may be tangentially related to the first act—*e.g.*, schoolchildren are permitted to purchase bicycles, the children are not permitted to ride their bicycles in lieu of attending school. Similarly, New York City public officials may obtain loans consistent with applicable laws, but they are not immune from having to comply with the City's ethical charter as a result.[28]

For these reasons, the Appellate Division properly affirmed the Board's finding that Holtzman's participation in the selection process at the time her loan was in default constitutes a violation of section 2604(b)(2).

III. THE APPELLATE DIVISION PROPERLY UPHELD THE BOARD'S DETERMINATION THAT HOLTZMAN VIOLATED SECTION 2604(b)(3) OF THE CHARTER

The Board found that Holtzman misused her public office for personal advantage in violation of section 2604(b)(3) by exercising authority over Fleet's co-manager application while her loan repayments were outstanding and imposing a "quiet period" to silence the Bank's recovery efforts. In response, Holtzman argues that (1) the imposition of the quiet period did not constitute a "use" of her office; (2) it was not foreseeable that she would benefit by imposition of the quiet period against the Bank; and (3) her quiet period policy was supposed to avoid appearances of impropriety, not create them. None of these arguments undermine the rational and considered conclusions of the Board.

---

[28] Holtzman's reliance on *Dilucia v. Mandelker*, 110 A.D.2d 260, 493 N.Y.S.2d 769 (1st Dep't 1985), *aff'd* 68 N.Y.2d 844, 501 N.E.2d 32, 508 N.Y.S.2d 424 (1986), is similarly misplaced. Holtzman Br. At 47-49. The Court in *Mandelker* held that political contributions from persons doing business with the City do not constitute "gifts" under the Charter. In reaching its decision, the Court relied on a Board of Ethics Advisory Opinion that was limited to a review of whether political *contributions* from entities doing business with the City were, *per se*, prohibited gifts under the City Charter. *See* Board Opinion No. 35 (Oct. 5, 1961). Thus, *Mandelker* stands simply for the pedestrian proposition that campaign contributions from interested parties are not *per se* illegal. That determination depends on the facts. But *Mandelker* in no way intimated that a campaign loan is a ticket to immunity from ethical scrutiny or an exemption from the City conflicts of interest laws.

A.   Holtzman's Conduct Constituted a "Use" of Her Public Office

Holtzman attempts to avoid the requirements of the Charter by contending that some form of official "action" should be required under section 2604(b)(3), and that she did not act with the intent to benefit herself. Holtzman Br. at 57-59. Putting aside the dubious factual presumptions in this argument, Holtzman purposely fails to comprehend that section 2604(b)(3) is violated by even "passive" conduct by an officeholder in a conflict position when that "passive" conduct provides a personal benefit. Here, her exercise of her Comptroller duties with regard to Fleet while simultaneously holding off any repayment discussions constituted a "use" of her office that personally benefitted her. Holtzman was personally engaged on both sides of a serious conflict situation. During the time period in question, she had critical decision-making authority over Fleet's application as an officeholder, and she owed Fleet hundreds of thousands of dollars as a debtholder. She utilized her official status (and the attending threat of her ability to choose co-managers) to suspend deeply troubling discussions regarding her delinquent payback obligations. Only by virtue of her official power over the selection did Holtzman get away with this (imagine a private citizen-debtor without authority over the selection process telling Fleet that there would be no discussions for several months). The Board rightly concluded that this set of facts gave rise to a violation of section 2604(b)(3), regardless of whether Holtzman expressly invoked her official authority in a private transaction or intended to benefit (or actually benefitted) from the use of her office. (A3999.)

Indeed, if section 2604(b)(3) does not apply to "passive conflicts" as well as intentional acts, public officials could avoid penalties by perpetually pleading ignorance with respect to the administration of their agency or permitting staff employees to undertake ethical misdeeds on their behalf, *even when they personally benefitted from the conflict.* This result would undermine the public confidence which the City Charter is designed to uphold by (i) permitting officials who appear to have engaged in inappropriate conduct to avoid discipline and (ii) weakening the public's confidence that their officials are actually competent and informed in their administration of City affairs. In light of the purpose of the City Charter, the Board's consistent interpretation of section 2604(b)(3) as regulating all conduct that creates an appearance of impropriety – both intentional and unintentional – is neither arbitrary nor capricious. *See* Board Opinion No. 92-38 (Nov. 9, 1992) (section 2604(b)(3) violated when actions "create the impression" of impropriety); Board Opinion No. 91-4 (July 18, 1991) (elected official should not accept honorarium to avoid creating the appearance of impropriety under section 2604(b)(3)).

Here, decisions relied upon by the Petitioner are distinguished on their facts in order to argue that they are inapplicable to the case.

The case law cited by Holtzman does not suggest anything to the contrary. Indeed, Holtzman's references to *U.S. v. Hall*, 110 F.3d 115 (5th Cir. 1997), and *Bailey v. U.S.*, 116 S.Ct. 501 (1995), are particularly inapposite. These cases concern the interpretation of the word "use" in relation to statutes prohibiting the "use" of firearms during the commission of other criminal acts. In *Bailey*, the Supreme Court noted that the word "use" "draws meaning from its context, and we will look not only to the word itself but also to the statute . . ." *Id.* at 505. The courts in both *Bailey* and *Hall* stressed that given legislators' careful selection of the word "use" rather than the words "possess" or "carry," which had been used in other provisions, the laws were intended to suggest an "active" connotation of the word. *Id.*; *Hall*, 110 F.3d at 1160. Holtzman has not even attempted to argue that such a legislative intent existed with respect to section 2604(3).[29] Holtzman's citation to *McGuire v. State Ethics Commission*, 657 A.2d 1346 (Pa. 1995), is similarly unhelpful. In *McGuire*, a Pennsylvania court concluded that the mistaken acceptance by public officials of paychecks for an amount higher than permitted under the applicable law was not a "use" of office because the officials had taken no action to increase the payments and were completely unaware that they were receiving excess compensation. Unlike the public employees in *McGuire*, Holtzman's actions were neither "clearly unintentional" nor were they the result of an "erroneous practice." *McGuire*, 657 A.2d at 1349, n.6. To the contrary, the Board's findings that Holtzman participated in the underwriter selection process and that she was or should have been aware she was enjoying the benefit of the "quiet period" are sufficient to establish Holtzman's use of her office for private gain.

More apposite to Holtzman's conduct is the discussion of the meaning of the word "use" in *Davidson v. Oregon Gov't Ethics Comm.*, 712 P.2d 87 (Ore. 1985). In *Davidson*, the court considered a conflict of interests provision virtually identical to section 2604(b)(3) and concluded that the term "use" included a public official "avail[ing] himself of" benefits provided to him by virtue of his position. The conduct at issue in *Davidson* was a public official's purchase of a car at a discounted price which he had not actually sought, but which was available to him only because of his position. In holding that the official's "avail[ing] himself of" the benefits obtained by virtue of his office even though he had not actively sought them constituted a "use", the court rejected the public official's argument that the term "use" could not be interpreted" in a passive sense" and that it "should be applied actively." *Id.* at 91. Even assuming, contrary to the Board's findings of fact, Holtzman did not actively engage in behavior that constituted an improper use of her position of Comptroller, the Board properly found that, at a bare minimum, Holtzman had availed herself of the benefits of that position and thereby ran afoul of the Charter's ethical provision. Indeed, wholly apart from an appearance of impropriety, Holtzman's misuse of her office constituted a clear violation of section 2604(b)(3), as demonstrated below.

---

[29] Holtzman's citation to *New York Magazine v. Metropolitan Transit* Auth., No. 97 Civ. 8792, 1997 WL 738610 (S.D.N.Y. Dec. 1, 1997) is equally inapposite. In *New York Magazine*, the court properly held that a magazine's unauthorized use of Mayor Giuliani's likeness in an advertising campaign to which the Mayor was opposed could not be the basis of finding that the Mayor had "used" his office for private gain. This holding was compelled by the fact that the Mayor not only was totally uninvolved in the decision by a commercial enterprise to use his likeness, but he then took affirmative steps to halt the use, including pursuit of the legal action underlying the case (despite public derision).

B.   Hotzman's Involvement in the Management Selection Process Was Reasonably Likely to Influence the Bank of Act Favorably Toward Her

There is ample factual support for the Board's conclusion that Holtzman violated section 2604(b)(3) because she exercised authority over the decision to select Fleet as a co-manager while the loan was in default, and her conduct was "*reasonably likely* to influence Fleet Bank to act favorably" toward Holtzman with respect to the loan. (A4000.) (emphasis added)

From the beginning, the loan was not treated in the ordinary course. The Committee did not apply for the loan through regular channels and instead directly approached Fleet's main lobbyist, Jim Murphy, who did not work at Fleet Bank and lacked lending authority. *See supra* pp. 10-11. Only with Murphy's repeated intervention on the Committee's behalf did the Bank award the Committee a $450,000 loan within twenty-four hours of Holtzman's loan application despite the minimal, unverified documentation the Bank possessed. See *supra* pp. 11-13.

The loan also violated the Bank's own lending policies in several important respects. Fleet's policies deemed political loans "undesirable" and required "undesirable loans" over $250,000 to have three approval signatures; Holtzman's loan received only one. *Supra* p. 13 n. 10. Moreover, Fleet's policies required that only certain Fleet officials can serve as "sponsoring agents"; Murphy, who served as "sponsoring agent" for Holtzman's loan, did not qualify as such an official. *Id.* In addition, the Bank clearly extended the loan to generate good will with the Comptroller's office, as the draft loan proposal indicated. *See supra* p. 14 n. 11. Based on these circumstances, the New York State Banking Department and the Board of Governors of the Federal Reserve System concluded that there were "serious questions as to whether the Bank would have extended the loan absent Murphy's involvement." *Supra* p. 13 n. 10.

In any case, as the Board properly found, it is not necessary for finding a violation of section 2604(b)(93) that Holtzman affirmatively intended to obtain a personal benefit from her office. Numerous Board Opinions hold that an official may not place himself ""in a position where his public office 'may be considered as a lure or as a pressure' by those with whom she is dealing." *See* Board Opinion No. 348 (finding that a solicitation by a City official on behalf of a charitable organization on official stationery may be improper because the official's public office might be considered a "'Lure or as pressure by those who receive his letter'"). For example, in addressing a situation in which a City official served on the board of directors for a real estate development corporation that was acquiring a property under the official's jurisdiction, the Board noted that any attempt to use an official position to secure favorable regulatory actions would be prohibited by Charter section 2604(b)(3) and that, "[a]t the very lease, the public servant's continued service as a Director of the Corporation would create an appearance of conflict . . . in violation of this section." Board Opinion No. 93-14 (May 17, 1993); Board Opinion No. 92-33 (Nov. 23, 1992) (acceptance of gifts could create an appearance of improper motivations in violation of section 2604(b)(3)); Board Opinion No. 91-1 9

(Feb. 8, 1991) (actions violate section 2604(b)(3) if they present "a significant risk of creating the appearance that the public servant's official position is being used to advance a private interest"). The Board's analysis of the Charter is also consistent with the analysis of similar conflict of interest provisions by courts in other jurisdictions. *See, e.g., Indiana State Ethics Commission v. Nelson,* 656 N.E.2d 1172, 1175 (1996) (in analyzing a public official's compliance with conflict of interest provisions, "[h]is good faith is of no moment because it is the policy of law to keep him so far from temptation as to insure the exercise of unselfish public interest").[30]

In sum, even if the Bank did not show actual favoritism, her participation in the selection process is exactly the type of "lure" or "pressure" that could have improperly affected the Bank's conduct in violation of section 2604(b)(3). The Board's conclusion is supported by substantial evidence.

C.   Imposition of the "Quiet Period" Was an Obvious Ethical Violation

Contrary to Holtzman's assertion, substantial evidence – and simple common sense—also support the Board's conclusion that Holtzman's exercise of authority over the co-manager selection process foreseeably led to an impermissible use of the "quiet period" in violation of section 2604(b)(3).

The "quiet period" initially was imposed by Deputy Comptroller O'Malley—not by "the Senate Campaign staff," as Holtzman contends, (Holtzman Br. at 56)—in January 1993. *See supra* p.19-20. O'Malley stated that he believed that the Committee members could not meet with Fleet to discuss repayment of the loan because Fleet responded to the RFP. *Id.* Consequently, on January 25, when Fleet telephoned the Committee to discuss repayment of the loan, Fleet was informed that a "rule or regulation" precluded the Bank from contacting Holtzman about the loan. *Id.* This is a highly unusual command that general members of the public cannot issue to their creditors.

Holtzman argues that the "quiet period" was a measure "designed to avoid appearance in her campaign." Holtzman Br. 54. Whatever the merits of the "quiet period" in the abstract, there can be no doubt that, as misused here, it not only failed to cure the conflict but actually constituted a very serious violation. Holtzman told Fleet it could not ask her to repay a sizable delinquent loan during the time period that she and her personnel decided the fate of Fleet's business application. To state this proposition is to concede the inherent ethical conflict. While Fleet Bank was understandably "outraged" by the enforced quiet period it abided by Holtzman's policy *because of Holtzman's office and*

---

[30]   65 N.Y.C. Charter § 2604(b)(12), relied upon by Holtzman, regulates political contributions, not loans. Holtzman Br. At 48-49. Thus, it is inapplicable here because the Board does not challenge the acceptance by Holtzman of political contributions from Fleet. Moreover, the mere fact that section 2604(b)(12) permits elected officials to solicit political contributions but bars non-elected employees from soliciting them has no bearing on the standard of moral conduct applied equally by the Charter to the job duties of elected and non-elected officials.

the power she wielded over the co-manager selection process.[31] (A442-43 (Fleet's letter referring to the Bank's inability to discuss the loan "because of Ms. Holtzman's position as Comptroller and her involvement in choosing banks for city underwriting").) Whether she did or did not exercise the power she projects does not matter.

It takes little imagination to envision the real world significance of the Comptroller's announcement to Fleet that "quiet" must ensue on the repayment front while her deliberations over the selection of co-managers went forward. To the creditor, and to the public, such an announcement would not be misunderstood as anything other than a blatant misuse of power. And it had the foreseeable effect of intimidating Fleet into inaction and provided a substantial benefit to Holtzman while her creditor stood frozen.

Substantial evidence supports the Board's finding that Holtzman was "on notice that her 'quiet period' policy" had been applied. As a direct result of the application of the "quiet period," on February 12, 1993, Fleet Bank's O'Connor wrote a letter to McDonald, advising that the loan was being transferred to the Bank's Managed Asset Department because of Holtzman's involvement with the RFP. *See supra* pp.21-22. McDonald acknowledged that he received and read the letter. Holtzman testified that she doubted that she had ever received the letter, and that even if she had, she would not have read it because she was listed only as a copy recipient. *Supra* p.22. Holtzman also suggests that, although the letter concerned an issue which was of grave concern to her, supra p.17, she did not read it because it was only one of "the thousands of letters sent to her." Holtzman Br. at 24. The Appellate Division properly affirmed the Board's finding that it is highly unlikely that Holtzman would have ignored a letter concerning a matter of such obvious personal interest to her.[32]

These damaging assertions regarding the Petitioner's case were included in the court's opinion.

Moreover, even if Holtzman did not know of the "quiet period," it is only logical that she would have questioned why—after weeks of intense pressure from Fleet Bank for repayment of the loan and threats that the Bank would enforce the personal guaranty and possibly force Holtzman into bankruptcy – the Bank abruptly halted negotiations regarding the loan.[33] What remains indisputably true is that Holtzman knew about the loan and knew about

---

[31] As noted above, the "quiet period" apparently did not prevent contact between Holtzman and Fleet when it benefited Holtzman.

[32] All of Holtzman's arguments with regard to *respondent superior* are irrelevant because the Board did not base its decision on this theory. Rather, the Board found that Holtzman had notice of the improper use of the quiet period.

[33] Holtzman's suggestion that the Board somehow based its finding on a theory of vicarious liability has no basis in the record. The Board found that Holtzman "knew of the Loan and the need for on-going communications with Fleet Bank regarding the pending loan extension deadline of February 1, 1993" (A4002), and her failure to recuse herself from the selection process "rendered it all but certain that the 'quiet period' policy would be applied to communications with the Bank." *Id.* Thus, far from finding that Holtzman acted innocently but was nevertheless responsible for the acts of an errant employee, the Board based its findings squarely on Holtzman's own conduct and her own knowledge.

the default, was charged with the duties of her office, failed to recuse herself in a conflict situation, ceased communicating with her creditor, signed the documents appointing her creditor to be co-manager and bought several months of time as a direct result. Thus, the Board's conclusion is supported by substantial evidence, and the Appellate Division properly affirmed its finding that Holtzman violated section 2604(b)(3).

IV.   NEITHER FECA NOR THE REGULATIONS PROMULGATED THEREUNDER PREEMPT THE APPLICATION OF NEW YORK CITY CONFLICTS OF INTEREST LAWS TO HOLTZMAN

In an attempt to avoid the facts of her inappropriate conduct, Holtzman contends that her candidacy for federal office exempts her from complying with the New York City ethical rules. Holtzman's argument rests on an untenable reading of the FECA's preemption provision. According to Holtzman, this provision means that a City employee who is a candidate for federal office need not comply with a single state or local law no matter how tangentially the City law affects the employee's campaign. Such a broad reading of FECA is unreasonable, unwarranted and unsupported by law.

A.   Preemption Of The City's Ethical Law Is Disfavored

Holtzman bears a "heavy burden" in her attempt to establish that Congress intended to preempt the City conflicts of interest laws. *Medical soc'y of the State of New York v. Cuomo*, 777 F. Supp. 1157, 1160 (S.D.N.Y. 1991), *aff'd*, 976 F.2d 812 (2d Cir. 1992); *see also Pac. Gas & Elec. Co. v. State Energy Resources and Dev. Co.*, 461 U.S. 190, 206 (1983) (party arguing preemption must prove that preemption was the "clear and manifest purpose of Congress"). As the Supreme Court has repeatedly held, there is a strong presumption that Congress did not intend to displace state law. *See, e.g., Medtronic Inc. v. Lohr*, 116 S.Ct. 2240, 2250 (1996) ("we have long presumed that Congress does not cavalierly pre-empt state-law causes of action"); *Maryland v. Louisiana*, 451 U.S. 725, 746 (1981) (noting strong presumption against preemption). This presumption is especially forceful where, as here, the area is one that is traditionally regulated by the state. *California v. ARC Am. Corp.*, 490 U.S. 93, 101 91989) (where area is one of traditional state regulation, there is additional burden in proving preemption); *Weber v. Heaney*, 793 F. Supp. 1438, 1443 (D. Minn. 1992), *aff'd*, 995 F.2d 872 (8th Cir. 1993) (traditional state interest in regulation of congressional elections creates especially high burden in establishing FECA preemption).

New York City's conflicts of interest laws regulate the ethical conduct of New York City's public officials. *See* 68 N.Y.C. Charter § 2600 *et seq*. No City law embodies a more compelling local interest than the statutory framework for protecting the integrity of official action. The preamble to the Charter clearly sets forth the City's compelling interest in regulating the ethical conduct of its employees:

> Public service is a public trust. These prohibitions on the conduct of public servants are enacted to preserve the public trust placed in the public servants of the city, to promote public confidence in government, to protect the

integrity of government decision-making and to enhance government efficiency.

68 N.Y.C. Charter § 2600. This compelling City interest is well-recognized by the courts. For example, in *Barry v. City of New York*, 712 F.2d 1554 (2d Cir.), *cert. denied*, 464 U.S. 1017 (1983), various City officials challenged as unconstitutional a law promulgated by the New York City Council requiring certain high-level City employees and candidates for those offices to file a financial report with the City Clerk. In rejecting that challenge, the Second Circuit Court of Appeals held:

> We think the statute as a whole plainly furthers a substantial, possible even a compelling, state interest. The purpose of the statute is to deter corruption and conflicts of interest among City officers and employees, and to enhance public confidence in the integrity of its government . . . . The Supreme Court has recognized a compelling state interest in the maintenance of an honest civil service . . . .

Id. At 1560. *See also Golden v. Clark*, 564 N.E.2d 611, 615, 563 N.Y.S.2d 1, 5 (1990) ("increas[ing] citizens' confidence in the integrity and effectiveness of their government is a legitimate governmental purpose); *Watkins v. New York State Ethics Comm'n*, 147 Misc. 2d 350, 355-56, 554 N.Y.S.2d 955, 960 (Sup. Ct. Albany County 1990) (there is a "compelling state interest in deterring governmental corruption and in fostering public confidence in our system of government"). In light of New York City's strong interest in regulating this area, Holtzman bears an especially heavy burden in attempting to demonstrate that the City's conflicts of interest laws are preempted by FECA. It is a burden Holtzman cannot meet.

B.   FEECA Does Not Preempt the City's Regulation of Holtzman's Activities in Office

FECA's preemption provision is narrow, displacing only state or local laws that regulate campaigns for federal office. Thus, section 453 of FECA provides:

> The provisions of this Act, and of rules prescribed under this Act, supersede and preempt any provision of State law *with respect to election to Federal office.*

2 U.S.C. § 453 (emphasis added). None of the Charter provisions at issue her purports to regulate such elections, or even mentions federal elections at all. Instead, these Charter provisions regulate the ethical conduct of City employees as *City employees*, an area traditionally and exclusively governed by the City. Congress specifically did not intend to prohibit the City from regulation the political activities of its employees, an area in which the City has a compelling interest. As a result, the City conflicts of interest laws lie far beyond the scope of FECA'S preemptive reach.

Since the plain language of section 453 clearly limits the scope of FECA's preemption, this Court need look no further. *See, e.g., Demarest v. Manspeaker*, 498 U.S.

184, 190 (1991) (where the statutory language is unambiguous, "judicial inquiry is complete except in rare and exceptional circumstances"). There is simply no indication that Congress intended to preempt state or municipal laws regulating the ethical conduct of public officials.

In accordance with Congress' express intent, the Federal Election Commission ("FEC") has promulgated rules which restrict the application of section 453 to election-related activities.[34] In its regulation setting forth FECA's "Effect on State Law," the FEC has set forth the limited, specific areas of state law that are superseded by FECA:

> (1) Organization and registration of political committees supporting Federal candidates; (2) Disclosure of receipts and expenditures by Federal candidates and political committees; and (3) Limitation on contributions and expenditures regarding Federal candidates and political committees.

11 C.F.R. § 108.7 (1997). These area all concern federal election activities.[35] None of them speaks to activities outside the electoral process or to conduct in office. None of them even mentions regulation of patent conflicts of interest that may arise *as a result* of campaign contributions or loans, and none purports to affect regulation of such conflicts. Certainly, the FECA preemption clause does not purport to invalidate state and local ethical standards appurtenant to campaign financing activities.

The courts too have recognized that states are empowered to regulate non-election-related activities of citizens. In *Stern v. General Electric Co.*, 924 F.2d 472 (2d Cir. 1991) – upon which the board properly relied – a shareholder filed a derivative action against the corporation's directors, alleging that the directors' payments from the corporation's treasury to a political support committee wasted corporate assets. In analyzing whether this claim was preempted under FECA, the court turned first to the language of section 453. In the court's view, the scope of the provision is "narrow," which "suggests

---

[34] Indeed, the FEC regulations expressly recognize that states have the authority to regulate certain election-related activities. 11 C.F.R. § 108.7(c) (1997) (states can regulate the manner of qualifying as a candidate or political party organization, dates and places of elections, voter registration, voting fraud and similar offenses, or candidates' personal financial disclosure); *see* also S. Conf. Rep. No. 1237, 93d Cong., 2d Sess. (1974), *reprinted in* 1974 U.S.C.C.A.N. 5618, 5668; H.R. Rep. No. 1438, 93d Cong., 2d Sess. 69 (1974).

[35] The legislative history similarly provides evidence that FECA's preemptive effect if limited to election-related activities. H.R. Rep. No. 1239, 93d Cong., 2d Sess. 10 (1974) ("[i]t is the intent of the committee to make certain that the Federal law is construed to occupy the field *with respect to elections to Federal office*") (emphasis added); S. Rep. No. 689, 93d Cong., 2d Sess. (1974), *reprinted* in 1974 U.S.C.C.A.N. 5587, 5587-88 (purpose of FECA is to provide "complete control over and *disclosure of campaign contributions and expenditures in campaigns for Federal elective office*") (emphasis added); H.R. Rep. No. 1438, 93d Cong., 2d Sess. 100-01 (1974) (Conference Report) ("It is clear that the Federal law occupies the field with respect to *reporting and disclosure of political contributions to and expenditures by Federal Candidates*") (emphasis added). Holtzman's repeated citations to *dicta* in *Buckley v. Valeo*, 424 U.S. 1 (1975), and *Colorado Republican Federal Campaign Committee v*. FEC, 116 S. Ct. 2309 (1996), do not contradict this legislative history.

that Congress did not intend to preempt state regulation with respect to non-election-related activities." *Id.* at 475.[36] The court further noted that Congress had not "occupied the entire field of corporate political spending, leaving no room for supplemental state regulation" and that, to the extent Congress had occupied this area, it had done so "to *limit* corporate political spending in order to preserve the integrity of the political process." Thus, "state-law regulations that tend to reduce a corporation's support of its political action committee do not impede the FECA's goals." *Id.* at 476 (emphasis in original). In sum, the *Stern* court ruled that Congress' presence in this area "does not preclude New York from pursuing its independent interest in ensuring that corporate directors exercise sound judgement in the expenditure of corporate funds." *Id.* at 475.[37]

Similarly, by applying the City conflicts of interest laws, the Board here seeks to enforce the City's "independent interest" in assuring that Holtzman acted ethically *as Comptroller.* These laws are not directed at, and this proceeding does not seek to regulate, any "election-related activities" by Holtzman. Thus, there is no preemption.

Holtzman's suggestion that the City's ethical rules are being used here to limit the sources of Ms. Holtzman's campaign loans and therefore must be preempted is a dangerous distortion of the law. Holtzman Br. At 50-53. Stated plainly, Holtzman's position is that the City law requirement that she act ethically and not use her position as Comptroller in a way that casts doubt and suspicion on her decision-making might impermissibly impinge upon her otherwise unfettered ability to obtain loans for her Senate campaign from companies interested in obtaining City business. Worse, Holtzman suggests that her supposed right to obtain loans from anyone and everyone takes complete precedence over her (purportedly now-preempted) obligation at least to recuse herself from the City's decision whether to award contracts to those same lenders.[38]

Finally, Holtzman suggests that having to recuse herself from certain duties as Comptroller as a result of her loan would "impose a considerable burden" that would pre-

---

[36] The Second Circuit also noted that, "[e]ven with respect to election-related activities, courts have given section 453 a narrow preemptive effect in light of its legislative history." *Id.* at 475 n.3 (*citing Reeder v. Kansas City Board of Police Comm'rs*, 733 F.2d 543, 545-46 (8th Cir. 1984))

[37] *Weber v. Heaney*, 995 F.2d 872, 875-76 (8th Cir. 1993), relied upon by Holtzman, is not to the contrary. Holtzman Br. At 41. The state law at issue in *Weber* directly limited campaign expenditures by candidates for *federal* office and was *expressly* aimed at supplementing what the State believed were the inadequate provisions of FECA. This exactly the type of state law FECA intended to preempt – a state law directly aimed at regulating federal elections. Thus, the court held that this state law fell within the narrowest parameters of section 453 and was preempted. *Id. Weber* in no way suggests that laws like the City Charter conflicts of interest provisions, which are aimed at regulating the day-to-day activities of City employees and do not even mention federal elections, are preempted by FECA.

[38] This argument betrays Holtzman's inverted view of her obligations. The minimum ethical requirement that Holtzman recuse herself from decisions involving Fleet, a City contractor to whom she personally owed several hundred thousand dollars, does not in any way limit her ability to obtain campaign loans. It only ensures that, after obtaining such a loan, Holtzman impartially carry out her official duties *as Comptroller.*

vent her from, for example, promoting "the selection women-owned and minority-owned firms." Holtzman Br. At 53-54. First, it is both difficult and troubling to imagine that the accomplishment of worthy public policy goals depends on a Comptroller's intimate involvement in every selection of underwriters, rather than on the existence of a general policy in the Comptroller's office. Second, the potential burden on Holtzman's duties from having to recuse herself from the selection of underwriters for a *limited* period of time while her loan was outstanding and *only* when Fleet had submitted an application, is quite small as compared to the overall duties of the Comptroller, which include managing the assets of five municipal pension systems and managing the rest of the City's debt financing program and the issuance of municipal bonds and notes. (A2003-2004, A1795.)[39] Third, whatever small burden is placed on a public official's duties as a result of having to avoid conflicts of interest is certainly no greater than the burden placed on those duties by that public official's decision to run for a higher office while retaining his or her present office. Fourth, perhaps the best evidence of the minimal burden imposed on the Comptroller by the Charter's conflict of interest provisions is that Holtzman *did* recuse herself from decisions involving Fleet after the appearance of press reports criticizing her, *supra* p.24, and she continued to function as Comptroller. Holtzman makes no allegation that she was hampered in her ability to perform her duties following her recusal, nor is there any evidence of such an effect. In short, whatever minimal impact these provisions may have on New York City public officials in performing the duties required of them as New York City public officials, it is difficult to imagine that any such impact would "unavoidably result in serious interference with the accomplishment and execution of the full purposes and objectives" of the United States Congress. *See Guice v. Charles Schwab & Co.*, 89 N.Y.2d 31, 45, 651 NY.S.2d 352, 359 (1996*), cert. Denied*, 117 S. Ct. 1250 (1997) (citation omitted) (discussing standards for preemption).[40]

Holtzman has not cited a *single* decision in which a state law not directed at regulating an election-related activity (*e.g.*, campaign fundraising and expenditures) was preempted. In addition, she has cited no authority purporting to preempt ethical rules governing conflicts of interest arising out of such activity. Rather, in every court and FEC advisory opinion cited by Holtzman in which preemption was found, the state laws at issue *directly* and *explicitly* regulated election-related activities, namely the acceptance

---

[39]   Furthermore, the finding of misconduct in this case does not arise solely from Holtzman's failure to recuse herself, but also, separately, from the imposition of the "quiet period" policy on Fleet Bank to delay the repayment of Holtzman's loan.

[40]   Nor does the Board's finding that City officials must recuse themselves from conflict- ridden decisions and the imposition of a $7,5000 fine for failure to do so constitute such a disproportionate penalty for ethical violations as to "shock the judicial conscience." *In re John Paterno*, Inc., 88 N.Y.2d 328, 336, 645 N.Y.S.2d 424, 428 (1996).

and use of campaign funds and political contributions.[41] None of them concern the *ethical* implications of official activities in local office in the context of such contributions. Thus, these decisions in no way support Holtzman's position that FECA preempts the City conflicts of interest provisions which are not directed at, and contain no explicit limitation on, a candidate's ability to raise or spend funds for federal campaigns.[42] In fact, in the only FECA case cited by Holtzman which involves state laws *not* directed at election-related activity, the court refused to find preemption. *Stern*, 924 F.2d at 476 (no FECA preemption for "state-law regulation that tend to reduce a corporation's support of its political action committee"); *cf. Morales v. Trans World Airlines, Inc.*, 504 U.S. 374, 390 (1992) (no preemption where state law affects matter regulated by federal government in a "tenuous, remote or peripheral" manner).

C.   The City Properly Regulates the Political Activities of its Officials

Further, under FECA, the City retains the authority to regulate the "political activities" of its own officials *as officials,* even when these activities relate to federal elections. FECA's legislative history clearly reveals Congress' intent to permit states to regulate the political activities of their own employees:

> It is the intent of the conferees that any State law regulating the political activities of State and local officers and employees *is not preempted* or superseded by the amendments to title 5, United States Code, made by this legislation.

S. Conf. Rep. No. 1237, 93d Cong., 2d Sess. (1974), *reprinted* in 1974 U.S.C.C.A.N. 5587, 5669 (emphasis added). The House Report similarly notes that "[t]he regulation of political activities of State and local employees *would be left largely to the States."* H.R. Rep. No. 1239, 93d Cong., 2d Sess. 11 (1974) (emphasis added). This legislative history reveals that Congress did not intend to preempt state "Hatch Acts" and other state ethics laws. *See Pollard v. Board of Police Comm'rs*, 665 S.W.2d 333, 337 (Mo. 1984). Thus, Congress clearly did not intend to preempt New York City's rules regulating the ethical conduct of public employees.[43]

---

[41]   *See Teper v. Miller*, 82 F.3d 989 (11th Cir. 1996) (Georgia statute imposed time limitations on when members of Georgia General Assembly could accept political contributions); *Bunning v. Kentucky*, 42 F.3d 1008 (6th Cir. 1994) (Kentucky Statute imposed limits on expenditures federal campaign committee could make); *Weber v. Heaney*, 995 F.2d 872 (8th Cir. 1993) (Minnesota law limited campaign expenditures for federal elections); FEC Advisory Opinion No. 1992-43 (Jan. 28, 1993) (Washington law prohibited raising contributions to retire federal campaign debt while state legislature was in session); FEC Advisory Opinion No. 1988-21 (May 16, 1988) (local ordinance limited contributions from "influence brokers").

[42]   Similarly, Holtzman's citations to *FEC V. Lance*, 617 F.2d 365 (5th Cir. 1980), FEC Advisory Opinion No. 1993-19 (Nov. 15, 1992), and *FEC v. Ted Haley Congressional Committee*, 852 F.2d 1111 (9th Cir. 1988), serve only as support for her argument that FECA applies to the receipt and repayment of federal election loans. This proposition, like Holtzman's conduct as Comptroller with respect to Fleet's application to serve as an underwriter and the imposition of the quiet period.

[43]   In Board Opinion Nos. 412, 412A and 603, the Board generally advised City employees that their political activities were subject to State and City regulation. These opinions set forth "Guidelines For Political Activity, Contributions To Political Funds and Seeking Public Or Political Office By City Employees."

Relying on this legislative history, courts have upheld states' regulations of their own employees' political conduct in federal elections. For example, in *Pollard*, 665 S.W.2d at 338, the court held that "Congress did not intend in enacting § 453, to preempt a broad field of state law," and thus, even a state law that flatly prohibits certain state employees from contributing to federal campaigns is not preempted by FECA. *Id.* at 338. Similarly, in *Reeder v. Kansas City Board of Police Commissioners*, 733 F.2d 543 (8th Cir. 1984), the Eighth Circuit construed section 453 narrowly and permitted Kansas to regulate the political activities of its own employees. There, an officer who had been dismissed from the police force for violating a Kansas statute prohibiting police officers from making political contributions argued that the statute was preempted by FECA. In rejecting that claim, the court noted that section 453 should not be construed to preempt every state law that could possibly be considered a "law with respect to election to Federal office." *Id.* at 545.

The authority of states to regulate the political activities of their employees applies even when the state employee is a candidate for federal office. Indeed, Holtzman's argument that the little Hatch Acts were designed to apply to non-elected government officials, (Holtzman Br. At 47-48), misses the mark entirely—elected officials are no more free to violate conflict of interest rules than non-elected officials. Running for office does not convey immunity for the behavior of public officials. For example, in FEC Advisory Opinion No. 1989-27 (Dec. 11, 1989), the FEC held that a state law that expressly restricts the funds available to candidates for federal office is not preempted by FECA. The FEC observed that, although FECA generally preempts state laws with respect to election to federal office, it does not preempt such laws where the state is regulating the political activity of its own employees. For this reason, the FEC ruled that, to the extent the state law prohibits "solicitation by the employee himself of herself of their personal receipt" of funds from a political committee—a rule designed to prevent conflicts of interest on the part of state employees—it is not preempted by FECA. *Id.*

Here, as discussed earlier, the City has an obvious and compelling interest in regulating the ethical conduct of its officials, including Holtzman while she was City Comptroller. By permitting the City to regulate the conduct of its own employees, even when engaged in political activities for federal elections, FECA enables the City to protect its compelling and independent interest. For all these reasons, FECA does not preempt the application of the City conflicts of interest rules to Holtzman's conduct in office.

V.   THE CONFLICT OF INTEREST PROVISIONS ARE NOT "A TRAP FOR THE UNWARY"

Holtzman contends that the conflict of interest provisions may be applied to her because they "failed to give warning of what is said to have been prohibited or required"

See Board Opinion No. 412 (Aug. 2, 1977); Board Opinion No. 412A (Aug. 2, 1977): Board Opinion No. 603 (June 24, 1981). Although not addressing the specific Charter provisions at issue here, these opinions inform City employees that the City Charter regulates their political activities.

and "failed to 'provide explicit standards' for law enforcement officials" to prevent arbitrary enforcement. Holtzman Br. At 64. Holtzman cites her supposed "goal . . . to comply with the law, not to violate it" as evidence that she was not on notice that her conduct could create an appearance of impropriety. Holtzman Br. at 65. This attempt to read an intent requirement into the conflict of interest provisions is unsupported by case law Moreover, as discussed above, the board never held that Holtzman acted in good faith. Simply because one knows the law does not necessarily make him more likely to follow it, particularly when he is confronted with grave financial obligations. *See, supra*, p. 17.

The Board's decision and reasoning followed clearly established Board precedent in interpreting section 2604(b) of the City Charter.[44] Holtzman's argument that the Board's decision reflects a novel application of the conflicts of interest laws ignores the wealth of Board decisions making it unmistakable that unethical behavior by public servants will not be tolerated. *See, e.g.*, Board Opinion No. 93-15 (May 20, 1993) (known and unknown conflicts could give rise to appearance of pressure, favoritism or unfair advantage in dealing with City agencies or officials); Board Opinion No. 91-10 (Nov. 18, 1991) (appearance of impropriety may be created if the nature of the official's involvement is perceived to be coercive or provides an inappropriate opportunity for access to officials).

Holtzman seizes on the Board's acknowledgement that conflicts of interest provisions, by their very nature, will apply to many factual scenarios in which an appearance of impropriety may arise to suggest that the law somehow is "standardless." Holtzman Br. at 66. Conflict of interest provisions stand in contrast to laws banning the possession of handguns or limiting the size of political contributions, in which analysis focuses on one specific prohibited act. For example, the Board has applied the law to such varied conduct as fundraising, working for not-for-profit organizations, and accepting airline tickets. *See* Board Opinion 93-6, February 1, 1993 (A4479-4482D); Board Opinion No. 92-83, September 15, 1992 (A.4462-4463); Board Opinion 93-4, January 20, 1993 (A4473-4478). Indeed, the Board recently applied the conflict of interest provisions to conduct arising from the solicitations of a loan by a City employee from her subordinate. *See Addendum* (Disposition, Board Case No. 97-225, December 10, 1997.) Simply because there is a broader array of conduct that may violate a conflict of interest provi-

Another instance where opinions relied upon by the Petitioner are distinguished on their facts.

[44]   *Girard v. City of Glens* Falls, 173 A.D.2d 113, 577 N.Y.S.2d 496 (3d Dep't 1991), which Holtzman cites for the proposition that a disciplinary decision may be annulled if it departs from prior administrative policy, is again totally distinguishable on the facts. Holtzman Br. at 65 n.37. In *Girard*, a firefighter became a Democratic committee member with the full knowledge of the Mayor of Glens Falls and thereafter sought election to the City Council. The Glen Falls Board of Public Safety later charged him with violating its regulations regarding the political activity of fire department members, tried the firefighter on the charge two working days after notifying him and "repeatedly prohibited petitioner from introducing evidence to support his defense" and from submitting closing briefs. *Id.* at 498, 173 A.D.2d at 117-18. In light of these facts, the court took the unusual step of annulling the administrative determination. *Id.* None of these circumstances is present with respect to the Board's determination that Holtzman violated the Charter.

sion than another type of law does not make laws regulating appearances of impropriety impermissibly vague. *See Hunt v. State*, 642 So.2d 999, 1029 (rejecting argument that conflict of interest law did not give sufficient notice that an official's conduct arising from his receipt of campaign loans was improper because "the focus of the Ethics Act" was not on such conduct), *aff'd* 642 So.2d 1060 (Ala. 1994).[45]

The Supreme Court has noted that a statute may not be condemned as vague merely because, with each set of given facts, its interpretation may be subject to scholarly debate. *Boyce Motor Lines, Inc. v. U.S.*, 342 U.S. 337, 72 S. Ct. 329 (1952). Accordingly, courts repeatedly have rejected challenges, such as that offered by Holtzman here, that conflicts of interest laws are impermissibly vague. *See Davidson*, 712 P.2d 87, 94 (where "the chief question concerns the correct interpretation of the verb 'use,'" conflict of interest law was not impermissibly vague); *U.S. v. Baird*, 29 F.3d 647, 652 (D.C. Cir. 1994) (conflict of interest law provided proper notice where "subtle legal analysis" was required to argue that the law did not apply); *Penn. State Assoc. of Township supervisors v. Thornburgh*, 437 A.2d 1 (Pa. 1981); *Rioux v. State Ethics Comm.*, No. CV 960472653, 1997 WL 120303 (Conn. Super. March 4, 1997).[46]

In particular, given the provision in most conflict of interest laws that allows officials to seek advisory opinions, courts have looked with disfavor upon the argument that these laws do not provide notice to officials that their conduct could constitute a violation. *See Penn. State Assoc. of Township Supervisors*, 437 A.2d at 6 ("it is . . . important . . . that the Commission has established a procedure by which an employee in doubt about the validity of a proposed course of conduct may seek and obtain advice from the Commission and thereby remove any doubt there may be as to the meaning of the law, at least insofar as the Commission itself is concerned") (quoting *Civil Service Comm. v.*

---

[45]   Holtzman's citations to *Keeffe v. Library of Congress*, 777 F.2d 1573, 1582 (D.C. Cir. 1985), and *Gentile v. State Bar of Nevada*, 501 U.S. 1030 (1991), provide no support for her argument that she was not on notice of the law. In *Keeffe*, there was a clearly new interpretation of a statute which contradicted a past opinion upon which the employee properly had relied. Neither of those factors exist here. In *Gentile*, the Supreme Court criticized the vagueness of a Nevada professional conduct rule applicable to attorneys based upon the "considerable deliberation" with which an attorney had tried to follow the rule, but still was found to have violated it. *Id.* at 1041. As demonstrated above, in this case, the Board properly found that Holtzman had not tried to follow the conflict of interest provision with "considerable deliberation," but that instead she had failed to take appropriate steps to prevent the appearance of impropriety.

[46]   Apparently acknowledging that courts have repeatedly upheld identical provisions against vagueness challenges, Holtzman attempts to challenge these provisions on the basis that they are impermissibly vague as *applied*. In doing so, however, she cites cases discussing whether standards are vague on their face. Holtzman Br. at 69 (citing *Geogia Pacific Corp. v. OSHRC*, 25 f.3d 999 (11th Cir. 1994)). In *Georgia Pacific Corp.*, the Eleventh Circuit upheld a vagueness challenge to a statute because not only could the administrators charged with interpreting it not determine what it meant, but outside experts also differed widely on its meaning. As demonstrated by the Board's consistent application of the Charter to situations in which officials create an appearance of impropriety through their actions, the Charter, like similar statues in other jurisdictions, does not suffer from a lack of clarity.

Letter Carriers, 413 U.S. 548, 580, 93 S.Ct. 2880, 2897 (1973)). This disfavor is particularly appropriate with Holtzman, since she has employed the procedure on previous occasions and even cited these instances as evidence of her good faith. Holtzman Br. at 65 n.36.

In short, Holtzman's argument that she should be excused from the consequences of her conduct because she was not on notice that her actions could be viewed as creating an appearance of impropriety is not supported by fact or law. As the Supreme Court has observed in connection with challenges that laws do not provide proper notice of prohibited conduct: "[N]o more than a reasonable degree of certainty can be demanded. Nor is it unfair to require that one who deliberately goes perilously close to an area of proscribed conduct shall take the risk that he may cross the line." *Boy Motor Lines, Inc.*, 342 U.S. at 340, 72 S.Ct. at 331.

CONCLUSION

Holtzman's position as Comptroller carried weighty responsibilities, including the duty to avoid event the appearance of impropriety and the misuse of her Office for her personal benefit. As the Board found, Holtzman's actions during 1992 and 1993 not only came "perilously close to an area of proscribed conduct," they clearly crossed the line. Holtzman did not live up to the duties imposed on her by virtue of the Charter and her position as Comptroller. The responsibility for Holtzman's conduct rests not on the alleged inadequacies of the Board or the Charter, but squarely on Holtzman herself.

For the foregoing reasons, this Court should issue an order affirming the decision of the Appellate Division, First Department.

Roy L. Reardon
425 Lexington Avenue
New York, NY 10017
(212) 455-2000

Attorney for Respondents-Respondents
Sheldon Oliensis, et al.

Robert F. Cusumano
Elizabeth A. Fuerstman
Lynn K. Neuner
David L. Lessing

Of Counsel

IN THE MATTER OF Elizabeth HOLTZMAN, Appellant,
v.
Sheldon OLIENSIS et al., Respondents.

Court of Appeals of New York

Argued March 25, 1998;

Decided April 30, 1998

Matter of Holtzman v Oliensis, 240 AD2d 254, affirmed.

APPEARANCES OF COUNSEL

Daniel F. Kolb, New York City, Nancy B. Ludmerer and Erika J. Adkins for appellant.

Roy L. Reardon, New York City, Robert F. Cusumano, Elizabeth A. Fuerstman, Lynn K. Neuner and David L. Lessing for respondents.

OPINION OF THE COURT

Levine, J.

Petitioner-appellant Elizabeth Holtzman, former Comptroller of the City of New York, challenges a determination of the New York City Conflicts of Interest Board (Board) that she violated the New York City Charter's conflicts of interest provisions. The following facts, as found by the Board, are supported by evidence in the record.

In 1992, while serving as Comptroller, petitioner also was seeking the Democratic Party's nomination for election to the United States Senate. When it became apparent that she likely would lose the September primary contest for that nomination unless her campaign garnered significant momentum, her campaign committee obtained a $450,000 unsecured loan from Fleet Bank, a subsidiary of Fleet Financial Group, Inc. and affiliate to Fleet Securities, Inc., to finance a last minute media promotion. Petitioner was required to guarantee the loan personally, which was to be repaid by September 30, 1992 from the proceeds of a September 9 fund raising event.

Contemporaneous with these events, Fleet Securities was engaged in public finance underwriting for the City of New York and was seeking to increase those business dealings. As Comptroller, it was petitioner's responsibility, inter alia, to work with the Mayor in selecting a management team to underwrite the City's bonds and notes. Both prior to and after petitioner obtained the loan from Fleet Bank, Fleet Securities had made overtures to the Comptroller's office concerning Fleet's desire to secure a position as a manager of the City's municipal bond offerings and pension funds. Petitioner personally attended a campaign breakfast meeting for herself on June 12, 1992 at which Fleet Securities unambiguously voiced its interest in a comanager position for the City's securities sales.

Petitioner's media campaign was unsuccessful, and ultimately she lost the Senate Democratic primary to Robert Abrams. In addition, after the September 9 fund raiser failed to meet her committee's expectations, petitioner's Fleet Bank loan went into default. At a December 15, 1992 meeting with petitioner, Fleet aggressively pressured for repayment of the loan, informing her that it was considering acting upon her personal guarantee. Nonetheless, the loan was extended until February 1, 1993 and petitioner and the bank's officers agreed to meet again in January to discuss a repayment schedule.

On December 22, 1992, the Comptroller's office issued a Request for Proposals (RFP) for selection of a new management team to underwrite the City's general obligations and Water Authority bonds, and Fleet Securities responded. Although petitioner designated another Comptroller staff member directly to oversee the RFP process, she did not recuse herself from participation in the selection or disclose her debtor/creditor relationship with the bank to others in her office. When members of the campaign committee informed the senior assistant comptroller (and petitioner's former campaign manager), Edward O'Malley, that they planned on meeting with Fleet Bank in January to discuss repayment of the loan, Mr. O'Malley informed them that because Fleet Bank had responded to the RFP, the committee could not do so. Specifically, Mr. O'Malley advised that, due to petitioner's general policy of imposing a "quiet period" during which her staff or representatives would have no communications with underwriting firms that had responded to an RFP to avoid the appearance of bias or preferential treatment, any such meeting with Fleet would have to be postponed until the management team was chosen.

Consequently, Fleet Bank was informed by the campaign committee that it could not communicate with petitioner regarding the loan during the quiet period. Moreover, despite plans to meet with the bank in January, and her awareness that her loan would once again go into default on February 1, 1993, petitioner made no attempt to contact Fleet Bank during this time. By letter dated February 12, 1993, with a copy to petitioner, Fleet Bank informed the campaign committee that the loan was being transferred to the bank's Managed Assets Department due to the inability to negotiate a restructure of the loan, specifically and expressly as a result of the imposition of the quiet period.

On recommendation from petitioner's office, on March 17, 1993, Fleet Securities was awarded a comanager position by the City. Petitioner personally signed a public "Tombstone" notice on April 1, 1993, which listed Fleet Securities as a comanager. Fleet's qualifications for that position are not in dispute.

Soon thereafter, press coverage of petitioner's debtor status with Fleet Bank apparently prompted her to recuse herself from further involvement in decisions of the Comptroller's office concerning the bank or its affiliates and, on May 13, 1993, then Mayor David Dinkins removed Fleet Securities as a comanager on the bond issue. On August 2, 1993, the bank issued a demand to petitioner's committee and to Holtzman, as guarantor, for immediate repayment of the outstanding loan principal. Petitioner and her committee finally reached an agreement with the bank in mid-August whereby the loan was extended and collateral was provided to secure the debt.

Based on these events, the Board charged petitioner with various ethical violations. After an 11-day hearing before an Administrative Law Judge at which over 150 exhibits were introduced and over 2,000 pages of testimony were taken, the Board concluded that by failing to recuse herself from the process of selecting managers on the City bond issue and, concomitantly, taking advantage of the quiet period to postpone loan repayment negotiations with Fleet, petitioner had violated section 2604 (b) (2) and (3) of chapter 68 of the New York City Charter, which define prohibited conflicts of interest on the part of public officials. Pursuant to the authority expressly granted to it in the Charter, the Board imposed a $7,500 fine on petitioner (see, NY City Charter § 2606 [b]).

Petitioner then commenced the instant CPLR article 78 proceeding, arguing that the Federal Election Campaign Act (2 USC § 453 et seq.) preempts application of the City Charter in this proceeding, and that the Board erred, on the law and the facts, in finding a violation of the City's conflicts of interest rules. The Appellate Division confirmed the Board's decision in all respects and dismissed the proceeding (240 AD2d 254). We granted petitioner leave to appeal, and now affirm.

I.

Turning first to the threshold question of whether the Federal Election Campaign Act (FECA) limits the Board's jurisdiction here, we begin with the presumption that Congress did not intend to preempt the States' power to regulate matters of local concern (see, *Medtronic, Inc. v Lohr*, 518 US 470, 484-485; *New York State Conference of Blue Cross & Blue Shield Plans v Travelers Ins. Co.,* 514 US 645, 654-655; *California v ARC Am. Corp.*, 490 US 93, 101), and then analyze whether this presumption is overcome by either an explicit or implicit manifestation of congressional preemptive intent in this case (see, *Guice v Schwab & Co.*, 89 NY2d 31, 39, *cert denied* 520 US 1118; *see also, Matter of Delta Air Lines v New York State Div. of Human Rights*, 91 NY2d 65, 70-71). Implied preemption may be established when "the Federal legislation is so comprehensive in its scope that it is inferable that Congress wished fully to occupy the field of its subject matter ('field preemption'), or because State law conflicts with the Federal law" (*Guice v Schwab & Co., supra*, at 39; *see, Barnett Bank of Marion County v Nelson*, 517 US 25, 30-31).

(1) Here, no express intent to foreclose State prohibitions of ethical misconduct by local officials is discernible from the language of FECA. That act provides:

> "The provisions of this Act, and of rules prescribed under this Act, supersede and preempt any provision of State law with respect to election *to Federal Office*" (2 USC § 453 [emphasis supplied]).

Thus, on its face, the statute's preemptive reach appears subject-specific, restricted to the regulation of the conduct and financing of campaigns for Federal elective office (see, *Stern v General Elec. Co.*, 924 F2d 472, 475; *see also, Matter of Delta Air Lines v New York State Div. of Human Rights, supra*, 91 NY2d, at 71).

Nor is FECA so pervasive that it reveals congressional intent to displace all ethical regulation of State and local officials while those officials are seeking election to Federal office. Indeed, the legislative history of the act supports the contrary:

"It is the intent of the conferees that any State law regulating the political activities of State and local officers and employees is not preempted or superseded by the amendments to title 5, United States Code, made by this legislation" (S Conf Report No. 1237, 93d Cong, 2d Sess, *reprinted in* 1974 *US Code Cong & Admin News* 5618, 5669 [emphasis supplied]).

Although FECA "occupies the field with respect to reporting and disclosure of political contributions to and expenditures by Federal candidates and political committees" (*see, id.*, at 5668), it does not prohibit other State regulation, such as "the manner of qualifying as a candidate, or the dates and places of elections" (id.), or a "[c]andidate's personal financial disclosure" (11 CFR 108.7 [c] [5]). Thus, it is apparent that Congress did not intend FECA's preemptive scope to reach official conduct discrete from Federal election fund raising, such as a City's ethical prohibitions (*see generally*, *Stern v General Elec. Co.*, 924 F2d, at 474, supra [holding that Congress did not intend to occupy the entire field of corporate political spending]).

Finally on the preemption issue, the Charter provisions under scrutiny here are not in conflict with FECA. "Implied conflict preemption may be found when it is impossible for one to act in compliance with both the Federal and State laws, or when 'the state law . . . "stan[ds] as an obstacle to the accomplishment and execution of the full purposes and objectives of Congress" ' " (*Guice v Schwab & Co.*, *supra*, 89 NY2d, at 39 [quoting *Barnett Bank of Marion County v Nelson*, *supra*, 517 US, at 31]). Here, the Charter provisions did not preclude petitioner, as a Federal candidate, from obtaining the loan, conduct which FECA expressly permits, but simply prohibited her from continuing to assert authority over a City decision in which her creditor was acutely interested. Unlike a State statute or regulation that directly conflicts with FECA's disclosure requirements and spending limits (*see, Bunning v Commonwealth of Ky.*, 42 F3d 1008, 1012; *Weber v Heaney*, 995 F2d 872, 876) the City's ethics laws do not limit petitioner's ability to fund her campaign and in no way infringe upon FECA's control over Federal campaign contributions and expenditures (*see, Reeder v Kansas City Bd. of Police Commrs.*, 733 F2d 543, 545-546 [Missouri law forbidding police officers to make campaign contributions not preempted]; *Pollard v Board of Police Commrs.*, 665 SW2d 333, 338 [Mo] [same], cert denied 473 US 907; *cf., Teper v Miller*, 82 F3d 989, 995 [State ethics law having the effect of limiting Federal fund raising preempted by FECA]). Indeed, the only conduct for which petitioner was sanctioned occurred after her race for Federal office had ended.

Thus, concluding that the New York City Charter's conflicts of interest prohibitions are not preempted by FECA, we turn to petitioner's substantive arguments.

II.

(2) Petitioner alternatively asserts that the Board erred in finding a violation of section 2604 (b) (3),* which provides:

> "No public servant shall use or attempt to use his or her position as a public servant to obtain any financial gain, contract, license, privilege or other private or personal advantage, direct or indirect, for the public servant or any person or firm associated with the public servant" (NY City Charter § 2604[b][3] [emphasis supplied]).

Petitioner claims that there was no factual basis upon which the Board could have concluded that she received an advantage from the imposition of the quiet period. The Board, however, readily could have inferred from the previously cited facts that the quiet period, in tandem with the pendency of Fleet's application to be appointed to a comanager position (over which petitioner officially and ostensibly retained authority), effectively forestalled Fleet's debt collection efforts for nearly three months. Thus, there was substantial evidence to support the Board's finding that petitioner obtained a personal advantage within the meaning of section 2604(b)(3) (*see*, CPLR 7803 [3]; *Matter of Jennings v New York State Off. of Mental Health*, 90 NY2d 227, 239).

Similarly unpersuasive is petitioner's claim that imposition of the quiet period, to thereby inhibit Fleet's collection-motivated communications with its debtor, did not constitute a use of her public office for which she should be held responsible. That this was a use of the Comptroller's power is indisputable, as the policy was created by petitioner in her capacity as Comptroller and carried out by her staff.

Nor is this conclusion obviated, as petitioner contends, because the Board did not explicitly make a finding that she actually was aware that Fleet's collection efforts had been deterred in this fashion. A City official is chargeable with knowledge of those business dealings that create a conflict of interest about which the official "should have known" (*see,* NY City Charter § 2604[a][6]). During her campaign, and at a campaign-related event, petitioner had been present on at least one occasion where Fleet importuned to become a comanager. Moreover, there is no dispute that members of her staff, including her top aide and former campaign manager, knew that Fleet responded to the RFP and, on prior occasions, had discussed with Fleet its ambition to increase its business dealings with the City. Petitioner also personally signed the Tombstone notice. Thus, it was hardly unreasonable for the Board to have concluded that petitioner at the least should have known that Fleet was an applicant for a managerial role in the next issuance of the City's bonds, to whom her all-pervasive quiet period rule would necessarily have been applied.

---

*   Although petitioner also was found to have violated section 2604(b)(2), she does not challenge that determination here except insofar as she argues that the City Charter provisions, in general, are inapplicable to her conduct.

Further, as to whether she should be charged with knowledge of the application of the quiet period to postpone Fleet's efforts to collect the debt, petitioner has not challenged the testimony of the Fleet officer that she was sent a copy of the February 12, 1993 letter, addressed to her campaign committee, expressly stating that the imposition of the quiet period prevented ongoing discussions for repayment of the loan. Moreover, it is reasonable to expect that she would have been alerted that the quiet period rule had been invoked against Fleet Bank's collection efforts in view of the loan department's otherwise inexplicable postponement without date of the January meeting that petitioner and the bank had agreed to on December 15, and its failure to take any action on the loan, not even contacting her, after the loan again went into default on February 1, 1993. Her only explanation for her inattentiveness to these facts was that she does not generally read mail merely copied to her (as to the February 12 letter), and that she may have psychologically blocked out the immediacy of the Fleet debt obligation and the bank's earlier collection efforts. Thus, she exhibited, if not actual awareness that she was obtaining a personal advantage from the application of the quiet period to Fleet Bank, at least a studied indifference to the open and obvious signs that she had been insulated from Fleet's collection efforts.

Under the foregoing compelling circumstances, the Board could reasonably read the Charter's conflicts of interest provisions to authorize charging petitioner with notice of, and responsibility for, the use of her quiet period rule to obtain an advantage through her public office regarding deferred collection of her Fleet debt. Indeed, any other conclusion would inevitably undermine enforcement of this important statutory scheme "to preserve the trust placed in the public servants of the city ... [and] to protect the integrity of government decision-making" (NY City Charter § 2600). Thus, the Board's interpretation in this respect was entirely reasonable and consistent with legislative purpose.

We also find no merit to petitioner's arguments that section 2604 (c) (3) exempts her conduct from the conflicts of interest rules. That provision states that the Charter does not prohibit "a public servant from obtaining a loan from any financial institution upon terms and conditions available to members of the public" (NY City Charter § 2604[c][3]). As discussed above, petitioner was not sanctioned for obtaining the loan, but for failing to recuse herself from the management team selection process while then availing herself of the quiet period. These activities clearly are not within the scope of the section 2604(c)(3) exemption.

Finally, petitioner's assertion that the City Charter provisions were insufficient for due process purposes to give her adequate notice that the conduct at issue here was prohibited is unpreserved for our review. Petitioner's remaining arguments are either unpreserved or wholly lack merit.

Accordingly, the judgment of the Appellate Division should be affirmed, with costs.

Chief Judge Kaye and Judges Titone, Bellacosa, Smith, Ciparick and Wesley concur.

Judgment affirmed, with costs.